The Epistemology of Group Disagreement

This book brings together philosophers to investigate the nature and normativity of group disagreement. Debates in the epistemology of disagreement have mainly been concerned with idealized cases of peer disagreement between individuals. However, most real-life disagreements are complex and often take place within and between groups. Ascribing views, beliefs, and judgments to groups is a common phenomenon that is well researched in the literature on the ontology and epistemology of groups. The chapters in this volume seek to connect these literatures and to explore both intra- and inter- group disagreements. They apply their discussions to a range of political, religious, social, and scientific issues. *The Epistemology of Group Disagreement* is an important resource for students and scholars working on social and applied epistemology; disagreement; and topics at the intersection of epistemology, ethics, and politics.

Fernando Broncano-Berrocal is a Talent Attraction Fellow at the Autonomous University of Madrid, Spain. He works mainly in epistemology, with an emphasis on virtue epistemology, philosophy of luck, social epistemology, and collective epistemology. He is the co-editor, with J. Adam Carter, of *The Epistemology of Group Disagreement* (Routledge, 2021). His work has appeared in such places as *Philosophical Studies, Analysis, Synthese*, and *Erkenntnis.*

J. Adam Carter is Reader in Philosophy at the University of Glasgow, UK. His expertise is mainly in epistemology, with particular focus on virtue epistemology, social epistemology relativism, know-how, epistemic luck, and epistemic defeat. He is the author of *Metaepistemology and Relativism* (2016); co-author of *A Critical Introduction to Knowledge-How* (2018); and co-editor, with Fernando Broncano-Berrocal, of *The Epistemology of Group Disagreement* (Routledge, 2021). His work has appeared in *Noûs, Philosophy and Phenomenological Research, Philosophical Studies, Analysis*, and the *Australasian Journal of Philosophy.*

Routledge Studies in Epistemology

Edited by Kevin McCain, University of Alabama at Birmingham, USA and Scott Stapleford, St. Thomas University, Canada

Well-Founded Belief
New Essays on the Epistemic Basing Relation
Edited by J. Adam Carter and Patrick Bondy

Higher-Order Evidence and Moral Epistemology
Edited by Michael Klenk

Social Epistemology and Relativism
Edited by Natalie Alana Ashton, Martin Kusch, Robin McKenna and Katharina Anna Sodoma

Epistemic Duties
New Arguments, New Angles
Edited by Kevin McCain and Scott Stapleford

The Ethics of Belief and Beyond
Understanding Mental Normativity
Edited by Sebastian Schmidt and Gerhard Ernst

Ethno-Epistemology
New Directions for Global Epistemology
Edited by Masaharu Mizumoto, Jonardon Ganeri, and Cliff Goddard

The Dispositional Architecture of Epistemic Reasons
Hamid Vahid

The Epistemology of Group Disagreement
Edited by Fernando Broncano-Berrocal and J. Adam Carter

For more information about this series, please visit: https://www.routledge.com/Routledge-Studies-in-Epistemology/book-series/RSIE

The Epistemology of Group Disagreement

Edited by
Fernando Broncano-Berrocal
and J. Adam Carter

Routledge
Taylor & Francis Group
NEW YORK AND LONDON

First published 2021
by Routledge
52 Vanderbilt Avenue, New York, NY 10017

and by Routledge
2 Park Square, Milton Park, Abingdon, Oxon, OX14 4RN

Routledge is an imprint of the Taylor & Francis Group, an informa business

Library of Congress Cataloging-in-Publication Data
A catalog record for this title has been requested

ISBN: 978-0-367-07742-6 (hbk)
ISBN: 978-0-429-02250-0 (ebk)

Typeset in Sabon
by codeMantra

Contents

1 The Epistemology of Group Disagreement

An Introduction

Fernando Broncano-Berrocal and J. Adam Carter

1.1 Group Disagreement: A Brief Overview

Disagreement is among the most thriving topics in mainstream and social epistemology.[1]

The research question responsible for initially launching the *epistemology of disagreement* as its own subfield in the early 2000s can be put very simply: suppose you believe some proposition, *p*, is true. You come to find out that an individual whom you thought was equally likely as you are to be right about whether *p* is true, believes *not-p*. What should you do? Are you rationally required, given this new evidence, to revise your initial belief that *p*, or is it rationally permissible to simply 'hold steadfast' to your belief that *p* with the same degree of confidence that you did before you found out your believed-to-be epistemic peer disagreed with you? Call this the *peer disagreement question*.

How we go about answering this question has obvious practical ramifications: we disagree with people we think are our peers often; knowing what we should do, epistemically, would be valuable guidance. But the peer disagreement question is also important for epistemologists to understand, theoretically speaking, given that it has direct ramifications for how we should understand disagreement itself as a form of evidence.

Unsurprisingly, responses to the peer disagreement question have fallen into two broadly opposing categories: those who think that discovering that an epistemic peer disagrees with you rationally requires of you some substantial kind of *conciliation*[2]—perhaps even agnosticism[3]—and those who think that it does not.[4] Interestingly, the past ten years or so have shown that—in the close orbit of the peer disagreement question—there are a range of related and interesting epistemological questions, questions that are perhaps just as epistemologically as well as practically significant.[5]

Just consider that the peer disagreement question is *individualistically framed*. It is a question about what rationality requires of an individual when they disagree with another individual about some contested proposition. Gaining an answer tells us, *at most*, and in short, what *individuals* should do in the face of epistemic adversity. But we also want to know what *groups* should do in the face of epistemic adversity. For example: what should a group—say, a scientific committee—do if it turns out that one of the members on the committee holds a view that runs contrary to the consensus?[6]

It would be convenient if answering questions about how individuals should respond to epistemic adversity *implied* answers to the interesting questions about how groups should do the same. Unfortunately, though, things are not so simple. This is because, to a first approximation, the epistemic properties of groups are not, as recent collective epistemology has suggested, always simply reducible to an aggregation of the epistemic properties of its members.[7] If we want to understand what *groups* should do, rationally speaking, when there is internal disagreement among members, or when there is disagreement between a group and individuals or groups external to the group, we cannot and should not expect to find the answers we need simply by looking to the results social epistemology has given us to questions that were *individualistically framed*.

The topic of this volume—the *epistemology of group disagreement*—aims to face the complex topic of group disagreement head on; it represents the first-ever volume of papers dedicated exclusively to *group disagreements* and the epistemological puzzles such disagreements raise. The volume consists of 12 new essays by leading epistemologists working in the area, and it spans a range of different key themes related to group disagreement, some established themes and others entirely new. In what follows, we offer brief summaries of these 12 chapters, drawing some connections between them where appropriate.

1.2 Overview of Chapters

In general, there are two epistemically significant ways in which intragroup disagreement can be resolved, i.e., in which members of a divided group can come to agree to let a certain view stand as the group's view: (i) they can deliberate and/or (ii) take a vote. Which is the best strategy and why? In 'Deliberation and Group Disagreement', we (Fernando Broncano-Berrocal and J. Adam Carter) open the volume by exploring the epistemic significance that the key difference between deliberative and voting procedures has for the resolution of intragroup disagreement: namely, the fact that only deliberation necessarily requires that group members communicate with each other and by doing so exchange their evidence. In order to make traction on this question, deliberation's epistemic effectiveness in resolving intragroup disagreement is assessed in some detail with respect to how well, in comparison with voting, it promotes (or thwarts the attainment of) a range of different epistemic goals, including truth, evidential support, understanding, and epistemic justice.

Javier González de Prado Salas and Xavier de Donato-Rodríguez, in their contribution 'Disagreement Within Rational Collective Agents', are primarily concerned with the question of what a group must do to be rational as a group when members of that group hold disagreeing views. One answer that they consider and reject holds that group attitudes are rational if they result from the application of appropriate judgement aggregation methods. On the proposal they favour, group (epistemic) attitudes are rational insofar as they are formed by responding competently or responsibly to the (epistemic) reasons available to the group as a group, where this requires the exercise of reasons-responding competences attributable to the group. In developing this proposal, González de Prado and de Donato-Rodríguez defend conciliationism as having an important role to play, and offer a positive characterization of group deliberation according to which deliberation in collective agents tends to facilitate the achievement of internal agreement, not only about what attitude to adopt collectively but also about the reasons for doing so.

Whereas González de Prado and de Donato-Rodríguez helpfully show the positive implications of conciliationism about group disagreement—in that it offers an optimistic picture of collective deliberation as a rational method for intragroup disagreement resolution—Mattias Skipper and Asbjørn Steglich-Petersen highlight its shortcomings. In particular, in their chapter 'When Conciliation Frustrates the Epistemic Priorities of Groups', Skipper and Steglich-Petersen argue that conciliatory responses on behalf of individual group members to intragroup disagreement—even if rational *qua* response types to individual disagreement—can have adverse epistemic consequences at the group level. In particular, as they see it, the problem is that such conciliatory responses to an internal disagreement can frustrate a group's epistemic priorities by changing the group's relative degree of reliability in forming true beliefs and avoiding false ones. Finally, Skipper and Steglich-Petersen suggest a solution to this epistemic priority problem that does not imply abandoning conciliationism.

The next two papers in the volume continue follow suit in investigating the relationship between group disagreement and conciliationism, albeit in different ways. In his chapter 'Intra-Group Disagreement and Conciliationism', Nathan Sheff's objective is to defend a form of conciliationism in the specific context of intra-group disagreements. Conciliationism in this context holds when an individual dissenter finds herself in disagreement with the other members of a deliberative group, the rational response for the disagreeing member is lowering confidence in their view. Sheff argues first that (i) intra-group conciliationism does not enjoy *ex ante* the intuitive plausibility that ordinary conciliationism, viz., individualistically framed, does, but (ii) difficulties facing the view can be overcome when we suitably appreciate, with reference to Margaret Gilbert's account of joint commitment,[8] the kind of normativity that constrains an individual dissenter in the predicament of an intragroup disagreement. In particular, they find themselves epistemically responsible for contradictory views: their own view, and that of the group and accordingly pulled in contrary directions. In this circumstance, Sheff argues, the rational response is at least to lower their confidence in their view.

In 'Bucking the Trend: The Puzzle of Individual Dissent in Contexts of Collective Inquiry', Simon Barker, like Sheff, is concerned with the predicament of an individual dissenter in her capacity as a group member. As Barker observes, there is pressure to suppose that when an individual dissents with intragroup members, the greater the number of one's peers against one, the more significance one should afford the disagreement—viz., what he calls the principle of collective superiority. At the same time, he notes, discussions of disagreement within collective inquiry have maintained that justified collective judgements demand methods of inquiry that permit and preserve (rather than eliminate) dissent—viz., a principle that Barker labels epistemic liberalism. Taken together, these principles seem to make different and incompatible demands, what Barker calls the 'puzzle of individual dissent'. Barker's objective in the paper is to sharpen this puzzle by tracing out the consequences of rejecting either of the two principles jointly responsible for the dilemma, and to assess the significance of the dilemma more widely in epistemology.

The next three papers in the volume engage in different ways with the social and power dynamics of group disagreement. In 'Gender, Race, and Group Disagreements' Mona Simion and Martin Miragoli take as a starting point two cases of group disagreement, one involving gender discrimination, the other involving the marginalization of racial and religious minorities. Both, they argue, feature a distinctive form of epistemic injustice at play, and further, that extant views in the epistemology of peer disagreement have difficulties accounting for what is defective about these cases. Against this background, Simion and Miragoli propose and defend a two-tiered solution to the problem that relies on an externalist epistemology and a functionalist theoretical framework.

Epistemic injustice is also a central theme in Mikkel Gerken's contribution to the volume, 'Disagreement and Epistemic Injustice from a Communal Perspective'. Gerken's central focus is on the epistemic pros and cons of disagreement for a community and on how the social structure of the community bears on these pros and cons. A central conclusion drawn is that disagreement has more epistemic costs at the communal level than is often recognized by those who follow Mill's emphasis on disagreement's positive social significance, and that these epistemic costs often yield epistemic injustice, especially given disagreement's capacity to defeat testimonial warrant.

In 'Group Disagreement in Science', Kristina Rolin explores, through the lens of scientific dissent, how relations of power influence perceived epistemic responsibilities. Rolin takes as a starting point the widespread view in the philosophy of science that a scientific community has an obligation to engage scientific dissent only when it is normatively appropriate from an epistemic point of view. One notable line of criticism to this standard line maintains that the norms constraining epistemically appropriate dissent are ambiguous. Rolin's objective is to respond to this concern by arguing that even when there is disagreement over the interpretation of such norms, a scientific community has a moral reason to respond to dissenters. On her favoured approach, there is a norm of epistemic responsibility—both an epistemic and moral norm—that defines mutual obligations for dissenters and the advocates of a consensus view.

The volume's next two chapters view the epistemology of group disagreement through a more formal lens. In 'Disagreement in a Group: Aggregation, Respect for Evidence, and Synergy', Anna-Maria Asunta Eder seeks to answer the following guiding question: How do members of a group reach a rational epistemic compromise on a proposition when they have different rational credences in the proposition? One way to settle this question is a standard Bayesian method of aggregation, a commitment of which is that the only factors among the agents' epistemic states that matter for finding the compromise are the group members' credences. In contrast, Eder develops and defends a different approach—one that makes use of a fine-grained method of aggregation—on which the members' rational credences are not the only factors concerning the group agents' rational epistemic states that matter for finding an epistemic compromise. This method is based on a non-standard framework for representing rational epistemic states that is more fine-grained than Standard Bayesianism, and which comports with a Dyadic Bayesian framework Eder has defended in a previous work.[9]

A different kind of Bayesian approach to group disagreement is explored by Erik J. Olsson in his paper 'Why Bayesian Agents Polarize'. A number of studies have concluded that ideal Bayesian agents can end up seriously divided on an issue given exactly the same evidence, which suggests that polarization may be rational. But even if this is right, a separate question is *why* do Bayesian agents polarize? Olsson engages with this question in the context of the Bayesian Laputa model of social network deliberation, developed by Angere and Olsson (e.g., 2017). According to recent work by Pallavicini, Hallsson, and Kappel (2018), on the Laputa model, polarization arises due to a failure of Laputa to take into account higher-order information in a particular way, making the model incapable of capturing full rationality. Olsson's objective is to reject Pallavinci et al.'s argument; on his preferred assessment, what drives polarization is expectation-based updating in combination with a modelling of trust in a source that recognizes the possibility that the source is systematically biased.

The volume rounds out with two new spins on traditional ways of thinking about groups and evidence in cases of (group) disagreement. In her paper 'The Mirage of Individual Disagreement: Groups Are All that Stand between Humanity and Epistemic Excellence', Maura Priest argues that a large number of important and long-standing disagreements that have typically been understood as between individuals, are actually disagreements between collectives. This conclusion marks a departure from orthodox thinking about individual disagreement. But, once this is appreciated, she argues, it is easier to then appreciate why such disagreements are often long-standing; further, Priest argues, many individual disagreements (properly understood as group disagreements) are likely to remain unresolved because the relevant parties are not properly motivated by epistemic ends.

The volume ends with Nikolaj Nottelmann's paper, 'A Plea for Complexity: The Normative Assessment of Groups' Responses to Testimony'. Nottelmann's central aim is to show that the epistemic evaluation of group performance in the face of testimony and disagreement is a more complex matter than has so far been explicitly acknowledged in the literature. In many cases, he argues, it is far from clear whether our evaluations of a group's responses to testimony are primarily epistemic or moral, and, in the latter case, how epistemic standards play into our moral assessment. In addition, Nottelmann maintains that what count as the relevant criteria of groupness, group membership, and group belief vary according to our evaluative interests and perspectives.[10]

Notes

1 For some representative recent work on disagreement in epistemology, see, for example, Carey and Matheson (2013); Christensen (2007, 2009); Elga (2007); Feldman (2007); Feldman and Warfield (2010); Goldman (2010); Hales (2014); Kelly (2005); Lackey (2013); Littlejohn (2013); MacFarlane (2007); Matheson (2009, 2015; 2016); Sosa (2011); Thune (2010a, 2010b); and Carter (2018).

2 This view is often described as 'conciliationism'. See, e.g., Feldman (2007) and Elga (2007).

3 See Feldman (2007); cf., Carter (2018).

4 For some representative 'non-conciliationist' views, see, e.g., Kelly (2005); Foley (2001), and Wedgwood (2007).

5 One notable example here concerns the *uniqueness thesis* (e.g., Kelly 2013; Dogramaci and Horowitz 2016; Matheson 2011) which holds that, with respect to a proposition p, your body of evidence, E, justifies at most one of the three attitudes of belief, disbelief, and withholding vis-a-vis p. For criticism of uniqueness, see, e.g., Kelly (2005); Ballantyne and Coffman (2011), and Goldman (2010).

6 For discussion on this issue, see, e.g., the essays in Lackey (2014) and Brady and Fricker (2016).

7 See, e.g., Gilbert (1996, 2013); Tollefsen (2006, 2007, 2015), Tuomela (1995, 2002, 2013), and Palermos (2015).

8 See, e.g., Gilbert (1996, 2013).

9 Brössell and Eder (2014).

10 Fernando Broncano-Berrocal is grateful to the BBVA Foundation for supporting this book, which was edited as part of a 2019 BBVA Leonardo Grant for Researchers and Cultural Creators—the BBVA Foundation accepts no

responsibility for the opinions, statements, and contents included in this book, which are entirely the authors' responsibility. J. Adam Carter is grateful to the Leverhulme Trust for supporting this book, which was edited as part of the Leverhulme-funded 'A Virtue Epistemology of Trust' (RPG-2019-302) project, hosted by the University of Glasgow's COGITO Epistemology Research Centre.

References

Angere, Staffan, and Erik J. Olsson. 2017. 'Publish Late, Publish Rarely!: Network Density and Group Performance in Scientific Communication'. In *Scientific Collaboration and Collective Knowledge*, edited by T. Boyer-Kassem, C. Mayo-Wilson, and M. Weisberg, 34–62. Oxford: Oxford University Press.

Ballantyne, Nathan, and E. J. Coffman. 2011. 'Uniqueness, Evidence, and Rationality'. Philosophers' Imprint 11 (8): 1–13.

Brady, Michael S., and Miranda Fricker. 2016. *The Epistemic Life of Groups: Essays in the Epistemology of Collectives*. Oxford: Oxford University Press.

Brössel, Peter, and Anna-Maria A. Eder. 2014. 'How to Resolve Doxastic Disagreement'. *Synthese* 191 (11): 2359–2381.

Carey, Brandon, and Jonathan Matheson. 2013. 'How Skeptical Is the Equal Weight View?: Brandon Carey and Jonathan Matheson'. In *Disagreement and Skepticism*, edited by Diego E. Machuca, 140–158. London: Routledge.

Carter, J. Adam. 2018. 'On Behalf of Controversial View Agnosticism'. *European Journal of Philosophy* 26 (4): 1358–1370.

Christensen, David. 2007. 'Epistemology of Disagreement: The Good News'. Philosophical Review 116 (2): 187–217.

———. 2009. 'Disagreement as Evidence: The Epistemology of Controversy'. *Philosophy Compass* 4 (5): 756–767.

Dogramaci, Sinan, and Sophie Horowitz. 2016. 'An Argument for Uniqueness about Evidential Support'. *Philosophical Issues* 26 (1): 130–147.

Elga, Adam. 2007. 'Reflection and Disagreement'. *Noûs* 41 (3): 478–502.

Feldman, Richard. 2007. 'Reasonable Religious Disagreements'. In *Philosophers without Gods: Meditations on Atheism and the Secular*, edited by Louise Anthony, 194–214. Oxford: Oxford University Press.

Feldman, Richard, and Ted A. Warfield. 2010. *Disagreement*. Oxford: Oxford University Press.

Foley, Richard. 2001. *Intellectual Trust in Oneself and Others*. Cambridge: Cambridge University Press.

Gilbert, Margaret. 1996. *Living Together: Rationality, Sociality, and Obligation*. London: Rowman & Littlefield Publishers.

———. 2013. *Joint Commitment: How We Make the Social World*. Oxford: Oxford University Press.

Goldman, Alvin I. 2010. 'Epistemic Relativism and Reasonable Disagreement'. In *Disagreement*, edited by Richard Feldman and Ted A. Warfield, 187–215. Oxford: Oxford University Press.

Hales, Steven D. 2014. 'Motivations for Relativism as a Solution to Disagreements'. *Philosophy* 89 (1): 63–82.

Kelly, Thomas. 2005. 'The Epistemic Significance of Disagreement'. *Oxford Studies in Epistemology* 1: 167–196.

Kelly, Thomas. 2013. 'Evidence Can Be Permissive'. In *Contemporary Debates in Epistemology*, edited by M. Steup and J. Turri, 298. Blackwell.

Lackey, Jennifer. 2014. *Essays in Collective Epistemology*. Oxford: Oxford University Press.

Lackey, Jennifer Amy. 2013. 'Disagreement and Belief Dependence: Why Numbers Matter'. In *The Epistemology of Disagreement: New Essays*, edited by D. Christensen and J. Lackey, 243–268. Oxford. Oxford University Press.

Littlejohn, Clayton. 2013. 'Disagreement and Defeat'. In *Disagreement and Skepticism*, edited by D. Machuca, 169–193. Routledge.

MacFarlane, John. 2007. 'Relativism and Disagreement'. *Philosophical Studies* 132 (1): 17–31.

Matheson, Jonathan. 2009. 'Conciliatory Views of Disagreement and Higher-Order Evidence'. *Episteme* 6 (3): 269–279.

———. 2011. 'The case for rational uniqueness'. *Logos & Episteme* 2 (3): 359–373.

———. 2015. *The Epistemic Significance of Disagreement*. Springer.

———. 2016. 'Moral Caution and the Epistemology of Disagreement'. *Journal of Social Philosophy* 47 (2): 120–141.

Pallavicini, Josefine, Bjørn Hallsson, and Klemens Kappel. 2018. Polarization in groups of Bayesian agents. *Synthese*. https://doi.org/10.1007/s11229-018-01978-w.

Palermos, Spyridon Orestis. 2015. 'Active Externalism, Virtue Reliabilism and Scientific Knowledge'. *Synthese* 192 (9): 2955–2986. https://doi.org/10.1007/s11229-015-0695-3.

Sosa, Ernest. 2011. 'The Epistemology of Disagreement'. In *Social Epistemology*, edited by A. Haddock, A. Millar and D. Pritchard. Oxford University Press.

Thune, Michael. 2010a. '"Partial Defeaters" and the Epistemology of Disagreement'. *The Philosophical Quarterly* 60 (239): 355–372.

———. 2010b. 'Religious Belief and the Epistemology of Disagreement'. *Philosophy Compass* 5 (8): 712–724.

Tollefsen, Deborah. 2007. 'Group Testimony'. *Social Epistemology* 21 (3): 299–311.

Tollefsen, Deborah Perron. 2006. 'From Extended Mind to Collective Mind'. *Cognitive Systems Research* 7 (2–3): 140–150.

———. 2015. *Groups as Agents*. Hoboken, NJ: John Wiley & Sons.

Tuomela, Raimo. 1995. *The Importance of Us: A Philosophical Study of Basic Social Notions*. Stanford University Press.

———. 2002. *The Philosophy of Social Practices: A Collective Acceptance View*. Cambridge University Press.

———. 2013. *Cooperation: A Philosophical Study*. Vol. 82. Dordrecht: Springer Science & Business Media.

Wedgwood, Ralph. 2007. *The Nature of Normativity*. Oxford: Oxford University Press.

2 Deliberation and Group Disagreement

Fernando Broncano-Berrocal and J. Adam Carter

2.1 Setting the Stage: Deliberative versus Non-Deliberative Agreement Following Intragroup Disagreement

Many disagreements take place in group settings. Over the years, religious groups (e.g., Christians) have internally disputed topics they consider significant (e.g., the real presence of Christ in the Eucharist). More often than not, political parties (e.g., the Tories) go through internal divisions over issues of societal importance (e.g., a no-deal Brexit). A brief look at the history of science reveals how scientists (e.g., physicists) disagree over factual issues in their fields (e.g., the Copenhagen vs. the many-worlds interpretation of quantum mechanics). More mundanely, disputes over practical matters are the order of the day in many families. On occasions, such internal disagreements end up badly, with a split in the relevant group or a punishment for the less influential. Sometimes, however, they result in a consensus[1] or an agreement of sorts to take a particular course of action or to let some view stand as the group's view.[2] It is this latter kind of intragroup disagreement we are interested in: the one that gets resolved.

How members of a group internally disagree matters for many reasons, not only for the stability or survival of the group but also *epistemically*. In general, there are two epistemically significant ways in which intragroup disagreement can be resolved, i.e., in which members of a divided group can come to *agree to let a certain view stand as the group's view*: (i) they can *deliberate* and/or (ii) take a *vote*.

In this chapter, we are interested in investigating the epistemic significance that the key difference between deliberative and voting procedures has for the resolution of intragroup disagreement: namely, the fact that only deliberation necessarily requires that group members communicate with each other and, more specifically, the fact that, by doing so, they exchange their evidence. Thus, the paper aims to assess, in general, the epistemic significance that such an exchange (or lack thereof) has for the resolution of intragroup disagreement.

This is of course not to say that deliberation and voting are mutually exclusive mechanisms for groups to resolve their internal disputes.

In practice, groups settle their disagreements by *mixed methods of decision-making*, i.e., methods that both involve deliberating and voting—as is, for instance, the mixed method for judging articles of impeachment in the United States House of Representatives.

That said, to better pin down the epistemic significance of each, it is best to keep them apart, at least theoretically. Thus, the kind of cases we will mainly focus on (whether real or ideal) have the following structures:

Deliberative cases of intragroup disagreement: Some operative members[3] of group *G* hold *p* and some not-*p* at t_1; at t_2, *G*'s operative members deliberate among themselves (i.e., they exchange reasons, evidence, arguments, and so on) with an eye toward settling whether *p* or else not-*p* should stand as *G*'s view; at t_3, as a result of this process, they settle on either *p* or not-*p*.

Non-deliberative cases of intragroup disagreement: Some operative members of *G* hold *p* and some not-*p* at t_1; at t_2, *G*'s operative members aggregate their views by taking a vote given some voting rule (e.g., majority rule), absent any communication among each other, with an eye toward settling whether *p* or else not-*p* should stand as *G*'s view; at t_3, as a result of this process, they settle on either *p* or not-*p*.[4]

Some clarifications are in order. First, at t_2, both in the case of deliberation and voting, members who initially believed that *p* should stand as *G*'s view *may change their opinion*, and vice versa. Second, we leave unspecified the *number of group members* that respectively hold *p* and not-*p* to make it compatible with several possibilities—as we will see, this factor marks a distinction in terms of reliability between deliberation and voting. Third, lack of communication among group members in the case of voting is compatible with there being common knowledge (perhaps implicit) of the existence of an internal disagreement or of the fact that it is to be solved by taking a vote.

Finally, certain cases will not be our main focus. Quite often, members of a group settle on a collective view pursuing *non-epistemic goals*—regardless of whether this collective agreement is reached by deliberation or vote. For example, the board of directors of a pharmaceutical company might settle on the view that a newly marketed drug is not the cause of the death of many, even if they know it, to prevent huge financial losses. A government might systematically deny that the country's secret services have been used for morally contentious surveillance activities, even if known to be true, to prevent protests and media pressure. A religious organization might conceal criminal activities by its members—and thus uphold the collective view that such activities never happened—to avoid criminal charges and loss of reputation.

The reason we won't focus on such cases is that deliberative and voting procedures have little or no epistemic value when aimed at non-epistemic goals.[5] Instead, the kind of cases we are interested in are cases of intragroup disagreement in which members of a group reach a collective agreement pursuing *epistemic goals*.[6] Although this certainly reduces the scope of our inquiry, by idealizing our focus in this way, we will be in a better position to rule out pragmatic noise when answering the two key *epistemological* questions of the paper.[7] For ease of reference, call these the *resolution question* and the *deliberation question*.

Resolution question: What is the most epistemically appropriate way to resolve intragroup disagreement: by means of deliberation or by taking a vote? More specifically, to what extent is it epistemically advantageous and disadvantageous that group members *exchange evidence* when it comes to reaching a collective agreement?

Deliberation question: Which conditions should *deliberative* disagreement comply with to be epistemically appropriate? More specifically, what would it take to overcome, or at least mitigate, the epistemic disadvantages of resolving intragroup disagreement by means of deliberation?

Our methodological approach to answering these questions is based on a simple *working assumption*: a group's collective endeavor to solve an internal dispute can be aimed at different (albeit not necessarily incompatible) epistemic goals. More carefully:

Assumption: Possibly, for two epistemic goals, E and E^*, and for two groups, G and G^*, members of G would let p or else not-p stand as the G's view only if the collectively accepted view has epistemic property E and members of G^* would let p or else not-p stand as G^*'s view only if the collectively accepted view has epistemic property E^*.

With this assumption in place, each epistemic goal can be interpreted as providing a particular *standard* for assessing the epistemic significance of deliberating and voting in the resolution of intragroup disagreement. More specifically, the way we propose to assess this epistemic significance is in terms of *goal-conduciveness*: for each goal, we can assess to what extent the fact that group members exchange (or refrain from doing so) reasons and evidence are conducive to it.

The following are four salient candidate epistemic goals we will consider, albeit they are not exhaustive (see n. 9). For any group G in which some operative members hold p and some hold not-p, in trying to settle whether p or else not-p should stand as G's view by means of method M, members of G would let p or else not-p stand as the group's view only if:

1. *Truth*: the collectively accepted view is true.
2. *Evidence*: the collectively accepted view is better supported by the best evidence individually possessed by group members than the opposite view.

3 *Understanding*: the collectively accepted view leads to more understanding than the opposite view.
4 *Epistemic justice*: the fact that G's members let such a view stand as G's view does not wrong any member specifically in her capacity as an epistemic subject (e.g., as a giver of knowledge, in her capacity for social understanding, and so on) or any other person outside the group in that capacity.[8,9]

Before assessing each epistemic goal, a final methodological caveat is in order. Our approach to the epistemic significance of deliberation and voting in terms of goal-conduciveness does not entail that the different epistemic goals are incompatible with each other, nor does it imply any stance on a number of debates, including (i) whether the relevant goals are finally or instrumentally valuable (or fundamentally or derivatively) in the case of collectives (cf., Goldman 1999; Fallis & Mathiesen 2013); or (ii) whether deliberation has a constitutive epistemic aim in terms of one of these goals; (iii) or whether deliberation has procedural in addition to instrumental epistemic value (cf., Peter 2013). Our results might of course be relevant to these debates, but we stay neutral on them.[10]

Here is the plan. In §2.2, we address the truth goal, explain what the different kinds of evidence involved in deliberation are and how they bear on the individual reliability of deliberators; compare the collective reliabilities of deliberation and voting drawing on social choice theory, and show how complex it is to give a straightforward answer to the question of whether deliberation is reliable due to, among other things, the existence of several reliability-undermining group phenomena—which are widely investigated in social psychology. In §2.3, we explain why it shouldn't be assumed that deliberation always achieves optimal results, nor that voting always produces suboptimal outcomes *vis-à-vis* the goal of evidence. In §2.4, we offer two interpretations of the understanding goal and argue that, on both interpretations, deliberation outperforms mere voting. In §2.5, we argue that voting is more efficacious than deliberation with respect to the goal of epistemic justice. In §2.6, we propose several ways to mitigate the potential epistemic disadvantages of solving intragroup disagreement by means of deliberation in relation to each epistemic goal.

2.2 Assessing for Truth

As we have seen, in settling for a collective view, groups may pursue non-epistemic goals (e.g., preventing financial losses), but they sometimes pursue epistemic goals. One example of an epistemically respectable goal, if not the most fundamental epistemic goal,[11] is *truth*.

In scientific disagreement, for example, members of a research group that internally disagree over some factual issue would not let a view stand as the group's view unless they considered it true, or at least, more likely to be true than any competing view. In a quiz show, members of a divided team would not let an answer stand as the team's answer unless they considered it correct (or likely to be correct). Thus, for any given method that members of a divided group may use to reach a collective agreement, we can assess its epistemic propriety in terms of how conducive toward truth this method is. Crucially, the *reliability* of deliberative and voting methods depends on the kind of individual and collective conditions under which they are employed. Fortunately, these conditions have been widely investigated in disciplines such as social psychology and social choice theory. That being so, we will review some of their results (with an eye on truth as the relevant epistemic standard) so as to provide an answer to the resolution question on a safe theoretical and empirical ground.

Before that, it is worth pointing out an *epistemic difference* concerning the reliability of deliberative and voting procedures in general. This will allow us to subsume some relevant results of the aforementioned disciplines under a broader epistemological framework. Consider, first, the following general idea: the reliability of a group in letting only a view that is true stand as the collective view is to some extent premised upon the reliability of individual group members in choosing the right view *both* in the case of deliberation and voting.

To see this, consider a group (e.g. a flat Earth society) such that all members are utterly unreliable (e.g., almost always, they get things wrong) regarding the question of whether *p* (e.g. whether Earth is flat or spherical). Suppose that this kind of group internally disagrees on whether *p* or else not-*p* should stand as the group's view. Even if all members aim at settling on the true view, most will end up defending the false view because of their utter unreliability, whereas those who unlikely end up upholding the right view, will do it by luck. In such a situation, it doesn't matter whether the group deliberates or takes a vote: whatever the procedure for settling their internal disagreement, it will be an unreliable one. Therefore, group members need to be individually reliable to a minimum degree for them to reliably reach a correct collective agreement as a group—in subsection 2.2.2, we will see what the minimum required degree of individual reliability is according to social choice theory.

Nonetheless, while the reliability of a group in letting only a view that is true stand as the collective view is to some extent premised upon the reliability of individual group members both in the case of deliberation and voting, individual reliability is fixed differently in deliberative and non-deliberative cases. The reason, as we will argue next, has to do with the fact that the former involve *different kinds of evidence* besides private evidence and hence different individual competences are required to evaluate them (this will also have a bearing on our discussion in §2.3).

2.2.1 *Individual Reliability*

In non-deliberative cases (at least as we have conceived them), the only evidence that group members use to establish which of the two options in a given dispute (*p* and not-*p*) is true (and therefore which one is the one that the group should uphold) is their own *private evidence*. In deliberative cases, by contrast, group members possess not only private evidence, but they are also exposed to *shared evidence*—i.e. evidence bearing on *p*/not-*p* shared by other group members during deliberation. In addition, as a consequence of this sharing process, they are also exposed to evidence about the distribution of opinions within the group, or *social evidence* for short—i.e. evidence that *n* number of group members are in agreement and *m* number in disagreement with one.

Thus, one plausible idea is that, for any given group member, her overall individual reliability concerning the disputed matter will be determined by how reliable she is in accurately judging to what extent *each* kind of evidence supports *p* or not-*p*. Interestingly, precisely because these are different kinds of evidence, the degree of reliability in assessing them need not coincide, hence the divergence with non-deliberative cases. Let's consider each in turn.

First, group members can be more or less reliable at seeing how relevant to the disputed matter their *private evidence* is, and on how much it supports or counts against the views in conflict. If, for instance, a group member's private evidence is misleading evidence for *p* because, say, it comes from a seemingly trustworthy but ultimately unreliable source, she will hardly assess in a reliable fashion that her evidence does not actually count in favor of *p*. Suppose that voting is the relevant procedure for resolving intragroup disagreement in a given case. In the difficult cases of misleading evidence just mentioned—as well as in cases where a group member has no evidence whatsoever—not voting for either option might be the best action to avoid collective error.

When it comes to *shared evidence*, matters are more complex. When group members put their private evidence on the table during deliberation, all involved members are exposed to two different things: (i) information that may back up, conflict, be redundant with or even irrelevant to their private evidence, and (ii) judgments from other group members to the effect that the shared information supports *p* or else not-*p* to such-and-such degree. Accordingly, and as in the case of private evidence, a group member can be more or less reliable at assessing to what extent the information provided by other members is relevant and corroborative of *p* or of not-*p*, and this can be done by, among other things, correctly assessing to what extent those other members are *competent* information-gatherers. Interestingly, as some have noted (e.g. Elga 2010; Weatherson 2013; Eder [this volume]), being competent at acquiring evidence is independent from being competent at correctly judging the confirmational import of the evidence. Thus, on top of being more or less reliable at assessing the evidence shared during deliberation, group members can be more or less reliable at assessing to what extent their fellow members' assessments of such shared evidence are accurate.

The last kind of evidence involved in deliberative cases, *social evidence*, is somehow different, as it does not directly bear on the question of whether *p*. As we have defined it, social evidence is evidence about, specifically, the distribution of opinions within the group, i.e., evidence about how many group members believe that *p* (or else not-*p*) should stand as the group's view because *p* (or else not-*p*) is true. Interestingly, social evidence can have a defeating effect on its own even if it does not directly bear on the question of whether *p*, and namely even if it carries no more information than that of assertions of the type "I think that *p* should stand as the group's view".

To see this, suppose that you have conclusive private evidence for the truth of *p* and that on that basis you believe that *p* should stand as the group's view. Furthermore, suppose that you are the only person in your group in possession of evidence that is relevant to the disputed matter. You share your evidence with your fellow members, which you regard as your epistemic peers. Suppose, next, that no one is moved and all of them (e.g., 999 members), except for you, individually assert "I believe that not-*p* should stand as the group's view because not-*p* is true". Many in the epistemological literature on disagreement agree that you should reduce your confidence in your belief simply because of being exposed to social evidence to the effect that a majority is in disagreement with you.[12] Furthermore, this defeating effect may occur even if private evidence directly bearing on *p*/not-*p* has not been put on the table yet.[13]

Turning to reliability, the kind of competence required to judge whether the social evidence available in the group is misleading or on the right track is a competence to judge whether the other group members are being *sincere* in asserting things such as "I believe that *p* should stand as the group's view". Suppose that, during deliberation, someone in your group asserts that. The questions you should ask yourself, *qua* group member, are like these: Is this person being sincere? Does she really care about the truth? Or is she making that assertion for strategic or pragmatic reasons? If one can answer these kinds of questions correctly for all (or at least many) group members, one is reliable at processing the group's available social evidence.[14] By contrast, if one conciliates with the majority for a non-epistemic reason such as social comparison (e.g., to maintain a socially favorable position within the group), one is not reliable at processing the group's social evidence.[15]

Which of these different bodies of evidence (i.e., private, shared, or social) and which of the corresponding degrees of reliability in processing them should have a greater weight in the overall individual reliability of a given group member is a question whose answer hangs to a great extent on the correctness of the different views of the epistemology of disagreement. In general, *steadfast theorists* will be more inclined to assign a greater weight to the group members' assessments of their own private evidence (or even of the shared evidence), whereas *conciliationists* will lean in the direction of giving a greater significance to the judgments of other group members and to the distribution of opinions within the group.[16]

To summarize the discussion so far, we've seen that there is a significant difference between how individual reliability is fixed in deliberative and non-deliberative cases of intragroup disagreement. This difference has to do with the fact that, in non-deliberative cases, group members only need to evaluate the confirmational import of their own private evidence to choose between the true and the false collective view. In deliberative cases, by contrast, group members need to process, besides their private evidence, the evidence shared by others as well as the available evidence about the distribution of opinions within the group, which can have a defeating effect by itself. In such deliberative cases, however, it is an open question which kind of evidence should carry more weight in fixing the individual reliability of group members, or what the interplay between these three types of evidence might be.

2.2.2 Group Reliability

One question we can ask concerning the reliability of deliberative and voting procedures is how reliable individual members of a group undergoing an internal dispute need be in order for one such procedure to reliably lead the group to settle on the true view. The results of social choice theory become useful on this score.

Let's consider voting first. In general, political scientists assess voting rules in terms of *fairness criteria*, i.e., how sensitive they are to all of the voter's opinions and preferences in the right way (Pacuit 2019). However, interestingly for our epistemological purposes, they can also be assessed in terms of how well they track the truth, i.e., in terms of how much the resulting collective view approximates it (List 2013; Pacuit 2019). A voting rule that is often referred to as a *collective truth-tracking device* in the two-option case (the one we are concerned with) is *majority rule* (see, e.g., List & Goodin 2001).

As it is well-known, one prominent argument for adopting majority rule comes from the Condorcet Jury Theorem (CJT), which maintains that, given two possible positions *p* and not-*p* with respect to a given topic (e.g., a verdict, a diagnosis, a factual issue), where only one of the options is correct given some standard (in our case, truth), the probability that a majority votes for the correct option increases and converges to one as the size of the group grows. Crucially, CJT is premised upon two conditions: (i) that the probability (viz. reliability) that each group member identifies the correct position is greater than 0.5 and the same for all voters (*voter competence condition*) and (ii) that all correct votes are mutually independent, conditional on the truth,[17] which is either *p* or not-*p* (*voter independence condition*).[18]

Whether or not majority rule reliably yields epistemically appropriate results (true or accurate group agreements) crucially depends on the voter competence and independence conditions being met. But this seldom happens. For instance, factors that have been cited as leading to correlated votes include opinion leaders, schools of thought, communication among voters, or common information (cf., e.g., Ladha 1992). Moreover, as Dietrich and Spiekermann (2020) point out, *any* common cause of votes is a potential source of dependence, including non-evidential (e.g., situational) factors such as distracting heat.[19]

Lack of independence has implications not only for whether or not CJT applies to a group that aims to resolve an internal dispute by taking a vote according to majority rule, but also for how the nature of such a disagreement should be conceived. After all, if the votes of every member in the two disagreeing subgroups are correlated, intragroup disagreement comes down to a one-to-one disagreement situation, as there would be two sets of mutually dependent votes: those for *p* and those for not-*p*. This is epistemically significant. For one epistemic benefit of CJT is that the *larger* the group, the *better* at tracking the truth it is. Therefore, if all votes are correlated in the two disagreeing subgroups, the size of the group no longer has a bearing on its reliability.

Turning to voter competence, multiple specific factors can bear on the individual reliability of voters. From a general epistemological point of view, the quality of their private evidence is probably the most significant factor. But note that voter reliability can be low even when the evidence privately possessed is good evidence. For the probability that a voter *correctly* judges that her good evidence is supportive of *p* rather than not-*p* is independent of the epistemic goodness of the evidence (e.g., someone with conclusive private evidence might fail to notice that the evidence is conclusive because of not being sufficiently attentive). Conversely, a voter with misleading evidence might uncritically follow her evidence, thus making it unlikely that she votes for the correct view. Finally, voters can also be unlikely to vote for the right view when they possess no evidence whatsoever (e.g., by casting their votes for *p* or not-*p* merely on the basis of the results of tossing coins that unbeknownst to them are independently biased in favor of the false view). Interestingly, all this can happen while all group members vote with the aim of choosing the correct view.

Lack of voter competence bears on the epistemic appropriateness of majority vote as a way of solving a group's internal dispute. One thing that the literature on CJT shows is that when the votes are independent but the competence of all voters is lower than 0.5 and the same for all, or when the average judgmental competence of voters in the group is lower than 0.5 (cf., e.g., Grofman et al. 1983), the probability that a majority votes for the correct option increases and converges to 0 as the size of the group grows. So majority rule can be an epistemically *inappropriate* procedure for solving intragroup disagreement after all.

Of course, the literature is filled with jury theorems that relax the independence (Ladha 1992, Dietrich & List 2004; Dietrich & Spiekermann 2013; Goodin & Spiekermann 2018) and the competence (e.g. Grofman et al. 1983; Boland 1989) conditions while still serving as truth-tracking devices, and hence as epistemically appropriate ways to resolve intragroup disagreement, at least in the case of large groups.[20] But, in general, voters need to be individually reliable to a sufficient degree, where in most cases this means being better than random.[21]

For some internal disputes, when individual reliability is an issue, groups can opt for some sort of proxy voting system that allows delegation of the votes to the most competent or well-informed in the group, or to weighted majority rules (e.g., expert rules) that assign different weights to different competence distributions (e.g., more weight to the votes of the most competent members). In general, for any competence distribution, there will be an optimal voting truth-tracking procedure for the group to solve its internal disagreement (for optimal voting rules see, e.g., Nitzan & Paroush 1982; Gradstein & Nitzan 1986; Dietrich 2006).

Beyond specific voting rules groups might use to resolve their internal disputes, one question we can ask is this: does communication and evidence sharing among group members represent a significant epistemic advantage over members simply taking a vote on the basis of her private evidence? What are the epistemic benefits and drawbacks of deliberation in general *vis-à-vis* the goal of reaching a true collective agreement?

One way to answer these questions is to offer a formal analysis of deliberation and compare it with voting procedures. Hartmann and Rafiee Rad (2018) do precisely this and show that deliberation is truth-conducive in a similar way as majority voting as per CJT. It is worth considering their proposed Bayesian model of deliberation, not only because its results are relevant to the subject matter, but also because it will serve to illustrate the many complexities that communication among group members may give rise to and, therefore, that any formal model of deliberation might need to incorporate if deliberation is to be compared to voting in a realistic way.

Hartmann and Rafiee Rad's Bayesian model of deliberation is based on several assumptions. First, all evidence is put on the table *before* deliberation (i.e., no extra evidence shows up during deliberation, so all evidence is shared evidence). Second, group members are assigned a first-order reliability value that measures how correctly they judge the disputed matter. Third, they are assigned a second-order reliability value that reflects how well they estimate the first-order reliability of the other group members. The latter is kept fixed during the course of deliberation, while the former may increase as members learn to better judge the reliability of other group members. In this way, deliberation, as they model it, consists in the following process:

> The group has to decide on the truth or falsity of a hypothesis H. Each group member assigns a certain probability to H. Then each group member casts a vote on the basis of this probability. Then each group member updates her probability on the basis of the votes of the other group members, weighted according to the estimated reliabilities (...). The procedure is iterated, and in each round the second order reliabilities are increased which leads to a more accurate estimation of the reliability of the votes of the other group members. After a number of rounds, this process converges.
>
> (Hartmann & Rafiee Rad 2018: 1278)

Their results show that the truth-tracking properties of deliberation are very similar to those of majority vote. As they summarize them:

> The deliberation process results in a consensus and correctly tracks the truth for groups of large size in the following cases: (i) homogeneous groups with a first order reliability greater than 0.5 and with a high second order reliability (ii) inhomogeneous groups with average first order reliabilities above 0.5 and with a high (initial) second order reliability. In this sense the deliberation procedure manifests the same epistemic properties as the majority voting while adding the benefit of a group consensus (...) We furthermore provided simulation results that indicate that the deliberation procedure tracks the truth even in cases that do not fall under the conditions stated in the Condorcet Jury Theorem for majority voting as well as for groups with low second order reliabilities.
>
> (Hartmann & Rafiee Rad 2018: 1289)

In sum, if Hartmann and Rafiee Rad are right, although majority vote may be more easily implemented as a procedure for solving intragroup disagreement in the case of large groups, deliberating *vis-à-vis* the goal of reaching true collective agreements is roughly as epistemically appropriate as voting by majority rule. This gives an answer to the resolution question. As we will see next, however, this answer is incomplete, since real-life deliberation cases may involve many complexities that make giving a general, straightforward answer to that question a complex matter.

2.2.3 Deliberation in Non-Idealized Conditions

Formal models are surely a great approach to the question of whether deliberation or voting is the most reliable way to solve intragroup disagreement. But deliberation involves many complexities—not present in voting cases—that have a bearing on its reliability as a collective method for solving intragroup disagreement, and which can make it difficult to give a straightforward answer. To illustrate this, consider Hartmann and Rafiee Rad's model again. As they acknowledge, in order to capture the reliability of more realistic deliberative situations, several assumptions of the model need to be relaxed, such as the assumption that the deliberators are independent, i.e., that the only cause for a group members' verdict is the truth or falsity of the hypothesis in question—whereas other members' verdicts are evidence for the truth or falsity of that hypothesis that don't necessarily break such an independence. Indeed:

i In real-life deliberation cases, the individual judgments of members of deliberating groups may not be independent from each other.

Or the assumption that the first-order reliability of group members remains unchanged during deliberation. After all:

ii In real-life deliberation cases, the probability that a given group member is right or wrong about the disputed matter may change along the deliberative process.

Or the assumption that the first-order reliability of group members is independent from their second-order reliability. However:

iii In real-life deliberation cases, how well a group member estimates how reliable, concerning the disputed matter, other group members are may be influenced by the judgment of those other members.

Other complications that a formal model of deliberation might need to incorporate to better reflect how deliberation compares with voting in real cases include the following. For instance, one crucial assumption of Hartmann and Rafiee Rad's model is that there is full disclosure of the evidence among all group members before deliberation. But:

iv In real-life deliberation cases, group members may gradually disclose their private evidence to other group members, and may not even disclose any evidence at all.

This is relevant, because in so proceeding deliberating groups can and often times fall prey to *shared information bias*, a tendency to discuss shared evidence, i.e., evidence that most group members possess, in detriment to discussing potentially relevant evidence privately possessed by individual members or only shared by a few of them (cf., Stasser & Titus 1985). If group members have good private evidence, but they do not draw on it during discussion—a situation that is often referred to as a *hidden profile*—the reliability of the deliberative process can be compromised. Several factors can help groups overcome shared information bias (see §2.3). Interestingly, the kind of groups we are concerned with—those whose goal is to find a correct answer—see this bias diminished by devoting more of their discussions to considering critical clues thus becoming more likely to adopt a correct view when relevant private information remains unshared (Stasser & Stewart 1992).

Another crucial assumption of Hartmann and Rafiee Rad's model is that deliberation proceeds in a series of iterations in which each group member first assigns a probability to the hypothesis in question, then casts a vote, and then each member updates her probability on the basis of the votes of other group members, weighted according to the estimated reliabilities. However:

v In real-life deliberation cases, group members may discuss the relevant issue one or several times and then take one final single vote to decide which view should stand as the group's view, or simply reach consensus without voting at all.

Other complexities have to do with the different types of evidence distinguished in §2.1. For example, during deliberation group members put their private evidence on the table, which becomes shared evidence. The complication, as we have already pointed out, is that:

vi In real-life deliberation cases, group members may need to assess two things: how good the evidence shared by other members is (e.g., by judging, among other things, how reliable those members are in gathering good evidence) and how good those other members' assessments of their own shared evidence are (e.g., by judging how reliable they are in assessing the confirmation import of their evidence).

This means that a more realistic model may need to include two measures of second-order reliability, instead of one (see Eder, this volume, for this kind of approach).

In addition, as we have also argued, social evidence—i.e., evidence about the distribution of opinions within the group—can have a defeating effect on its own (i.e., independent of the group's shared evidence) even if it carries no information directly bearing on the question of whether p (like shared evidence does). Relatedly, the very distribution of the disagreement matters and, in particular, when the relevant intragroup disagreement is between a majority and a minority. This is illustrated by extensive research in social psychology on group conformity pressures, and in particular, on *majority influence*. For example, in a famous study by Sherif (1936), subjects were asked to perform a visual task. Subjects whose estimations diverged from those of the majority gradually converged to the latter after being exposed several times to the opinions of the majority. In later studies by Asch (e.g., 1952), the relevant visual task had an obvious correct answer and conformity to the majority was also observed (although to a lesser extent). Accordingly, it is plausible that:

vii In real-life deliberation cases, group members who hold a different view to the one held by most members of the group may conform to the majority opinion by repeatedly being exposed to it.

Judging whether a disagreeing majority is right or wrong might be a complex issue. In particular, to judge whether majority influence is epistemically appropriate, one needs to determine whether it is informational (i.e., due to the fact that there is more evidence supporting the relevant opinion) or normative (e.g., due to a desire to fit and avoid social exclusion). Incorporating a corresponding realistic measure of reliability in a formal model of deliberation might accordingly be a complex issue as well.

The issue is even more complex considering the fact that *minorities* also exert influence on majorities. For instance, Moscovici and Zavalloni (1969) observed this kind of effect in a visual task with an obvious correct answer when a minority of subjects gave consistent and unanimous answers that diverged from those of the majority. Thus:

viii In real-life deliberation cases, group members who unanimously hold a different view to the one held by most members may make the latter conform to their opinions by consistently exposing it to them.

The existence of minority dissent is not necessarily negative at the collective level. Quite the contrary: minority dissent previous to group discussion has been observed to improve the quality of the resulting collective judgments and decisions (e.g., Hightower & Sayeed 1996; Brodbeck et al. 2002; Schulz-Hardt et al. 2005).

Another specific condition widely investigated in social psychology that may affect the reliability of deliberation is the *group polarization* phenomenon (e.g., Stoner 1961; Burnstein & Vinokur 1977; Isenberg 1986)[22]:

ix In real-life deliberation cases, the individual members of like-minded groups may adopt, on average, more extreme views after group discussion than those held before deliberation.

This means, for instance, that in an intragroup disagreement where most group members lean, on average, toward *p* and only a few toward not-*p* chances are that if group members discuss whether *p* or not-*p* should stand as the group's view, the group's average will more strongly lean toward *p*. This is a source of collective unreliability, at least in the cases where *p* is false. Thus, the initial distribution of opinions in a group featuring an internal disagreement matters for how reliable deliberation is in solving it.

Finally, when it comes to the different kinds of evidence involved in deliberation, the most difficult issue to solve is this:

x In real-life deliberation cases, it may be unclear what exactly the interplay between the different kinds of evidence (private, shared or social) is, and which one should play a more significant role in whether a group ends up adopting a true or else a false view following deliberation.

As we noted in §2.1, it is an open question which of these three kinds of evidence should have a greater weight in fixing the reliability of individual deliberators. This question might be difficult to address with formalization or empirical research only, and further philosophical investigation is required.

So where does this leave us? Is deliberation as appropriate as a method to solve intragroup disagreement *vis-à-vis* the truth goal as voting is when CJT-style theorems apply? According to Hartmann and Rafiee Rad's model, the answer is 'yes'. However, this answer to the resolution question, albeit on the right track, is not (as they also acknowledge) fully satisfactory: deliberating groups can be affected by a variety of factors that bear negatively (but also positively) on the reliability of deliberation. Some such factors that we have discussed are: (i) the interdependence between the judgments of group members; (ii) changes in their first-order reliability along the deliberative process; (iii) the first-order and second-order reliabilities of group members not being independent; (iv) shared information bias and hidden profile situations; (v) different modes of deliberating, such as several iterations of deliberation and voting, deliberation followed by a single final vote, or deliberation followed by consensus absent voting; (vi) the group members' need to assess the epistemic quality of the evidence shared by others and of the judgments they make about such evidence; (vii) majority influence; (viii) minority influence; (ix) group polarization; and (x) the complex interplay between private, shared, and social evidence. If anything involves complexity, that is the question of whether deliberation is a truth-conducive method for solving intragroup disagreement.

2.3 Assessing for Evidence

Truth is not the end of the story, however. It is not unusual that members of a group featuring an internal disagreement are not merely interested in settling on a true collective view, but on a view that is supported by the best evidence individually possessed by them. Of course, the truth and evidence goals are not incompatible and are in fact oftentimes pursued simultaneously, so that members of a group would let a certain view stand as the group's view only if it were true and supported by the best private evidence available in the group.

However, the two goals are also independent from each other and cases of groups whose primary goal is not truth but evidential support are conceivable. For example, consider a group of high-profile members of the Bush administration back in 2003 having a disagreement about the exact location of Saddam Hussein's weapons of mass destruction. Even if all are aware or suspect that there are no WMDs, they might still be interested in collectively agreeing on the view that is supported by the best evidence privately possessed by them (such as the most credible military reports about the possible locations of WMDs). Or consider a tobacco company's board of directors back in the 1950s having a disagreement on which kind of evidence provides the best epistemic justification against the (now proven) fact that there is a causal link between smoking and lung cancer. Each board member might be in possession of different bodies of evidence, such as different statements from physicians against that fact or different scientific reports to the effect that there is no conclusive scientific proof of a link between smoking and cancer. Even if all board members might individually suspect that smoking causes cancer, they might still be more interested in agreeing on a collective view that is false yet supported by their best private evidence than on a true collective view with worse or no intragroup evidential support.[23] The motives of these groups might be non-epistemic—e.g., convincing the public opinion that Saddam Hussein has WMDs or that smoking is not causally linked to lung cancer—but their goals, insofar as they prime evidential support, can be considered epistemic.[24]

Thus, with the goal of evidence (not truth) in mind, we can ask: what method for solving intragroup disagreement is best *vis-à-vis* the evidence goal: deliberation or voting? At first sight, deliberation seems a better method for solving intragroup disagreement when a group is mainly seeking evidential support. After all, it is at the core of any deliberative process that group members communicate their opinions and share their evidence with other members. Thus, in ideal deliberative conditions, no collective decision is made or no collective view is adopted unless all members share their private evidence and everyone processes it.

By contrast, not all voting rules seem well-suited to reach collective views that are supported by the best evidence privately possessed within the group. Consider majoritarian rules. Suppose that a group of physicians disagree about whether they should give treatment A or B to a patient. All except one believe that they should apply A. Their opinions are based on their own physical examination of the patient and their clinical judgment. By contrast, the only dissenter in the group is in possession of conclusive evidence for applying B (e.g., evidence from randomized clinical trials). Without prior deliberation (something admittedly rare for medical decisions), the group takes a vote and they collectively accept that they should apply treatment A. This view, however, is not supported by the best evidence privately possessed within the group: the dissenter's evidence is discounted as a result of the voting procedure.

Of course, this neither implies that deliberation always achieves optimal results, nor that voting always produces suboptimal outcomes *vis-à-vis* the goal of evidence. As the social choice theory literature shows, some voting rules are conducive to this goal. In addition, as the social psychology literature demonstrates, deliberating groups often operate in non-ideal conditions that prevent them from exploiting the full potential of deliberation.

Let's consider voting first. In a recent paper, Bozbay et al. (2014) propose a quota rule that aims to make correct collective decisions (or judgments) while being efficient in light of all the information privately possessed by group members. As Dietrich and List (2007: 392) explain, quota rules are judgment aggregation rules such that "a proposition is collectively accepted if and only if the number of individuals accepting it is greater than or equal to some threshold". Bozbay et al. focus on cases in which groups need to settle on the correctness of two propositions, e.g., a jury on whether a contract was broken and whether it is legally valid, or a hiring committee on whether a candidate is good at research and good at teaching. Their proposed quota rule for these simple preferences (i.e., choosing between a correct and an incorrect decision, making a right or a wrong judgment) is based on the idea that for any of these propositions to be more probably true than false given all information, at least a number of group members above a certain threshold—which they define formally—need to possess evidence for that proposition. This rule, they argue, effectively uses all the private evidence available in the group assuming that group members aim for correct decisions and judgments. In sum, even if majoritarian rules are not appropriate for the goal of evidence, voting cannot be discarded out of hand as a procedure for solving intragroup disagreement with the aim of settling on an evidentially well-supported collective view.

Let's consider deliberation now. While it is true that there are voting rules that are appropriate for the goal of evidence, it is also true that deliberation may not be conducive to it. As we have seen, deliberating groups often fall prey to shared information bias—recall: the tendency to discuss evidence that most members possess in detriment of' discussing potentially relevant evidence privately possessed by individual group members or only shared by a few of them. When a group undergoes this kind of bias and the unshared evidence is the best or at least relevant evidence (a hidden profile situation), solving an internal dispute by deliberating may not be more conducive to the evidence goal than voting by majoritarian rules.

We have also seen that groups that aim to find a correct answer (at the truth goal), see this bias diminished because they devote more discussion time to consider critical clues (Stasser & Stewart 1992). Other factors that help reduce shared information bias include the involvement of team leaders (Larson et al. 1996) as well as of members with experience in the subject matter (Wittenbaum 1998)—they pay more attention to unshared information—low time pressure or having access to sheets that either indicate which pieces of information are shared and unshared—rather than discussing the relevant issue from memory—(Bowman & Wittenbaum 2012). However, the most relevant factor in the context of intragroup disagreement is, precisely, the existence of dissent within the group.

For instance, in a study by Brodbeck et al. (2002) they observed that groups featuring dissent before deliberation shared more information during discussion. In another study, Schulz-Hardt et al. (2005) found that groups featuring dissent are more likely to arrive at a correct collective decision or judgment than homogeneous groups—especially when someone in the group advocates the right solution—by, among other things, increasing discussion intensity and better pooling of unshared evidence. Interestingly, they also established a correlation between pre-deliberation dissent and better collective outcomes and less shared information bias in groups where none of the members favored the right solution—e.g., groups like the high-profile members of the Bush administration disagreeing about the possible locations of Saddam Hussein's WMDs or the tobacco company's board of directors disagreeing about which evidence best proves that there is no causal link between smoking and lung cancer. Another study by Greitemeyer et al. (2006) further confirmed the positive effects of intragroup disagreement, this time with artificially fostered controversy within target groups. In their study, they implemented an advocacy procedure in which each group member acted as an advocate for each alternative for some time independently of their individual preferences. This procedure resulted in an increased exchange of both unshared and shared information.

Thus, if it is at the core of any deliberative process that private evidence is shared among group members and the very existence of intragroup disagreement is already a factor that cancels out (perhaps in combination with other factors we've seen) shared information bias, we have good reason to think that deliberating is an appropriate way to solve intragroup disagreement with the primary aim of settling on an evidentially supported collective view.

2.4 Assessing for Understanding

Suppose that members of a group, *G*, aim to let *p* or else not-*p* stand as the group's view only if it facilitates *understanding*. Understanding—at least, as it is typically discussed in epistemology—is a genus with (at least) two distinct species: (i) *understanding-why* (e.g., I understand why the house burnt down, I understand why Caesar crossed the Rubicon) and (ii) *objectual understanding* (I understand chemistry, I understand Australian Rules football). It is an open question how these two species are related.

Moreover, it is a point of contention whether either of these species of understanding *reduces* to propositional knowledge, or to each other.[25] For the present purposes, we will remain neutral on these points. One assumption we will make, however, is that understanding involves—in some suitably specified sense—*grasping*. In the case of *understanding-why*, what one grasps when one understands why something is so is the relation between the *explanans* and the *explanandum*. In the case of *objectual understanding*, what one grasps when one understands something, X, which can be treated as a subject matter, is the explanatory and coherence-making relations between propositions making up the relevant body of information (e.g., Kvanvig 2003, Ch. 8; Gordon 2017).

In *both* cases, truth plays a constraining role, even if true beliefs don't suffice for understanding of either variety. For example, you don't understand why the house burnt down if the explanation you grasp is itself false—e.g., *The house burnt down because of arson* (false) versus *The house burnt down because of faulty wiring* (true). Likewise, in the case of objectual understanding, one doesn't understand combustion even if one grasps the coherence and explanatory relations between the (mostly false) propositions making up phlogiston theory—and this is so even if one, by such grasping this body of information, understands, merely, the phlogiston *theory* of combustion.

If true beliefs are necessary for understanding, why are they not sufficient? Here is the importance of grasping to understanding. A child might, for example, believe truly (e.g., via testimony from a parent) that the house burnt down due to faulty wiring without *understanding why* this is so, on account of failing to suitably grasp how the *explanans* relates to the *explanandum*. Likewise, one might fail to understand algebraic geometry even if one has memorized true axioms and formulae, if one fails to grasp how the relevant axioms and formulae hang together, e.g., by failing to grasp how the axioms and formulae are mutually supporting.

Against this (albeit brief) background: let's consider how voting and deliberation, respectively, fare as a means to achieving a group's aim to let *p* or else not-*p* stand as the group's view only if it facilitates *understanding*. For simplicity, we will focus on understanding *why*—using as a reference case the following: suppose the mayor of a city has appointed a committee to determine why city hall mysteriously burned to the ground in a fire. The two salient alternatives the committee are evaluating as the cause are faulty wiring and arson. Let 'Case 1' be a case where the group simply takes a vote (e.g., 'yea' for fire, 'nay' for arson), and let 'Case 2' be a case featuring deliberation. Which best facilitates understanding?

Interestingly, there are two very different senses in which a vote or a deliberation *vis-à-vis* arson or faulty wiring might (broadly speaking) 'facilitate' understanding, which need to be separated. Suppose, for example, the mayor goes further to instruct the committee to not settle on a group view (*vis-à-vis* arson or faulty wiring) *until* the group understands why the hall burnt down. In such a situation, the settled view should be made *on the basis* of a certain kind of epistemic credential, and regardless of whether taking that vote *promotes* the group's understanding—e.g., regardless of whether reaching a settled view will *itself* help the group come to understand the cause of the fire, or to increase that understanding.

On this interpretation of the understanding goal, *merely* voting will be inefficacious, and this is so even if voters antecedently meet voter competence and voter independence conditions, and thus, even if voting would further the truth aim. Deliberation by comparison does much better. Put another way, the probability that the group will be positioned to reach a verdict on the basis of understanding conditioned on deliberation is higher than on voting, even if it is *not* particularly high in cases where subjects prior to deliberation fail to meet competence and independence conditions.

The rationale for why voting will do worse in comparison to deliberation (*vis-à-vis* the above interpretation of the understanding goal) is that the mere registering (by group members) *that* each member holds certain views [either the 'yea' or 'nay' view] is simply not the sort of thing that could ensure that a group *grasps* why something is so; deliberation, by contrast is. On this point, Kenneth Boyd's (2019) analogy between a group's physically grasping something and cognitively grasping something is helpful:

> [...] consider again the way in which individuals rely on one another in the case of physical group grasping: they rely on each other insofar as they are aware both that they must direct effort towards the same goal, and that if any other let go then they would not be able to pull their friend to shore safely on their own. In the epistemic case the situation is analogous: if the goal of the group is to understand (why/how/that) p, then members of the group are mutually p-reliant in the case that they recognize both that they are contributing towards the relevant goal (perhaps in the form of representing reasons and relationships between reasons), and that they would not be able to achieve that goal on their own (given the circumstances).
>
> (2019: 15–16)

Boyd's idea here is that kind of grasping that is germane to a group's understanding something involves, necessarily, some kind of *group reliance*, viz., reliance between group members on each other's contributions toward the common goal, as well appreciation that each other's contributions is necessary. Mere voting in the absence of sharing evidence is a paradigmatic example of a *non-reliant* contribution to a common goal. If group members fail to understand why city hall burnt down prior to voting, so they will fail to understand why after voting, and will thereby simply *register* viewpoints that are reached unreliantly on other group members' influences. Deliberation, by contrast, offers at least the kinds of conditions that could make such reliance possible, especially when deliberation involves the sharing of evidence and reasons.

The above articulates the situation, at least, if the idea is that the settled view of the group should be made *on the basis* of a certain kind of epistemic credential—viz., understanding. Interestingly, with respect to the understanding goal, we end up with the same result (viz., deliberation beats voting) even if we reject that the settled view should be made *on the basis* of a certain kind of understanding and instead ask whether voting or deliberation better *promotes* the group's understanding.

Voting does look, initially at least, as though it could promote understanding. Returning to our illustrative case of the committee appointed by the mayor to determine why city hall burned (viz., arson or fire): even if the committee simply takes a vote, with no deliberation whatsoever, group members, in virtue of their appreciation of what each other has voted, might gain some kind of intellectual traction on the situation. For example, if I am on the committee and antecedently think that other committee members satisfy a voter competence condition, then my coming to find out that there is a near-unanimous vote favoring the arson explanation might lead me to think it's more likely than not that it was arson rather than faulty wiring. In fact, on the basis of simply gaining knowledge of this revealed voting distribution, I might even become highly epistemically justified in believing this.

However, no matter how high we raise my antecedent knowledge of the extent to which other voters on the committee satisfy a competence condition, and no matter how large the group size agreement is (e.g., no matter how many people there are on the committee whose votes align with the same explanation), it remains that the kind of intellectual improvement I might attain by simply learning what a voting pattern is, is going to fall short of understanding. The same, however, does not apply in the case of deliberation.

The argument for this is as follows. The first premise says that expert testimony does not suffice for individual-level understanding-why. This premise (defended in various places by Duncan Pritchard, e.g., 2009, 2014) gains support from the following kinds of cases. Suppose you want to understand why the dinosaurs went extinct, and you ask an expert paleontologist. The paleontologist is in a hurry and simply tells you that they went extinct because of an asteroid. You then come (in the absence of any undefeated defeaters for this expert testimony) to believe the proposition "the dinosaurs went extinct because of an asteroid". While it is uncontentious (regardless of whether one is a reductionist or anti-reductionist in the epistemology of testimony) that you can come to gain *propositional knowledge* on the basis of this kind of testimonial exchange, Pritchard's line is that such testimony isn't enough to secure understand-why given that (i) understanding-why requires a suitable grasp of the how the relevant cause and effect relationship, and (ii) such a grasp is not something one gains *simply* by accepting someone's word, even an expert's.

The second premise of the argument then draws an analogy between testimony from experts and testimony from intragroup members, where the latter is effectively what one gleans by coming to learn that there was a majority voting pattern in favor of one explanation (e.g., arson) over another. The claim is that *if* the former doesn't suffice for understanding, then neither does the latter. That is: if expert testimony to the effect that some causal claim is true doesn't suffice for understanding *why* that claim is true (even if it suffices to furnish justification or even knowledge), then neither will the testimony to the effect that some causal claim is true when the source of that testimony is an aggregation of voting choices by individuals one regards to be competent. Taken together, the two premises imply that mere voting is not going to facilitate group understanding-why—or, at least, not any more than *mere* expert testimony facilitates understanding-why.

It's worth noting of course that deliberation is importantly different from mere voting in exactly the kind of respect in which mere voting was shown to (like relying on testimony) be incapable of engendering understanding-why. This is because when a group deliberates about why something, X, is so, the sharing of evidence (and indeed, in some cases, the critical discussion of shared evidence) engages with not *merely* the matter of *what* caused X (e.g., arson caused the fire, an asteroid caused the dinosaurs' extinction, etc.), but *how* it did so. For example, the mayor-appointed committee, upon sharing evidence, will discuss such things as whether the building had enough flammable material to have burnt simply through a burning wire, what an arsonist would have had to do to have brought about the fire in the way it was brought about, etc. Such considerations are, of course, exactly the thing that (*à la* Pritchard) one would have to have some command of if one is to grasp the connection between the relevant cause and effect. And, moreover, by *relying* on one another for such considerations (and not merely for the *verdicts*), group members are grasping an explanation as a group in a way that is (*à la* Boyd) analogous to the way a group might physically grasp something together.

Bringing this all together: we've seen in this section that there are two ways we might plausibly measure the effectiveness of voting as opposed to deliberation in light of the epistemic aim of understanding. The first way is to ask which is more effective if the objective is for the group to reach a settled view about why X only if the group understands why X. The second is to ask which is more effective if the objective is to promote the group's understanding. In both cases, we've seen (for different reasons) that deliberation outperforms mere voting.

2.5 Assessing for Epistemic Justice

Thus far, we've been considering how voting versus deliberation fare with respect to the following kinds of goal-conduciveness: truth, evidence, and understanding. Each of these goals is a traditional epistemic goal.

As recent work in social epistemology has shown, there are important connections between epistemic goals and social power and pressures, connections which can give rise to what Miranda Fricker (2007) terms *epistemic injustice*. Put generally, an injustice to someone is an epistemic injustice if it involves their being wrongfully disadvantaged in their capacity as an epistemic subject (e.g., a potential knower). A central species of epistemic injustice is *testimonial injustice*, for example, when prejudice leads a hearer to give a deflated level of credibility to a speaker's word.[26] In a group setting, we might imagine, for instance, a female or minority juror's viewpoint being disregarded on the basis of sexist prejudice or, more subtly, being accepted but being given less weight than the viewpoint of an equally or less competent male juror.

Given the prevalence of these kinds of prejudices and the epistemic harms they lead to, one kind of epistemic value which groups might aspire to in settling the matter is to settle it in a way that mitigates, or is free from, epistemic injustices to individual members of the group. More precisely, let us suppose that a group adopts the following aim: to let *p* or else not-*p* stand as the group's view only if their doing so does not wrong any member specifically in her capacity as an epistemic subject (e.g., as a giver of knowledge, in her capacity for social understanding, and so on) or any other person outside the group in that capacity. Such a group, for short, adopts the aim of *epistemic justice*.

Of course, a group's aiming to issue an epistemic just verdict does not in any way *preclude* aiming at other epistemic goods, and in fact, it would be natural to expect that this aim will generally be paired with other aims. For example, a group might combine this aim with the aim of truth. In which case, the group aims to let *p* or else not-*p* stand as the group's view only if (i) *p* or else not-*p* is true, and (ii) their doing so does not wrong any member specifically in her capacity as an epistemic subject or any other person outside the group in that capacity.

Does voting or deliberation better facilitate epistemic justice? Let's begin by considering the following simple argument for voting: epistemic injustice (at least, of the testimonial variety of epistemic justice we're interested in) depends on testimonial exchange. Voting, but not deliberation, forecloses the possibility of testimonial exchange; so, voting, but not deliberation, forecloses a condition on which testimonial injustice depends. Therefore, voting better facilitates epistemic justice—specifically, by (unlike deliberation) blocking a condition necessary for its manifestation.

If the above argument is sound, then it looks as though voting should be favored to deliberation on epistemic justice grounds, even if it turns out that deliberation beats voting with respect to other epistemic goals.

Put perhaps there is space for the proponent of deliberation to press back along the following lines: even if deliberation is a precondition for epistemic injustice of the testimonial variety to occur, it remains that it is unlikely that testimonial injustice *will* occur in ordinary structured voting groups, e.g., such as juries, where there are norms in place already to give appropriate weight to individual viewpoints. For example, as this line of thought might go, juries are read instructions prior to deliberation that are meant to combat an epistemically irresponsible assessment of evidence, of which testimonial injustice is an instance. Likewise, other groups, particularly those with internal decision procedures that are structured around an office and a charter (Kallestrup 2016; cf., Pettit & Schweikard 2006), specify within that charter the *rules* by which a group will proceed toward its (joint) aims. So long as such rules demand a fair evaluation of evidence during deliberation, they will *de facto* block epistemic injustice. Or so the thought might go.

The above reply is met with a rather straightforward counterreply. Empirical studies by Waters and Hans (2009) show how deliberation often does engender testimonial injustice in the case of juries (particularly those using unanimity rules), where the rules for evaluating evidence are, and *paradigmatically* so, meant to be impartial ones. What Waters and Hans (2009) found was that (in a study of 3,500 jurors in four urban courts) 38% of juries contained at least one juror who succumbed to social pressure by voting along with the rest despite being such that they would have voted differently had they voted privately (Waters & Hans 2009: 520). And, as Brian Hedden (2017) notes, such pressures are "likely to have a disproportionate impact on "low status" jurors, that is, females, members of minority ethnic groups, jurors with less education, jurors of low socioeconomic status, and the like" (2006: 7). Hedden reaches this conclusion on the basis of studies from, in particular, Christensen and Abbott (2000) and Hastie et al. (1983), which report findings that lower status jurors speak less, share less evidence, exert less influence, and are less likely to be elected as a jury foreperson.

These considerations support a presumptive case for thinking that deliberation will be positively correlated with epistemic injustice in a way that mere voting will not. However, even if this is granted, the proponent of deliberation has a card still to play: perhaps even if deliberation leads to epistemic injustice through the kinds of mechanisms described, it also facilitates at the same time epistemic *justice*—viz., perhaps deliberation is on the whole *more* epistemically just than it is unjust, even granting the kinds of considerations Hedden draws attention to.

One attempt to advance this kind of an argument draws from considerations about the *procedural value* of deliberation. According to Fabienne Peter (2013), there is a procedural epistemic value to deliberation which does not simply reduce to the epistemic value deliberation might have in so far as it brings about epistemic values such as truth, knowledge, etc. The idea is as follows: deliberation (particularly when it involves epistemic peers), brings about relationships of *mutual accountability*, relationships that are characterized by (among other things) a respect for epistemic *equality* among group members. As Peter (2013) puts it:

> deliberative parties who count each other as peers ought to recognize each other as such. It is then not permissible to give extra weight to one's own beliefs simply because they are one's own. This condition ensures that the participants are each aware of their own fallibility and acknowledge the possibility that their own beliefs may be wrong while their peers might be correct [...].
>
> (2013: 1264)

Peter emphasizes that the value of this kind of mutual accountability, which is grounded in respect for epistemic equality, along with a "willingness to enter deliberation and to explicate one's beliefs; and [...] uptake" (2013: 1264), is procedural in that it does not "reduce to the value of its result" (2013: 1263). So, for Peter, the procedural value that mutual accountability adds to a correct group stance (e.g., p) is not 'swamped' by the value of that group's correct stance that *p*.

There are two worries for this argument. The first has to do with the swamping claim. It is not clear, without further argument, why the procedural value of Peter-style mutual accountability, in so far as this procedural value is meant to be *epistemic* (as opposed to, say, moral) is not simply swamped by the value of an epistemic end such as accuracy, truth, etc., toward which mutual accountability contributes. Second, the matter of how we *ought* to regard individuals we take to be epistemic peers and how we *in fact* are likely to treat such individuals can come apart. For example, even if juries ought to exhibit mutual accountability, it is a separate question whether they are inclined to meet this normative demand. The kinds of results Hedden draws attention to indicate that this normative demand is, in practice, often not met.

A proponent of deliberation might lean back, at this point, to a final kind of consideration: mere voting, absent deliberation, is a form of *silencing* (e.g., Barrett forthcoming; cf., Langton 1993; Tanesini 2019), in that one's assertions of one's reasons are *de facto* suppressed via the denial of the opportunity for any kind explanation of one's position. This silencing is injust, epistemically, in so far as it is suppressive; it suppresses one's capacity to justify her view—capacity that might arguably be viewed as a kind of epistemic *right* (e.g., Watson 2018)—as well as the possibility of having any such justification make a difference. The argument then proceeds as follows: the epistemic injustice of silencing through mere voting is a greater epistemic injustice than the kind of testimonial injustice brought about by deliberation.

While there is some intuitive pull to this line of thinking, it's not clear that it ultimately holds up. The reasoning is as follows: even if we grant that mere voting is a form of silencing, it is unclear that silencing is unjust, at least, in so far as it involves the *de facto* suppression of an opportunity to explain one's view. The thesis that a denial of the opportunity to explain or justify one's view (whenever one is permitted to register that view) constitutes unjust silencing overgeneralizes such as to generate the result that almost all standard presidential and political voting in liberal democracies involves unjust silencing. Second, beyond the overgeneralization worry, there is further reason to resist thinking that mere voting involves any epistemically unjust form of silencing. The argument is that whether or not a given restriction on the extent to which one may justify her view is unjust is context dependent. In the context where a group's views must all be taken into account, a better example of unjust silencing is *disenfranchisement* as opposed to voting in the absence of a capacity to provide additional reasons. And this is so even if the suppression of the opportunity to justify one's view does constitute unjust silencing in the context of a parent-teacher meeting, or a criminal trial.

In summary, we've seen in this section that epistemic justice is an epistemic aim that a group might reasonably adopt, along with any other epistemic aim (or set of epistemic aims), in its endeavor to settle a group view. With respect to this aim, deliberation was shown not only to be a precondition for a central species of epistemic injustice—testimonial injustice—but further, that there are reasons to expect that deliberation will in fact—and regularly does—contribute to this form of injustice in practice (Hedden 2017). In response to this worry for deliberation, we looked at whether the positive procedural value brought about by deliberation might compensate for this epistemic injustice (Peter 2013), and concluded in the negative. Finally, we considered whether there might be an epistemically pernicious form of *silencing* (Barrett *forthcoming*) that is brought about by mere voting that might be in itself a kind of epistemic injustice that is more serious than what is engendered by deliberation, and the argument for this suggestion was ultimately unconvincing. With respect to the aim of epistemic justice, then, it looks as though voting is going to be more efficacious than deliberation.

2.6 Ways to Mitigate the Epistemic Disadvantages of Deliberative Intragroup Disagreement

In this section, we will address the *deliberation question*—recall: what would it take to overcome or at least mitigate the epistemic disadvantages of solving intragroup disagreement by means of deliberation? Given the pluralist approach to deliberation that we have adopted in this paper, namely that a group's collective endeavor to solve an internal dispute can be aimed at different (albeit not necessarily incompatible) epistemic goals, it comes as no surprise that this question has no unique answer. To put it differently, for each epistemic goal a divided group might aim at when settling on a collective view, there are specific deliberative conditions that can make that view fail to satisfy that goal. Indeed, for some such goals we have concluded that deliberation is *not*, after all, an epistemically appropriate procedure for groups to solve their internal disputes.

This doesn't mean, of course, that there is nothing groups can do to overcome the epistemic shortcomings of deliberative processes. To put things into perspective, let us briefly summarize our main conclusions on deliberation for the four epistemic goals we have considered and, on that basis, and also on the basis of empirical results, provide some answers to the deliberation question for each of the goals.

2.6.1 The Truth and the Evidence Goals: The Epistemic Significance of Being Divided

Concerning the truth goal, we have seen—drawing on social choice theory—that deliberating *vis-à-vis* the goal of reaching true collective agreements is roughly as epistemically appropriate as voting by majority rule in relatively idealized conditions (this is the result of Hartmann and Rafiee Rad's Bayesian model of deliberation). However, we have also seen—drawing on empirical social psychology—that real-life deliberative situations may involve an array of factors that bear on the reliability of deliberation.

Among those factors, two phenomena that operate at the group level constitute two particularly significant threats to the reliability of deliberation: group polarization and shared information bias. We have also seen, however, that these two reliability-undermining phenomena lose their influence in groups featuring internal disagreements (albeit perhaps not to the point of disappearing).

This results in a rather paradoxical situation: groups whose members would only settle their internal disagreements if the resulting settled views were true can more reliably achieve this goal when their disagreements are pronounced. To put it differently, groups whose members are starkly divided over some issue (e.g., with a 50/50 distribution) might be in a more solid epistemic position to avoid such reliability-undermining phenomena and thus to solve their internal disputes reliably than groups that feature less pronounced disagreements.

Groups can intensify their internal disputes in a number of ways. By way of illustration, a group of 100 members such that, e.g., 99 hold the false proposition *p*, whereas one holds that not-*p* might avoid or mitigate reliability-undermining group phenomena such as group polarization or shared information bias (i) by increasing the number of members who defend not-*p*[27]; (ii) by making some members play the devil's advocate role in defense of the minority view[28]; or (iii) by implementing the previously discussed *advocacy procedure*, tested by Greitemeyer et al. (2006), according to which each group member acts as an advocate for each alternative for some time independently of their individual preferences.

As we have seen in previous sections, increased disagreement within the group (e.g., by means of the just-mentioned advocacy procedure) results in better pooling of the evidence—including the group members' private evidence, which raises the chances that the collectively accepted view is supported by the best evidence available within the group, which would satisfy the evidence goal.

Accordingly, one answer to the deliberation question could be the following: the very fact of being internally divided makes groups featuring internal disagreements be more protected from group phenomena that make it less likely that they solve their internal disagreements in such a way that they meet the truth and the evidence goals.

Of course, this might not be enough for deliberation to be conducive to such goals and there are certainly more things that groups can do to ensure a better pooling of the evidence and increased accuracy—such as involving team leaders and members with experience at the relevant task in the deliberative process, giving enough time for discussion or having direct access to the evidence (as we have seen in §2.3). The bottom line, at any rate, is this: what might be considered a disadvantage for many reasons—viz., that a group is internally divided over some issue—turns out to be an epistemic advantage when the group aims to solve such a dispute by means of deliberation with an eye on reaching a true and evidentially well-supported collective agreement.

2.6.2 The Understanding Goal: Individual Competence and the Explanatory Value of the Evidence

We have offered two interpretations of the understanding goal. On the first interpretation, members of a group would only let a view stand as the group's view if the settled view is made *on the basis* of the group's understanding; on the second interpretation, only if it *promotes* the group's understanding. We have argued, in both cases, that deliberation is superior to voting. However, this doesn't mean that deliberation is always epistemically appropriate.

Consider the first interpretation of the goal. When group members are individually incompetent, it is unlikely that they will grasp the relevant issue in the way required by the goal. Accordingly, one way in which a group can mitigate this shortcoming is by increasing the individual competence of its members. This can be done in several ways. For example, changes can be made to group membership, and incompetent members be excluded from the group, or perhaps, only, from discussion. Another way is to ensure that internal or external experts explain the relevant subject matter to incompetent group members.

Consider now the second goal, for example, in the case of understanding-why. We've argued that one epistemic advantage of deliberation over voting is that the sharing of evidence engages with not *merely* the matter of *what*, e.g., caused X, but *how* it did so, which better contributes to reaching the goal of promoting understanding among group members. However, whether or not deliberation is capable of this does not only depend on the sharing of the evidence, but also on its explanatory value.

Not all evidence is equally explanatory, where this might depend on several factors. For example, sharing with one's group a newspaper article on why SARS-CoV-2 is as infectious as it is is not as explanatory as sharing the specific studies that pin down the particular transmission channels. In some cases, by contrast, e.g. when group members are not particularly competent or lack the relevant expertise, sharing *less* detailed information might facilitate that they grasp the relevant issue more easily than sharing very detailed information they are in no position to understand. Sometimes, it is the *amount* of evidence, not just its quality, that matters for its explanatory value: sharing too much information with group fellows, even if high-quality, can lead to information overload, which rather than promoting group understanding may hinder it.

In this way, two things groups can do to overcome or at least mitigate the epistemic limitations of deliberation *vis-à-vis* the understanding goal is to increase, first, the degree of individual competence of their members and, second, the explanatory value of the evidence, where this will depend, among other things, on increasing the quality of the information shared as well as on controlling the amount of information shared.

One way to improve on both factors (individual competence and the explanatory value of the evidence) and thus to facilitate group understanding is to implement a method akin to the advocacy procedure discussed in §2.3—to our knowledge, this has not been empirically tested. In the advocacy procedure, each group member acts as an advocate for each alternative for some time independently of their individual preferences. In the method we envisage—call it the *pedagogical procedure*—the competent members of the group (if any), or all members in groups of competent epistemic peers, act as pedagogues for the rest in the following way: all take care of explaining to fellow members the specifics of the collective views in dispute, in the best of their capacity and drawing on the best of their evidence. In cases where this policy cannot be applied, e.g., because no one in the group is competent, groups can resort to external experts who can give such a pedagogical service to group members.

2.6.3 The Epistemic Justice Goal: Smaller Discussion Groups and Computer-Mediated Communication

Concerning the aim of epistemic justice, we've argued that deliberation is epistemically inappropriate for it in that deliberation is not only a precondition for testimonial injustice, but also regularly contributes to this form of injustice in practice. As empirical studies on juries have shown, deliberation puts social pressure on jurors to vote differently than if they had voted privately, makes lower status jurors speak less, share less evidence, exert less influence, and be less likely to be elected as a jury foreperson.[29]

One way in which participation can be enhanced during group discussion—thus minimizing the risk of testimonial injustice—is by reducing the size of the group (e.g., by splitting discussion into smaller subgroups). As it turns out, the bigger the group, the more unequal participation is; and the smaller the group, the more equal it is (Bonito & Hollingshead 1997).

In addition, since group members with lower status participate less and are less influential than those with higher status—which can no doubt lead to testimonial injustices if low status is allocated on non-epistemic grounds (e.g., prejudice, implicit bias)—then one way to mitigate this epistemic flaw of deliberation is to prevent deliberators from accessing those cues that make them attribute status to other group members, including demographic cues such sex, race, or age. Unsurprisingly, face-to-face communication makes such cues more readily accessible to deliberators, which can cause testimonial injustices more easily. By contrast, one way to make participation levels more equal—and thus mitigate testimonial injustice—is computer-mediated communication, which makes the cues that serve to allocate status private, at least in the short term until online group hierarchies emerge (Hollingshead 2001).[30]

2.7 Concluding Remarks

Deliberation can be assessed from many angles. We have assessed it epistemically. In particular, we have investigated to what extent it is epistemically advantageous and disadvantageous that groups whose members disagree over some issue use deliberation in comparison with voting as a way to reach collective agreements. The way we have approached this question is from a pluralist perspective. We have assumed that a group's collective endeavor to solve an internal dispute can be aimed at different, albeit not necessarily incompatible, epistemic goals, namely the goals of truth, evidence, understanding, and epistemic justice. For the goals of truth and evidence we have explained, drawing on social choice theory, that deliberation and voting are epistemically on a par. But we have also shown how complex it is to give a straightforward answer to the question of how reliable deliberation is as a method for solving intragroup disagreement. This complexity, we have argued, has to do with the interplay between the different kinds of evidence involved in deliberation as well as with several group phenomena widely investigated in empirical social psychology such as group polarization and shared information bias. Concerning the goal of understanding, we have given two interpretations of the goal (the goal of reaching a collective view about why X only if the group understands why X and the goal of reaching a collective view only if it promotes the group's understanding). In both cases, we have argued, deliberation outperforms mere voting. Concerning the epistemic justice goal, however, we have concluded that voting is more efficacious than deliberation. Finally, we have discussed several ways to mitigate the potential epistemic disadvantages of solving intragroup disagreement by means of deliberation in relation to each epistemic goal.[31]

Notes

1 Collective agreement is a gradable notion: the more members of a group *G* agree on *p*, the broader the collective agreement. When a collective agreement is complete (all members of *G* agree on *p*) or else when it is broad (many members of *G* agree on *p*), we call it 'consensus' (see Tucker 2003: 509–510 for the former view; Miller 2013 for the latter). For our purposes, the kind of collective agreement we are interested in need not be consensual, but sufficiently broad for the relevant view to be considered the group's view.

2 That members of a group agree to take a certain course of action, φ, as a group is a special case of letting a view stand as the group's view, namely the view that the group will or ought to φ.

3 *Operative members* are, according to Lackey, those who "have authority or power to determine certain outcomes for the group as a whole" (Lackey 2016: 350). In contrast, *passengers* are group members with no or little authority or power that simply go along with the resolutions and decisions of operative members (cf. Fricker 2010).

4 For simplicity, we will not consider the third kind of view members of deliberative and non-deliberative groups might agree on to feature as the group's view: *suspension of judgment*, i.e., neither endorsing *p*, nor not-*p*.

5 In §2.3, we will consider borderline cases of groups that are motivated by non-epistemic reasons but that nevertheless pursue epistemic goals.

6 For discussion on how groups can aim at epistemic goals *qua* groups, see Fallis (2007).

7 For a similar methodological approach to a different question (whether or not deliberation has procedural in addition to instrumental value), see Peter (2013: fn. 12).

8 Epistemic justice, as a goal, is not purely epistemic: epistemic *in*justice, as Fricker (2007) conceives it, involves both epistemic and moral harm. Still, given the significance of this notion in recent epistemological theorizing, it is interesting to assess what kind of method to solve disagreement fares better with respect to it: deliberation or voting.

9 Other epistemic goals might be the following: the collectively accepted view (CAV) is known by the group as a whole (*non-summativist knowledge*); CAV is epistemically justified (*justification*); CAV coheres better with other collective views of the group than the opposite view (*coherence*). CAV is a view upon which individual group members would justifiedly place her trust (*epistemic trust*).

10 For example, if veritism (see fn. xi) is correct and truth is the primary epistemic goal so that the epistemic value of other goals is merely instrumental to it, then if, let's suppose, taking a vote is more conducive to truth than deliberation, we should certainly prefer the former.

11 The thesis that truth is the fundamental epistemic goal is often referred to as *veritism* (e.g., Goldman 1999). Cf., Kelp (2014) and Kvanvig (2013) for criticism.

12 See Lackey (2013) and Carey and Matheson (2013) for the epistemic significance of numbers in responding to disagreement.

13 In non-deliberative cases, social evidence can be part of the group members' private evidence (e.g., evidence from polls). However, social evidence is not always available in the case of voting as it is in the case of deliberation.

14 Of course, the kind of admittedly idealized deliberative cases we are considering are cases in which group members aim to reach a collective agreement pursuing the epistemic goal of truth. This plausibly suggests that all group members are sincere in their assertions. Still, even in these idealized cases, other group members can still *incorrectly* judge that fellow members are not being sincere, which can potentially lead to unreliable assessments about the distribution of opinions within the group.

15 Exposing group members to the positions of other group members in the absence of any other information has been observed to make them shift their own positions in a direction that is consistent with the average position of the group, where this is explained by social comparison mechanisms (Goethals & Zanna 1979).

16 For a comprehensive critical review of the different positions in the epistemology of disagreement, see Matheson (2015). For how the implications of conciliationism for intragroup disagreement, see Sheff (this volume) and Skipper Rasmussen and Steglich-Petersen (this volume).

17 See Dietrich and Spiekermann (2020) for an explanation of why this sort of conditionalization is needed.

18 As List and Spiekermann (2016) helpfully explain the two conditions in an informal fashion: "[The competence condition] says that each voter is better than random at identifying the truth, and that different voters are equally reliable. Furthermore, this holds irrespective of whether the truth is [*p* or not-*p*]. (…) "[The independence condition] says that once we hold the truth in question fixed—thereby conditionalizing either on [*p* or not-*p*]—learning the votes of some voters does not give us any information about the votes of others" (List & Spiekermann 2016: 221).

19 To remedy this, Dietrich and Spiekermann (2013) distinguish causal from probabilistic independence, and formulate a version of CJT that conditionalizes on any common cause.

20 As Dietrich and Spiekermann (2020) helpfully explain, one thing that many jury theorems aim to establish is what they call the *growing reliability thesis*,

namely that larger groups are better truth-trackers, in the sense that they are more likely to select the correct alternative (by majority) than smaller groups or single individuals.

21 Note, however, that, in the case of large groups, an increase in individual reliability doesn't necessarily translate into an increase in collective reliability. As Goodin and Spiekermann (2018: 138) point out, "For a large group, any mean individual competence level appreciably above random will have *almost* 'maxed out' the 'wisdom of crowds' effect already. Increasing mean individual competence further does not, therefore, have much effect for large groups".

22 For a book-length of the philosophical aspects of group polarization, see Broncano-Berrocal and Carter (*forthcoming*). See also Olsson (this volume).

23 These cases differ with respect to the cases we've been considering so far in that the propositions in dispute are both false, while the previous examples are such that the relevant disagreement is between a proposition and its negation.

24 This kind of position is not far from internalism in traditional individualistic epistemology: after all, many internalists rank higher a false justified belief (e.g., the perceptual beliefs of brains in vats) than a true unjustified belief (e.g., a lucky guess in normal circumstances).

25 For defenses of the thesis that understanding-why is a species of propositional knowledge, see, for example, Grimm (2006), Sliwa (2015), Lipton (2004), and Woodward (2002). See Kelp (2015, 2017) and Sliwa (2015) for a defense of the view that objectual understanding reduces to propositional knowledge.

26 A separate strand of epistemic injustice, which we'll set aside for the present purposes, is called *hermeneutical injustice*, which occurs when individuals are deprived in unjust ways of the opportunity to conceptualize their own experiences.

27 Concerning group polarization more specifically, there is an extensive empirical literature on why groups polarize (see Broncano-Berrocal and Carter *forthcoming*, Ch. 2., for a review), but not so many studies on group depolarization—for some exceptions, see Abrams et al. (1990) and Vinokur and Burnstein (1978). Yet, group polarization has been observed in homogeneous groups, not in diverse ones, which gives reason to think that increasing group diversity translates into less polarization.

28 But see Nemeth et al. (2001), who demonstrate that authentic dissent leads to better information processing and decision-making than the devil's advocate strategy.

29 See Devine et al. (2000) for a comprehensive review of the empirical research on jury deliberation.

30 As Levine and Moreland (2006) point out, a particular technology for which there is strong evidence of equalizing participation and priming informational over normative influence is email.

31 Carter's contribution to this chapter was conducted as part of the Leverhulme-funded 'A Virtue Epistemology of Trust' (RPG-2019-302) project, which is hosted by the University of Glasgow's COGITO Epistemology Research Centre, and he is grateful to the Leverhulme Trust for supporting this research. Broncano-Berrocal's contribution was conducted as part of a 2019 Leonardo Grant for Researchers and Cultural Creators, BBVA Foundation. The BBVA Foundation accepts no responsibility for the opinions, statements, and contents included in this chapter, which are entirely the authors' responsibility.

References

Abrams, D., Wetherell, M., Cochrane, S., Hogg, M. A., & Turner, J. C. (1990). Knowing what to think by knowing who you are: Self-categorization and the nature of norm formation, conformity and group polarization. *British journal of social psychology*, 29(2), 97–119.

Asunta Eder, Anna-Maria. 2020. *Disagreement in a Group: Aggregation, Respect for Evidence, and Synergy*. In Eds. F. Broncano-Berrocal and J.A. Carter, The Epistemology of Group Polarization, Routledge, 184–210.

Boland, P. J. (1989). 'Majority Systems and the Condorcet Jury Theorem'. *The Statistician* 38 (3): 181–189.

Bonito, J., & Hollingshead, A. B. (1997). 'Participation in Small Groups'. *Annals of the International Communication Association* 20 (1): 227–261.

Boyd, K. (2019). 'Group Understanding'. *Synthese*: 1–22. doi:10.1007/s11229-019-02492-3

Bozbay, I., Dietrich, F., & Peters, H. (2014). 'Judgment aggregation in search for the truth'. *Games and Economic Behavior* 87: 571–590.

Brodbeck, F. C., Kerschreiter, R., Mojzisch, A., Frey, D., & Schulz-Hardt, S. (2002). 'The Dissemination of Critical, Unshared Information in Decision-Making Groups: The Effects of Pre-Discussion Dissent'. *European Journal of Social Psychology* 32 (1): 35–56.

Broncano-Berrocal, F., & Carter, J. A. (2020). *The Philosophy of Group Polarization*. London: Routledge.

Burnstein, E., & Vinokur, A. (1977). 'Persuasive Argumentation and Social Comparison as Determinants of Attitude Polarization'. *Journal of Experimental Social Psychology* 13 (4): 315–332.

Bowman, J. M., & Wittenbaum, G. M. (2012). 'Time pressure affects process and performance in hidden-profile groups'. *Small Group Research* 43 (3): 295–314.

Carey, B., & Matheson, J. (2013). 'How Skeptical Is the Equal Weight View?' In D. Machuca (Ed.), *Disagreement and Skepticism*. New York: Routledge: 131–149.

Christensen, C., & Abbott, A. S. (2003). '10 Team Medical Decision Making'. In G. B. Chapman & F. A. Sonnenberg (Eds.), *Decision Making in Health Care: Theory, Psychology, and Applications*. 267. Cambridge, UK.

Devine, D. J., Clayton, L. D., Dunford, B. B., Seying, R., & Pryce, J. (2001). 'Jury Decision Making: 45 Years of Empirical Research on Deliberating Groups'. *Psychology, Public Policy, and Law*, 7 (3): 622.

Dietrich, F. (2006). 'General Representation of Epistemically Optimal Procedures', *Social Choice and Welfare*, 26 (2): 263–283.

Dietrich, F., & List, C. (2004). 'A Model of Jury Decisions Where All Jurors Have the Same Evidence'. *Synthese* 142 (2): 175–202.

——— (2007). 'Judgment Aggregation by Quota Rules: Majority Voting Generalized'. *Journal of Theoretical Politics* 19 (4): 391–424.

Dietrich, F., & Spiekermann, K. (2013). 'Epistemic Democracy with Defensible Premises'. *Economics and Philosophy* 29 (1): 87–120.

——— (2020). 'Jury Theorems'. In M. Fricker, P. J. Graham, D. Henderson, and N. J. L. L. Pedersen (Ed.), *The Routledge Handbook of Social Epistemology*. New York and Abingdon: Routledge: 386–396.

Elga, A. (2010). 'How to Disagree about How to Disagree'. In R. Feldman & T. Warfield (Eds.), *Disagreement*. New York: Oxford University Press.

Fallis, D. (2007). 'Collective Epistemic Goals'. *Social Epistemology* 21: 267–280.

Fallis, D., & Mathiesen, K. (2013). 'Veritistic Epistemology and the Epistemic Goals of Groups: A Reply to Vähämaa'. *Social Epistemology* (27): 21–25.

Fricker, M. (2007). *Epistemic Injustice: Power and the Ethics of Knowing*. Oxford: Oxford University Press.

——— (2010). 'Can There Be Institutional Virtues?' In T. Szabo Gendler & J. Hawthorne (Eds.), *Oxford Studies in Epistemology*. Oxford: Oxford University Press: 235–252.

Goethals, G. R., & Zanna, M. P. (1979). 'The Role of Social Comparison in Choice Shifts'. *Journal of Personality and Social Psychology* 37: 1469–1476.

Goldman, A. I. (1999). *Knowledge in a Social World*. New York: Oxford University Press.

Goodin, R. E., & Spiekermann, K. (2018). *An Epistemic Theory of Democracy*. Oxford University Press.

Gordon, E. C. (2017). Understanding in epistemology. Internet Encyclopedia of Philosophy. https://iep.utm.edu/understa/

Gradstein, M., & Nitzan, S. (1986). 'Performance Evaluation of Some Special Classes of Weighted Majority Rules'. *Mathematical Social Science* 12: 31–46.

Greitemeyer, T., Schulz-Hardt, S., Brodbeck, F. C., & Frey, D. (2006). 'Information sampling and group decision making: the effects of an advocacy decision procedure and task experience'. *Journal of Experimental Psychology: Applied* 12 (1): 31.

Grimm, S. R. (2006). Is understanding a species of knowledge?. *The British Journal for the Philosophy of Science*, 57(3), 515–535.

Grofman, B., Owen, G., & Feld, S. (1983). 'Thirteen Theorems in Search of the Truth'. *Theory and Decision* 15 (3): 261–278.

Hartmann, S., & Rad, S. R. (2018). 'Voting, deliberation and truth'. *Synthese* 195 (3): 1273–1293.

Hastie, R., Penrod, S., & Pennington, N. (1983). *Inside the Jury*. Cambridge, MA: Harvard University Press.

Hightower, R., & Sayeed, L. (1996). 'Effects of Communication Mode and Prediscussion Information Distribution Characteristics on Information Exchange in Groups'. *Information Systems Research* 7: 451–465.

Hollingshead, A. B. (2001). 'Communication Technologies, the Internet, and Group Research'. In M. A. Hogg & R. S. Tindale (Eds.), *Blackwell Handbook of Social Psychology: Group Processes*. Malden, MA: Blackwell: 557–573.

Isenberg, D. J. (1986). 'Group Polarization: A Critical Review and Meta-Analysis'. *Journal of Personality and Social Psychology* 50 (6): 1141.

Kallestrup, J. (2016). 'Group Virtue Epistemology'. *Synthese*, 1–19. doi: 10.1007/s11229-016-1225-7

Kelp, C. (2014). 'Two for the Knowledge Goal of Inquiry'. *American Philosophical Quarterly*, 51 (3): 227–232.

Kelp, C. (2015). 'Understanding phenomena'. *Synthese*, 192 (12): 3799–3816.

Kelp, C. (2017). 'Towards a knowledge-based account of understanding'. In S. R. Grimm, C. Baumberger, & S. Ammon (Eds.), *Explaining Understanding: New Perspectives from Epistemology and Philosophy of Science*. New York: Routledge: 251–271.

Kvanvig, J. L. (2013). 'Curiosity and the Response-Dependent Special Value of Understanding'. In T. Henning & D. Schweikard (Eds.), *Knowledge, Virtue and Action: Putting Epistemic Virtues to Work*. London: Routledge: 151–174.
Lackey, J. (2013). 'Disagreement and Belief Dependence: Why Numbers Matter'. In D. Christensen & J. Lackey (Eds.), *The Epistemology of Disagreement: New Essays*, Oxford: Oxford University Press: 243–268.
——— (2016). 'What Is Justified Group Belief'. *Philosophical Review* 125: 341–396.
Ladha, K. (1992) 'The Condorcet Jury Theorem, Free Speech and Correlated Votes'. *American Journal of Political Science* 36 (3): 617–634.
Langton, R. (1993). 'Beyond a pragmatic critique of reason'. *Australasian Journal of Philosophy* 71 (4): 364–384.
Levine, J. M., & Moreland, R. L. (Eds.). (2006). *Small Groups: Key Readings*. Psychology Press.
Lipton, P. (2004). *Inference to the Best Explanation*. Taylor & Francis.
List, C. (2013). 'Social Choice Theory'. In E. N. Zalta (Ed.), *The Stanford Encyclopedia of Philosophy* (Winter 2013 Edition). https://plato.stanford.edu/archives/win2013/entries/social-choice/.
List, C., & Goodin, R. E. (2001). 'Epistemic Democracy: Generalizing the Condorcet Jury Theorem'. *Journal of Political Philosophy* 9: 277–306.
List, C., & Spiekermann, K. (2016). 'The Condorcet Jury Theorem and Voter-Specific Truth'. In H. Kornblith & B. McLaughlin (Eds.), *Alvin Goldman and His Critics*. Oxford: Wiley Blackwell: 219–231.
Matheson, J. (2015). *The Epistemic Significance of Disagreement*. Dordrecht: Springer.
Miller, B. (2013). 'When Is Consensus Knowledge Based? Distinguishing Shared Knowledge from Mere Agreement'. *Synthese* 190: 1293–1316.
Moscovici, S., & Zavalloni, M. (1969). 'The group as a polarizer of attitudes'. *Journal of Personality and Social Psychology* 12 (2): 125.
Nemeth, C., Brown, K. and Rogers, J. (2001). 'Devil's Advocate versus Authentic Dissent: Stimulating Quantity and Quality'. *European Journal of Social Psychology* 31: 707–720.
Nitzan, S., & Paroush, J. (1982). 'Optimal Decision Rules in Uncertain Dichotomous Choice Situations'. *International Economic Review* 23(2): 289–297.
Pacuit, E. (2019). 'Voting Methods'. In E. N. Zalta (Ed.), *The Stanford Encyclopedia of Philosophy* (Fall 2019 Edition). https://plato.stanford.edu/archives/fall2019/entries/voting-methods/.
Peter, F. (2013). 'The Procedural Epistemic Value of Deliberation'. *Synthese* 190: 1253–1266.
Pettit, P., & Schweikard, D. (2006). 'Joint Actions and Group Agents'. *Philosophy of the Social Sciences* 36 (1): 18–39.
Pritchard, D. (2009). 'Knowledge, Understanding and Epistemic Value'. In A. O'Hear (Ed.), *Epistemology* (Royal Institute of Philosophy Lectures). Cambridge: Cambridge University Press.
Pritchard, D. (2014). 'Knowledge and Understanding'. In A. Fairweather (Ed.), *Virtue Epistemology Naturalized: Bridges Between Virtue Epistemology and Philosophy of Science*. Dordecht: Springer.
Schulz-Hardt, S., Fischer, P., & Frey, D. (2005). Confirmation bias in accuracy-motivated decision-making: A cognitive explanation for biased information seeking. Unpublished manuscript.

Sheff, Nathan. 2020. Intra-Group Disagreement and Conciliationism. In Eds. F. Broncano-Berrocal and J.A. Carter, The Epistemology of Group Polarization, Routledge, 90–102.

Sherif, M. (1936). *The Psychology of Social Norms.* New York: Harper.

Skipper, Mattias and Steglich-Petersen, Asbjørn. 2020. When Conciliation Frustrates the Epistemic Priorities of Groups. In Eds. F. Broncano-Berrocal and J.A. Carter, The Epistemology of Group Polarization, Routledge, 68–89.

Sliwa, P. (2015). 'IV—Understanding and Knowing'. *Proceedings of the Aristotelian Society* 115 (1): 57–74.

Stasser, G., & Stewart, D. (1992). 'Discovery of Hidden Profiles by Decision-Making Groups: Solving a Problem versus Making a Judgment'. *Journal of Personality and Social Psychology* 63 (3): 426–434.

Stasser, G., & Titus, W. (1985). 'Pooling of Unshared Information in Group Decision Making: Biased Information Sampling During Discussion'. *Journal of Personality and Social Psychology* 48 (6): 1467–1478.

Stoner, J. A. F. (1961). *A Comparison of Individual and Group Decision Involving Risk.* Cambridge, MA: Massachusetts Institute of Technology.

Tanesini, A. (2019). 'Silencing and Assertion'. In S. Goldberg (Ed.), *The Oxford Handbook of Assertion.* Oxford: Oxford University Press: 749–769.

Tucker, A. (2003). 'The Epistemic Significance of Consensus'. *Inquiry* 46: 501–521.

Vinokur, A., & Burnstein, E. (1978). 'Novel argumentation and attitude change: The case of polarization following group discussion'. *European Journal of Social Psychology* 8 (3): 335–348.

Waters, N., & Hans, V. (2009). 'A Jury of One: Opinion Formation, Conformity, and Dissent on Juries'. *Cornell Law Faculty Publications*, Paper 114.

Watson, L. (2018). 'Systematic Epistemic Rights Violations in the Media: A Brexit Case Study'. *Social Epistemology* 32 (2): 88–102.

Weatherson, B. (2013). 'Disagreements, Philosophical and Otherwise'. In J. Lackey & D. Christensen (Eds.), *The Epistemology of Disagreement: New Essays.* Oxford, UK: Oxford University Press: 54–76.

Wittenbaum, G. M. (1998). 'Information sampling in decision-making groups: The impact of members' task-relevant status'. *Small Group Research* 29 (1): 57–84. Woodward, J. (2005). Making things happen: A theory of causal explanation. Oxford: Oxford university press.

Woodward, J. (2005). Making things happen: A theory of causal explanation. Oxford: Oxford university press.

3 Disagreement within Rational Collective Agents

Javier González de Prado Salas and Xavier de Donato-Rodríguez

3.1 Introduction

Groups are often treated as (collective) rational agents. More specifically, it is common to attribute to groups epistemic states and attitudes, such as knowledge or justified belief and acceptance. Imagine, for example, a speaker saying that a certain company knows that its products are especially popular among young people. Not only does this way of talking accord with ordinary discourse, but it is also vindicated by several authors in the literature (for instance, List and Pettit 2011; Bird 2014; González de Prado and Zamora-Bonilla 2015; Kallestrup 2016; Hedden 2019; see Tollefsen 2015 for a survey). In this essay, we will assume that groups sometimes count as rational agents.

The question we want to address is what it takes for groups to constitute rational epistemic agents. The members of a group often hold disagreeing views. How can a group rationally move from such situations of internal disagreement to a unified group attitude? A possible answer is that group attitudes are rational if they result from the application of appropriate judgment aggregation methods. In Section 3.2, we discuss some problematic aspects of this answer, and then, in Section 3.3, we present an alternative proposal, according to which group (epistemic) attitudes are rational insofar as they are formed by responding competently or responsibly to the (epistemic) reasons available to the group as a group (this will require exercises of reasons-responding competences attributable to the group). In Section 3.4, we explore the idea that bare judgment aggregation methods have to be combined with collective deliberation in order for groups to be able to respond competently to reasons. In Section 3.5, we discuss the extent to which collective deliberation can be expected to solve internal group disagreements, paving the way for the adoption of coherent, reasons-responsive group attitudes. We suggest that conciliationist approaches to disagreement offer an optimistic picture of collective deliberation, as a method for bringing about internal group consensus. However, we will also explore possible limitations to the application of the conciliationist picture to realistic instances of group deliberation. Finally, in Section 3.6, we examine the role of dissensus and consensus in epistemically virtuous group deliberations.

3.2 Disagreement and Aggregation-Procedures in Groups

Groups that constitute rational collective agents can take part in epistemic practices in a similar way to individual agents. In particular, collective agents can engage in testimonial exchanges and be involved in arguments and disputes with others. Think for instance of a company arguing in court, or a national government disagreeing with the views of some international institution. Thus, once we allow for the possibility of collective agency, it is natural to think that groups can disagree with other agents (whether individual or collective). This type of disagreement would be with agents that are not acting as members of the group, so let us call it *external collective disagreement*. External collective disagreement would be analogous to standard cases of disagreement among individual agents.

We want to argue, however that a crucial difference between collective and individual agents is that *internal disagreement* is a far more common occurrence in the former than in the latter. By internal collective disagreement we will refer to cases in which there is disagreement *within the group*. So, internal disagreement will take place in a group when its members disagree among themselves while acting as members of the group.[1] At least at certain stages of collective decision-making, some level of internal disagreement is common in most groups. In this way, mechanisms of judgment aggregation such as voting are devised to generate judgments at the collective level starting from situations of internal disagreement among the group's members.

By contrast, internal disagreement does not typically happen in individual agents. Or, less controversially, if it happens, it plays a far less general and pervasive role than in groups. Possible situations of internal disagreement in individuals seem interestingly different from the ordinary forms of internal disagreement in groups discussed in the previous paragraph.[2] An individual may vacillate or be in a situation of uncertainty, but in normal cases there are no disagreements *within* individuals. Individual deliberation does not normally involve disagreements among voices or attitudes internal to the individual, since individuals are not composed of agents with potentially disagreeing stances (for a similar point, see Epstein 2015: 248). The goal of individual deliberation is precisely to make up the individual's mind, by settling what attitudes she ought to adopt, rather than being a process aimed at aggregating preexisting attitudes or judgments of the individual. In the case of groups it is possible to make a clear distinction between the judgments of the group at the collective level and the judgments of its members (in particular, disagreeing judgments at the level of the members can in principle co-exist with a single, unified judgment at the collective level). No such distinction can be made in normal individual agents.

To be sure, individual epistemic deliberation is sometimes seen as a matter of assessing and weighing the evidence available (more generally, a process of balancing the epistemic reasons accessible to the agent). One might think that such weighing deliberations can be modeled as processes with the aim of solving disagreements among different pieces or sources of evidence. More specifically, one can be tempted to characterize individual deliberations by analogy to judgment aggregation methods, and in particular voting procedures. On this model, the votes in favor and against a certain attitude would be determined by the strength of the evidence for and against it.

However, we should be wary of taking this voting analogy other than in a metaphorical way. First of all, it is not clear whether (individual) epistemic deliberation is adequately characterized by appeal to the picture of the balance of reasons, that is as a process of weighing evidential reasons for and against the relevant attitudes (see Titelbaum 2019; González de Prado 2019a). Anyway, even if we accept this picture, it seems that evidence weighing and amalgamation just does not work like standard processes of voting for different options (or, more generally, like judgment aggregation methods taking as inputs disagreeing judgments). Obviously, pieces or sources of evidence are not agents casting votes expressing their judgments or preferences. Less trivially, evidential reasons interact among themselves in ways that are not easily captured by standard voting methods.

One first way in which reasons may interact is by rebutting or outweighing each other. Reasons for a given option are outweighed when there are stronger opposing reasons against that option. Outweighing may perhaps be conceived of by analogy with voting procedures – stronger reasons would be associated with more votes, and would therefore defeat weaker reasons bringing in fewer votes. However, reasons can also undercut or attenuate each other (Pollock 1987; Dancy 2004; Schroeder 2007). An attenuator is a consideration that reduces the strength or weight of a certain reason. In the extreme cases of attenuation, the reason ends up having no weight at all and is said to be undercut or disabled. Undercutting is a common phenomenon in epistemic deliberation. For instance, a testimonial report will lose its evidential weight if it is found that the testifier is unreliable or has deceiving intent. Likewise, the measurements made by some thermometer will stop being counted as providing evidential reasons to form beliefs about the environmental temperature if we know that the thermometer is broken.

Undercutting and attenuation are not easily captured by accounts of individual deliberation framed in terms of standard voting methods. In a voting procedure, cases analogous to undercutting defeat would be situations where the votes of certain agents stop being counted because of the votes casted by other voters. That is, certain votes would have the effect of disenfranchising some other voters who were in principle granted suffrage. Note, moreover, that these disenfranchising powers would depend not only on who the voters are (i.e. the content of the relevant epistemic reasons and defeaters), but also on the issue voted (i.e. the options the agent deliberates about). Furthermore, reasons and defeaters interact in complex, holistic ways: undercutting defeaters can be themselves undercut, and whether a certain consideration has undercutting power may depend in open-ended ways on surrounding features of the issue deliberated about (Dancy 2004). Perhaps it is possible to come up with exotic voting methods that mimic the holistic, occasion-sensitive features of interactions among reasons. Yet, these methods would be so far away from standard voting systems that it would stop making sense to appeal to the voting analogy.

It is well known, on the other hand, that standard judgment aggregation methods sometimes lead to incoherent, or otherwise irrational collective judgments or attitudes despite taking as inputs perfectly rational individual attitudes. An illustrative example is what Pettit calls the *discursive dilemma* (Pettit 2001; List and Pettit 2011). Imagine that we aggregate the judgments of a group of agents on several propositions using a majority voting method on each of them, so that a proposition is accepted if and only if the majority of the group members accept it. Let us apply this method to the propositions *p*, *q*, and *p&q*. It is possible to have a group composed only by members with rational attitudes such that 55% of the group accepts *p*, 55% accepts *q*, but only 10% accepts *p&q*. In this case, the group would end up with incoherent collective attitudes, since it would accept *p* and it would accept *q*, but nonetheless it would reject *p&q*. This problem generalizes to more sophisticated judgment aggregation strategies. As List and Pettit (2011) have shown, for a large class of judgment aggregation methods, there will be cases in which rational attitudes at the level of the members of the group will lead to an irrational aggregated attitude at the collective level. This pessimistic thesis mirrors similar results in social choice theory, such as Arrow's impossibility theorem.

Thus, judgment aggregation methods like voting are not just unsuited as models for individual deliberation; it seems that, in addition, such methods are not always, on their own, good means to form rational, coherent collective attitudes in groups (Buchak and Pettit 2014; Hedden 2019). One could conclude that this reveals a limitation in the rationality of groups: groups can have irrational attitudes even when they are formed by aggregating individual attitudes that are themselves rational, and that were adopted by the members by responding properly to their epistemic reasons. An alternative view is that what makes the collective attitudes of a group rational is not so much whether they were formed following some particular judgment aggregation method, but rather whether they properly respond to the reasons accessible to the group as a collective agent. We will explore here this type of approach, which has been recently advocated by Hedden (2019; also González de Prado and Zamora-Bonilla forthcoming).

3.3 Group Rationality as Reasons-Responsiveness

Among the different ways of thinking about rationality discussed in the literature, it is possible to distinguish two main trends. On the one hand, there is coherence-based rationality. According to this first approach, rationality is a matter of satisfying coherence requirements, such as avoiding inconsistent beliefs (for instance, Broome 2007a, 2007b). On the other hand, there is reasons-based rationality. On this second approach, being rational amounts to responding properly to one's (apparent) reasons (Schroeder 2007; Parfit 2011; Kiesewetter 2017; Lord 2018).

We will focus here on this second conception of rationality, first because we think that it leads to a more attractive picture of group rationality, and second because coherence-rationality can arguably be derived from a view of rationality as reasons-responsiveness.[3] From the perspective of this approach to rationality, the natural thing to say, following Hedden (2019), is that a group is rational insofar as its attitudes are properly sensitive to the reasons available to the group *as a collective agent*. As is customary to do, we will think of normative reasons as considerations that favor or recommend a certain attitude. On our preferred account, a certain attitude is rational for a (collective or individual) agent if and only if such an attitude is sufficiently supported by the agent's *apparent* reasons, that is by the considerations that appear to the agent as reasons for the attitude (Schroeder 2007; Parfit 2011; for different ways of understanding the notion of apparent reason, see Whiting 2014; Sylvan 2015). According to this view, an attitude can be made rational by considerations that merely appear to be reasons to the agent (e.g. false beliefs supported by convincing but ultimately misleading evidence). However, for our purposes in this paper, it is also possible to adopt the view that rationally permissible attitudes are those sufficiently supported by *actual* available reasons (not by merely apparent ones). This type of view has been recently defended by Kiesewetter (2017) and Lord (2018). For the sake of simplicity, we will assume this latter view here. Nothing substantial hangs on this choice.

As pointed out above, a plausible idea is that coherence is an offshoot of reasons-responsiveness, in the sense that responding properly to one's reasons ensures that one's attitudes are coherent (Kolodny 2007; Kiesewetter 2017; Hedden 2019; Lord 2018). The idea is that incoherent attitudes cannot receive decisive support from the same set of reasons. For instance, the belief that p and the belief that $\neg p$ cannot both receive decisive support from the same body of epistemic reasons, and therefore it can never be rational for an agent to hold beliefs she takes to be inconsistent (it can never appear to the agent that her reasons support a combination of beliefs she knows to be inconsistent). If this idea is on the right track, it will apply generally to attitudes formed by responding properly to some set of reasons, regardless of whether they are individual or collective attitudes. Hedden (2019) has argued that this is the case: as long as a collective agent adopts its attitudes by responding properly to the set of reasons it has access to, the resulting attitudes will avoid the threat of incoherence associated with standard judgment aggregation.

If reasons-responsiveness guarantees coherence, it may seem puzzling that judgment aggregation methods can lead to incoherent collective attitudes, despite taking as inputs individual attitudes that are properly responsive to the reasons possessed by the members. We should note, however, that different members of a group may have access to different sets of reasons. And attitudes that are supported by different sets of reasons can be incoherent when taken together (e.g. your evidence may support believing that *p*, while mine supports suspending judgment). Thus, the individual attitudes of the different members of a group may be jointly incoherent, so that the application of judgment aggregation methods leads to incoherent collective attitudes. By contrast, a single set of reasons available to the group (as a collective agent) will not support incoherent collective attitudes, or at least it will not make it rational for the group to adopt simultaneously incoherent attitudes.[4]

The crucial point is that, on the view of rationality we are exploring here, whether an attitude is rational for a given agent is determined by those reasons the agent has access to, but not by reasons *unavailable* to the agent (see Schroeder 2007; Parfit 2011; Kiesewetter 2017; Lord 2018; González de Prado 2019b). As we have just seen, the reasons accessible to a group at the collective level may differ from the reasons accessible to its members. In this way, it may well be that an attitude that is rational for a member of the group (as an individual agent) is irrational for the group (as a collective agent). For instance, a member of the group can possess evidence that she does not want to share with the other members. As a result, it may happen that such evidence is not available for the group as a collective agent.[5]

What reasons count as available to some group? This will depend on the type of group and its structure. In normal cases, when a reason is available (in the relevant sense) to a group, the group will be in a position to guide its behavior by relying on such a reason, and to appeal properly to that reason in justificatory practices. In turn, the group will become open to challenges and criticism if it does not respond correctly to reasons available to it (that is, the group will be treated as *answerable* to the reasons it has access to).

Arguably, whether a reason is accessible to a given group depends on the epistemic position and competences of the group (Sylvan 2015; Kiesewetter 2017; Lord 2018; González de Prado 2019b). First, a reason is accessible to a (collective or individual) agent only if the consideration constituting it is within the agent's epistemic ken. So, rational doxastic attitudes do not have to respond to evidence constituted by facts the agent has no way of knowing (if you are not in a position to know any fact that constitutes evidence about whether it is raining in Sidney, you may rationally suspend judgment on that issue). Moreover, it is plausible to think that the agent also has to be capable of properly recognizing that the consideration constituting the reason offers support to the relevant attitude (Sylvan 2015; Lord 2018; González de Prado 2019b). For instance, the premises of a sophisticated mathematical deduction may not be accessible to the layperson as reasons to endorse the conclusion of the deduction (it can be perfectly rational for the layperson to suspend her judgment about the truth of that conclusion, even if she knows the premises of the deduction).

On the way of seeing things we will favor here, a reason is available to an (collective or individual) agent only if that agent is in a position to respond competently to the reason – that is, just in case the agent is in a position to respond to the reason in a way that manifests a reliable, virtuous competence to be guided only by good reasons (Sylvan 2015; González de Prado 2019b; also Lord 2018). The manifestation of this type of competence will involve displaying a reliable disposition to be guided by, and only by actual reasons (see Sylvan 2015). In other words, the agent has to be capable of manifesting sufficient sensitivity to the relevant reasons in order to count as answerable to them and, more generally, to count as properly evaluable in terms of rationality (Pettit 2001: 283). In this way, entities that are totally insensitive to reasons, such as inanimate objects, are taken to be *arrational*, this to say, beyond rational evaluation. Only agents that are minimally competent in responding to reasons count as rational at all. The question we want to address now is what it takes for a group to possess sufficient competence as a follower of reasons.

3.4 Group Deliberation

Kallestrup (2016) has offered an account of the epistemic competences of groups in terms of the competences of their members. We could follow suit here and analyze the reasons-responding competences of a group by reference to the rational competences of its members and the way the group is structured. The idea would be that, in order for a group to behave as a rational agent, its members need to manifest their competence in contributing to the group's aim of responding to reasons reliably (Kallestrup 2016: 13; also Silva 2019).[6] So, as a result of the competences manifested by its members, a rational group will adopt collective attitudes in ways that reveal reliable dispositions to treat certain considerations as reasons only in case they are (and to refrain from doing so when they are not). The individual competences manifested by the members of the group could involve, for instance, a competence in collecting and pooling evidence, knowing how to engage in team reasoning, the ability to trust instruments and inferential methods only when they are reliable enough, or the capacity to defer competently to expert members in their areas of specialization. While the resulting group-level competences may not be shared by any of its members, they arise from the combination of the different individual competences of the members. Accordingly, as we will see below, the reasons accessible to the group as a collective may not be accessible to any of its members.

With this picture of group epistemic competence in mind, we can ask ourselves what decision-making mechanisms should be implemented in a group in order to make it a competent follower of reasons. Hedden (2019) distinguishes explicitly this practical matter from the question of what attitudes are rationally permissible for a group (and he makes it clear that he is interested in addressing this latter question, and not so much the former practical issue). However, these two questions are not completely unrelated, given that the question about what attitudes are rational for a group presupposes that the group has some competence as a follower of reasons, and therefore is evaluable in terms of rationality. If we are not able to show that groups can function in ways that make them minimally competent followers of reasons, it does not make sense to ask ourselves what reasons are available to some group and what attitudes are rationally supported by those reasons (in the same way that it makes no sense to ask what reasons are accessible to arrational objects such as chairs and tables).

Our goal here is to examine what types of group organizations and dynamics can ground a collective competence to respond to group-level reasons. The answer to this question is not trivial. Arguably, the members of a group will often disagree about what evidential reasons are available to the group, and about what collective attitudes are supported by such reasons. What decision-making mechanisms should be introduced in the group in order to move from such internal disagreements to collective attitudes that are sufficiently sensitive to the group's reasons? If we try to settle these disputes by applying directly standard judgment aggregation methods, we will find again the problems discussed above: the resulting collective attitudes may be incoherent, even if the attitudes of the members are all rational. There is no guarantee that a group exhibiting this type of attitude-formation mechanisms will be in a position to respond to reasons in a competent, reliable way (more specifically, in a way that reliably avoids incoherence). Thus, there is no guarantee that such a group will count as a rational agent with access to reasons.

It may seem that a possible way of integrating judgment aggregation methods with a reasons-based approach to collective rationality is by resorting to judgment aggregation to fix the group's reasons. In this way, the members of the group could vote to select the set of propositions that is to count as the group's available reasons, in other words, as the premises from which the group's attitudes will be derived. In order to avoid incoherence, the candidate sets of reasons would be composed only by rationally independent propositions (i.e. no subset of the propositions sufficiently supports (dis)believing any proposition in the set not included in that subset). The group's rational attitudes would then be those that are sufficiently supported by the selected set of reasons.

This method is a version of the premise-based aggregation procedures explored by List and Pettit (2011), and it would ensure that the resulting attitudes are coherent, if it is granted that an agent cannot rationally derive incoherent attitudes from a coherent set of reasons. However, the implementation of this method is not straightforward. First, in principle, the members of a group may disagree about which sets of propositions are permissible inputs to the aggregation procedure, given that the members can disagree about which propositions are rationally related. Moreover, there can also be disagreements about what follows from the set of reasons acting as the group's premises. This may happen even if all the members behave rationally, insofar as rational individuals can have different inferential capacities and dispositions (disagreements about inferential support will be far from uncommon in cases involving ampliative, non-monotonic inferences). Now, remember that what attitude is rational for an agent depends on what reasons are accessible to the agent. And what reasons are accessible to the agent depends on the agent's inferential capacities (that is, on what reasons the agent can competently rely on). Yet it is not clear what inferential capacities we should attribute to a group, when its members disagree about what the group's reasons support.

How should these disagreements about the inferential implications of the group's reasons be settled? If we just resort again to judgment aggregation methods, the discursive dilemma and related problems will resurface. To see this, note that rational reasoners are not infallible. Arguably, it is possible to make a rational inference from true premises that nonetheless leads to false conclusions (say, because one resorts to a reliable, but defeasible piece of reasoning). If this is so, there can be a group where 55% of the members rationally take *p* to follow from the set of group reasons {E}, 55% of the members rationally think that *q* follows from {E} and nevertheless 80% rationally accept that *(p&q)* follows from {E}. This could happen if 40% infer *p&q* from {E}, 40% infer *p&*q and only 15% infer *p&q* (imagine that reaching these different conclusions involves manifesting different inferential skills and dispositions, not all of them shared by all members).

A natural reaction to the problems associated with bare judgment aggregation methods is to turn one's attention to deliberative mechanisms of collective decision-making (see Miller 1992; Sunstein 1993; Pettit 2001; Dryzek and List 2003; List 2007). In deliberative processes of collective attitude formation, the members of the group discuss among themselves in order to decide what collective attitude should be adopted. Through such deliberations, the members of the group would try to reach an agreement on what the group's reasons are, which conclusions are supported by them, and in what way these conclusions are so supported. Note that collective deliberation is an interpersonal activity, as opposed to individual deliberation, which only involves the deliberating agent. Again, a crucial difference between groups and individual agents is that only in the case of groups there can be internal collective deliberation among the different agents constituting the group.

An attractive possibility is to resort to judgment aggregation methods like voting only after the attitudes of the members of the group have been shaped by a process of inter-subjective deliberation. The hope is that collective deliberation will significantly reduce the initial disagreement and heterogeneity among the members' attitudes, so that a subsequent application of judgment aggregation methods will tend to deliver coherent collective attitudes. In other words, collective deliberation would foster the sorts of conditions that allow for well-behaved applications of judgment aggregation methods (see Dryzek and List 2003; also Bright, Dang and Heesen 2018).

It could even be expected that, after engaging in collective deliberation, groups will reach sufficient internal consensus, at least if certain conditions obtain. In best-case scenarios, collective deliberation will lead to complete consensus among the group members, not only about what attitude ought to be adopted, but also about what reasons there are for adopting it. Of course, it is trivial to apply judgment aggregation methods after this collective consensus has been achieved. The collective attitude of the group will be the attitude endorsed by all members as the group attitude. Similarly, the group's reasons for adopting that attitude will be those considerations agreed by the members to constitute such reasons. The group will count as responding competently to such reasons if, in reaching this inter-subjective agreement, the members of the group contribute to a group-level disposition to form collective attitudes that track reliably those (and only those) considerations that constitute reasons for those attitudes. Remember that in the previous section we characterized collective epistemic competences as arising from the contributions of the members to group-level reliable dispositions to pursue epistemic aims (in this case, the aim of forming collective attitudes that are supported by reasons).

In simple cases, the group will show proper sensitivity to its reasons because all the members are themselves in a position to recognize that the relevant considerations are reasons for the group's attitude. Note, however, that the type of consensus we are considering does not require that all members adopt, as individuals, the same attitude that is to be adopted collectively by the group, or that they have access as individuals to the group's reasons. The relevant form of agreement may come into place by virtue of there being members of the group that agree to defer to the judgment of other members, or to the outcomes of information-processing mechanisms to which they have no direct access. In this way, there can be members of the group who suspend judgment on the specific content of the resulting group attitude (and also members who cannot directly grasp the support relation between the group's reasons and its attitudes). Imagine, for instance, cases of distributed cognition, where the members of the group contribute to the collective attitude-forming process by providing different inputs for a complex inferential mechanism, even if perhaps many members have no access to the final outcomes of that mechanism (see Bird 2014; also Silva 2019). It may be that each member is an expert in a different domain and just produces a piece of knowledge pertaining to that domain, which is then passed on to other members, eventually leading to a unified group attitude.[7] Still, all the members can agree that the group attitude will be determined by the outcomes of this complex inferential procedure. Moreover, by so agreeing, the members could be manifesting their competence as a collective in treating such a procedure as responding reliably (only) to epistemic reasons. As suggested above, a key part of this competence would be knowing when to defer to the expertise of other members, and when to trust the outcomes of the relevant information-processing mechanisms (including, for instance, the outcomes of computer calculations).

It might be argued that full internal consensus is needed for rational collective agency.[8] At any rate, if collective deliberation manages to bring a sufficient level of homogeneity and agreement among the member's attitudes, it seems that the group will be in a good position to adopt rational, coherent collective attitudes. In the next section we discuss to what extent we can expect collective deliberation to result in sufficient group consensus.

3.5 Consensus and Group Deliberation

One may think that the possibility of reaching full group consensus is extremely far-fetched. Arguably, this is the case for practical collective deliberation about what aims are worth pursuing and what actions ought to be performed. On a common view, evaluative questions are non-factual, in the sense that there is no guarantee that there is evidence about what the facts are that will settle an evaluative debate among fully rational agents.[9] According to this non-factualist view, evaluative disagreements would be underlain at bottom by conflicts of preferences and values that cannot always be settled rationally (at least not by appealing to facts or pieces of information that all parties to the disagreement can recognize). Thus, even if the members of a group get to share the same body of evidence after deliberating among themselves, they may still have different preferences and disagree about evaluative issues. It can be argued that judgment aggregation methods such as voting offer the only fair (even if imperfect) way of making practical decisions in groups involving recalcitrant internal evaluative disagreements.

The situation is more promising in relation to epistemic collective deliberation. Epistemic deliberation is generally treated as addressing objective matters of fact. Therefore, epistemic disagreement among rational agents will in principle be solvable by appealing to sufficient evidence about what the facts are. Indeed, according to the view known as *uniqueness*, there is a unique attitude rationally permitted as a response to a given body of evidence (see for instance White 2005; Feldman 2007; Greco and Hedden 2016). On this view, two equally rational agents sharing all their evidence will adopt the same attitude. Insofar as collective deliberation allows for the sharing of information among group members, it should promote group consensus, at least if the members respond rationally to such shared evidence.

What happens if the members of a group take themselves to be rational but find that they disagree with each other (despite appearing to share the same evidence)? Certain approaches to epistemic disagreement offer further support to the idea that collective deliberation should result in group consensus. According to *conciliationist* accounts of peer disagreement, rational agents should reduce their initial confidence in their views when they realize that their epistemic peers disagree with them, despite sharing the same evidence and having considered the issue with care (Christensen 2007; Elga 2007; Feldman 2007; Matheson 2009). This is so because the fact that an agent disagrees with her (equally well-informed) peers should be taken by that agent as a reason to think that she may be mistaken, and therefore to adopt a somewhat cautious attitude toward her initial conclusion. In particular, according to Elga's *Equal Weight* view (Elga 2007), if two agents are initially equally reliable about a certain issue, and they come to endorse incompatible conclusions in the face of the same evidence, they should revise their attitudes assigning equal weight to each other's conclusions (that is, they should regard each other as equally likely to have been right). In turn, if your (equally well-informed) disagreeing peer is taken initially to be more reliable than you about the issue discussed, then the possibility that she is right should be assigned higher probability than the possibility that you are. Thus, rational agents sharing the same evidence (including evidence about their respective reliability), and behaving in accordance with Equal Weight, will (ideally) converge toward the same conciliated consensus attitude after realizing that they disagree about some issue.

Collective deliberation would be a way of ensuring that group members recognize the same relevant evidence (including evidence about the reliability of each member). If the members respond rationally to such evidence, they will (again, ideally and according to uniqueness) come to adopt the same consensus attitude. And, on a conciliationist picture, if they find that they keep endorsing different views, they will allow for the possibility that they are mistaken, and will reduce their initial confidence accordingly. In particular, if Equal Weight is right, it can be expected that the members of the group will tend to converge upon a shared consensus attitude after deliberating.

According to a plausible way of understanding conciliationism, agents engaged in peer disagreement should conciliate because they should revise their original reasoning commitments or inferential dispositions (Brössel and Ede 2014; Rosenkranz and Schulz 2015; González de Prado 2019b). The fact that you and your reliable peers fail to draw the same conclusions from the same body of evidence constitutes a reason to doubt the correctness of the inferential dispositions you were relying on. Thus, if you are epistemically humble, you should revise your inferential dispositions, in a way that acknowledges the possibility that your original inference was mistaken and your peers' was right. For instance, you may assign certain degrees of expected reliability to your and your peers' original inferential dispositions (for details, see Brössel and Ede 2014; Rosenkranz and Schulz 2015; also Schoenfield 2018). Insofar as your peers are also humble and revise their original inferential dispositions in analogous ways, you will end up following similar inferential rules, or at least inferential rules that are closer to each other than the original ones. Thus, by conciliating after collective deliberation, the members of a group would not just move toward agreement on what attitudes should be endorsed, but also toward agreement on the inferential rules that lead from the group evidence to those attitudes.

There are reasons, however, to think that this conclusion is too optimistic, at least beyond very idealized scenarios. First, conciliationism, and in particular Equal Weight are not uncontroversial views (see Kelly 2010; Coates 2012; Titelbaum 2015). And, even if Equal Weight is accepted, there is no guarantee that the members of a group will treat each other as peers, or, more generally, that they will agree on their assessments of the expected reliability of each member (as Klein and Sprenger 2015 remind us, recognition of expertise is often deeply problematic). It should also be noted that one could reject uniqueness and argue that members with different norms and values may rationally adopt different doxastic attitudes, despite sharing the same evidence and having similar inferential competences. For instance, different members may be willing to undertake different degrees of inductive risk (Magnus 2013).

To make things more complicated, members of a group may be motivated by practical, non-epistemic reasons in order to steer the group toward a given collective attitude, even if they do not take that attitude to be supported by the available evidence. An extreme, but not rare, example of this is Sunstein's figure of polarization entrepreneurs or professional polarizers (Sunstein 2000: 97). In general, collective deliberation among the members of a group can be affected by practical interests in a way that individual epistemic deliberation is not (see González de Prado and

Zamora-Bonilla forthcoming). For instance, the members of a group may have practical reasons not to share some of their evidence with the rest of the group,[10] or to argue or vote for a view they know not to be supported by the group's evidence. It is important to note that members that manipulate group deliberations in these ways can behave rationally (as individuals), insofar as they act in response to their practical reasons. It may be perfectly rational to believe (as an individual) that p, but to intend that a group you belong to adopts a collective belief in $\neg p$ (say, because this will have positive practical consequences).

Thus, practical interests and ethical considerations can play an important role in processes of collective deliberation by setting the hidden agenda of the members that participate in such deliberations. Take as an example a company board where some members hide or manipulate information moved mainly by economic interests (see Hendriks, Dryzek, and Hunold 2007). Of course, it will often be the case that the members of a group try to convince each other purely on epistemic grounds. Still, there can be other cases in which non-epistemic factors exert a decisive influence in collective deliberation and group attitude-formation processes.

Moreover, phenomena such as group polarization and the endowment-effect can make one question how realistic the prospects of reaching (epistemically virtuous) consensus via collective deliberation are. It has been claimed that processes of group formation in our current societies can be subject to factors that facilitate and stimulate the agglutination of like-biased individuals (Shapiro 1999; Sunstein 2002). According to well-established results, deliberation in ideologically biased groups may result in severe forms of polarization, so that agents will tend to align their views with the most extreme discussants whose biases are similar to their own (Hafer and Landa 2006; see Blumenthal 2012 for a study of the endowment-effect in group deliberation). As a result of such polarization, after deliberating, agents will reinforce their original attitudes, rather than moderate them in the face of disagreeing stances. This is just the contrary of what one would expect to happen according to a conciliationist picture of rational deliberation. The use of Bayesian simulation models suggests that this polarization phenomenon does not always result from shortcomings in the rationality of group members, but can be a predictable consequence of deliberation among ideally rational agents (Olsson 2013 and this volume).

Still, we should not undervalue the epistemic benefits of resorting to deliberation when trying to solve internal group disagreements, no matter whether consensus is effectively reached. Aikin and Clanton (2010: 410) have argued that the flow of information during the deliberation process generally improves the epistemic position of the discussants in relation to the evidence. A non-biased argumentative exchange also tends to enhance the quality of the basis on which the different positions are shaped.

Of course, the success of deliberation processes strongly depends on the fact that the individuals participating in the deliberation exhibit certain deliberative virtues such as honesty, sincerity, temperance, empathy, or truth-aiming (see Aikin and Clanton 2010). If discussants do not exhibit these virtues, or fall into vicious attitudes, it is clear that deliberation will not produce desirable effects.

The epistemic virtues of deliberative consensus have been highlighted as well with respect to truth-conductivity. Using Bayesian models, Hartmann and Rad (2018) show that, under not particularly demanding conditions regarding the reliability of the discussants (including their reliability in assessing other discussants' reliability), reaching a consensus via deliberation is a better truth-tracking strategy than majority voting. In addition, Hartmann and Rad argue that deliberative consensus has the further benefit of ensuring the satisfaction of group members, in contrast to voting procedures, which may leave those members who voted for the losing option unsatisfied.

3.6 Consensus and Dissensus in Groups

Regardless of how easy it is to promote group consensus, we can ask ourselves whether it is always desirable to do so. It may be argued that dissent plays a valuable epistemic role, which risks being overshadowed by an excessive emphasis on group consensus. Take the example of science. Although a great part of the classical philosophy of science was pro-consensus, some later authors, with Feyerabend at the head, have stressed the importance of dissent in scientific debates.[11] It is often argued that, at least in some fields, it is convenient, if not necessary, to work with a diversity of scientific models in order to produce different kinds of predictions, all of which may be relevant. In this way, model pluralism is customarily accepted in climate modeling. Climate scientists often take into consideration different simulation models when investigating climate change, even if such models make incompatible assumptions (Parker 2006). Similarly, it is not uncommon in the history of science to find cases of prominent scientists working in competing research programs at the same time. For instance, Kragh (1999: 199–200) mentions the case of Heisenberg and Dirac, who, during the crisis of quantum electrodynamics in the 1930s, combined a revolutionary and a conservative strategy: at the same time that they were developing new theoretical hypotheses, they were also introducing small corrections in the old theory. This combination of attitudes, at least in certain cases, proved to be a productive and stimulating path for scientific advance.

One of the risks involved in group deliberation is the apparition of groupthink. Groups affected by groupthink tend to rush to judgment or to accept, in a fast and unreflective way, the opinion manifested by the majority of the group. Unfortunately, mental laziness is often a vice that lies behind many cases of agreement. In these situations, dissent is generally excluded acritically, and alternative views are often undervalued. Indeed, taking consensus to be in itself an ultimate aim of deliberation may have the negative effect of fostering a sort of non-rational conformism (Mackie 2006: 285; also Friberg-Fernros and Schaffer 2014; Landemore and Page 2015). Thus, deliberative agreement should not be reached exclusively in response to practical reasons, such as shortening the time of deliberation. Friberg-Fernros and Schaffer (2014) have discussed further epistemic shortcomings of prioritizing consensus for its own sake: for example, the fact that, after agreement, the discussants often cease to develop new arguments, whose consideration could alter that agreement, or tend to forget the already discarded theses.

In order to avoid groupthink, Solomon (2001, 2006) has favored aggregation procedures over group deliberation, particularly in the case of science. But, precisely by examining in detail the way in which scientific discussions are held, authors like Tollefsen (2006), Wylie (2006), and Wray (2014) adopt a more optimistic attitude toward group deliberation. According this optimistic outlook, the dangers of groupthink can be mitigated if every group member behaves as a critical deliberant that carefully examines, under the scrutinizing gaze of the other members, every reasonable option and contrasts it against the background of available evidence (see Janis 1972; Tollefsen 2006; Wray 2014). Tollefsen (2006: 45) adds that dissent is tolerable in group deliberations as long as it is not pervasive and it does not threaten the stability of the group by questioning its most important principles and norms.

Eschewing a simplified opposition between consensus and dissensus, Beatty and Moore (2010) emphasize the importance of dissent in reaching robust forms of consensus beyond mere aggregation. By highlighting the role of dissenting voices, they follow Elster's (1986) considerations about the democratic force of minorities. Elster claims to have more confidence in the outcome of a decision if a minority voted against it than if it was a unanimous decision (Elster 1986/1997: 16, quoted in Beatty and Moore 2010: 198). As strange as it may initially sound, this idea becomes plausible if we take into account that the mere presence of dissenting opinions in a debate is in principle a guarantee of more careful decision processes in which at least more than a single option was considered. Accordingly, Beatty and Moore (2010: 209) vindicate a qualified way of understanding consensus, in which ideas or decisions are accepted after a virtuous process of deliberation with dissenting parties.

Dissent, however, is not always acceptable or epistemically beneficial. When based on unreasonable grounds or against the available evidence, dissent should be avoided or overcome. Actually, it could be argued that an excessive tolerance of dissent will encourage epistemic conformism, insofar as individuals will not try to assess critically the dissenting views of others.[12] Even in contexts where a certain level of dissent within a group is admitted, deliberative process should aim to remove disagreements that have as their source incomplete or mistaken evaluations of the evidence available. This claim is compatible with granting that the value of consensus over disagreement depends on the task deliberators set out to perform (Landemore and Page 2015: 246). In this respect, we should distinguish groups that constitute collective agents and groups that do not. Arguably, the need to reach agreements will be more pressing in the former than in the latter, since a collective agent needs to adopt, at some point, unitary cohesive attitudes, under penalty of dissolving or becoming paralyzed by internal conflicts. This can be clearly seen in the case of political parties, where internal dissenting voices are badly tolerated and tend to end up being obliterated by a uniform view coalescing around the positions endorsed by the leaders of the party.

Thus, whereas dissent may be epistemically fruitful at different stages of collective deliberation, groups constituting collective agents will need to reach eventually some agreement on what group attitude to adopt, in the face of the total evidence available (see Wray 2014). Accordingly, rational collective agency will often involve deciding in advance the optimal way to respond to internal disagreement. It should be noted, however, that the final agreement reached by the members of the group may reflect the existing internal dissent in the group. The members may consensually agree that there are dissenting voices in the group, so that no strong view can be collectively endorsed. Rather, the group as a collective will adopt a cautious attitude that properly recognizes the plurality of stances within the group.

We cannot expect groups to be always in a position to reach full internal consensus about a certain topic. Sometimes, the best the members of the group can do is to agree that they disagree, and that therefore the group's collective attitude cannot settle conclusively the issue under discussion (for instance, the group may agree to suspend judgment until more substantial consensus is reached). In particular, this will happen when the time available for deliberation is limited and it is clear that agreement is not going to be easily reached. If, in these situations, a practical decision has to be made anyway, the group can resort to bare judgment aggregation methods as helpful heuristic tools, despite their shortcomings – in the same way that individual agents may resort to heuristics and rules of thumb when making quick decisions. At any rate, in order for the group's use of bare judgment aggregation methods to be rational, it has to be subject to top-down deliberative supervision, so that possible incoherences are suitably revised (see Buchak and Pettit 2015).

3.7 Conclusions

As we have seen, engaging in collective deliberation does not always guarantee that the group as an agent will respond rationally to the evidence available, among other reasons because group members may be rationally motivated by practical, non-epistemic considerations when participating in collective deliberation. However, group deliberation in collective agents will tend to facilitate the achievement of internal agreement, not only about what attitude to adopt collectively but also about the reasons for doing so. If consensus among group members is not reached at a first stage, further deliberation about their assumptions, inferential dispositions, evidence, and epistemic values may help the members assess the nature of the underlying disagreement, so that the collective attitude adopted collectively is properly sensitive to the epistemic position of the group (including its uncertainty). Even in cases in which a consensus has been easily reached from the beginning, deliberation in further stages may reveal new arguments or aspects of the evidence that had been overseen, making the group more responsible and competent in responding to the available reasons.

Notes

1 Note that, in general, individuals may have different attitudes when acting as members of a group (say, when engaging in the group's decision-making) and when acting as individual agents in pursuit of their own goals.

2 Of course, an agent may disagree with her past views. A rational agent may also hold views that are disagreeing in the sense that they are inconsistent. In particular, in non-transparent situations a rational agent may be unaware that she is actually believing inconsistent contents (think of Kripke's belief puzzles). Likewise, an agent may believe inconsistent contents when appreciating their inconsistency requires sophisticated logical skills (although, arguably, in these cases she will not be perfectly rational). However, it is harder to find cases where an individual agent believes simultaneously contents that she recognizes as inconsistent.

3 This last point is argued for, among others, by Kolodny (2007), Kiesewetter (2017), and Lord (2018). For dissenting views, see for instance Broome (2007a, 2007b) and Worsnip (2018).

4 The last part of this sentence is intended to leave room for Permissivism, that is the view that a set of reasons may support either of a set of incompatible attitudes (Kelly 2014; Schoenfield 2014). We will express our sympathies for Uniqueness, the negation of Permissivism (see White 2005; Feldman 2007), but for the time being, we just need the claim that a coherent set of reasons cannot make it rational for an agent to adopt at the same time two attitudes that are incoherent. This is something compatible with Permissivism.

5 As we will see below, the evidence available to the group may but in principle need not be evidence available to all group members.

6 Kallestrup's view relies on Sosa's AAA account of performance assessment (Sosa 2007).

7 Maybe the last step is to introduce all the information gathered in a computer, which then produces automatically the result that is to become the group's attitude. In this case, it could be that all members ignore the content of the final attitude adopted collectively by the group, even if they agree that it will be whatever result is delivered by the computer.

8 Wray (2014) defends this view in relation to scientific co-authorship. For a critical discussion of this idea, see Solomon (2006). Bright, Dang, and

Heesen (2018) distinguish between collective belief and collective assertion, in particular, the type of (rational) collective assertion involved in co-authored scientific papers. They argue that consensus is not necessary for the latter.

9 In general, this non-factualism or non-cognitivism has been defended for evaluative or normative discourse. The position has been defended in moral philosophy and metaethics as well as in aesthetics. Examples of non-cognitivism about morality are Blackburn's (1998) metaethical quasi-realism, Gibbard's (1990) norm-expressivism, or Stevenson's (1944) moral emotivism.

10 In relation to this, we have the well-known phenomenon of hidden profiles (see, for example, Stasser and Titus 1985, 2003), where, in addition to a common body of information shared by everyone in the group, some of the members possess further unshared pieces of information. This often leads to suboptimal group decisions, especially in groups manifesting shared information bias, in which deliberations tend to revolve around information already shared by the members of the group.

11 Other notable proponents of this view include Longino (2002) and Solomon (2001, 2006).

12 See Rolin (this volume) for an extended discussion of this issue.

Bibliography

Aikin, S.F., & Clanton, J.C. (2010). Developing group-deliberative virtues. *Journal of Applied Philosophy, 27*(4), 409–424.

Beatty, J., & Moore, A. (2010). Should we aim for consensus? *Episteme, 7*(3), 198–214.

Bird, A. (2014). When is there a group that knows? Scientific knowledge as social knowledge. In J. Lackey (ed.), *Essays in collective epistemology.* Oxford: Oxford University Press, 42–63.

Blackburn, S. (1998). *Ruling passions: A theory of practical reason.* Oxford: Oxford University Press.

Blumenthal, J.A. (2012). Group deliberation and the endowment effect: An experimental study. *Houston Law Review, 50*(1), 41–71.

Broome, J. (2007a). Wide or narrow scope? *Mind, 116*(462): 359–370.

Broome, J. (2007b). Does rationality consist in responding correctly to reasons? *Journal of Moral Philosophy, 4*(3), 349–374.

Brössel, P., & Eder, A.M.A. (2014). How to resolve doxastic disagreement. *Synthese, 191*(11), 2359–2381.

Buchak, L., & Pettit, P. (2015). Reasons and rationality: The case of group agents.' In I. Hirose and A. Reisner (eds.), *Weighing and reasoning: Themes from the philosophy of John Broome.* New York: Oxford University Press, 207–231.

Christensen, D. (2007). Does Murphy's Law apply in epistemology? Self-doubt and rational ideals. *Oxford Studies in Epistemology, 2*, 3–31.

Coates, A. (2012). Rational epistemic akrasia. *American Philosophical Quarterly, 49*(2), 113–124.

Dancy, J. (2004). *Ethics without principles.* Oxford: Oxford University Press.

Dryzek, J., & List, C. (2003). Social choice theory and deliberative democracy: A reconciliation. *British Journal of Political Science, 33*(1), 1–28.

Elga, A. (2007). Reflection and disagreement. *Noûs, 41*(3), 478–502.

Elster, J. (1986/1997). The market and the forum: Three varieties of political theory. In J. Bohman and W. Rehg (eds.), *Deliberative democracy*. Cambridge, MA: MIT Press, 3–34.

Epstein, B. (2015). *The ant trap. Rebuilding the foundations of the social sciences*. Oxford: Oxford University Press.

Feldman, R. (2007). Reasonable religious disagreements. In L. Antony (ed.), *Philosophers without gods*. Oxford: Oxford University Press, 194–214.

Friberg-Fernros, H., & Schaffer, J.K. (2014). The consensus paradox: Does deliberative agreement impede rational discourse? *Political Studies, 62*(S1), 99–116.

Gibbard, A. (1990). *Wise choices, apt feelings*. Cambridge, MA: Harvard University Press.

González de Prado, J. (2019a). No reasons to believe the false. *Pacific Philosophical Quarterly*. https://doi.org/10.1111/papq.12271

González de Prado, J. (2019b). Dispossessing defeat. *Philosophy and Phenomenological Research*. https://doi.org/10.1111/phpr.12593

González de Prado, J., & Zamora-Bonilla, J. (2015). Collective actors without collective minds: An inferentialist approach. *Philosophy of the Social Sciences, 45*(1), 3–25.

González de Prado, J., & Zamora-Bonilla, J. (forthcoming). Rational golems: Collective agents as players in the reasoning game. In L. Koreň, H.B. Schmid, P. Stovall, and L. Townsend (eds.), *Groups, norms and practices. Essays on inferentialism and collective intentionality*. Springer.

Greco, D., & Hedden, B. (2016). Uniqueness and metaepistemology. *The Journal of Philosophy, 113*(8), 365–395.

Hafer, C., & Landa, D. (2006). Deliberation and social polarization. *SSRN Electronic Journal*. https://ssrn.com/abstract=887634

Hartmann, S., & Rad, S.R. (2018). Voting, deliberation and truth. *Synthese, 195*, 1273–1293.

Hedden, B. (2019). Reasons, coherence, and group rationality. *Philosophy and Phenomenological Research, 99*(3), 581–604.

Hendriks, C.M., Dryzek, J.S., & Hunold, C. (2007). Turning up the heat: Partisanship in deliberative innovation. *Political Studies, 55*(06), 362–383.

Janis, I. (1972). *Victims of groupthink*. Boston, MA: Houghton Mifflin.

Kallestrup, J. (2016). Group virtue epistemology. *Synthese*. https://doi.org/10.1007/s11229-016-1225-7

Kelly, T. (2010). Peer disagreement and higher-order evidence. In R. Feldman and T.A. Warfield (eds.), *Disagreement*. Oxford: Oxford University Press, 111–174.

Kelly, T. (2014). Evidence can be permissive. In M. Steup, J. Turri, and E. Sosa (eds.), *Contemporary debates in epistemology*. Oxford: Wiley-Blackwell, 298–311.

Kiesewetter, B. (2017). *The normativity of rationality*. Oxford: Oxford University Press.

Klein & Sprenger (2015). Modelling individual expertise in group judgments. *Economics and Philosophy, 31*(2015), 3–25.

Kolodny, N. (2007). State or process requirements? *Mind*, 116(462), 371–385.

Kragh, H. (1999). *Quantum generations. A history of physics in the twentieth century*. Princeton, NJ: Princeton University Press.

Landemore, H., & Page, S.E. (2015). Deliberation and disagreement: Problem solving, prediction, and positive dissensus. *Politics, Philosophy & Economics, 14*(3), 229–254.

List, C. (2007). Deliberation and agreement. In S.W. Rosenberg (ed.), *Deliberation, participation and democracy: Can the people govern?* New York: Palgrave, 64–81.

List, C., & Pettit, P. (2011). *Group agency*. Oxford: Oxford University Press.

Longino, H. (2002). *The fate of knowledge*. Princeton, NJ: Princeton University Press.

Lord, E. (2018). *The importance of being rational*. Oxford: Oxford University Press.

Mackie, G. (2006). Does democratic deliberation change minds? *Politics, Philosophy & Economics, 5*(3), 279–303.

Magnus, P.D. (2013). What scientists know is not a function of what scientists know. *Philosophy of Science, 80*(5), 840–849.

Matheson, J. (2009). Conciliatory views of disagreement and higher-order evidence. *Episteme, 6*(3), 269–279.

Miller, D. (1992). Deliberative democracy and social choice. *Political Studies, 40*(Special Issue), 54–67.

Olsson, E.J. (2013). A Bayesian Simulation Model of Group Deliberation and polarization. In F. Zenke (ed.), *Bayesian argumentation, Synthese Library* New York: Springer, 113–134.

Olsson, E.J. (2020). This volume.Parfit, D. (2011). *On what matters*. Oxford: Oxford University Press.

Parker, W.S. (2006). Understanding pluralism in climate modeling. *Foundations of Science, 11*(4), 349–368.

Pettit, P. (2001). Deliberative democracy and the discursive dilemma. *Philosophical Issues, 11*, 268–299.

Pollock, J.L. (1987). Defeasible reasoning. *Cognitive science, 11*(4), 481–518.

Rollin, K. (2020). This volume.

Rosenkranz, S., & Schulz, M. (2015). Peer disagreement: A call for the revision of prior probabilities. *Dialectica, 69*(4), 551–586.

Schoenfield, M. (2014). Permission to believe: Why permissivism is true and what it tells us about irrelevant influences on belief. *Noûs, 48*, 198–218.

Schoenfield, M. (2018). An accuracy based approach to higher order evidence. *Philosophy and Phenomenological Research, 96*(3), 690–715.

Schroeder, M. (2007). *Slaves of the passions*. Oxford: Oxford University Press.

Shapiro, I. (1999). Enough of deliberation: Politics is about interests and power. In S. Macedo (ed.), *Deliberative politics*. Oxford: Oxford University Press, 28–38.

Silva, P. (2019). Justified group belief is evidentially responsible group belief. *Episteme, 16*(3), 262–281.

Solomon, M. (2001). *Social empiricism*. Cambridge, MA: MIT Press.

Solomon, M. (2006). Groupthink vs. the wisdom of the crowds: The social epistemology of deliberation and dissent. *Southern Journal of Philosophy, 44*, 28–42.

Sosa, E. (2007). *A virtue epistemology: Apt belief and reflective knowledge*. Oxford: Oxford University Press.

Stasser, G., & Titus, W. (1985). Pooling of unshared information in group decision making: Biased information sampling during discussion. *Journal of Personality and Social Psychology, 48*(6), 1467–1478.
Stasser, G., & Titus, W. (2003). Hidden profiles: A brief history. *Psychological Inquiry, 14*(3/4), 304–313.
Stevenson, C. (1944). *Ethics and language.* New Haven, CT: Yale University Press.
Sunstein, C.R. (1993). *The partial constitution.* Cambridge, MA: Harvard University Press.
Sunstein, C.R. (2000). Deliberative trouble? Why groups go to extremes. *The Yale Law Journal, 110*(1), 71–119.
Sunstein, C.R. (2002). The law of polarization. *The Journal of Political Philosophy, 10*(2): 175–195.
Sylvan, K. (2015). What apparent reasons appear to be. *Philosophical Studies, 172*(3), 587–606.
Titelbaum, M. (2015). Rationality's fixed point (or: In defense of right reason). *Oxford Studies in Epistemology, 5*, 253–294.
Titelbaum, M. (2019). Reason without reasons for. In R. Shafer-Landau (Ed.), *Oxford Studies in Metaethics (Vol. 14*). Oxford: Oxford University Press, 189–215.
Tollefsen, D. (2006). Group deliberation, social cohesion and scientific teamwork: Is there room for dissent? *Episteme, 3*(2), 37–51.
Tollefsen, D. (2015). *Groups and agents.* Cambridge: Polity.
White, R. (2005). Epistemic permissiveness. *Philosophical Perspectives, 19*(1), 445–459.
Whiting, D. (2014). Keep things in perspective: Reasons, rationality and the a priori. *Journal of Ethics & Social Philosophy, 8*(1), 1–22.
Worsnip, A. (2018). The conflict of evidence and coherence. *Philosophy and Phenomenological Research, 96*(1), 3–44.
Wray, K.B. (2014). Collaborative research, deliberation, and innovation. *Episteme, 11*(3), 291–303.
Wylie, A. (2006). Socially naturalized norms of epistemic rationality: Aggregation and deliberation. *Southern Journal of Philosophy, 44*, 43–48.

4 When Conciliation Frustrates the Epistemic Priorities of Groups

Mattias Skipper and Asbjørn Steglich-Petersen

4.1 Introduction

Here is a question to which epistemologists have devoted much attention in recent decades: does the disagreement of others give you epistemic reason to reduce your confidence in your own views? Here is a relatively modest answer to this question: "Yes, at least sometimes." Let's stipulate that any epistemological theory of disagreement that entails this answer (or something stronger) counts as a version of conciliationism.

Conciliationism, even in this minimal form, is a controversial view, and we won't here try to make a final judgment on it.[1] Rather, our aim is to draw attention to what we see as a disturbing feature of conciliationism, which has (as far as we're aware) gone unnoticed in the literature. Roughly put, the trouble is that conciliatory responses to in-group disagreement can lead to the frustration of a group's *epistemic priorities*: that is, the group's favoured trade-off between the "Jamesian goals" of *truth-seeking* and *error-avoidance*. We'll say more about what this "Epistemic Priority Problem" (as we'll henceforth call it) amounts to later on. But before we dive into the details, we'd like to put the problem into a slightly broader context.

One of the most exciting ideas to have emerged from the recent flurry of work in collective epistemology (and one of the main reasons, to our mind, why collective epistemology is an interesting and important field of study in its own right) is that epistemically well-performing individuals might make up epistemically ill-performing groups and that, conversely, epistemically well-performing groups might be made up of epistemically ill-performing individuals. This idea, broadly construed, is what Mayo-Wilson et al. (2011) refer to as the "Independence Thesis." The idea has been defended in various forms not only in the epistemological literature but also in the philosophy of science and social choice theory. For example, Goodin (2006) has argued that biased individuals may be able to pool their information in ways that give rise to unbiased groups; Zollman (2010) has argued that scientists who hold on to their theories despite strong evidence against them may help ensure that the broader scientific community doesn't abandon those theories prematurely; and numerous authors have contributed to the now extensive literature on the "wisdom of crowds" (see Lyon and Pacuit (2013) for an overview).

The Epistemic Priority Problem, as we will describe it, can be seen as lending further support to the Independence Thesis: it illustrates, in yet another way, how a seemingly rational epistemic practice at the individual level—namely, the practice of conciliating with those who disagree with us—can have adverse epistemic effects at the group level. Whether this result constitutes a problem for conciliationism *per se*, or whether it simply shows that the true epistemic norms for individual believers can have adverse epistemic consequences at the group level is not a question that will occupy us much. As we see it, the problem raised is an important one to address, even if it doesn't give us reason to doubt that conciliationism is true.

For the sake of clarity and definiteness, we'll embed our discussion of the Epistemic Priority Problem within a general "belief aggregation" framework (more on this framework below). This is not to suggest that the problem is specific to the aggregation-based way of understanding the relationship between the beliefs of a group and those of its members. Indeed, we suspect that very similar problems will arise for alternative ways of understanding group belief as well (though we won't try to defend this claim here). But the aggregation framework provides a simple and tractable way of making the Epistemic Priority Problem vivid.

Here, then, is the plan of attack. In §4.2, we begin by covering some basics of the belief aggregation framework, and explain in more detail what we mean by saying that a group can have "epistemic priorities." In §4.3, we go on to show, in a preliminary way, how, given certain idealizing assumptions, the Epistemic Priority Problem can arise as a consequence of conciliatory responses to in-group disagreement. In §4.4, we generalize the problem by showing how it can arise even if we relax the various idealizing assumptions. At this point we'll have established our main negative lesson. We close on a more positive note in §4.5 by offering a tentative proposal for how to solve the problem raised without rejecting conciliationism.

4.2 Preliminaries on Belief Aggregation

As many authors have pointed out, groups are often said to believe things.[2] For example, a jury might be said to believe that the defendant is guilty; UNESCO might be said to believe that education is a human right; and so on. This raises a natural question: how (if at all) do the beliefs of a *group* relate to those of its *members*?

According to a familiar answer, a group's belief state is (or may be represented as) a *function*, or *aggregate*, of the belief states of its individual members. This "aggregation model" of group belief has featured prominently in the literature on the "doctrinal paradox" and related impossibility results (Kornhauser and Sager 1986; List and Pettit 2002), but has also been used to investigate questions about, e.g., the epistemic merits of co-authorship (Bright et al. 2017), the nature of group justification (Goldman 2011), and the normative significance of group disagreement (Skipper and Steglich-Petersen 2019).[3] Here we'd like to use the aggregation framework to illustrate how the Epistemic Priority Problem can arise as a consequence of conciliatory responses to disagreement among the members of a group. Below we introduce some nuts and bolts that will facilitate the discussion.

Let a *belief state* be a set of propositions (intuitively: the set of propositions believed by the agent in question), and let a *Belief Aggregation Function* (henceforth just a "BAF") be a function from sets of belief states to single belief states (intuitively: the function taking the belief states of the individual group members as input and returns the belief state of the group as a whole). Familiar BAFs include majority voting, unanimity voting, and dictatorship, but there are many other BAFs that a group might in principle use, and we won't make any limiting assumptions at the outset about which BAFs are admissible. For example, we won't assume that a group believes a proposition, *p*, only if a large enough proportion of its members believe that *p*. Moreover, we won't assume that the members of a group must be explicitly aware of which BAF they adhere to. For all we are concerned, a group's BAF might rather be a tacit feature of the group's practice.

To simplify the discussion, we'll assume that each group member must either believe or disbelieve any given proposition (suspension of judgment isn't allowed). Accordingly, we'll count any credence above 50% as a belief, and we'll count any credence below 50% as a disbelief (a credence of exactly 50% isn't allowed). Needless to say, this is a rather strained use of the ordinary term "belief." But as we'll see, nothing of importance is going to turn on this simplification.

Though not uncontroversial, the aggregation model of group belief is a highly general one, and one that comes with very few substantive assumptions about the metaphysical nature of group belief. For example, as hinted above, it doesn't commit us to a "summativist" view of group belief, according to which a group's believing that *p* is just a matter of all (or a sufficiently high proportion) of its members' believing that *p*.[4] Indeed, for all the aggregation model says, a group might believe those and only those propositions that its members unanimously agree are false. This would obviously require an odd BAF (one saying that the group believes *p* if all of the group members believe ~*p*). But, in principle, the aggregation framework is general enough to accommodate any BAF you like.

The aggregation model is also silent on whether groups literally have minds of their own, or whether our talk of group belief should be understood in a less metaphysically committal way. To ease the exposition, we'll continue to talk as if groups, like their members, have genuine beliefs. But all we assume on the official story is that a group's belief state, whatever its metaphysical status, may be usefully represented as a function of the belief states of its members.

Just as individuals can be more or less epistemically reliable, groups can be more or less epistemically reliable as well: that is, their beliefs can "line up" with the truth in more or less accurate ways. They can do so in (at least) two different ways, corresponding to two different kinds of reliability. On the one hand, there is an agent's *positive reliability*: that is, the probability that the agent believes that *p* given that *p* is true. On the other hand, there is the agent's *negative reliability*, that is, the probability that the agent doesn't believe that *p* given that *p* is false. Formally (cf. List 2005):

Positive reliability: $Pr(Bp|p)$
Negative reliability: $Pr(\sim Bp|\sim p)$

As William James (1896) famously pointed out, these two kinds of reliability do not always go hand in hand. In fact, they can come arbitrarily far apart. A highly credulous agent—someone who is willing to believe even the most improbable of propositions—will have a very high positive reliability, but a very low negative reliability. Such an agent will rarely miss out the truth, but at the cost of forming lots of false beliefs. Conversely, a highly incredulous agent—someone who is unwilling to believe even the most probable of propositions—will have a very low positive reliability, but a very high negative reliability. Such an agent will rarely form false beliefs, but at the cost of often missing out on the truth.

Here is an uncontroversial fact that will be important for what follows: different BAFs contribute in different ways to a group's positive and negative reliability. To take a simple example, consider a group with *n* members, where each member has the same positive and negative reliability, *r*. Given this, the group's positive and negative reliability will vary quite significantly, depending on what BAF the group uses. For example, unanimity voting will tend to yield a much higher negative reliability than majority voting, whereas majority voting will tend to yield a much higher positive reliability than unanimity voting (see Table 4.1 and Figure 4.1).[5]

Table 4.1 A group's positive and negative reliability as a function of its size (n) and member reliability (r), depending on whether the group uses unanimity or majority voting

BAF	*Positive reliability*	*Negative reliability*
Unanimity voting	r^n	$1-(1-r)^n$
Majority voting	$\sum_{i=.5(n+1)}^{n} \frac{n!}{i!(n-i)!} r^i (1-r)^{n-i}$	

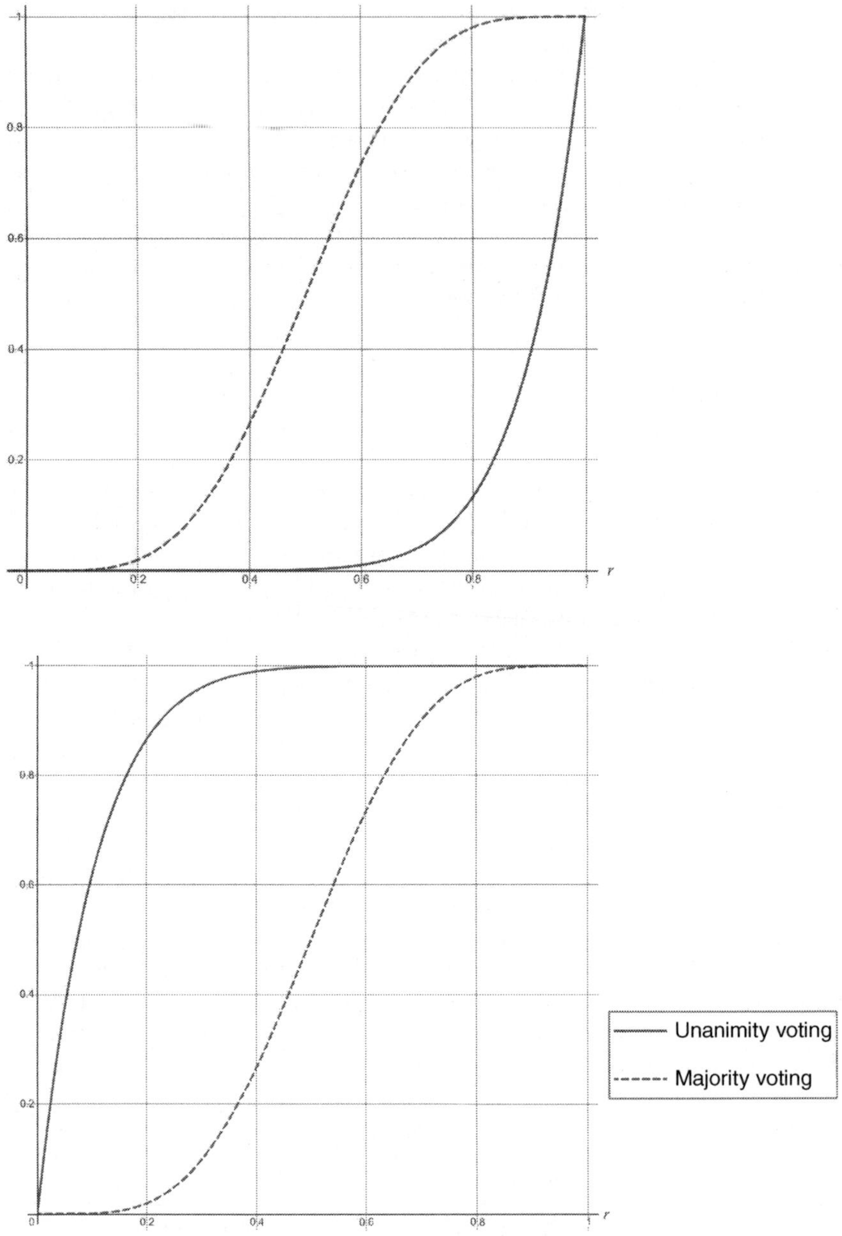

Figure 4.1 A group's positive reliability (top graph) and negative reliability (bottom graph) as a function of the members' reliability, r (setting $n = 9$, for illustration).

We take this to suggest that what BAF it is advisable for a group to use depends, at least in part, on the group's *epistemic priorities*: that is, the group's preferred trade-off between *believing what is true* and *not believing what is false* (or: the group's preferred trade-off between positive reliability and negative reliability). For example, if the group described above (consisting of n members with identical positive and negative reliability, r) places more weight on negative reliability than positive reliability, unanimity voting will be preferable to majority voting. By contrast, if the group places equal weight on positive reliability and negative reliability, majority voting will be preferable to unanimity voting.

So far, so good. But what is the *right* trade-off between positive and negative reliability? In other words, what epistemic priorities *should* a group have? A natural first reaction to this question would be to say, on grounds of uniformity, that groups should simply have whatever epistemic priorities *individuals* should have. And many epistemologists have been inclined to think that individuals should be epistemically *risk-averse*, that is, that they should place more weight on error-avoidance than on truth-seeking.[6] If so, it would be natural to think that groups should likewise be epistemically risk-averse, that is, that they should place more weight on negative reliability than on positive reliability.

However, we don't think this parity between individuals and groups can be easily maintained. Note that the idea that individuals should place more weight on error-avoidance than on truth-seeking is usually motivated on distinctly *epistemic* grounds, e.g., by appeal to considerations about the irrationality of contradictory beliefs (Dorst 2019, p. 185), the rationality of suspending judgment (Easwaran 2016, p. 824), or the rationality of imprecise credences (Konek forthcoming). By contrast, the kinds of considerations that are naturally taken to bear on questions about what BAF it would be advisable for a group to use are often *practical* in nature. Here are three hypothetical (but, we hope, not too far-fetched) examples:

Criminal Trial: The jury in a criminal trial must reach a collective verdict about whether the defendant is guilty. The jury is required to deem the defendant guilty iff all of the jurors believe that the defendant is guilty beyond reasonable doubt. This unanimity procedure is justified on the grounds that it is much more important to avoid punishing the innocent than it is to punish the guilty.

Quiz Show: A group of friends appear on a quiz show. The host asks the group to collectively answer *yes*, *no*, or *pass* in response to a series of questions. Each right answer gives +1 point, each wrong answer gives –1 point, and no points are awarded or subtracted if the group says "pass." The friends decide to base their answers on simple majority voting on the grounds that they suspect this to maximize their expected score.

Anti-Terror Unit: An anti-terror police unit must decide whether to treat an apparent threat as real. The unit conforms to a policy of treating apparent threats as real as long as at least *one* member of the unit believes that the threat is real. The rationale behind this policy is that it's much worse to treat a real threat as merely apparent than to treat a merely apparent threat as real.

In each case, the group's choice of BAF seems perfectly reasonable given the circumstances in which the group is to form a collective verdict. Yet, only in the first case does the group place more weight on negative reliability than on positive reliability. In the other two cases, the group places at least as much weight on positive reliability as on negative reliability.

We take this to suggest that, whatever might be said about the epistemic priorities of individuals, there isn't is a unique trade-off between positive and negative reliability that groups should always try to make. It seems much more plausible to suppose, as we'll henceforth do, that different contexts call out for different epistemic priorities, and hence different BAFs.[7]

4.3 The Epistemic Priority Problem

With these preliminaries in place, we are now ready to show how the Epistemic Priority Problem can arise within a simple aggregation framework. We begin by making some additional idealizing assumptions, which will help to simplify the exposition (the assumptions will be relaxed later on).

First, we assume that the *agenda*—that is, the set of propositions that the group members are to form beliefs about—consists of just a single proposition, p. This allows us to sidestep certain problems that can arise when the agenda contains two or more logically interconnected propositions (as exemplified in the famous *doctrinal paradox*).[8] These problems are of obvious interest and importance in their own right, but they are orthogonal to our present concerns.

Second, we assume that all group members are (and consider themselves to be) *epistemic peers* with respect to p. We will take this to mean that all group members have the same positive and negative reliability: that is, no two members differ in their positive reliability, and no two members differ in their negative reliability.[9] Furthermore, we'll assume that each group member has the same positive and negative reliability, r, where $r > 50\%$ (which is just to say that the group members are at least slightly more reliable than the flip of a fair coin).

Third, we assume that all group members practice a particularly strong form of conciliationism akin to the familiar "Equal Weight View" defended by Christensen (2007), Elga (2007), and others. More specifically, we'll assume that the group members "split the difference" in response to peer disagreement. This is clearly not the only available interpretation of the Equal Weight View, nor perhaps the most plausible one.[10] But the exact interpretation of the Equal Weight View won't matter for present purposes. As we'll see, the Epistemic Priority Problem can in any case arise in much less conciliatory environments.

Fourth, we assume that the reliability of any given member doesn't depend on how confident that member is that his or her opinion is correct. In other words, members with *more* extreme credences are assumed to be neither more nor less reliable than members with *less* extreme credences. This assumption may seem egregiously unrealistic. (Wouldn't it be more realistic to assume that people who are highly confident in their opinion on some matter are also more likely to be correct about that matter?) But the assumption isn't meant to be realistic, since (as we'll see) the Epistemic Priority Problem can in any case arise without it. For now, we are just looking to make things as simple as possible.

Finally, we'll work with a very sparse set of possible degrees of confidence (or "credences"). More specifically, we will assume that each group member is either *slightly more* confident of p than $\sim p$ (which we'll write as "$Cr(p) > Cr(\sim p)$") or *much more* confident of p than $\sim p$ (which we'll write as "$Cr(p) \gg Cr(\sim p)$"). The converse is obviously also allowed: members may be *slightly less* confident of p than $\sim p$ (written "$Cr(p) < Cr(\sim p)$") or *much less* confident of p than $\sim p$ (written "$Cr(p) \ll Cr(\sim p)$"). One small complication of this way of modeling credences is that it doesn't involve real numbers, which means that the idea of "splitting the difference" can't be taken to mean "taking the arithmetic mean." All we need to assume in what follows, however, is that if you're *much less* confident of p than $\sim p$ while I'm *slightly more* confident of p than $\sim p$, then the way for us to split the difference is by both becoming *slightly less* confident of p than $\sim p$. And, conversely, if you're *much more* confident of p than $\sim p$ while I'm *slightly less* confident of p than $\sim p$, then the way for us to split the difference is by both becoming *slightly more* confident of p than $\sim p$.

Taken together, these assumptions make for a highly idealized setting in which to study the Epistemic Priority Problem. This should not be taken to suggest that the Epistemic Priority Problem is a mere theoretical curiosity with little practical relevance. As already mentioned, we'll eventually argue that the problem can arise under much less idealized circumstances as well. But we'd like to begin by showing how the problem can arise in a very clean and simple setting.

To show this, we'll proceed in a case-based manner. Each of the cases will feature a group whose members start out with a given set of individual credences in p—we'll call them their *pre-conciliation* credences. The group will then undergo a *conciliation process*, whereby the members learn about each other's credences and respond to any potential disagreements by splitting the difference in the way described. As a result, the members end up with identical credences in *p* once the conciliation process is completed—we'll call them their *post-conciliation* credences.

That's the basic setup. Now for the cases (of which there are three).

4.3.1 Case 1: Unanimity Voting

Consider a group with the following characteristics (in addition to those listed above):

i The group consists of two same-sized subgroups, g_1 and g_2.
ii The group members' pre-conciliation and post-conciliation credences in *p* are as stated in Table 4.2.
iii The group uses unanimity voting: that is, the group believes *p* iff all of its members believe *p*.

Let's begin by asking: what does the group believe about *p* before and after the conciliation process? Before the conciliation process, all members of g_1 are more confident of *p* than *~p*, and so they all believe *p*. By contrast, all members of g_2 are more confident of *~p* than *p*, and so they all believe *~p*. Hence, due to the lack of unanimity, the group as a whole neither believes *p* nor believes *~p*.

However, note that the members of g_1 all start out being *much more* confident of *p* than *~p*, whereas the members of g_2 start out being only *slightly more* confident of *~p* than *p*. As a result, the members of g_1 and g_2, after having conciliated with each other, all end up being slightly more confident of *p* than *~p*. Consequently, the group as a whole ends up believing *p* after the conciliation process is completed.

This change in the group's belief state may not seem like much of a problem. But consider what has happened to the group's positive and negative reliability, respectively. Recall that the distinctive feature of unanimity voting is that it secures a high negative reliability in comparison to other BAFs (e.g., in comparison to majority voting, as illustrated by Figure 4.1). In other words, unanimity voting is supposed to be an

Table 4.2 Before the conciliation process, all members of g_1 are much more confident of *p* than *~p*, whereas all members of g_2 are slightly more confident of *~p* than *p*. After the conciliation process, all group members are slightly more confident in *p* than *~p*

	g_1	g_2
Pre-conciliation	$Cr(p) \gg Cr({\sim}p)$	$Cr(p) < Cr({\sim}p)$
Post-conciliation	$Cr(p) > Cr({\sim}p)$	

effective guard against false belief. But the conciliation process puts a crack in the guard: it leads the group to form a new belief, which, in turn, introduces a new error-possibility. Now, the mere introduction of a new error-possibility obviously isn't enough to show that the group's negative reliability has decreased as a result of the conciliation process. We also need to consider whether any existing error-possibilities have been eliminated. This would be the case if the conciliation process made the group drop an existing belief. But since the group starts out neither believing p nor believing $\sim p$, there is no such belief to be dropped.[11] This is the qualitative reason why the conciliation process harms the group's negative reliability: it introduces a new error-possibility without eliminating any existing ones.

How significant is this problem from a quantitative point of view? To get a feel for this, let's put some numbers on the table. Suppose that g_1 and g_2 each have five members ($n = 10$), and suppose that all members have a positive reliability and negative reliability of 70% ($r = .7$). We can then ask: once the conciliation process is completed, how likely is it that the group's belief that p is false? In other words, how likely is it that p is false given the members' post-conciliation beliefs about p? On the face of it, this might seem like an intractable question, since we haven't said anything about how the conciliation process might affect the reliability of the group members. But we can approach the question in a more indirect way, by considering a slightly different question: how likely is p to be false given the members' pre-conciliation beliefs about p? This is a question that we *can* answer. But before we do, let's explain why the two questions must have the same answer.

Suppose that you're a third party—someone not a member of the group in question—who seeks to use the group members' beliefs about p as evidence bearing on p. And let's say that, upon learning about the group members' pre-conciliation beliefs about p, you should have such-and-such a credence in p. Now suppose you learn that the group members have been through a conciliation process: that is, you learn that the group members have adopted their average credence in p (and that's *all* you learn). Should you revise your credence in p in light of this new piece of information? It seems not. After all, the mere fact that the group members have conciliated doesn't seem to have any bearing on whether p is true or false. This suggests that there is no difference between, on the one hand, the probability that p is false given the group members' *post-conciliation* beliefs about p, and, on the other hand, the probability that p is false given the group members' *pre-conciliation* beliefs about p. Hence, to determine the former probability, we need only determine the latter.

What, then, *is* the probability that p is false given the group members' pre-conciliation beliefs about p? In the case at hand, the answer is simple—50%—since there are equally many, equally reliable members who believe p and $\sim p$ respectively.[12] Consequently, the group ends up believing a proposition that, by the lights of its own members, is no more likely to be true than false. This already looks like a severe blow to the group's negative reliability.

We can harden the blow even more by considering just how unlikely $\sim p$ would have to be in order for the group to believe p *before* the conciliation process. The relevant scenario is one where all ten group members falsely believe p, which, in spite of their relatively modest reliability, is extremely unlikely: $(1 - r)^n = (1 - .7)^{10} = .000006$. Thus, the conciliatory effects of in-group disagreement can in fact have a very significant, adverse impact on a group's negative reliability.

There is, however, a positive flip side: the *decrease* in negative reliability is accompanied by an *increase* in positive reliability. The qualitative reason is the same as above: given that the group uses unanimity voting, it isn't possible for the conciliation process to eliminate any existing, potentially true beliefs. By contrast, it *is* possible for the conciliation process to introduce a new, potentially true belief. Hence, the group's positive reliability goes up.

This also brings out a more general lesson about the problem we're facing. The problem isn't so much that the conciliatory effects of in-group disagreement can harm a group's *overall* reliability (although this may sometimes be the case, depending on how we determine an agent's "overall" reliability on the basis of the agent's positive reliability and negative reliability). Rather, the problem is that the conciliatory effects of in-group disagreement can lead to the frustration of a group's preferred trade-off between positive and negative reliability. That's why we began by naming it the "Epistemic Priority Problem."

4.3.2 *Case 2: Inverse Unanimity Voting*

The same general problem can arise for groups that place more weight on positive reliability than negative reliability. Consider a group with the same characteristics as the one above except that it uses a different BAF:

- i The group consists of two same-sized subgroups, g_1 and g_2.
- ii The group members' pre-conciliation and post-conciliation credences in p are as stated in Table 4.2.
- iii The group uses (what we'll call) "inverse" unanimity voting: that is, the group believes p iff at least one of its members believes p.

The operative BAF here—inverse unanimity voting—is less familiar than, say, unanimity voting or majority voting. It has some rather odd properties. For example, it entails that a group believes both p and $\sim p$ whenever its members do not unanimously agree about whether p is true or false. Yet, this is precisely what makes inverse unanimity voting conducive to a high positive reliability: just as unanimity voting is an effective way of avoiding false beliefs, inverse unanimity voting is an effective way of gaining true ones.

Let's ask again: what does the group believe about *p* before and after the conciliation process, respectively? Before the conciliation process, the group believes both *p* and ~*p*, since the members do not unanimously agree about whether *p* is true or false (more specifically: all members of g_1 believe *p*, whereas all members of g_2 believe ~*p*). But after the conciliation process is completed, the members unanimously agree that *p* is true. As a result, the group drops its belief in ~*p*, but retains its belief in *p*.

What has happened to the group's positive and negative reliability here? On the one hand, the group's positive reliability has decreased, since the group has dropped a potentially true belief without forming any new ones. On the other hand, the group's negative reliability has increased, since the group has eliminated an existing error-possibility without introducing any new ones. Thus, the group's epistemic priorities are once again frustrated.[13]

4.3.3 Case 3: Majority Voting

What about groups that place *equal* weight on positive and negative reliability? Can the problem arise for such groups as well? The short answer is "yes." But the details are a bit different from the previous two cases. Consider a group with the following characteristics:

- i The group consists of two subgroups, g_1 and g_2, where g_1 has 4 members, and g_2 has 5 members.
- ii The group members' pre-conciliation and post-conciliation credences in *p* are as stated in Table 4.2.
- iii The group uses majority voting: that is, the group believes *p* iff more than half of its members believe *p* (which secures an equal weighing of positive and negative reliability, as illustrated by Figure 4.1).

What does the group believe about *p* before and after the conciliation process, respectively? Before the conciliation process, the group believes *p*, since all members of the majority group, g_2, believe *p*. But since the members of the minority group, g_1, are *much more* confident of ~*p* than *p*, whereas the members of g_2 are only *slightly more* confident of *p* than ~*p*, the result of the conciliation process is that all members of the combined group end up being slightly more confident of ~*p* than *p*. So, after the conciliation process is completed, the group believes ~*p*.

What has happened to the group's reliability here? Consider first the group's *negative* reliability. One effect of the conciliation process is that the group drops its belief in *p*, which eliminates an existing error-possibility. But the group also forms a new belief in ~*p*, which introduces a new error-possibility. These opposing effects might be thought to "cancel each other out," so as to leave the group's negative reliability unaffected. But things are a little more complicated than that.

Here is why: before the conciliation process, the majority group is more likely than the minority group to be right (assuming, as we do, that $r > 50\%$).[14] Thus, the conciliation process effectively leads the group to trade a belief that is *less likely* to be false for a belief that is *more likely* to be false, which means that the group's negative reliability decreases. The same goes for the groups' positive reliability: it also decreases, since the group effectively trades a belief that is *more likely* to be true for a belief that is *less likely* to be true. This stands in contrast to the previous two cases, where the group's positive/negative reliability decreased, whereas the group's negative/positive reliability increased, thereby leaving the group's *overall* reliability (at least potentially) untouched.[15]

However, this result should be taken with a pinch of salt. As we'll see in the next section, the result is sensitive to our background assumptions in a way that the previous two results are not. (More specifically: it doesn't fully generalize to settings where a high level of confidence is indicative of a high reliability.) Thus, we still take the main upshot of the foregoing considerations to be that the conciliatory effects of in-group disagreement can lead to the frustration of a group's epistemic priorities (rather than necessarily damage the group's overall reliability).

4.4 Generalizing the Epistemic Priority Problem

We have now seen how the Epistemic Priority Problem can arise in a highly idealized setting. The next thing we'd like to do is to generalize the problem by showing how it can arise even without the various idealizing assumptions introduced in the previous section. We will skip over some of the assumptions that clearly aren't responsible for the problem (e.g., the assumption that suspension of judgment isn't allowed, and the assumption that there are only two levels of comparative confidence). This leaves us with three assumptions to consider.

The first assumption is the one saying that the reliability of any given member is independent of how confident that member is that his or her opinion is correct. There are two general ways in which this assumption might be modified: either (i) by assuming that members with more extreme credences are more reliable than members with less extreme credences or (ii) by assuming that members with more extreme credences are less reliable than members with less extreme credences. While the latter of these dependencies might well obtain in certain kinds of situations,[16] we'll focus our attention on the former dependency here, since this carries no obvious presumption of irrationality on part of the individual group members.[17]

So, let's assume that members with more extreme credences are also more reliable, and let's ask: how, if at all, does this change affect the results from the previous section (other things being equal)? There are three cases to consider.

In Case 1, the Epistemic Priority Problem still shows up, albeit with mitigated strength. The basic mechanism is the same as before: the group's negative reliability decreases, since the group forms a new belief, which introduces a new error-possibility. But since the members of g_1 are more confident (and hence, by present assumptions, more reliable) than the members of g_2, the group's negative reliability doesn't suffer as much as before. In particular, the group now ends up with a belief that, by the lights of its own members, is at least slightly more likely to be true than false (unlike the original case where the group ended up with a belief that, by the lights of its own members, was no more likely to be true than false).

The same goes, *mutatis mutandis*, for Case 2: the group's positive reliability still decreases, since the group drops a belief, which eliminates an existing possibility of being right. But since the members of g_1 are more confident (and hence, by present assumptions, more reliable) than the members of g_2, the group's positive reliability doesn't suffer as much as before.

By contrast, the Epistemic Priority Problem need no longer arise in Case 3. The reason for this is that the members of the minority group, g_1, are (by present assumptions) more reliable than the members of the majority group, g_2, which means that it's no longer clear that the majority group is initially (that is, prior to the conciliation process) more likely to be right than the minority group. Rather, what subgroup is more likely to be right is going to depend on how much more reliable the members of the g_1 are assumed to be than the members of g_2. Thus, although the Epistemic Priority Problem will still arise on *some* ways of filling in the details of the case, the problem is no longer inevitable.

The next assumption we'd like to consider is the one saying that all group members are epistemic peers. As many authors have pointed out, this condition is rarely (if ever) met in real life.[18] It is therefore natural to wonder whether the Epistemic Priority Problem is affected (one way or the other) by relaxing the peerhood assumption. So, let's assume that the group members may differ in reliability, and let's also assume (which seems reasonable from an epistemic viewpoint) that members who are more reliable are also accorded more weight by the group's BAF. How, if at all, does this change affect the Epistemic Priority Problem (other things being equal)?

In Case 1, the Epistemic Priority Problem still arises with unmitigated strength. The reason for this is that the introduction of differential weights has no effect on the output of unanimity voting: all members still have to agree on p in order for the group to believe p. In consequence, the group's negative reliability still decreases as a result of the group forming a new belief, which introduces a new error-possibility.

And, at least insofar as there is no reason to think that the members of g_1 are systematically more or less reliable than the members of g_2, there is no reason to think that the group's negative reliability suffers any more or less than in the original case.

The same goes, *mutatis mutandis*, for Case 2: the introduction of differential weights has no effect on the output of inverse unanimity voting, which means that the group's positive reliability still decreases as a result of dropping an existing, potentially true belief. And given that there is no reason to think that the members of g_1 are systematically more or less reliable than the members of g_2, there is no reason to think that the group's positive reliability suffers any more or less than in the original case.

Things get a bit more complicated in Case 3, since the introduction of differential weights *can* affect the output of majority voting. Whether it *does* affect the output in the case at hand depends on the specific weight allocation. It would take us too far astray to enter a detailed discussion of how different types of weight allocation would affect the Epistemic Priority Problem. But we'd like to consider one particularly natural weight allocation (or class of weight allocations) which turns out to have the potential to mitigate the Epistemic Priority Problem, at least to some extent. On this way of allocating weight, members with more extreme credences are given more weight than members with less extreme credences. The rationale behind this weight allocation is supposed to be that people who are more confident in their beliefs are also more likely to be right in their beliefs. As mentioned, this dependency might not always hold true. But we find it realistic enough in many cases for it to be worthwhile considering how the Epistemic Priority Problem might be affected by it.

The first thing to observe is that it's no longer clear what the group believes before the conciliation process, since the members of the minority group have more extreme credences (and hence, given present assumptions, are given more weight) than the members of the majority group. Rather, whether the group as a whole initially (that is, prior to the conciliation process) agrees with the majority group or the minority group is going to depend on how much more weight is placed on the beliefs of the minority group than on the members of the majority group. This gives us two cases to consider.

The first (and simplest) case is the one where the group as a whole initially agrees with the minority group. Here it's clear that the Epistemic Priority Problem no longer arises, since the conciliation process leads to no change in the group's belief state, and hence leaves the group's positive and negative reliability unaffected.

The second (and slightly more complicated) case is the one where the group as a whole initially agrees with the majority group. Given this, the conciliation process *does* lead to a change in the group's belief state, since all members still end up agreeing with the minority belief once the conciliation process is completed. However, given that the members of the minority group are more reliable than those of the majority group, it's not immediately clear whether the group's reliability increases or decreases. Rather, whether the group's reliability increases or decreases depends on whether the majority group is initially more or less likely to be right than the minority group. And this, in turn, depends on just how much more reliable the members of the minority group are assumed to be than those of the majority group. Thus, the Epistemic Priority Problem may or may not arise, depending on how we fill in the details of the case.

The third (and final) assumption we want to discuss concerns the particular version of conciliationism practiced by the group members. Until now, we have assumed that the group members practice a form of "splitting the difference." However, there are various weaker versions of conciliationism which have been defended in the literature (perhaps the best-known example being Kelly's (2010) "Total Evidence View"). This makes it natural to wonder whether the Epistemic Priority Problem can also arise in more moderate conciliatory environments. So, let's suppose that the group members practice a moderate form of conciliationism: that is, they don't split the difference, but they do revise their credence at least to some extent in the face of peer disagreement. How, if at all, does this change affect the Epistemic Priority Problem (other things being equal)?

The answer, to a first approximation, is the same in all three cases: the Epistemic Priority Problem can still arise, but it does so in a more limited range of cases. A little more precisely: the Epistemic Priority Problem still shows up as long as the members practice a form of conciliationism that is strong enough to ensure that all members end up favouring the same proposition once the conciliation process is completed. What counts as "strong enough" is going to depend on the pre-conciliation credences of the group members. For example, in Case 1, a fairly weak form of conciliationism will suffice to generate the Epistemic Priority Problem, since all members of g_1 are *much more* confident of p than $\sim p$, while all members of g_2 are only *slightly more* confident of $\sim p$ than p. By contrast, if some of the members of g_2 had instead been *much more* confident of $\sim p$ than p, we would have needed a stronger form of conciliationism to generate the problem. Thus, although the Epistemic Priority Problem is most prevalent in highly conciliatory environments, it can arise in more moderate conciliatory environments as well.

4.5 Solving the Epistemic Priority Problem

Although not the main focus of the chapter, we'd like to close on a more positive note by offering a tentative proposal for how to solve the Epistemic Priority Problem without rejecting conciliationism. The proposal relies on a distinction that has come up in various forms in the recent "higher-order evidence" literature: a distinction between, on the one hand, an agent's *credence* in *p*, and, on the other hand, (what we'll call) the agent's *first-order judgment* as to whether *p*.

An agent's first-order judgment as to whether *p*, as we'll understand it, is the agent's judgment of how likely it is that *p* is true given the first-order evidence available to the agent.[19] We won't here try to say anything very precise about what counts as "first-order evidence," but, as a minimum, the mere fact that someone disagrees with you is supposed to *not* count as first-order evidence, but is rather supposed to count as a (higher-order) reason for you to doubt the reliability of your judgment of what your first-order evidence supports.[20]

Now, in many cases your credence in *p* will line up (at least roughly) with your first-order judgment as to whether *p*. For example, if it seems to you on the basis of your visual experience that it's raining outside, you will normally be quite confident that it's raining outside. Sometimes, however, your credence may come apart from your first-order judgment, precisely because you have reason to doubt the accuracy of your own first-order judgment. This is what can happen in cases of disagreement.

Suppose, for example, that you disagree with a trusted colleague about how strongly a given body of meteorological data supports the proposition that (*p*) it's going to rain this afternoon. In your judgment, the data strongly supports *p*. In your colleagues judgment, the data strongly supports ~*p*. Setting aside the fact that your colleague disagrees with you on this particular occasion, you don't consider your judgment to be any more or less likely to be accurate than your colleague's. Thus, you adopt a relatively low credence in *p* (say, around 50%), not because you have been persuaded by your colleagues first-order considerations, but because the disagreement itself has led you to doubt the accuracy of your own first-order judgment.

Distinction in hand, here is the proposal in rough outline: rather than aggregating the group members' *credences* in *p*, let's instead aggregate their *first-order judgments* as to whether *p*. Doing so would block the Epistemic Priority Problem by preventing the conciliatory effects of in-group disagreement from having any impact on the group's belief state in the first place (since the group members' first-order judgments are not supposed to be sensitive to higher-order considerations). And it would at the same time allow the group to take advantage of various other deliberative activities like knowledge sharing and critical argumentation (since the group members' first-order judgments are supposed to be sensitive to first-order considerations).

The hope, then, is that by aggregating first-order judgments rather than credences, we can at once (i) avoid the Epistemic Priority Problem, (ii) retain conciliationism, and (iii) reap the epistemic benefits of group deliberation. Needless to say, there are various concerns one might have about the concrete implementation of this proposal. Most obviously, it is not immediately clear how easy it will be to elicit people's first-order judgments in real-world settings (say, a typical voting scenario). We are not ourselves in a position to give an informed assessment of the practical feasibility of the proposed solution. For now, we are content to leave the proposal on the table for our joint consideration.

4.6 Conclusion

Here, then, is the main takeaway: conciliatory views of disagreement have a disturbing feature. The trouble is that conciliatory responses to in-group disagreement can lead to the frustration of a group's *epistemic priorities*: that is, the group's favoured trade-off between the "Jamesian goals" of truth-seeking and error-avoidance. This is what we called the "Epistemic Priority Problem." The problem is most prevalent in highly conciliatory environments, but it can in principle arise whenever the members of a group practice at least a minimal form of conciliationism. Thus, we take the problem raised to flow from all versions of conciliationism, albeit with different severity.

As mentioned at the outset, this is not to say that conciliationism, understood as a view about how individuals should revise their beliefs in response to disagreement, is undermined (partly or wholly) by the Epistemic Priority Problem. The considerations put forth in this chapter might just show that the true epistemic norms for individual believers sometimes have adverse epistemic consequences at the group level. If so, a solution along the lines of the one outlined in §4.5 may be particularly apt, since it doesn't force us to give up conciliationism. But in any case, it seems to us that we need to face up to the problem raised in one way or another.

Acknowledgments

We'd like to thank Fernando Broncano-Berrocal and Adam Carter for providing very helpful comments on an earlier version of this chapter.

Notes

1 Different versions of conciliationism have been defended by Christensen (2007), Elga (2007), Kelly (2010), Lackey (2008), among others. For critics of conciliationism, see Titelbaum (2015), Tal (forthcoming), Smithies (2019), and Weatherson (2019).
2 For some good entry points into the literature on group belief, see Gilbert (1987, 1989), Tuomela (1992), List and Pettit (2011), and Lackey (2016).
3 For a general introduction to the theory of belief aggregation, see Pigozzi (2016).

4 See Gilbert (1989) for an early discussion of summativist vs non-summativist views of group belief.
5 Here and elsewhere we assume that the group members are independent of each other: that is, any given member's belief about p isn't affected by any other member's belief about p.
6 See, e.g. Dorst (2019) and Easwaran (2016). See also Skipper (2020a), Steinberger (2019), and Hewson (2020) for critical discussion of this idea.
7 There are also less practically founded reasons to think that no one BAF will fare well in all contexts; reasons coming from various impossibility results in social choice theory (see List (2013) and Pacuit (2019) for overviews). See also Kelly (2013), Horowitz (2017), and Pettigrew (2016) for recent discussions of how rational individuals might trade off the Jamesian goals of truth-seeking and error-avoidance in different ways.
8 See List and Pettit (2002).
9 One might instead adopt an "evidentialist" notion of epistemic peerhood, whereby two agents are said to be epistemic peers with respect to p iff they have the same evidence about p and are equally competent at judging how that evidence bears on p. This notion of epistemic peerhood has often been operative in the "peer disagreement" literature (e.g., Christensen 2007). As previously noted, we suspect that the Epistemic Priority Problem (or a very similar problem) will arise equally for such an evidentialist notion of peerhood, but we won't here try to defend this claim in any detail.
10 See, e.g., Fitelson and Jehle (2009) and Rasmussen et al. (2018).
11 More generally: as long as the group uses unanimity voting, it's impossible for the conciliation process to eliminate any existing error-possibilities, since, if the members unanimously agree on a proposition prior to the conciliation process, they will also unanimously agree on that proposition after the conciliation process.
12 Assuming that the prior probability of p is 50%.
13 For a quantitative example pertaining to Case 2, the calculations provided in connection with Case 1 carry over, mutatis mutandis, to the present case. We omit the details.
14 This is a consequence of Condorcet's famous jury theorem (Condorcet 1785). For an accessible modern discussion of the result and its implications, see Goodin and Spiekermann (2018).
15 A different but related point has been made by Hazlett (2016), who argues that the probability with which majority voting yields the correct result may be harmed if the voters defer to each other's beliefs prior to voting, because this compromises the "independence" assumption underlying the Condorcet jury theorem.
16 For example, one might wonder whether the dependency is sometimes obtained as a consequence of the well-documented "Dunning-Kruger" effect, whereby (roughly) people who are less competent on a given matter are more prone to overestimating their own competence (Dunning and Kruger 1999).
17 A small aside on this point: psychological studies have documented a robust and widespread "overconfidence bias," whereby people's confidence in their answers to a wide range of tests tends to exceed the actual frequency with which their answers are correct (Lichtenstein et al. 1982; Hoffrage 2004). In other words, of the answers people are n% confident in, less than n% are true. One might be tempted to see this overconfidence effect as evidence against the claim that a high confidence is typically indicative of a high reliability. However, this would be too quick. Something much stronger would be needed to show this, namely, that if we compare the answers people are

n% confident to the answers they are >n% confident in, a higher proportion of the former answers are true. As far as we know, there is no evidence to support this stronger claim.

18 See, e.g., King (2012).

19 Variations on the notion of a first-order judgment have been employed by, e.g., Barnett (2019, §4) who talks about your "disagreement-insulated inclination" toward p, and Worsnip (ms, §4) who talks about your "personal take" on whether p.

20 For more detailed characterizations of the distinction between "first-order evidence" and "higher-order evidence," see Christensen (2010), Lasonen-Aarnio (2014), and Skipper (2019, 2020b).

References

Barnett, Z. (2019): "Philosophy without Belief." In: *Mind* 128, pp. 109–38.

Bright, L., H. Dang, and R. Heesen (2018): "A Role for Judgment Aggregation in Coauthoring Scientific Papers." In: *Erkenntnis* 83, pp. 231–52.

Christensen, D. (2007): "Epistemology of Disagreement: The Good News." In: *The Philosophical Review* 116, pp. 187–217.

Christensen, D. (2010): "Higher-Order Evidence." In: *Philosophy and Phenomenological Research* 81, pp. 185–215.

Condorcet, N. (1785): *Essai sur l'Application de l'Analyse à la Probabilité des Décisions Rendues à la Pluralité des Voix*. Paris: De l'Imprimerie royale.

Dorst, K. (2019): "Lockeans Maximize Expected Accuracy." In: *Mind* 138, pp. 175–211.

Dunning, D. and J. Kruger (1999): "Unskilled and Unaware of It: How Difficulties in Recognizing One's Own Incompetence Lead to Inflated Self-Assessment." In: *Journal of Personal and Social Psychology* 77, pp. 1121–34.

Easwaran, K. (2016): "Dr. Truthlove Or: How I Learned to Stop Worrying and Love Bayesian Probabilities." In: *Noûs*, 50, pp. 816–53.

Elga, A. (2007): "Reflection and Disagreement." In: *Noûs* 41, pp. 478–502.

Fitelson, B. and D. Jehle (2009): "What is the 'Equal Weight View'?" In: *Episteme* 6, pp. 280–93.

Gilbert, M. (1987): "Modelling Collective Belief." In: *Synthese* 73, pp. 185–204.

Gilbert, M. (1989): *On Social Facts*. New York: Routledge.

Goldman, A. (2011): "Social Process Reliabilism: Solving Justification Problems in Collective Epistemology." In J. Lackey (ed.), *Essays in Collective Epistemology*. Oxford: Oxford University Press, pp. 11–41.

Goodin, R. (2006): "The Epistemic Benefit of Multiple Biased Observers." *Episteme* 3, pp. 166–74.

Goodin, R. and K. Spiekermann (2018): *An Epistemic Theory of Democracy*. Oxford: Oxford University Press.

Hazlett, A. (2016): "The Social Value of Non-Deferential Belief." In: *Australasian Journal of Philosophy* 94, pp. 131–51.

Hewson, M. (2020): "Accuracy Monism and Doxastic Dominance: Reply to Steinberger." In: *Analysis* 80, pp. 450–56.

Hoffrage, U. (2004): "Overconfidence." In R. Pohl (ed.), *Cognitive Illusions: A Handbook on Fallacies and Biases in Thinking, Judgement and Memory*. Hove and New York: Psychology Press, pp. 235–254.

Horowitz, S. (2017): "Epistemic Utility and the Jamesian Goals." In J. Dunn and K. Ahlstrom-Vij (eds.), *Epistemic Consequentialism*. Oxford: Oxford University Press, pp. 269–89.

James, W. (1896): "The Will to Believe." In Cahn (ed.), *The Will to Believe: And Other Essays in Popular Philosophy*, New York: Longmans, Green, and Co., pp. 1–15.

Kelly, T. (2010): "Peer Disagreement and Higher Order Evidence." In A. Goldman and D. Whitcomb (eds.), *Social Epistemology: Essential Readings*. Oxford: Oxford University Press, pp. 183–217.

Kelly, T. (2013): "Evidence Can Be Permissive." In M. Steup, J. Turri, and E. Sosa (eds.), *Contemporary Debates in Epistemology*. Oxford: Blackwell.

King, N. (2012): "Disagreement: What's the Problem? *or* A Good Peer is Hard to Find." In: *Philosophy and Phenomenological Research* 85, pp. 249–72.

Konek, J. (forthcoming): "Epistemic Conservativity and Imprecise Credence." In: *Philosophy and Phenomenological Research*.

Kornhauser, L. and L. Sager (1986): "Unpacking the Court." In: *Yale Law Journal* 96, pp. 82–117.

Lackey, J. (2008): "A Justificationist View of Disagreement's Epistemic Significance." In A. Millar, A. Haddock, and D. Pritchard (eds.), *Social Epistemology*Oxford: Oxford University Press, pp. 145–54.

Lackey, J. (2016): "What is Justified Group Belief?" In: *The Philosophical Review* 125, pp. 341–96.

Lasonen-Aarnio, M. (2014): "Higher-Order Evidence and the Limits of Defeat." In: *Philosophy and Phenomenological Research* 88, pp. 314–45.

Lichtenstein, S., B. Fischhoff, and L.D. Phillips (1982): "Calibration of Probabilities: The State of the Art to 1980." In D. Kahneman, P. Slovic, and A. Tversky (eds.), *Judgment under Uncertainty*. Cambridge: Cambridge University Press, pp. 306–34.

List, C. (2005): "Group Knowledge and Group Rationality." In: *Episteme* 2, pp. 25–38.

List, C. (2013): "Social Choice Theory." In E. N. Zalta (ed.), *Stanford Encyclopedia of Philosophy*. https://plato.stanford.edu/archives/win2013/entries/social-choice/

List, C. and P. Pettit (2002): "Aggregating Sets of Judgments: An Impossibility Result." In: *Economics and Philosophy* 18, pp. 89–110.

List, C. and P. Pettit (2011): *Group Agency: The Possibility, Design, and Status of Corporate Agents*. Oxford: Oxford University Press.

Lyon, A. and E. Pacuit (2013): "The Wisdom of Crowds: Methods of Human Judgement Aggregation." In P. Michelucci (ed.), *Springer Handbook for Human Computation*. New York: Springer, pp. 599–614.

Mayo-Wilson, C., K. Zollman, and D. Danks: "The Independence Thesis: When Individual and Social Epistemology Diverge." In: *Philosophy of Science* 78, pp. 653–77.

Pacuit, E. (2019): "Voting Methods." In E. N. Zalta (ed.), *Stanford Encyclopedia of Philosophy*. https://plato.stanford.edu/archives/fall2019/entries/voting-methods/

Pettigrew, R. (2016): "Jamesian Epistemology Formalized: An Explication of 'The Will to Believe'." In: *Episteme* 13, pp. 253–68.

Pigozzi, G. (2016): "Belief Merging and Judgment Aggregation." In E. N. Zalta (ed.), *The Stanford Encyclopedia of Philosophy*.

Rasmussen, M.S., A. Steglich-Petersen, and J.C. Bjerring (2018): "A Higher-Order Approach to Disagreement." In: *Episteme* 15, pp. 80–100.

Russell, J., J. Hawthorne, and L. Buchak (2015): "Groupthink." In: *Philosophical Studies* 172, pp. 1287–309.

Skipper, M. (2019): "Higher-Order Defeat and the Impossibility of Self-Misleading Evidence." In M. Skipper and A. Steglich-Petersen (eds.), *Higher-Order Evidence: New Essays*. Oxford: Oxford University Press.

Skipper, M. (2020a): "Belief Gambles in Epistemic Decision Theory." In: Philosophical studies. Online first.

Skipper, M. (2020b): "Does Rationality Demand Higher-Order Uncertainty?" In: Synthese. Online first.

Skipper, M. and A. Steglich-Petersen (2019): "Group Disagreement: A Belief Aggregation Perspective." In: *Synthese* 196, pp. 4033–58.

Smithies, D. (2019): *The Epistemic Role of Consciousness*. Oxford: Oxford University Press.

Steinberger, F. (2019): "Accuracy and Epistemic Conservatism." In: *Analysis* 79, pp. 658–69.

Tal, E. (forthcoming): "Is Higher-Order Evidence Evidence?" In: *Philosophical Studies*.

Titelbaum, M. (2015): "Rationality's Fixed Point (Or: In Defense of Right Reason)." In: *Oxford Studies in Epistemology* 5, pp. 253–94.

Tuomela, R. (1992): "Group Beliefs." In: *Synthese* 91, pp. 285–318.

Weatherson, B. (2019): *Normative Externalism*. Oxford: Oxford University Press.

Worsnip, A. (ms): "Compromising with the Uncompromising: Political Disagreement Under Noncompliance." Unpublished Manuscript.

Zollman, K. (2010): "The Epistemic Benefit of Transient Diversity." In: *Erkenntnis* 2, pp. 17–35.

5 Intra-Group Disagreement and Conciliationism

Nathan Sheff

Conciliationists about peer disagreement claim that, when epistemic peers (that is, people who are equally intelligent, aware of the same relevant evidence, and so on) disagree, the rational response is for each to lower their confidence in their initial views – perhaps even suspending judgment on the matter entirely.[1] While conciliationism in cases of disagreement among individual peers remains controversial, the case for conciliation in other types of disagreement has been underexplored. This chapter aims to explore this territory, making the case for conciliationism in *intra-group* disagreements. An intra-group disagreement occurs when a deliberative group of epistemic peers comes to believe that *p*, while at least one of the members of that group persists in believing *not-p*. Conciliationism about intra-group disagreement holds that, in cases where group members disagree with their group's judgments, the rational response for any disagreeing members is lowering confidence in their view.

Intra-group conciliationism has not received the attention that peer-to-peer conciliationism has and may not seem intuitively plausible. So, in order to make the case for intra-group conciliationism, I will start by discussing Margaret Gilbert's joint commitment theory of collective intentionality. Joint commitment provides the normativity that makes group action possible, even group belief. Once the Gilbertian account of what happens in deliberating groups is laid out, we can appreciate the epistemic predicament someone is in when, over the course of settling a question with their group, the group as such settles on a view that dissenting members personally disagree with. They find themselves epistemically responsible for contradictory views: their own personal view and the view of the group. They find themselves pulled in contrary directions. The rational response is to at least lower their confidence in their view.

5.1 Joint Commitment

What is the difference between walking side-by-side and walking together (Gilbert 1990)? In general, the former involves no shared intention or common purpose, while the latter does involve it, but the nature of that shared element has been a matter of debate.[2] Walking together, and other shared activities, seem to require some form of collective intentionality, where two or more people can act together for a common end, but the mechanism of collective intentionality can be obscure. What, exactly, is happening in the minds of people who are acting as a group? Are we forced to say there are "group minds"?

Margaret Gilbert answers this problem by positing joint commitments as the mechanism of collective intentionality, but in explaining joint commitment, it helps to consider personal commitments first.[3] Commitments, generally speaking, are the output of deliberative processes. When I decide to go to the grocery store for peanut butter, I thereby give myself a reason to go to the store and get peanut butter. I become committed to going to the store because of my decision to do so. In this way, a personal commitment has a world-to-mind direction of fit, in the mold of Anscombe (1957). While beliefs have a mind-to-world direction of fit, in that their function is to align their contents to the world, commitments are world-to-mind in that their function is to make the world match their contents. Commitments have a directive-like character; their contents function like imperatives. Directives in general – even directives given to oneself – inherit their function from the relationship between their producers and consumers, and the normative role that each has. In producing a commitment, the producer determines what is to be done. The producer has the authority to set the agenda and the authority to revise or rescind it. Meanwhile, the consumer's job is to carry out what the producer says. Consumers answer to producers; they are responsible for carrying out the agenda. Correspondingly, the producer can criticize or demand compliance from the consumer. This is a teleosemantic account of commitment; the producer/consumer analysis comes directly from Ruth Millikan's account of intentionality (Millikan 1984).

Analyzing the capacity for commitment into two normative roles shows how some commitment-related phenomena arise. Unlike other mental states with a world-to-mind direction of fit, commitments are normatively robust in the following sense. Desires and intentions can form and dissolve without giving me a lasting reason to act on them. If I have a sudden desire for a cup of tea but then forget to get up and make it, I haven't acted irrationally in any way. But, Gilbert points out, when we fail to act on our commitments, we're liable to self-criticism, taking ourselves to task for failing to do what we decided to do. If I remember later that I had briefly wanted tea and never made any, I won't hold myself accountable, but if I committed to going to the store, forgot to go, and later remember my commitment, I will upbraid myself. The Millikanian producer-consumer analysis makes sense of this easily. Since this was a personal commitment, I was both the producer and the consumer of the directive. I set the agenda for myself to go to the store, and I never unmade that agenda.

As the consumer of the directive, I was responsible for carrying it out, and I failed to do so. I'm using my authority to criticize myself, insofar as I am the producer of the directive, and in being criticized, I'm answerable as the consumer for not carrying out the agenda.[4] Self-chastisement, even disappointment with oneself, might seem like an inexplicable personality quirk at first glance, but it emerges as a natural consequence of the structure of accountability set up by a commitment.

Commitments create structures of responsibility and accountability, and they come in two forms, either as personal commitments or as joint commitments. If I am personally committed to going to the store, then I am responsible to myself, and myself alone, for carrying out the plan. However, if you and I are jointly committed to going to the store together, I am responsible both to you and to myself for going to the store, and you likewise are responsible both to yourself and to me for going to the store.

To better understand this last point, consider the simple case of us going on a walk together. I invite you to take a break from your work and take a walk on campus. You agree, and after mulling over our options, we decide to head towards the lake. We have not only jointly committed to going for a walk; we have also committed to a destination. If I suddenly broke off towards a campus coffee shop without warning, I would be acting irrationally (not to mention strangely). You could rightly say, "Hey, weren't we going to the lake?" This is because, when we make a joint commitment, we create a structure of responsibilities towards ourselves and each other. By accepting my invitation, your normative situation changes in two ways. You, insofar as you are the commitment's consumer, become both accountable to yourself and accountable to me for going on the walk. But when you accept my invitation, my normative situation changes as well: I'm accountable to myself and to you, also, as a consumer. And both of us have authority over one another insofar as we are both producers of the commitment. So, when we jointly commit to going on a walk together, it is no longer up to either of us individually to cancel the plans. Even if I really want to get coffee instead of walking to the lake with you, I cannot simply go it alone and make the decision to undo the joint commitment for both of us. In a case of personal commitment, after all, the responsibilities to yourself do not simply disappear if you forget about them. They can only be unmade by a new decision process. Likewise, canceling or revising a joint commitment must be done jointly. I'm a producer of the commitment, but so are you, and I'm as answerable to you as I am to myself in this matter. In light of our commitment, if I really want to get coffee instead of walking to the lake, the responsible thing for me to do is ask you to reconsider our plans.

Once our joint commitment creates a structure of accountability and responsibility, we together become appropriate targets of praise or blame. We become creditable for our successes or failures at what we committed to doing together. If I personally commit to bringing cookies to the party, I can be credited for my success if I succeed or held accountable for failing to do so if I don't. The same holds for joint commitment: we can be praised or blamed together, depending on the outcomes of the action(s) produced by our joint commitment(s).

5.2 Group Belief

When two or more people jointly commit to doing something, they are, for as long as the commitment persists, a group.[5] People come together as groups in order to carry out what they've committed themselves to, but carrying out their projects requires more than merely making the right commitment. Successful action requires both goals and beliefs about how to accomplish them. For instance, obtaining a glass of cold brew coffee requires a commitment to obtaining one and believing truly that there is cold brew coffee in the refrigerator. So, just as a personal commitment must be paired with the relevant beliefs to move an individual person to action, a joint commitment must be paired with the relevant beliefs to move jointly committed individuals to act.

With an individual's actions, it is the individual's beliefs that inform action, but whose beliefs inform a group action? Gilbert answers that the beliefs of the *group* inform action, not necessarily the beliefs of the members. Suppose you and I jointly commit to making pasta dough. Further questions now arise. Should we use a food processor? Assuming we're using egg yolks, do we have enough eggs? With these answers in hand, we can direct our joint activity together.

But how do group beliefs get fixed in the first place? Occasionally, a group belief that *p* might consist in the right number of group members believing *p*. Perhaps, for you and me, it goes without saying that, when we commit to making pasta dough, we believe that we'll be making it in the very kitchen where we made our commitment, and that's enough for us to believe, as a group, that we'll make the dough there. That's not always the case, however. Groups often have to be more explicit in fixing their beliefs; this process has to occur out in the open, between the members, in order for it to work. Everyone has to have a good idea of what *we* believe.

According to Maura Priest and Margaret Gilbert (2013), many group beliefs are formed by means of negotiation between the members. Consider the following dialogue, in which you and I are making pasta dough:

I: Two cups of semolina flour should make the dough nice and pliable.
YOU: That's at least one cup too much. Two cups of semolina will make the dough really dry.
I: Hmm, maybe that's right. Would ¾ of a cup work?
YOU: Yes, it would.

Gilbert and Priest would interpret this dialogue as follows. As we make pasta together, I make a proposal for what to believe about the semolina content of our dough. You reject that proposal (for good reason), so I try again with another proposal, which you accept. According to Gilbert and Priest's Negotiation of Collective Belief thesis, we have successfully negotiated one of the beliefs necessary for our joint project. Indeed, according to them, most group beliefs are negotiated in this manner. Some negotiations are comparatively quiet (e.g. someone makes a proposal, nobody objects, and the proposal becomes the group position), but negotiation is the main mechanism for fixing group belief. Once our belief is fixed, we are jointly committed to acting together as a body that so believes. When we believe *as a group* that ¾ cup of semolina will work, we are jointly committed to acting *just like a person* who believes that ¾ cup of semolina will work. We will take it for granted in our activity together.

Joint commitment might seem like an idle cog here, but it helps explain particular intra-group behaviors. Imagine that, as we start getting our pasta flours together, I say, "Two cups of semolina it is!" That would be strange, even irrational, since we had just settled on a very different view, and our joint commitment explains why contradicting the group belief is irrational. I might personally believe that two cups would be fine, but, in our joint activity, I can't gainsay the position we've settled on. When we jointly commit to the belief that ¾ cup will work, we become accountable to ourselves and each other just as we do in any other joint commitment. If I wanted to change our mind on this matter, I couldn't do it by myself; that would be up to both of us, not just me.[6] Thus, it's the structure of accountability made by our joint commitment that enables you to remind me that, actually, *we* had said that two cups wouldn't work. The joint commitment that makes our group belief possible also makes that belief stable.

Joint commitment also explains how our group can settle on a belief that no member believes as an individual. A group believes p when the group is jointly committed to treating p as true in further deliberations and actions, and to acting like a single body that believes p.[7] When we negotiate ourselves into the position that ¾ cup will work, we do not necessarily commit ourselves to that view as individuals. Nothing in the negotiation requires each of us to personally believe it. I might continue believing that two cups will work; you might be sure that two cups is too much. As long as we are jointly committed to acting as one body that believes ¾ cup is good, we believe it as a group, despite neither of us believing it as individuals.

5.3 Disagreement in Group Epistemic Enterprises

While the psychological possibility of making pasta together provides a lot of material for philosophical reflection, the main takeaway is that group belief arises from the need to take certain things for granted in joint activity, and the normative structure of joint commitment (i.e. responsibility to oneself and each other) regulates these beliefs. A lot of joint activity involves little interpersonal friction, and few cross-purposes, so that the resulting negotiation of belief is cut and dry. In some cases, though, where the stakes are higher and opinions differ, and as groups grow in size, negotiations can take on a more pointed character, though it is not necessarily acrimonious or combative.

Disagreement between scientists offers a case in point. Let's illustrate the issue by considering two principal investigators on a research project: Rada and Jessica. Rada and Jessica are part of the same field, both have doctorate degrees, and they have collaborated in the past on papers relating to their lab's current project. By any measure, they are epistemic peers, and, (one would hope) as partners, they recognize one another as such, meaning that each knows of the other that she is as informed, as capable of interpreting evidence, and generally as intellectually virtuous as herself. But suppose a controversy emerges between them in this very expensive laboratory setting, concerning the prospects of their future research. Let's imagine that, since they're studying limb regeneration in salamanders, they are considering new techniques for stimulating and inhibiting stem cells. Given their previous experiences with a particular technique, Jessica thinks that further research on this particular laboratory method promises results; they could even use it in enticing grant proposals. Rada, however, is pessimistic about the research prospects on that route. At the risk of oversimplifying, let's say there is a crucial proposition M which they disagree about:

> M: The new research method is a promising avenue of research.

Rada denies M; Jessica is confident in it. As scientists who take a deep interest in the same questions, they will discuss it, and as research partners whose reputations are tied up in their shared work, they have a practical interest in figuring out what *they* will believe. And this will not be a conversation where either party is likely to back down easily. They each take their own position on M to be backed with good reasons, even conclusive reasons, and they both draw from the same well of evidence. At this point, they're in a position that Richard Feldman calls disagreement after full disclosure (Feldman 2006). They recognize each other as epistemic peers; they understand each other's reasons and how those inform their conclusions, yet they still disagree. What now?

From the perspective we've developed so far in this paper, we can look at their situation through the negotiation lens. In their disagreement with one another, Jessica and Rada are negotiating what *they* think of M, and whether *they shall take M to be true together*, as they are in charge of the lab. (In real life, there would also be postdocs and graduate students working in the lab. One would hope they would be accounted for in real life.) Since their disagreement does not initially move either of them, it's safe to say that negotiations for their collective belief about M more or less stall. Rada offers a proposal and her reasons, which Jessica rejects in favor of her own counter-proposal. This is, in turn, rejected by Rada, and the cycle begins again. Eventually, they decide to postpone settling the M issue until another time.

If group beliefs are settled by means of negotiation, yet a particular group tries but fails to negotiate a group belief (regarding M, for example), what is the result? I suggest that it's a suspension of judgment or something very close. The question of M's truth is left open. They together have failed to establish a position one way or the other. The only thing they *have* settled on is to try again another time, which is to say they don't (yet) affirm or deny M. Jessica and Rada are still jointly committed to working together, so the failure to commit jointly to M doesn't dissolve their larger commitments. If we were considering a single person who was exhibiting this kind of behavior – going back and forth, weighing reasons for and against, but not reaching a conclusion – we would likely say the same, so it seems appropriate here in the group case. If neither Rada nor Jessica budge, they will postpone making any decisions which M would bear on until absolutely necessary. This makes sense if they have suspended judgment on M *as a group*.

So, the disagreement between Rada and Jessica results in them suspending their judgment about M as a group. This is a claim about *how group belief gets fixed*, not about what's rational for the group to believe after negotiation. As noted above, the fact that *they together* suspend judgment about M logically implies nothing about Rada's nor Jessica's beliefs about M as individuals. The group's suspending judgment also does not *ipso facto* make the group members suspend judgment. I don't take the case as described so far to imply anything about Rada's epistemic standing, or Jessica's, or the group's. Nothing has emerged yet about the rational course of action for anyone. So far, we've only made the case for understanding the fixation of group belief as the outcome of negotiation between group members. Nothing yet has been claimed about the epistemically responsible thing to do in light of Jessica's and Rada's group suspension of judgment about M. But let's turn to that now.

5.4 Intra-Group Conciliationism

Rada and Jessica are equally intelligent and mutually aware of the same body evidence; they recognize how they are each drawing their conclusions, but they disagree anyway. As a group, they have decided to suspend judgment about M in light of their stalled negotiations. But consider how things might seem to Jessica later on, reflecting on M in a cooler hour. She had entered the negotiation with Rada convinced of M, and during the negotiation, she put forward her best case for M. As far as she could tell, the case for M was still satisfying, even if it didn't convince Rada. Jessica built up a good case for M and had herself convinced. She was *epistemically responsible* in her confidence in M's truth. But then, the negotiations began with Rada, and Jessica was working to stake out not just her own personal belief but the belief of her group. In carrying out their joint activity, Jessica and Rada negotiated each other to a standstill. Over the course of discharging her responsibilities *vis-a-vis* her joint commitment with Rada, Jessica was *epistemically responsible* in bringing about her group's suspension of judgment about M.

Jessica finds herself in a difficult position, then. On the one hand, she is epistemically responsible in forming her own belief that M is true, but on the other hand, she is epistemically responsible in helping her group to suspend judgment about M. She is creditworthy for her own belief in M, but, because of the normative structure of her joint commitment with Rada, she is just as creditworthy for their suspension of judgment. She finds herself equally creditworthy for establishing contrary attitudes: belief that M in herself and suspended judgment about M for her and Rada. For a reflective person, this kind of equipollence ("I could just as well believe M as suspend judgment about it") puts one in a bind. There seems to be some pressure to change one's mind.

In the disagreement literature, conciliationists (like Feldman (2006)) claim that the rational response to peer disagreement after full disclosure is suspension of judgment or, at the very least, some lowering of credence in one's initial position. For conciliationists, the fact of disagreement puts pressure on the epistemic peers to change their minds. The case of Jessica and Rada helps us see where this rational pressure can come from. When two or more people are trying to answer the same question together – not in competition but in cooperation – they are responsible to themselves and each other in determining what they will think. With this normative structure in place, it becomes possible for the jointly committed parties to come to conclusions together which neither person individually believes. And if someone has really put in the effort, in private and in the group, they can, like Jessica, be in position to take equal credit for contrary attitudes. If Jessica's private conclusion is creditworthy, and her conclusion with Rada is creditworthy, but she can't endorse both conclusions, some sort of reconciliation is necessary to avoid cognitive dissonance. This is a form of conciliationism. When a person disagrees with the judgment they reach with their group, and when they regard their own activity and the activity of the group as epistemically responsible, the rational response to the disagreement is conciliation.

5.5 Objections and Replies

I've argued that, in cases where a member of a group disagrees with the position they've helped their group to establish, they become epistemically creditable for taking contrary attitudes, and the rational response to this form of dissonance is conciliation between their personal view and the view of their group. This view is non-committal on how these conflicting views are reconciled in the conflicted agent (perhaps they suspend judgment or simply lower their confidence), believing only that reconciliation is the rational response.

But one might object here that, in cases of conflict between one's own attitudes, reconciliation is not necessarily the uniquely rational response. Many of us often feel at odds with our own attitudes as different aspects of our personalities or identities come into conflict. Baxter (2018) sees such a case in Medea's conflict: insofar as she is a spurned wife, she wants to kill her children to spite Jason, but insofar as she is a mother, she does not want to kill her children to spite Jason. These two aspects make her differ from herself, but the self-differing doesn't exactly resolve itself in the disappearance of one side. As Baxter sees it, we should not be misled into thinking that Medea is, in one instant, wholeheartedly one way (for killing) and then, in the next instant, wholeheartedly the other way (against killing): "When we are torn, one side may predominate temporarily but the other side does not vanish" (Baxter 2018, p. 902).

Lahroodi (2007) considers a case involving differing beliefs. Suppose an administrative committee for a church, known for its opposition to gay rights, is staffed by committee members who are all, as individuals, in favor of gay rights. Each member, *as an individual*, is in favor of gay rights, but, at the same time, each member, *as a member of the church committee*, opposes gay rights. Each person takes differing attitudes keyed to different aspects of their identities. My view would imply that they're under rational pressure to reconcile their beliefs. Are they really? Do they need to feel the kind of dissonance experienced by Rada or Medea?

I would caution against putting too much weight on understanding Rada as torn between two sides of herself. It's not quite that she suspends judgment about M insofar as she is a member of the laboratory but not insofar as she is an individual. We can discuss how her commitments made her accountable in different ways, though. She formed one view on her own and the other *in cooperation with* Jessica. These are both things that *she* did; Rada herself is responsible for conflicting views. They are not, first and foremost, distinct sides of herself or aspects of herself in different roles. She gets sole credit for one view but shares credit with Jessica for the other. This is to say that it's not so easy to sequester one belief into one side of oneself and another conflicting belief into another side. Rada herself is epistemically responsible for conflicting views. That's why she herself feels conflicted, and reconciliation is the way in which to resolve the conflict.

The issue remains whether we're epistemically required to reconcile conflicting attitudes that we're equally responsible for. What am I supposed to do if I argue myself into believing *p* and also argue myself into denying *p*? Certain kinds of dialetheists wouldn't be opposed in principle to believing *p* and denying *p*. But, supposing we're not dialetheists, we might try to resolve the inner conflict by simply giving up one of the conflicting attitudes. This is easier said than done, however. To give up my denial of *p*, I will have to argue myself into it or encounter some epistemically irrelevant biasing factors that will turn me off denying *p* (maybe I learn that Trump denies *p*, and I automatically affirm *p* more powerfully than ever). I assume, though, that, in the ordinary case where we're aware of a conflict between our beliefs, we need to resolve the conflict through reconciliation. This is a major commitment to the view I'm defending here about the epistemic import of disagreeing with one's group. If reconciliation isn't required of us in cases where our attitudes pull in opposing directions, then the narrow conciliationism I've outlined loses a significant supporting strut. Unfortunately, a full defense of this commitment is beyond the scope of this paper. Suffice it to say that I agree with Sextus Empiricus: in cases where one is presented with opposing equipollent views, suspending judgment is necessary.

Another issue arises with the limits of my example. Jessica and Rada are two in number, and many groups are not. In a group this small, there might not be that much space between Rada arguing on her own behalf and Rada contributing to the making of the group attitude. Her participation in the negotiation of her group's view on M seems awfully close to her arguing for her own view. We might wonder whether Rada's change of heart later would be due to her interaction within the group or due to ordinary peer-to-peer conflict. Where exactly is the line between negotiating the group view and arguing for your own view?

These are admittedly blurry lines, but we can appreciate how what happens in groups can come apart from what participants believe. Jessica and Rada might have very different personal views from what they actually say in negotiation. For instance, neither of them might have a firm, settled view on M, but they each end up picking a side in their discussion. Rada might make the case for not-M, and Jessica the case for M, while neither has made up her mind. It's a feature, not a bug, of non-summative views of group belief that group beliefs have no necessary connections with what their members believe (see (Gilbert 1994; Gilbert 2002; Gilbert & Pilchman 2014)). In principle, then, there's no problem separating the negotiation of group belief from a debate between committed partisans insofar as we can distinguish between what group members say in negotiation and what those members personally believe.

A problem arises when, over the course of a larger project (like the direction of a laboratory), people argue on behalf of their own considered views. What's the difference between an argument between Jessica and Rada as group members and an argument between two epistemic peers having a peer-to-peer disagreement? It comes down to the nature of the joint commitment between them and what they are trying to do with their conversation. Conversations and debates normally require a joint commitment to sustain them. This means that, whether they are negotiating the group view or having a simple disagreement, what they are doing is sustained by a joint commitment. What marks the difference between defending one's own view in a peer-to-peer disagreement and helping to build a group view will be the joint commitment that sustains the shared activity. Peer-to-peer disagreements in conversation require a joint commitment, but the content of that joint commitment can sometimes involve nothing more than commitment to talking. It need not involve establishing a group view at all, or determining what the group shall take for granted in their activity, since there may not be any activity for the group beyond mere conversation. Jessica and Rada might say all the same things that they would say if they were having an ordinary peer-to-peer disagreement, but what makes their disagreement a negotiation is the content of the joint commitment in the background. They're not arguing for the sake of arguing. They're arguing for the sake of their shared scientific undertakings. Their shared activity is constructive, not just conversational, and this marks the difference between a mere peer-to-peer disagreement and a substantive negotiation of group belief.

5.6 Conclusion

Whenever we do anything together, we undertake joint commitments with one another and thereby become responsible to ourselves and each other. And when we do this, we often need to form beliefs as a group, things *we* can take for granted in order for our shared activity to go on. We form these beliefs by negotiating the group view; what *we* believe emerges as the result of the members' back-and-forth. It sometimes happens that groups will reach conclusions that disagree with those of the individual members. What should a person do if they disagree with a group they're a part of? If their joint commitment has led them to drawing contrary, yet epistemically responsible, conclusions, the dissonance caused by those contrary attitudes has to be dealt with by reconciling the opposing views in some way.

The case of Jessica and Rada is a special case, to be sure. They have a laboratory; they have a history of working together; there's a lot of money on the line. We might think, then, that intra-group conciliationism is interesting but narrow in scope. But we've also seen that joint commitment phenomena are everywhere – even a conversation between strangers can create a joint commitment between them, however ephemeral.

The last section concluded that we can distinguish between disagreements by looking at the joint commitments sustaining the conversation. Sometimes, these distinctions won't make much of a practical difference. People who dare to talk politics with the strangers sitting next to them on a plane are engaged in a shared activity, and this shared activity becomes more epistemically significant as each party puts in more effort and does their best to be epistemically responsible. These exchanges might not convince anyone of anything in the moment, but the fact of what they established – or failed to establish – in conversation will remain.[8]

Notes

1 Some prominent defenses of conciliationism include Feldman (2006) and Christensen (2007).

2 Rival accounts of intentionality include Bratman's shared intention account (most recently defended in Bratman (2014)) and Tuomela's we-intention account (Tuomela 2003). Schweikard and Schmid (2013) provide an excellent overview of the debate. For an overview of Gilbert's view specifically, see her recent Gilbert (2013).

3 I'm not claiming in this section that personal commitment is in any way prior to joint commitment. I've defended the view elsewhere that neither personal nor joint commitment is first in the order of knowing or being. This contrasts with views like Bratman's, which understands collective intentions as built up from complexes of personal intentions. On Gilbert's view, personal and joint commitment share a homologous normative structure, which explains why we can fruitfully understand joint commitment by starting with personal commitment.

4 The "self-criticism" point comes from Gilbert, but the Millikanian analysis comes from my dissertation (Sheff 2017) and is not endorsed by Gilbert herself.

5 The metaphysics of groups is complicated, but when I talk about groups here, I principally have in mind jointly committed people, not larger corporate entities (like AT&T), mere collections (the set of all left-handed students at the University of Connecticut), or social kinds (professional gardeners). See Ritchie (2015) for a strategy on how to distinguish between these different senses of "group".

6 Some groups have an internal structure for delegating certain tasks, like making a decision or answering a question for the group, to particular group members. Such groups would have somewhat more complicated joint commitments in play. For the sake of brevity, we'll consider groups without a complex inner structure.

7 Gilbert's critics often target her analysis of group belief, saying it is at best an account of *acceptance*, not belief proper (see Wray (2001)). A discussion of this would take us too far afield, but readers interested in this debate can refer to Chapter 3, sections 5 and 6, of Sheff (2017).

8 Thanks to the editors of this volume, Adam Carter and Fernando Broncano-Berrocal, for a number of helpful comments and criticisms which improved this paper.

References

Anscombe, G. E. M. (1957). *Intention* (Vol. 57). Cambridge, MA: Harvard University Press.

Baxter, D. L. M. (2018). Self-Differing, Aspects, and Leibniz's Law. *Noûs*, 52, 900–920.

Bratman, M. E. (2014). *Shared Agency: A Planning Theory of Acting Together*. Oxford: Oxford University Press.

Christensen, D. (2007). Epistemology of Disagreement: The Good News. *Philosophical Review*, *116*(2), 187–217.

Feldman, R. (2006). Epistemological Puzzles about Disagreement. In S. Hetherington (Ed.), *Epistemology Futures* (pp. 216–236). Oxford: Oxford University Press.

Gilbert, M. (1990). Walking Together: A Paradigmatic Social Phenomenon. *Midwest Studies in Philosophy*, *15*(1), 1–14.

Gilbert, M. (1994). Remarks on Collective Belief. In F. F. Schmitt (Ed.), *Socializing Epistemology: The Social Dimensions of Knowledge* (pp. 235–256). Lanham, MD: Rowman & Littlefield.

Gilbert, M. (2002). Belief and Acceptance as Features of Groups. *ProtoSociology, 16*, 35–69.

Gilbert, M. (2013). *Joint Commitment: How We Make the Social World*. Oxford: Oxford University Press.

Gilbert, M., & Pilchman, D. (2014). Belief, Acceptance, and What Happens in Groups. In J. Lackey (Ed.), *Essays in Collective Epistemology* (pp. 189–212). Oxford: Oxford University Press.

Lahroodi, R. (2007). Collective Epistemic Virtues. *Social Epistemology*, *21*(3), 281–297.

Millikan, R. G. (1984). *Language, Thought, and Other Biological Categories* (Vol. 14). Cambridge, MA: MIT Press.

Priest, M., & Gilbert, M. (2013). Conversation and Collective Belief. In A. Capone, F. Lo Piparo, & M. Carapezza (Eds.), *Perspectives on Pragmatics and Philosophy* (pp. 1–34). New York: Springer.

Ritchie, K. (2015). The Metaphysics of Social Groups. *Philosophy Compass*, *10*(5), 310–321.

Schweikard, D.P. & Schmid, H.B. (2013). Collective Intentionality. In E. N. Zalta (Ed.), *The Stanford Encyclopedia of Philosophy* (Summer 2013 Edition), https://plato.stanford.edu/archives/sum2013/entries/collective-intentionality/.

Sheff, N. (2017). *Thinking Together: Joint Commitment and Social Epistemology* [Dissertation]. Storrs, CT: University of Connecticut.

Tuomela, R. (2003). The We-Mode and the I-Mode. In F. Schmitt (Ed.), *Socializing Metaphysics: The Nature of Social Reality* (pp. 93–127). Lanham, MD: Rowman & Littlefield.

Wray, K. B. (2001). Collective Belief and Acceptance. *Synthese*, *129*(3), 319–333.

6 Bucking the Trend

The Puzzle of Individual Dissent in Contexts of Collective Inquiry

Simon Barker

6.1 Introduction

The primary focus of the literature on the epistemology of disagreement has been upon the question of how one ought to respond to the realisation of disagreement. Largely, this question has been considered in relation to cases of disagreement between two individuals who are epistemic peers. Whilst there are good methodological reasons for the focus on two-person peer disagreement, the class of philosophically interesting disagreements is not exhausted by these. As the current collection attests, another kind of disagreement worth special philosophical attention is that of disagreements involving and between groups. Just as we can ask how individuals ought to respond to disagreement with other individuals, we can ask how groups ought to respond to disagreement with other groups. Depending on the correct ontology of 'group' or 'collective' epistemic agents, this question may differ in significant ways from the question about two-person disagreements. Keeping on the group line, a further kind of disagreement worth considering is that in which an individual finds themselves in disagreement with a group. Depending on the nature of the group and the individual's relationship to that group, the normative implications of such cases may well differ quite significantly from simple two-person cases. One situation in which we might think this likely to be the case is when the individual is themselves an active participant in the group with which they disagree. We might call these cases of 'individual dissent'. In cases of individual dissent, the epistemic practices by which the individual reached their beliefs are likely to be both partly dependent upon and partly constitutive of the epistemic practices of the group. Consequently, the dissenter might accrue epistemic obligations both in respect to their status as an individual epistemic agent and in respect to their status as an active participant in the collective epistemic practices of the group. What is interesting about such cases, then, is that questions about the significance of the disagreement arise for the dissenter in respect to both these roles. Thus, not only can we ask of the dissenter:

1 How ought they respond to the disagreement *qua* individual?

But also:

2 How ought they respond to the disagreement *qua* group member?

To illustrate the tension between these two questions, this paper considers a puzzle that arises when we situate the literature on the epistemology of disagreement within a wider corpus of work on disagreement. I call this 'The Puzzle of Individual Dissent'. This puzzle follows from accepting two independently plausible principles – one of individual rationality and one of collective rationality.

The first principle comes out of the epistemological literature. Whilst epistemologists disagree on the question of how disputants ought to respond to disagreement with a single peer,[1] there is wider acceptance that the greater the number of one's peers one disagrees with, the more significance one should afford the realisation of disagreement. In section 6.1, I build upon this idea and introduce a principle I call 'Collective Superiority' or CS. One consequence of CS is that there can be situations in which an individual dissenter ought – *qua* individual rationality – to *accede* to the collective judgement. The second principle comes from discussions of the role of disagreement within collective inquiry in political philosophy, feminist philosophy of science, and social psychology. In this context, and in contrast to the epistemological literature, much attention has been paid to the epistemic benefits of disagreement and dissent. In section 6.2, I build upon such arguments to introduce a principle of collective rationality that I label 'Epistemic Liberalism' or EL. Roughly, EL says that collective judgements will not be justified if they are reached by practices that do not permit and preserve dissent within the collective. If CS and EL are both true, I suggest, there will be cases in which an individual dissenter ought – *qua* individual agent – to accede to the group on the disputed propositions and ought – *qua* group member – to stay steadfast in dissent. This is the puzzle of individual dissent. Whilst such conflicts between normative domains are familiar, I argue in section 6.3 that this kind of case would represent a rift within epistemic rationality that any plausible account of disagreement must resolve. To do so we must reject one or the other or both of 'Collective Superiority' and 'Epistemic Liberalism'. I conclude by considering the significance of rejecting 'Collective Superiority' within the epistemology of disagreement.[2, 3]

6.2 Examples and Assumptions

Let's start with some scene setting. First, an example:

THINK TANK

Indy is a skilled political analyst working for a political think tank. The think tank is a surprisingly principled research institution and

> Indy has every reason to believe that her colleagues and higher-ups are all competent and trustworthy researchers. Indy is one of several analysts tasked with assessing the data relevant to determining the viability of policy-X. On the basis of that assessment, Indy concludes that X is not viable. Indy submits her analysis to the group prior to a meeting to decide upon the recommendations to be included in a final policy paper on X. As the meeting goes on, and despite their awareness of Indy's analysis and conclusions, the group begins to coalesce around the conclusion 'X is viable'.

Let's say that this is a case of 'individual dissent'. Like any such toy-example it is somewhat idealised, but it should serve the purposes of this discussion, nonetheless. With example in hand, it will also help to clarify two points about the terminology I employ in the following discussion.

As noted, the puzzle of individual dissent arises when we consider how a dissenter ought to respond to disagreement *qua* individual and *qua* member of the group. For the purpose of the discussion, I treat these as questions about how the dissenter should respond to the evidence they acquire on realising the disagreement. In that light, I employ the vernacular of 'epistemic justification' throughout – where I take justification to refer to the kind of epistemic support that corresponds to following the evidence or believing on the basis of the right reasons. Having said that, I remain neutral on what is the best way of theorising justification so understood. Thus, I remain neutral also on whether *either* question is a matter of maintaining internal coherence between evidence and conclusions, accurately representing objective relations between evidence and conclusions, employing reliable methods in assessing evidence, and so on.

Second, since the puzzle of individual dissent follows, in part, from consideration of the literature on peer disagreement, it will be useful to have an idea of what it means to be epistemic peers. Broadly speaking, the idea is employed to pick out cases in which none of the disputants enjoy any clear advantage when it comes to determining the truth about the disputed propositions – whether that advantage comes from the quality of disputants' evidence, differences in their competence in the relevant domain, or features of the specific context that might impair or enhance the epistemic performance of one or another disputant. Whilst there are a number of different definitions of this relationship in the literature,[4] the problem I shall discuss does not turn on any of these. Thus, I shall employ the following catch-all definition:

> If S and R are competent in the domain relevant to p and disagree about p, S and R are **epistemic peers** *iff*, independent of the substance of their disagreement, neither S nor R have the *relative epistemic advantage* vis-à-vis p.[5]

With these provisory notes made, let's turn to the two principles that generate the puzzle of individual dissent. I'll start with 'Collective Superiority'.

6.2.1 Collective Superiority

'Conciliationist' views of disagreement say that, upon finding oneself in disagreement with a single peer, one ought to revise one's attitudes toward the disputed propositions in the direction of one's interlocutor's attitudes. The idea that greater significance should be given to the realisation of disagreement as the numbers stack up against one is a natural extension of that view. So, Adam Elga argues:

> If one really has 99 associates who one counts as peers who have independently assessed a given question, then one's own assessment should be swamped. This is simply an instance of the sort of group reliability effect commonly attributed to Condorcet.
>
> (Elga 2007: 494)

And Jon Matheson:

> [W]hat you are justified in believing is a matter of your higher-order evidence [...] Evidence about additional parties' opinions on a disputed matter is additional higher-order evidence that is relevant to what you are justified in believing about the disputed propositions.
>
> (Matheson 2015a: 126)

Whilst it is unsurprising that conciliationists endorse the idea that 'numbers matter', authors who reject conciliationism have expressed similar thoughts. For example, Thomas Kelly argues for the 'Total Evidence View', in which the appropriate response to disagreement depends upon a *substantive judgement* of the combination of first- and higher-order evidence available. Kelly's view is opposed to conciliationism's uniform diagnosis of two-person peer disagreement. Nonetheless, he writes:

> As the number of peers increases, peer opinion counts for progressively more in determining what it is reasonable for the peers to believe [...] At some point, when the number of peers grows large enough, the higher-order psychological evidence will swamp the first-order evidence into virtual insignificance.
>
> (Kelly 2010: 144–5)

Jennifer Lackey's 'Justificationist' view is also opposed to concilationism. According to this view, in some cases, disputants might ground a steadfast response to disagreement in 'personal information' they possess about their own lack of cognitive malfunction (see Lackey 2010). Nonetheless, Lackey writes elsewhere that:

> [N]umbers do matter in cases of disagreement, even in the absence of independence.
>
> (Lackey 2013: 245)

Others who oppose conciliationism to some degree yet echo these sentiments include Enoch (2010), Pettit (2006), and van Inwagen (2010). On the basis of this sample, then, it seems fair to say that the idea that 'numbers matter' – or, perhaps more accurately, 'numbers matter most' – is widespread in the literature on disagreement – and on all sides of the debate about simple two-person peer disagreements. As per the quote from Elga, the core motivations for this line of thought can be expressed by reference to Condorcet's Jury Theorem, which states that, if:

1. A group is voting on a choice between two options
2. One of those two options is 'correct'
3. The members of the group make their choices independently of each other
4. The members of the group are all more likely than not to make the correct choice and are equally likely to do so

   Then the likelihood that the majority decision is correct will increase as the size of the group increases.

The general result is a simple consequence of the law of large numbers applied to group decision-making under the conditions described.[6] Questions about the theoretical value of the theorem, thus, do not concern its correctness but whether the conditions of that result can be met in an interesting range of real-world situations. Putting these questions aside, however, we can see Condorcet's theorem as a useful theoretical encapsulation of the 'numbers matter' intuition.

As a first-pass at applying the insights behind Condorcet's theorem to the epistemology of disagreement we might posit the following principle:

> Principle of Many Peers (POMP): If S believes p, S belongs to group G, all the other members of G are S's epistemic peers, S is aware that the members of G have all reached their conclusions about p independently and that the majority have concluded that ~p, then, S ought to significantly revise her attitude toward p in the direction of the majority opinion. If G is large enough, S ought to accede to the majority opinion that ~p.

(I leave it to the reader to see how POMP extends to cases of individual dissent and how it corresponds to the conditions of Condorcet's theorem. Hopefully, both are clear enough.)

How interesting POMP is – just as with Condorcet's theorem – depends largely upon how well the principle corresponds to real-world cases. And, just as with Condorcet's theorem, we might have significant doubts that it corresponds to any interesting range of cases. For one thing, the condition that all members of the group are peers is extremely demanding. In any reasonably sized group, individuals will differ in their levels of competence and be aware of these differences. More problematic is the 'Independence' condition. Defining what it means for group members to reach their conclusions in ways that are probabilistically independent of each other will depend upon the specific contours of the issue under consideration. But even on the assumption that there are some cases in which independence is achievable, many (if not most) collective judgements are reached in ways that are not even intended to preserve full independence. Since POMP won't apply to those cases, its correspondence to real-world cases is limited at best.

Nonetheless, neither of these points give us reason to doubt the basic insight behind POMP. As far as the competence condition goes, Condorcet's original theorem applies strictly to cases where the members of the group are *equally* competent. Yet similar results have been demonstrated for variants of the theorem that relax the condition of parity and allow for unequal levels of competence amongst group members (for discussion, see List 2013). Likewise, social choice theorists have shown that the independence condition can be relaxed in various ways, with similar results to the original theorem still following. For instance, Estlund (1994) shows that Condorcet's theorem can accommodate qualified deference to opinion leaders; Ladha (1992) shows that it can accommodate the influence of dominant 'schools of thought'; and Dietrich and Spiekermann (2014) show that it can accommodate deliberation between group members on a topic, so long as deliberation increases group members 'problem-specific competence'. Also relevant here are Lackey's philosophical arguments in favour of relaxing independence. To quote her main conclusions:

> When the dependence in question is only partial in a case of peer disagreement, additional evidence relevant to the belief in question can be possessed by the dependent party, thereby necessitating doxastic revision that goes beyond that required by the original source's belief. When the dependence is complete but autonomous, additional epistemic force can be brought to the disagreement in various forms, such as through the hearer monitoring the incoming information for defeaters, possessing beliefs about the reliability and trustworthiness of the source, and bearing the responsibility of offering a flat-out assertion in the first place.
>
> (Lackey 2013: 265)

I won't rehearse Lackey's arguments in full, but I find this compelling. The general insight that the Condorcet considerations captures more formally is that a group of inquirers is typically able to draw from a greater pool of expertise and resources in its epistemic practices than any individual member of that group.[7] As Lackey points out, however, the range of relevant expertise, competence, and evidence that group members bring to an inquiry need not be confined to evidence and expertise that bear directly on its central topic. Imagine, for instance, that Indy's think tank includes an individual, Dep, who has no grasp of policy but is great at the data-stuff. Dep has no substantive input on the think tank's actual policy recommendations but plays a crucial role in double-checking the quality of the data on which those recommendations are based. Given his lack of wonkishness, Dep will be heavily dependent upon the other members of the team when it comes to questions about the viability of specific policy positions. Nonetheless, his acceptance of a collective policy position would imply that he found no problems with the data on which that position is based; his not accepting it would imply that he did find problems with the data. Given Dep's expertise, then, the group's policy positions will be on better justificatory standing if the group in some way conditionalizes on Dep's responses to its judgements than if it does not. To echo Lackey's conclusions, if the benefits of collective inquiry can be accrued even where the dependence relationships are this pronounced, we do not need to include an independence condition on any principle along the lines of POMP.

Taking these points about the reliability and independence conditions seriously, then, we might endorse a principle, similar in spirit to POMP, but not one so demanding that it fails to correspond to real-world cases. For, other things being equal, it seems reasonable to suppose that the advantages that come from pooling and expertise will place the collective in comparatively *superior* epistemic standing vis-à-vis the substance of disagreement to any individual member of the group – even if its procedures for reaching collective judgements do not satisfy the more stringent conditions of Condorcet's theorem (as in the Dep case). And, to return to a theme, whilst there is disagreement about the appropriate response to disagreement with a single peer – there is wider consensus that one ought to afford disagreement with one's *epistemic superior* comparably more significance than disagreement with one's peer.

In that light, let's say that G is S's **collective epistemic superior** vis-a-vis p, *iff*, independently of the substance of disagreement over p, G has the relative epistemic advantage over S vis-à-vis p. On that basis, we might posit the following condition on cases of individual dissent:

> **Collective Superiority (CS)**
> If S believes p, S belongs to G, S is aware that G has collectively judged that ~p, and, G is S's collective epistemic superior, S ought to significantly revise her attitude toward p in the direction of the collective judgement. If G's advantage over S vis-a-vis p is sufficiently great, S ought to accede to G that ~p.

Given the points made in this section, I take it that CS is a plausible principle. For sure, different accounts of disagreement, as articulated around two-person cases, are likely to differ on the degree of disparity between the individual and the group at which the requirement to accede comes into effect. Nonetheless, I would suggest for now that the onus of proof will be on any account that looks to reject this principle.

That gives us our first principle. To get our second, let's turn to the topic of dissent in the context of collective rationality.

6.2.2 *Epistemic Liberalism*

> [T]he peculiar evil of silencing the expression of an opinion is, that it is robbing the human race; posterity as well as the existing generation; those who dissent from the opinions, still more than those who hold it. If the opinion is right, they are deprived of the opportunity of exchanging error for truth: if wrong, they lose, what is almost as great a benefit, the clearer perception and livelier impression of truth, produced by its collision with error.
>
> (Mill 1859/2003: 87)

This passage from *On Liberty* is perhaps the most famous expression of the idea that dissent has special value within collective inquiry. The preservation of dissent, Mill seems to suggest, keeps alive the possibility that errors on the part of the group can be corrected. It also provides a resource against which to test the ideas and arguments that the group have endorsed – even when those arguments and ideas are correct, and it is the dissenter who is in the wrong. Following Mill's line of thought, we might say that dissent improves collective inquiry in terms of both reliability and rationality.

Similar claims have been widely made within the philosophy of science, political philosophy, and feminist and social epistemologies, finding further support in the data from social psychology. In this section, I shall focus on three such claims:

1. Dissent counters the effect of 'groupthink' and 'group-polarization' in amplifying individual epistemic shortcomings in collective inquiry.
2. The permission of and preservation of dissent is necessary for 'objective' collective inquiry.
3. The permission of and preservation of dissent is necessary for 'fallibilistic' collective inquiry – understood as inquiry that is sensitive to the possibility of error.

6.2.2.1 *Groupthink and Group-Polarization*

The suggestion earlier was that groups can enjoy significant epistemic advantages over their individual members by drawing on a wider pool of expertise, competence, and evidence than is available to any individual group member. The flipside of this is that the group also draws on a wider pool of biases and prejudices, misleading evidence, and other epistemic shortcomings than any individual group member. After all, group members remain fallible, and those fallibilities might surface in collective inquiry just as they might surface in the individual's personal practices. Depending on the way the group conducts collective inquiry, then, the influence of these negative attributes, traits, and information may come to outweigh or undermine benefits that come from the pooling of resources. When that happens, collective judgements will fail to be justified, as will individual beliefs that are unduly influenced by such factors.

Two well-evidenced phenomena that highlight how limiting dissent can amplify individual shortcomings at the collective level are 'groupthink' and 'group-polarization'.

In his 1971 article of the same name, Irving Janis describes 'groupthink' as 'the mode of thinking that persons engage in when concurrence-seeking becomes so dominant in a cohesive ingroup that it tends to override realistic appraisal of alternative courses of actions' (Janis 1971: 43). Groupthink, so described, refers to an irrational and epistemically pernicious tendency toward consensus in contexts of collective inquiry – not the tendency rational agents might have toward a consensus position when presented with evidence for that position. Correspondingly, positions that are reached via groupthink will fail to be justified, either because they fail to be properly based upon good epistemic reasons or simply because they are unreliable.

Importantly, the evidence from psychological data suggests that individuals can be susceptible to groupthink even when (i) the task is simple, (ii) the majority is clearly in error, and (iii) there is no discussion or deliberation on the task.[8] In respect to this evidence, we might suppose that groupthink is not a special consequence of specific methods of collective inquiry but rather an inherent danger of collective inquiry as a category, requiring specific measures to be mitigated or avoided. Crucially to the current discussion, the psychological data provides evidence that the presence of in-group dissent – even individual dissent – can significantly countermand the groupthink effect.[9] Thus, methods, policies, or norms that accommodate and even encourage dissent, including individual dissent, can, in general, be seen as effective measures for avoiding the pernicious effects of groupthink in collective inquiry. Correspondingly, methods, policies, or norms that preclude dissent – even if only individual dissent – impede a significant way in which those effects might be mitigated or prevented.

'Group-polarization' is closely related to groupthink. If 'groupthink' describes an irrational tendency toward consensus, irrespective of content and prior attitudes, 'group-polarization' describes an irrational tendency for the views of and within the group to shift in specific directions. As

Cass Sunstein describes it, '[G]roup polarization means that members of a deliberating group move toward a more extreme point in the direction indicated by the members "predeliberation tendencies."' (Sunstein 2002: 176) Examples of group-polarization under experimental conditions include: moderately feminist women becoming more strongly feminist, citizens of France becoming more critical of the United States, and whites with a predisposition to racial prejudice coming to disagree more vehemently with the statement that white racism has contributed to the detrimental conditions faced by urban African-Americans (Sunstein 2002: 218). As these examples illustrate, the kind of predisposition amplified by deliberation may be epistemically neutral or well-founded (as I take a predisposition to favour feminist arguments to be), or they may themselves be evidence of epistemically significant shortcomings (as racial prejudice is on principle epistemically, as well as morally, problematic).

Sunstein (2002: 179) describes two theoretical explanations for group-polarization from the psychological literature:

i Social comparison: Individuals move their position to match others who they see favourably and want to be seen favourably by.

ii A limited argument pool: Like-minded groups have access to fewer arguments and arguments that tend to favour one direction; positions that are more widely defended in the group will have a greater influence on group and individual positions irrespective of the quality of those arguments.

Also prominent is:

iii Social Identity and Self-Categorization theory: Social influence (including group-polarization) occurs through awareness of norms and stereotypes associated with one's social identity, social identity comes from 'a process of self-categorization whereby the person perceives him- or herself as a group member, and thus as possessing the same characteristics and reactions as other group members' (Abrams et al. 1990: 98)

Crucially, in all three theorisations, group-polarization occurs not because deliberation has unveiled the previously hidden epistemic significance of the predispositions in play but as a by-product of deliberation and discussion with others who share those predispositions. Correspondingly, echoing the discussion of groupthink, evidence of group-polarization is evidence of a tendency for deliberation in homogenous groups to amplify individual members' irrational attitudes, subjective inclinations, biases, and prejudices.

As with groupthink, I would suggest that susceptibility to group-polarization can compromise any justification a group might otherwise have for its collective judgements. As far as the current discussion goes, the crucial point to emphasise is that, by its nature, group-polarization is a threat within groups that do not feature the right kind of diversity in beliefs, predispositions, social relationships, identities, and so on (Sunstein 2002). Thus, any group that does not allow at least some space for disagreement and dissent within its structure, or enact alternative measures to counteract those effects, will be susceptible to group-polarization effects.[10]

The phenomena of groupthink and group-polarization point to a close connection between collective justification and dissent. Yet, whilst psychological data suggests that dissent is an effective remedy to both groupthink and group-polarization, this does not entail that measures to encourage dissent are *necessary* to counter either phenomena. (A group might, for instance, *both* consist of individuals who follow CS and enact other measures to counter groupthink and group-polarization.) I consider motivations for that stronger claim in the next section.

6.2.2.2 Objectivity and Fallibilism[11]

Theoretical motivations for including a 'dissent' condition on collective justification can be found in Helen Longino's philosophy of science and Elizabeth Anderson's work on the epistemic dimensions of democratic decision-making. Disagreement plays a crucial role in each with respect to objectivity in scientific inquiry and a 'fallibilistic' approach to conducting collective decision-making, respectively. In so far as it is reasonable to suppose that there are close connections between objectivity, fallibilism, and epistemic justification, these two discussions provide complementary theoretical motivations for a 'dissent' condition on collective justification.[12]

Helen Longino's long-term project in the philosophy of science draws upon feminist critiques of traditional conceptions of 'rationality' and 'objectivity' to develop an ameliorative conception of scientific inquiry.[13] She distinguishes between two conceptions of objectivity: As a relationship between the theoretical claims made in science and external reality, and as a feature of 'modes of inquiry [...] achieved by reliance on non-arbitrary and non-subjective criteria for accepting and rejecting [...] hypotheses and theories...' (Longino 1989: 264). The feminist critiques of rationality, Longino suggests, motivate a rejection of (i) the idea that objectivity of the first kind requires and follows from objectivity of the second kind and (ii) the illusion that an individual inquirer can ever fully escape the influence of non-epistemic influences upon their work. She argues, however, that the lesson to be learned here is not that objectivity of the first kind is an illusion but rather that scientific inquiry is a social and collective enterprise, not an individualistic one. Once we recognise this, Longino suggests, we can see how scientific inquiry – as normatively well-conducted collective inquiry – can still produce knowledge. As she explains:

> [I]f scientific knowledge is understood as the simple sum of finished products of individual activity, then there is no way to block or

> mitigate the influence of subjectivity. Only if the finished products are understood to be formed by the kind of critical discussion that is possible among a plurality of individuals about a commonly accessible phenomenon, can we see how the production of scientific knowledge can be objective.
>
> (Longino 1989: 266)

Critical discussion between practitioners is thus, according to Longino's account, a constitutive feature of 'objective' scientific inquiry. In that light, she argues that it is necessary that groups engaged in scientific inquiry, and the scientific community as a whole, have robust institutions and procedures for the promotion of critical discussion – and that the community as a whole be responsive to criticism from within. Genuinely robust critical discussion, however, would seem to entail the possibility for scientists to authentically disagree and express disagreement with each other as well as with the community as a whole. I would suggest, then, that, per Longino's account, objective scientific inquiry is collective inquiry that *permits and preserves dissent*. Supposing, then, that there is a connection between 'objectivity' and epistemic justification, Longino's account includes a genuine dissent condition on collective epistemic justification.

Elizabeth Anderson's account of the epistemic dimensions of democracy similarly ties dissent and disagreement into the normativity of collective inquiry. The general idea is captured in the following passage, in which Anderson warns against norms of public discourse that demand consensus either before or after a decision is reached:

> Consensus implies that everyone agrees that all objections to a proposal have been met or at least overridden by more important considerations. The parties to a consensus are therefore expected to hold their peace once a decision is made, on the pretense that all their reservations were met. The norm suppresses public airing and responsiveness to the continuing reservations individuals may have about the decision. [...] Minority dissent [reminds] us that any given decision remains beset by unresolved objections.
>
> (Anderson 2006: 16)

Anderson's concern in this paper is to identify the kinds of democratic practice and institutions required to justify treating political decisions as accurate representations of the collective/public will. In this context, we might note, the epistemic goal of collective inquiry is tied closely to the interests of the members of the group. For example, if 'democratic' referenda tend to result in decisions that do not reflect the interests of the members of the polity, despite the fact that the referendum may seem a procedurally democratic form of decision-making, they will fail to be a reliable way of securing a key epistemic goal of democracy. Given this, it is reasonable to suppose that a democratic decision-making practice that fails to properly represent individual or minority group perspectives and opinions will, in principle, not be epistemically fit for the task. Correspondingly, in the political context, it is plausible that the best evidence of error will be dissent. Thus, it is also reasonable to suppose that dissent is the fundamental mechanism by which the political body, or decision-makers within that body, remain sensitive to the possibilities for error in the decisions and judgements they reach. In the political context, then, these considerations give us reason to think that dissent is necessarily related to collective justification just because – to borrow Anderson's terminology - dissent is necessary for democratic decision-making to be conducted in ways that 'instutitionalize fallibilism and an experimental attitude with respect to state policies' (Anderson 2006: 14).

There is a question here as to whether the observation that dissent is the *fundamental* mechanism of fallibilistic inquiry extends to domains other than the political. Putting that aside, however, it seems clear that the underlying insight about the importance of affirming fallibilism within inquiry does generalise. For whilst it is unusual to political decision-making that epistemic success is so closely tied to the interests of group members, it is not unusual thatpolitical decision-making can be prone to error. Humans are fallible inquirers, so any inquiry they engage in – individual or collective – is susceptible to error. Thus, if the methods employed over the course of *any kind of* collective inquiry preclude the appreciation of or recognition of the possibility of error, I would suggest, positions reached via those methods will fail to be justified.

One way in which we might theorise this is in terms of a failure to respect significant kinds of evidence. Any group (or members of a group) will over time acquire some evidence of the fallibility of the methods, procedures, and policies it employs in coming to collective judgements. Evidence of the fallibility of a method, though, is evidence relevant to determining the likely truth of the outputs of those methods. If, then, the methods employed by a group preclude recognition of the possibility of error, they will also preclude recognition of an important kind of evidence that is likely to be available to any group engaged in collective inquiry. Judgements that are reached on the presumption of infallibility, then, will be judgements that almost certainly fail to respect a significant kind of evidence. Such judgements will fail to be justified.[14]

This is just one way in which we might theorise Anderson's emphasis on the importance of affirming fallibilism in collective inquiry. Whatever the underlying epistemology, though, the point is that fallibilism so conceived has normative significance across domains, not just in the context of political decision-making. Now, as noted, the question remains whether dissent is the *best* evidence of the possibility of error in domains other than the political. But, if we have already accepted the connection between justification and fallibilism in collective inquiry, I would suggest that we can motivate a 'dissent' condition on collective justification whilst circumventing this question. For whether or not dissent is the *best evidence* of error in all forms of collective inquiry, *reasonable* dissent will be *relevant* evidence of error, no matter the domain.[15] That being so, it seems reasonable to presume that there will be some cases in any domain in which the *only* evidence of error is in the form of (reasonable) dissent – even if there are better forms of evidence available in other cases. If we accept that, in some cases, dissent will be the only available evidence of collective error, however, then we should also accept that collective inquiry conducted according to methods, policies, or norms that do not permit dissent will, in those cases, preclude *recognition* of the only evidence of error available to the group. That, I would suggest, would be enough to deem those methods inimical to conducting fallibilistic inquiry. And, if that is so, and accepting the general points about fallibilism, it would also be enough to deem those methods inimical to producing justified collective judgements.

With these last two arguments considered, I take it that we have enough motivation to posit a genuine condition of dissent on collective justification. Here is one way in which we might conceive that:

Say that collective inquiry 'permits and preserves dissent' if none of the methods, norms, or policies employed in that inquiry require *reasonable* dissenters to revise the relevant beliefs or act as if they have revised the relevant beliefs. That being so, we might recognise a principle along the following lines:

> **Epistemic Liberalism (EL)**
> If G collectively judges p, that judgement will be justified for G only if the methods of inquiry employed over the course of reaching that judgement permit and preserve dissent.

EL is the second piece in the puzzle of individual dissent. With both pieces in hand, we can now properly formulate that puzzle.

6.2.3 The Puzzle of Individual Dissent

To reiterate:

CS says:

> If S believes p, S belongs to G, S is aware that G has collectively judged that ~p, and G is S's collective epistemic superior, S ought to significantly revise her attitude toward p in the direction of the collective judgement. If G's advantage over S vis-a-vis p is sufficiently great, S ought to accede to G that ~p.

EL says:

> If G collectively judges that p, that judgement will be justified for G, only if the methods of inquiry employed over the course of reaching that judgement permit and preserve dissent.

To see how these two principles conflict, let's consider how they pertain to the two questions I introduced at the beginning of this discussion. Namely, how ought the individual dissenter respond to the disagreement *qua* individual? And how ought they respond to the disagreement *qua* group member?

Consider Indy in THINK TANK. Let's stipulate that the think tank is not only Indy's collective epistemic superior but has a significant enough advantage over her to satisfy the antecedent of the second conditional in CS. This being so, if CS is true, Indy ought to – *qua* individual – accede to the collective judgement that 'X is viable'. Moreover, given the stipulation about the think tank's comparative advantage over Indy, she ought to shutter her dissent in this way as a matter of epistemic policy. For just that reason, however, EL prescribes that Indy – as an active contributor to the think tank's research programme – ought not to follow the prescriptions of CS but should instead stay steadfast in her belief that 'X is not viable'. Since Indy cannot both accede to the rest of the group that 'X is viable' and stay steadfast in her belief that 'X is not viable', CS and EL conflict. Likewise for any other case in which CS recommends that the individual dissenter ought to accede to the collective.

There are three ways in which we might respond to this conflict:

1 Accept that individual and collective rationality make conflicting recommendations in these kinds of case.
2 Reject/revise EL.
3 Reject/revise CS.

At first blush, the obvious response is the first. After all, the idea that different normative domains can give conflicting recommendations is one that we are quite familiar with – even when those recommendations concern what we ought to believe.[16] Indeed, even *within* the domain of individual epistemic rationality, it has been suggested that we should accept that there can be dilemmas in which satisfying one norm or ideal of rationality will entail violating another. Srinivasan (2015) comes close to this view when arguing that, if there are no fully transparent norms, then 'any norm can be *blamelessly* violated by a competent agent who knows the norm' (Srinivasan 2015: 285 [italics added]). More explicitly, Christensen suggests that misleading higher-order evidence places one in a position in which one cannot trust one's (good) appreciation of logical or explanatory support relations, so 'respecting that evidence may require… violating certain rational ideals' (Christensen 2010: 212). Finally, Nick Hughes (2019) considers cases in which there is a conflict between a norm to only believe truths and a norm to be epistemically rational. He concludes that, whilst in such cases, both norms cannot be satisfied concurrently, this is no reason to reject either norm. On this basis, he posits an overarching view of epistemic normativity called 'epistemic dilemmism', which admits the possibility of a variety of cases in which genuine but competing epistemic requirements issue an *all things considered* obligation to both believe P and not believe P.

What is common to all of these discussions, however, is that they concern cases in which (i) it is possible to satisfy one or another of the competing requirements or ideals in play, yet (ii) it is not possible to satisfy all of the competing requirements or ideals at once. However, the conflict generated by the puzzle of individual dissent is not like this. In these cases, I shall argue, the domains of individual and collective rationality are linked in such a way that if CS and EL are both true, the dissenter has no good option *from either perspective*. Consequently, they encounter not so much an epistemic *dilemma* as a rift in epistemic rationality that needs to be resolved.

Consider the perspective of collective rationality. As per EL, any group G with a significant enough advantage over its individual members for the 'accession' clause of CS to kick in in all cases of individual dissent will not want all of its members to follow CS as a matter of policy. For, if they do, all judgements reached by G will be reached partly by way of a policy that precludes (reasonable) dissent. Thus, no judgements reached by G will be collectively justified. If CS is true, then, EL requires at least some members of G to fail to act according to the dictates of individual rationality. At first blush, this is not so troubling. None of us is *perfectly* rational, so it is not unusual that a group would consist of members who all fail to be *perfectly* rational. Whilst that is surely true, however, it is also true that disagreement is a ubiquitous and significant feature of our epistemic lives. Correspondingly, I would suggest, individuals who consistently contravene true principles of disagreement (*qua* individual rationality) will display serious and significant epistemic failings as individuals. If that is the case, though, EL requires at least some of the members of G to have serious and significant epistemic failings. And, whilst there is evidence that groups can in fact benefit epistemically from properly channelled failings among their members at the level of individual rationality,[17] I would suggest that groups should not rely upon this kind of effect to the exclusion of asking for general competence amongst their members. Rather, *ceteris paribus*, a group comprised of individuals without serious and significant epistemic failings will be epistemically more competent than a group containing such epistemic miscreants. But, if that is right, the puzzle of individual dissent represents a potential loss to the group, no matter how its members respond to the relevant kinds of case. For, if they follow CS, the collective judgements will fail to be justified. But if they follow EL, the groups' collective competency will be compromised – and so too, at some point, will its judgements be rendered unjustified.

Though less acute, similar conflicts arise at the individual level. Here are two:

First, if EL and CS are both true, S's following the prescriptions of CS can put her in a position of rational instability. Consider: If S accedes to G that ~p, and by doing so undermines the justification of the collective judgement, then G ought to revise its collective judgement of p. But if G revises the judgement, as per CS, S also ought to revise her belief to match G's new position. But, if S follows that prescription, she will undermine whatever justification G has for the new position. Thus, G ought to revise that position accordingly. And so on. Presuming that this kind of rational instability is an unwelcome consequence of any theory of rationality, I take this as a significant mark against accepting the conflict between EL and CS.

Second, as G is S's epistemic superior, S stands to benefit epistemically from relying upon the judgements of G. Indeed, the idea that S might so benefit is an important part of the motivation for CS. However, by following CS as a matter of policy – which S ought to if CS is true – S puts those benefits at risk. This is because, by following CS, S may to some degree make G less competent when it comes to collective inquiry, thereby compromising the very epistemic resource that she relies upon and benefits from. To act in a way that may worsen one's epistemic situation, however, would appear to be epistemically irrational.

Just as at the collective level, then, if CS and EL are true, conflicts are thrown up, not just across domains but within the domain of individual rationality.

Given these points, then, I think there is a reason to see the puzzle of individual dissent as a genuine problem in the epistemology of disagreement *and* collective inquiry – and not one that we can accept as we may other normative dilemmas. If that is so, then either CS, EL, or both must be rejected or revised. I won't argue the case here, but my inclination is to jettison CS. In that light, I conclude with some observations upon the significance of doing so within the epistemology of disagreement.

6.3 Conclusion

As I have presented it, the conflict between CS and EL arises because of the specific content of CS – not simply because it precludes rational dissent in some cases. It is important to note that, as formulated, EL does not require the presence of actual dissent, only that the methods of inquiry employed by a group do not preclude reasonable dissent outright. Thus, it remains possible that the principles of individual rationality as they pertain to disagreement might rule out dissent under some conditions without coming into conflict with EL. This is important in so far as it seems reasonable to demand of any plausible account of disagreement that it accommodate the intuition that, *generally speaking*, we ought to afford greater significance to disagreement with a group than to disagreement with a single individual. And, thus, any plausible account of disagreement should admit that there are *some* cases in which dissent is rationally forbidden. What is specifically problematic with CS is not that it accommodates this intuition but that it does so by specifying conditions that forbid dissent, irrespective of the content and context of a particular disagreement. Importantly, however, this aspect of CS is a straightforward consequence of a more general assumption that, for at least some significant class of disagreements, the appropriate response will be entirely determined by what the disputants should believe about their relative competence, independently of the case at hand.

Crucially, this assumption does not entail any specific position on the normative significance of standard two-person peer disagreements. The assumption is that there is some point of comparison at which the relative competence levels cancel out other features of the disagreement, not at what point that is. Thus, whilst the thought lends itself naturally to conciliationism, it also fits with the kinds of comment we saw about multi-party disagreements from anti-conciliationists in Section 6.2. However, it is this assumption that underwrites both: the move from 'numbers matter' to 'numbers matter most' that bequeathed us POMP and the thought that one ought always to afford greater significance to disagreement with an epistemic superior than to disagreement with an epistemic peer. Since CS followed as a kind of hybrid of these ideas, any view of disagreement that makes this assumption is committed to CS as a matter of course.

Outside of the current discussion none of these ideas seem particularly objectionable – and so this underlying assumption about the terms of the debate seems eminently plausible. Yet, if we are to avoid the puzzle of individual dissent by revising CS, it seems that it is just that assumption that needs to go. Recanting it, however, would appear to entail rejection of *any* in-principle restrictions upon relying upon the fact of disagreement in determining how to respond to disagreement. Or, at least, any determined solely by what the disputants are independently justified in believing about their comparative epistemic standings. That, on its own, would be a significant implication within the epistemology of disagreement. At the same time, rejecting CS in this way would require us to find new resources with which to respect a number of familiar intuitions about the significance of disagreement, not least that disagreement with a group, or an epistemic superior, generally speaking, will have greater significance than disagreement with a single peer. In respect to both these points, then, avoiding the puzzle of individual dissent by revising

CS would require a significant reconfiguration of the whole debate about the significance of disagreement. And, in that sense, the puzzle of individual dissent is not just a theoretical oddity but a core problem within the epistemology of disagreement.

Notes

1 Roughly, the literature is divided between *conciliationists* and *non-conciliationists*. *Conciliationists* argue that one ought to revise one's attitudes toward the disputed propositions in the direction of one's peer's (e.g. Christensen 2007; Elga 2007; Matheson 2015a). Non-conciliationists fall into two camps: Those who argue that one has default reason to stay *steadfast* in one's beliefs in case of peer disagreement (e.g. Enoch 2010, Schafer 2015) and those who argue that the appropriate response to peer disagreement varies between cases (e.g. Kelly 2010; Lackey 2010).

2 Since the aim of this paper is only to lay out the contours of this puzzle, I shall table questions about the nature of group agency. However, I should point out that we may have to put those questions back on the table if we want to *resolve* the puzzle. For instance, in a joint commitment model of collective agency, a group's status as agent depends upon group members' upholding joint commitments to act in certain ways 'as a body' (see esp. Gilbert 2013). Correspondingly, individual failures to uphold joint commitments may compromise that status. Thus, the epistemic obligations of the dissenter *qua* group member may depend partially upon the content of the relevant joint commitments. If such commitments run counter to EL, providing a full account of the normativity of dissent would require us to consider how the various obligations *qua* group member balance out. (Thanks to Fernando Broncano-Berrocal for raising these points.)

3 See Matheson (2015b) for discussion of a related, but narrower, tension between psychological data on the role of disagreement in group inquiry and *conciliationist* views of disagreement. The problems raised in this paper differ from Matheson's concerns in two important ways: (i) They are faced by all accounts of disagreement, not only conciliationism, and (ii) they emerge specifically when we consider the obligations which an *in-group* dissenter may accrue with respect to the rationality of the group's collective judgements.

4 For example, Lackey (2010) defines peers such that they have fully disclosed their evidence to each other, are equally familiar with that evidence, and are equals in cognitive ability. Kelly (2010), Christensen (2007), and Matheson (2015a) all suggest that someone is your peer when you *have reason to believe* they are your intellectual and evidential equal. Elga (2007) and Enoch (2010) suggest that someone is your peer with respect to p when you think that, conditional on your disagreeing with them, they are equally as likely to be mistaken about p as you.

5 The competence condition rules out cases in which neither S nor R are likely to be right about p to start with. Generally, such cases are not seen as epistemologically interesting.

6 For a good overview of this and other related theorems within social choice theory, see List (2013).

7 As Fernando Broncano-Berrocal has pointed out to me, this insight also runs through the so-called Diversity Trumps Ability Theorem (see Hong and Page 2004).

8 The classic demonstration of this is Solomon Asch's (1951) 'conformity experiment'. In the initial experiments, participants were shown two slides: One marked with a single line and a second with three lines. One line on the second slide was equal in length to that on the first; the others were clearly not. When shown the slides in isolation, the participants picked out the matching line with near universal success. When placed in groups, each including six to eight 'plants' in unanimous agreement on some other clearly erroneous answer, around 37% of the genuine participants agreed with the majority. A meta-analysis (Bond et al. 1996) of replications of the line study under different experimental conditions suggested that the effect remained to some degree of significance across different conditions. For an approachable discussion of these and other psychological works on dissent, see Nemeth (2018).

9 For discussion of the relevant studies, see Nemeth (2018), Ch. 2.

10 What if the group has a high general level of competence, its initial collective judgement is a rational response to the evidence, and the dissenter's opinion is not? Would any check on group polarization via the presence of dissent, then, be detrimental to the justification of the collective judgement? Only, I think, if we deny that justified beliefs/judgements must be properly based on the relevant evidence. However, even staunch reliabilists do not deny this (see, for example, Goldman, 2012: 82, 85–6). Since group polarization effects are the result of epistemically irrelevant social-influences, I take it that changes in collective judgements caused by group polarization will fail to be properly based on the relevant evidence. Thus, at least in so far as it is a check on such effects, even irrational dissent will at worst be neutral with respect to collective justification. (Thanks to Fernando Broncano-Berrocal for raising the possibility of this kind of case.)

11 Another place in which we might hope to find support for an authentic dissent condition is social psychology. Here, there is evidence, for instance, that (i) 'authentic dissent' outperforms simple devil's advocate strategies when it comes to the outcomes of group inquiry tasks (Schulz-Hardt 2002), and (ii) simple devil's advocate strategies promote the kinds of reasoning that we would associate with cognitive biases and prejudices, whilst 'authentic dissent' promotes the kinds of reasoning that we would associate with combatting biases and prejudices (Nemeth et al. 2001). I won't focus on these studies here, but for close discussion of some of these findings in relation to conciliationist views of disagreement, see Matheson (2015b).

12 Other theorists who argue in favour of dissent include Kitcher (2001) and Solomon (2001).

13 See Longino (1989, 1990, 2002).

14 This explanation echoes the literature on 'higher-order evidence', where an agent's higher-order evidence in respect to p is evidence of potential error in the practices by which that agent came to believe p. Skipper and Steglich-Petersen (2019) brings together many of the main contributors to this literature. For cautionary remarks about the kind of view of the relationship between higher-order evidence and justification I allude to here, see Schoenfield (2015); for a whole-hearted rejection of it, see Lasonen-Aarnio (2014).

15 For discussion of the standards of reasonable and unreasonable dissent, see Kappel (2018). Roughly speaking, the standards of 'reasonable dissent' do not preclude all rational error but do preclude expressions of dissent in bad-faith or arrived at via ignorance or epistemic vice (Thanks to Fernando Broncano-Berrocal for bringing this point to my attention.)

16 See especially discussion of the potential conflicts between practical/prudential reasons for belief and epistemic reasons for belief – as famously represented by Pascal's (1670) pragmatic argument for belief in god. For a useful survey of contemporary discussions of such conflicts, see Howard (2019).

17 See, for instance, Dawson et al. (2002).

Bibliography

Abrams, D., Wetherell, M., Cochrane, S., Hogg, M. A., and Turner, J. C. (1990). Knowing what to think by knowing who you are: Self-categorization and the nature of norm formation, conformity and group polarization. *British Journal of Social Psychology* 29: 97–119.

Anderson, E. (2006). The epistemology of democracy. *Episteme* 3 (1–2): 8–22.

Asch, S. E. (1951). Effects of group pressure on the modification and distortion of judgments. In H. Guetzkow (Ed.) *Groups, leadership and men*. Carnegie Press: Pittsburgh, PA. 177–190.

Bond, R., and Smith, P. B. (1996). Culture and conformity: A meta-analysis of studies using Asch's (1952b, 1956) line judgment task. *Psychological Bulletin* 119: 111–137.

Christensen, D. (2007). Epistemology of disagreement: The good news. *Philosophical Review* 116: 187.

Christensen, D. (2010). Higher order evidence. *Philosophy and Phenomenological Research* 81 (1): 185–215.

Dawson, E., Gilovich, T., and Regan, D. (2002). Motivated reasoning and performance on the Wason selection task. *Personality and Social Psychology Bulletin* 28 (10): 1379–1387.

Dietrich, F. and Spiekermann, K. (2013). Epistemic democracy with defensible premises. *Economics and Philosophy* 29 (1): 87–120.

Elga, A. (2007). Reflection and disagreement. *Noûs* 41: 478–502.

Enoch, D. (2010). Not just a truthometer: Taking oneself seriously (but not too seriously) in cases of peer disagreement. *Mind* 119 (476): 953–997.

Estlund, D. M. (1994). Opinion leaders, independence, and Condorcet's Jury Theorem. *Theory and Decision* 36 (2): 131–162.

Gilbert, M. (2013). *Joint commitment: How we make the social world*. Oxford University Press: Oxford.

Goldman, A. (2012). *Reliabilism and contemporary epistemology: Essays*. Oxford University Press: Oxford.

Hong, L. and Page, S. (2004) Groups of diverse problem solvers can outperform groups of high-ability problem solvers. *Proceedings of the National Academy of Sciences* 101 (46): 16385–16389

Howard, C. (2020). Weighing epistemic and practical reasons for belief. *Philosophical Studies* 117: 2227–2243

Hughes, N. (2019). Dilemmic epistemology. *Synthese* 196 (10): 4059–4090.

Janis, I. L. (1971). Groupthink. *Psychology Today* 5 (6): 43–46, 74–76.

Kappel, K. (2018). Dissent: Good, bad and reasonable. In C. R. Johnson (Ed.) *Voicing dissent: The ethics and epistemology of making disagreement public*. Routledge: New York. Ch. 4.

Kitcher, P. (2001). *Science, truth, and democracy*. Oxford University Press: Oxford.

Kelly, T. (2010). Peer disagreement and higher order evidence. In R. Feldman and T. Warfield (Eds.) *Disagreement*. Oxford University Press: Oxford. 111–174.

Lackey, J. (2010). A Justificationist view of disagreement's epistemic significance. In A. Haddock, A. Millar, and D. Pritchard (Eds.) *Social epistemology*. Oxford University Press: Oxford. 298–325.

Lackey, J. (2013). Disagreement and belief dependence: Why numbers matter. In D. Christensen and J. Lackey (Eds.) *The epistemology of disagreement: New Essays*. Oxford University Press: Oxford. 243–268.

Ladha, K. (1992). The Condorcet Jury Theorem, free speech and correlated votes. *American Journal of Political Science* 36: 617–634.

Lasonen-Aarnio, M. (2014). Higher-order evidence and the limits of defeat. *Philosophy and Phenomenological Research* 88 (2): 314–345.

List, C. (2013). Social choice theory. In E. N. Zalta (Ed.) *The Stanford encyclopedia of philosophy*. (Winter 2013 Edition). https://plato.stanford.edu/archives/win2013/entries/social-choice/.

Longino, H. E. (1989). Feminist critiques of rationality: Critiques of science or philosophy of science? *Women's Studies International Forum* 12 (3): 261–269.

Longino, H. E. (1990). *Science as social knowledge: Values and objectivity in scientific inquiry*. Princeton University Press: Princeton, NJ.

Longino, H. E. (2002). *The fate of knowledge*. Princeton University Press: Princeton, NJ.

Matheson, J. (2015a). *The epistemic significance of disagreement*. Palgrave: Basingstoke.

Matheson, J. (2015b). Disagreement and the ethics of belief. In J. Collier (Ed.) *The future of social epistemology: A collective vision*. Rowman & Littlefield International: Lanham, MD. 139–148.

Mill, J. S. M. (1859) [2003]. *On liberty* (D. Bromwich and K. George, Eds.). Yale University Press: New York.

Nemeth, C. (2018). *No! The power of disagreement in a World that wants to get along*. Atlantic: Glasgow.

Nemeth, C., Rogers, J., and Brown, K. (2001). Devil's advocate vs. authentic dissent: Stimulating quantity and quality. *European Journal of Social Psychology* 31: 707–720.

Pascal, B. (1670) [1995]. *Pensées*. Penguin Press: London.

Pettit, P. (2006). When to defer to majority testimony – And when not. *Analysis* 66 (3): 179–187.

Schafer, K. (2015). How common is peer disagreement? On self-trust and rational symmetry. *Philosophy and Phenomenological Research* 91: 25–46.

Schoenfield, M. (2015). A dilemma for calibrationism. *Philosophy and Phenomenological Research* 91 (2): 425–455.

Schulz-Hardt, S., Jochims, M., and Frey, D. (2002). Productive conflict in group decision making: Genuine and contrived dissent as strategies to counteract biased information seeking. *Organizational Behavior and Human Decision Processes* 88 (2): 563–586.

Skipper, M. and Steglich-Petersen, A. (Eds.) (2019). *Higher-order evidence: New essays*. Oxford University Press: Oxford.

Solomon, M. (2001). *Social empiricism*. MIT Press: Cambridge, MA.

Srinivasan, A. (2015). Normativity without Cartesian privilege. *Philosophical Issues* 25 (1): 273–299.

Sunstein, C. R. (2002). The law of group-polarization. *Journal of Political Philosophy* 10 (2): 175–195.

van Inwagen, P. (2010). We're right. They're wrong. In R. Feldman and T. Warfield (Eds.) *Disagreement*. Oxford University Press: Oxford. 10–28.

7 Gender, Race, and Group Disagreement

Martin Miragoli and Mona Simion

7.1 Introduction

A hotly debated question in mainstream social epistemology asks what rational agents should believe when they find themselves in disagreement with others.[1] Although special attention has been paid to disagreement between *individuals*, recent developments have opposed this trend by broadening the focus to include cases of disagreement between *groups*. We argue that this shift is interesting because the phenomenon of inter-group disagreement (such as the disagreement that occurs between opposing political parties or countries) raises some distinctive challenges for our methodological choices in the epistemology of disagreement. To do that, we look at two cases of group disagreement – one involving gender discrimination, the other involving the marginalisation of racial and religious minorities – and argue that mainstream epistemology of peer disagreement essentially lacks the resources to explain what is going wrong in these cases. In this paper, we advance a two-tiered strategy to tackle this challenge by drawing on an inflationist account of group belief and an externalist account of the normativity of belief in the face of disagreement.

Here's the structure of this paper. We start off the discussion by presenting two examples of discrimination in cases of group disagreement, then offer a diagnosis of the distinctive form of epistemic injustice at play (#2). We then proceed to examine the prospects of extant views in the epistemology of peer disagreement to address the problem raised in the first section and conclude that these views have difficulties accounting for what went wrong in these cases (#3). We suggest that the problem lies at the methodological level and advance a two-tiered solution to the problem that relies on an externalist epistemology and a functionalist theoretical framework (#4).

7.2 Gender, Race, and Group Peer Disagreement

Consider the two following cases:

SEXIST SCIENTISTS: During a conference on the impact of climate change on the North Pole, a group of male scientists presents their most recent result that *p*: 'The melting rate of ice has halved in the last year'. In the Q&A, a group of female scientists notes that the study doesn't take into account the results of a study published by them, which supports not-*p:* 'It is not the case that the melting rate of ice has halved in the last year'. Not-*p* is, as a matter of fact, true, but the group of male scientists continue to disregard this option solely on the grounds that the other research group was entirely composed by female scientists.

RACIST COMMITTEE: In a predominantly Christian elementary school, the Teachers Committee convenes to discuss what food should be served for lunch during the upcoming semester. As it turns out, exclusively white schoolteachers of Christian faith compose the committee. After a brief discussion, the committee comes to believe, among other things, that *q*: 'Children should be served pork on Wednesdays.' A small group of non-white Muslim parents, informed of the outcome of the meeting, raise a number of independent formal complaints against this decision of the Teachers Committee on the grounds that it doesn't respect the dietary restrictions of their religion and arguing for not-q: 'It is not the case that children should be served pork on Wednesdays.' Due to racial prejudice, however, the Teachers Committee ignores the complaints, and no action is taken to amend the decision.

In the first case, the group of male scientists dismisses a relevant piece of evidence based on their prejudice against women. Because of their gender, the women's team fails to be rightly perceived as a peer. In the second case, the group formed by the parents is discriminated against because they constitute a racial and religious minority.

It is crucial to note that, although moral harm is definitely at stake in these cases as well, the kind of harm perpetrated is distinctively *epistemic* in that both discriminated groups are harmed in their capacity as knowers (Fricker 2007). What is common between the two cases is that both manifest some form of *epistemic injustice* – i.e., the discriminated groups don't succeed, due to their hearers' prejudices, in their attempt to transmit a piece of information they possess. Moreover, the epistemic harm at stake here is the result of a fundamental epistemic failure on the part of the oppressive groups. The group of scientists and the school representatives don't simply *happen* to fail to notice some relevant piece of information, nor is it the case that they aren't in a position to easily access it. Instead, upon being presented with the relevant piece of evidence, they discount it for no good epistemic reason; in this, the oppressor groups fail to be properly responsive to evidence (Simion 2019a).

The above cases represent instances of disagreement between groups whereby the disagreement is resolved in a bad way: the oppressor group ignores or dismisses the information that the oppressed group attempts to transmit, and this happens by virtue of the social dynamics that are particular to the two types of case; it is the prejudices that the male group of scientists have towards women, and that the RACIST COMMITTEE has towards minorities, that prevents them from perceiving their interlocutors as their peers.

We strongly believe that the epistemology of disagreement should be able to account for what is going wrong in these cases. Furthermore, we think that, if our epistemology is not able to do so – i.e., if we don't have resources to explain the arguably most ubiquitous and harmful among epistemic failures, of which these cases are prime examples – our epistemology requires a swift and radical methodological change. For this reason, an important question that such examples raise is the following: are extant accounts in the epistemology of disagreement sensitive enough to actual social dynamics to be capable of explaining what went wrong in these problem cases?

7.3 A (Problematically) Narrow Methodological Choice

Epistemology at large is concerned with what is permissible to believe[2]; given this, it is a matter of surprising historical contingency that the vast majority[3] of the literature in the epistemology of disagreement concerns itself with a much narrower question: 'What is rational to believe in the face of disagreement with an epistemic peer?' (henceforth, the question).[4] The question is narrow in two crucial ways. First, in that it is explicitly conceived as concerning an internalist, accessibilist notion of rationality[5]: the version of the question that the vast majority of the literature concerns itself with is 'Given all and only reasons accessible to me, what is rational for me to believe in the face of disagreement with an epistemic peer?'

A second crucial way in which the question is narrow is that it is not primarily concerned with real cases of everyday disagreement but rather restricts focus to highly idealised cases in which one disagrees with one's epistemic peer. The thought is that, if we answer the question for perfect peerhood, we can then 'upload context' and figure out the right verdict for cases of real-life disagreement as well. Here is how David Christensen puts it:

> The hope is that by studying this sort of artificially simple socio-epistemic interaction, we will test general principles that could be extended to more complicated and realistic situations, such as the ones encountered by all of us who have views–perhaps strongly held ones–in areas where smart, honest, well-informed opinion is deeply divided.
> (Christensen 2009: 231)

One notable difficulty for these accounts is how to define the notion of peerhood at stake in the question. In the literature, epistemic peerhood is typically assessed along two main lines: cognitive equality and evidential equality.[6] Agents are taken to be evidential peers if they ground their confidence in a proposition *p* on pieces of evidence that are epistemically equivalent, while cognitive peers are typically taken to have the same cognitive abilities.[7] No matter the correct account, though, it is crucial to note that, *as a matter of principle*, on pain of normative misfit, the notion *cannot* feature externalist elements. After all, if the question regards a purely internalist notion of rationality, the corresponding notion of peerhood should follow suit: it should concern perceived peerhood rather than *de facto* peerhood. To see this, consider the following case:

> EXPERT CHILD: My six-year-old son (weirdly enough) disagrees with me about whether the closure principle for knowledge holds. Intuitively, it seems fine for me to hold steadfast: after all, discounting him as an epistemic peer on the issue seems like the rational thing to do. Surprisingly, however, my son *is*, unbeknownst to me, my epistemic peer on this topic (he is extraordinarily smart, and he's been reading up on the matter).

If we allow this unknown fact in the world to matter for our peerhood assignments, on conciliatory views of disagreement we're going to get the implausible result that I'm internalistically irrational to discount his testimony. That seems wrong. An internalist question about peer disagreement requires an internalist notion of peerhood.

On the other hand, a purely internalist notion of peerhood obstructs the prospects of coming to account for the phenomenon of disagreement between groups. Consider again the problem cases presented at the outset: SEXIST SCIENTISTS and RACIST COMMITTEE. By stipulation, in both cases the oppressor groups are not taking the oppressed groups to be their peers due to sexist and racist prejudice, respectively. As such, views on how to respond to peer disagreement internalistically conceived will not straightforwardly apply to the cases above since they will not count as cases of peer disagreement to begin with.

Recall, though, that focussing on the narrow question was not supposed to be the end of the road in the epistemology of disagreement. After all, cases of perfect peer disagreement are rare, if not non-existent. The thought was that, as soon as we figure out the rational response in these idealized cases, we could upload context and get the right result in real-life cases as well. So, maybe once we do that for the cases at hand – i.e., upload context - things will start looking up?

Unfortunately, there is reason to believe otherwise. There are two broad families of views in the literature on peer disagreement: *conciliationist views*[8] and *steadfast views*.[9] Conciliationists claim that disagreement compels rational agents to decrease their confidence about p when faced with peer disagreement; steadfasters deny this claim and argue that, in such situations, rational agents are entitled to hold on to their beliefs.

What is the verdict these views give us on the examples discussed at the outset? The case is quite straightforward for steadfasters: if a rational agent (in this case, a group) is entitled, in the face of disagreement with a *peer*, to stick to their guns, then, *a fortiori*, they are also entitled to do so when they disagree with someone whose epistemic position they take to be *inferior* to theirs. Such is indeed the case in both examples above. In SEXIST SCIENTISTS, the team of female scientists is not perceived as a peer by the group of male scientists by virtue of gendered prejudice; similarly, in RACIST COMMITTEE, the school representatives judge the complaint not worthy of consideration precisely because it is made by a group they take to be epistemically inferior to them by virtue of racial prejudice. Steadfasters, then, would conclude that both the group of male scientists and the school representatives are entitled to hold on to their beliefs and discount the minority groups' testimony on the grounds that such testimony isn't recognised as being produced by a peer group.

According to conciliationism, in the face of disagreement with a peer, one should revise one's beliefs. What ought one to do, epistemically, when one doesn't take the disagreeing party to be their peer, though? The question remains open. Conciliationism does not offer any prediction: peerhood is sufficient for conciliation; we don't know, though, whether it's also necessary.

In conclusion, then, it looks as though the two main accounts of peer disagreement in the literature aren't able to explain what is going wrong in the two examples presented at the outset. Even worse, in fact, we have identified two major, interrelated methodological problems that prevent the vast majority of our epistemology of disagreement from explaining what is going wrong in garden-variety group epistemic injustice cases. First, by virtue of solely asking a question pertaining to internalist standards of rationality, the oppressor groups come out as justified in discounting the testimony of the oppressed groups. Second, by virtue of employing an internalistic account of peerhood moulded out of disagreements between individuals, the literature fails to account for the intuition that the oppressed groups are, intuitively, the epistemic peers of the oppressor groups on the question at hand, irrespectively of their social features.

We take these two problems to motivate the corresponding two desiderata for any satisfactory account of group peerhood and group disagreement. Here they are:

Peerhood Constraint: Accounts of the relation of epistemic peerhood among groups should be able to account for peerhood in cases of minority groups and socially oppressed groups.

Normative Constraint: Accounts of peer disagreement should be capable of providing the normative grounds on which the beliefs of oppressive groups in cases of epistemic injustice can be negatively evaluated (namely, that they be capable of recognising that the oppressive groups believe something they should not).

The two desiderata are independent in that they concern different spaces in theory: the first sets a minimal requirement for accounts of group epistemic peerhood by asking that they be capable of identifying minority groups and groups discriminated against as epistemic peers when they are so. The second desideratum, in turn, asks that accounts of group disagreement possess the required normative toolkit to identify the epistemic harm at play in frustrating the attempt of a peer group to transmit a piece of information by virtue of prejudice against them.

7.4 A Functionalist Solution

In what follows, we make the case for a functionalist theoretical framework that, with the resources made available from an inflationist account of group belief and an externalist account of the normativity of belief in the face of disagreement, can deliver both goods. In previous work (Simion 2019b, Broncano-Berrocal & Simion 2020, Miragoli 2020), we independently developed (1) a functionalist account of the nature of group belief and (2) a functionalist account of the normativity of belief in the face of disagreement. In the following sections, we will explain how our functionalist accounts deliver on both the desiderata identified above.

7.4.1 The Peerhood Constraint: A Functionalist View of Group Belief

To begin with, it is important to note that, even if we move away from an essentially internalist overall notion of the peerhood relation – i.e. targeting perceived peerhood – to an externalist one – targeting de facto peerhood – the latter might not yet be fitting to capture the epistemic dimension of the social dynamics at play in the examples above. We want minority groups – which, by definition, are smaller groups, numerically – to be able to count as epistemic peers, i.e., we want groups that are *numerically* inferior to not thereby be considered inferior *epistemically*.

Furthermore, disagreement might occur between different types of groups: it must be possible, on the account at stake, to recognise cultural minorities that do not form established groups (either because their structure isn't sufficiently sophisticated or because they are not recognised to be such) as being the epistemic peers of more highly organised collectives. We can take this as suggesting that it must be possible for the relationship of peerhood to hold between different group-types.

The debate surrounding the epistemology of groups features two main camps: *deflationism*[10] and *inflationism*.[11] The former argues that the belief of a group is nothing more than the sum of the individual beliefs of its group members. To say that Swedes believe that Volvos are safe is equivalent to saying that all (or most) Swedes believe this is so.[12]

In contrast, inflationists argue that group belief is independent of the beliefs of the group members. The jury's belief that the defendant is guilty, for instance, is typically taken to hold irrespectively of the individual beliefs of its members.[13] There are two main inflationist views available on the market: that groups form beliefs by the joint acceptance[14] of a common view or that they do so, distributively, by collaborating organically to the production of a belief.[15] The former focuses on beliefs formed in established groups, such as juries, committees, institutions, and so on,. So, for instance, according to the Joint Acceptance Account (or JAA), we have a genuine group belief when the European Commission representatives agree that the member states will halve the CO_2 emissions by 2025, and their agreement is conditional on the acceptance of the other members. The latter view, instead, takes as paradigmatic the beliefs formed by organic groups, such as teams, agencies, crews, and cooperations. Proponents of the Distributive Model (or DM) argue that genuine group belief is the result of the group members' collaboration and relies on division of labour. Take, for instance, a team of scientists working together: the work is divided among the group members according to their expertise, in such a way that the final belief is the product of their organic cooperation.

It is easy to see that deflationist views will have trouble meeting the Peerhood Constraint. After all, deflationism suggests that the belief of a group *deflates to* the individual beliefs of (some of) its members. This means that, when we compare the beliefs of two groups that are equal in every other respect (i.e., cognitively or evidentially), we are still comparing two unequal sets of beliefs. That is because, according to deflationism, group belief **just is** the sum of individual beliefs (plus some aggregation function). This means that, when there are two groups that disagree with each other, the clash between two group beliefs is, in deflationary terms, a clash between two sets of individual beliefs, each constituted by the sum of the individual beliefs of the group members.

From the perspective of deflationism, then, it is hard to see how the two groups can qualify as peers. To see why, note that numbers do matter, epistemically: if one reliable testifier tells me that *p*, while four other reliable testifiers tell me that not-*p*, all else being equal, it is intuitive that I should lean towards believing not-*p*. As such, if we reduce group belief to the beliefs of individuals, it is unclear how the Peerhood Constraint can be met.

Inflationism, on the other hand, seems, at first glance, to fare better than deflationism on this score. Inflationists take group belief to be irreducible to individual belief. For them, it is by relying on some distinctive principle of composition (joint acceptance or organic labour) that the group members *collectively* (i.e., *as one epistemic agent*) form a belief. So, while for deflationists the believing subjects are as many as the *believers* in each group, for inflationists they are as many as the *groups* involved in the disagreement, irrespective of the group size. As a result, all else being equal, on an inflationist reading, beliefs formed by minority groups won't be considered epistemically inferior to majoritarian ones simply by virtue of being backed by an inferior number of believers.

However, upon closer inspection, it is not just *any* inflationist account that will do the work. Recall that, in RACIST COMMITTEE, the group of parents don't file a collective complaint, but, rather, each family raises the issue with the school individually. Here, you have an example of disagreement between a formalised group – the committee – and a mere aggregate (the sum of individual parents). If our account doesn't recognise that different group-types can host genuine group beliefs, it will also fail to recognise that such groups can be epistemic peers on the matter at hand. On the Joint Acceptance account, for instance, since the parents do not get together to 'shake hands' on the issue, they don't count as a genuine believing group to begin with. As such, an account that cannot accommodate aggregates delivers the result that what is at stake in RACIST COMMITTEE is, once more, a series of disagreements between a group and separate individuals. It is easy to see how the peerhood relation might not obtain under such circumstances: after all, it seems intuitively right that, if I disagree with my entire group of friends on a topic of common expertise, it is I that should lower my credence in the relevant proposition. Clearly, however, it must be possible to recognise minorities that do not form established groups (either because their structure isn't sufficiently sophisticated or because they are not recognised to be such) as peers. What we are looking for, then, is an inflationist account that is versatile enough to accommodate different types of groups.

In previous work, one of us has developed a functionalist view of the nature of group belief (Miragoli 2020). In a nutshell, Group Belief Functionalism (henceforth, GBF) defines group belief in terms of the role the belief plays in the agent host. According to this view, a group believes something when the belief attributed is individuated via a Ramsey sentence by a set of inputs – e.g., perception or reflection – and outputs – typical corresponding behaviour – that identify the role it occupies in the group host.[16] The principle of composition of such an agent (aggregation of individual beliefs, joint commitment or organic labour), then, imposes restrictions on the way in which the role is implemented. As a result, for example, mere aggregates will generate group beliefs via simple belief aggregation, and established and organic groups will do so via more elaborate systems, involving some sort of mechanic or organic collaboration among group members.

A special advantage of relying on a functionalist framework is the versatility it affords. GBF licences that beliefs are attributed to each group-type according to the belief forming mechanism that is most suitable to their sociological structure. For example, if the principle of composition of a group is the acceptance of a certain system of norms or sanctions, then GBF allows that such a group can naturally form beliefs via the joint acceptance of a common view. On the other hand, where the sociological structure of the group is such that its members are held together by a common goal and the fact that they work together to achieve it, in this case GBF allows that the group will be able to form beliefs via organic collaboration. On such a view, it is sometimes the case that a group forms its beliefs via a 'deflationist' mechanism, meaning that the main condition the group has to satisfy in order to count as a believing subject is that all group members have the relevant belief. Sometimes, the belief will be formed along inflationist lines, meaning that other more sophisticated conditions will have to be met (e.g. that all group members jointly commit to the propositions at hand or that they cooperate organically).

GBF meets the Peerhood Constraint nicely precisely in virtue of its functionalist details. Since it denies the deflationist claim that group belief reduces to the sum of individual beliefs, GBF enjoys the inflationist advantages with respect to group peerhood. Furthermore, it accommodates multiple realizability, which allows that genuine group beliefs can be formed by the aggregation recipe peculiar to any group-type (aggregates, categories, and established and organic groups).

Returning to our examples, then, we can see how GBF reaches the right verdict in both cases. As noted, in SEXIST SCIENTISTS and RACIST COMMITTEE, the belief of the oppressed group was discounted on the grounds that it was formed by a racial or gender minority. According to GBF the doxastic status of a group agent is determined independently of its numerical and sociological characteristics (i.e., the size and type of the group). As such, granted that the symmetric epistemic conditions are in place, GBF can accommodate our peerhood intuitions in the cases above.

7.4.2 *The Normative Constraint: A Functionalist View of the Epistemology of Disagreement*

In previous work, one of us developed a functionalist account of the normativity of belief in cases of disagreement, the Epistemic Improvement Knowledge Norm of Disagreement (EIKND; Simion 2019b, Broncano-Berrocal & Simion 2020). In a nutshell, the account looks into what has been left out of the equation so far in the epistemology of disagreement and what, arguably, defines the subject matter: the fact that the doxastic attitudes of disagreeing parties never have the same overall *epistemic status: one of them is right and the other one wrong*. This *fundamental asymmetry* present in all cases of disagreement is an asymmetry concerning evaluative normativity – i.e., how good (epistemically) the doxastic attitudes of the disagreeing parties are. In this way, by accounting for the rational response to disagreement in terms of what all cases of disagreement have in common, the account can easily address all possible cases of disagreement, independently of whether they are instances of peer or everyday disagreement. Indeed, that a given case is a case of peer or everyday disagreement is orthogonal to the distribution of epistemic statuses.

On this view, knowledge is the function of the practice of inquiry. Social epistemic interactions such as disagreements are moves in inquiry; therefore their function is to generate knowledge. If that is the case, in cases of disagreement one should make progress towards achieving knowledge.

On EIKND, one should (i) improve the epistemic status of one's doxastic attitude by conciliating if the other party has a doxastic attitude with a better epistemic status and (ii) stick to one's guns if the other party's doxastic attitude has a worse epistemic status. In turn, the quality of the epistemic status at stake is measured against its closeness to knowledge: given a value ranking R of epistemic states with respect to proximity to knowledge, in a case of disagreement about whether p, where, after having registered the disagreement, by believing p, S is in epistemic state E_1 and, by believing not-p, H is in epistemic state E_2, S should conciliate if and only if E1 is lesser than E2 on R and hold steadfast iff E1 is better than E2 on R. This view has several crucial advantages over extant views in disagreement literature: (i) it accounts for the epistemic significance of disagreement as a social practice, i.e., its conduciveness to knowledge, and (ii) it straightforwardly applies to everyday disagreement rather than to idealised, perfect-peer disagreement cases and thus does not face the transition problem exemplified above.

It is easy to see that this view will also lead to the right results in the cases of gender and race group discrimination we are looking at: by stipulation, both of the above cases are cases in which the asymmetry in epistemic status favours the oppressed groups – the epistemic status of their beliefs is closer to knowledge than the epistemic status of the beliefs of their oppressors. After all, by stipulation, the oppressed groups are wrong about the matter at hand. As such, in these cases, EIKND delivers the right result that the oppressors should conciliate in order to improve the epistemic status of their beliefs.

7.5 Conclusion

This paper has put forward a two-tiered functionalist account of group peer disagreement. This strategy is primarily made possible by a radical methodological shift: *contra* extant accounts that rely on internalist notions of epistemic peerhood and belief permissibility, we have advanced an externalist approach motivated by cases of epistemic injustice in group peer disagreement (SEXIST SCIENTISTS and RACIST COMMITTEE). We have shown that such cases set two desiderata (what we called the Peerhood and Normative Constraint) that can be elegantly met by appealing to a functionalist view of group belief (GBF) and group justification (EIKND). GBF guarantees that minority groups are considered epistemic peers, despite the social prejudices to which they are systematically subject in real cases of disagreement. EIKND, in turn, provides the normative framework to evaluate the conduct of the disagreeing parties and recognise instances of epistemic injustice.

Notes

1 Lackey (2010), Christensen (2009), Feldman & Warfield (2010), Matheson (2015), Kelly (2005), and Elga (2007).
2 See Steup & Neta (2020).
3 But see Broncano-Berrocal & Simion (2020) and Hawthorne & Srinivasan (2013) for exceptions.
4 Lackey (2014).
5 Internalist accessibilism is the view that epistemic support depends exclusively on factors that are internal to the subject and accessible through reflection alone (e.g. Chisholm 1977: 17)
6 Lackey (2010).
7 There is ongoing debate on how to spell out the notion of cognitive or evidential equality. The former is typically understood in terms of sameness of reliabilist (i.e., a well-functioning cognitive system) or responsibilist (e.g., open-mindedness, humility) virtues. The latter is sometimes taken to require 'rough sameness' of evidence and mutual knowledge of the relevant differences (Conee 2010). However, neither route is fully satisfactory. For a useful discussion of the prospects and problems of this problem see Broncano-Berrocal & Simion (2020).
8 Bogardus (2009), Christensen (2007), Elga (2007), Feldman (2006), Matheson (2015).
9 Kelly (2005), Bergmann (2009), van Inwagen (2010), Weatherson (2013), Titelbaum (2015).
10 Quinton (1975), List & Pettit (2011).
11 Gilbert (1987), Lackey (2016), Tuomela (2013) and Tollefsen (2015).
12 The number of individuals that suffices to make up a group belief differs depending on the aggregation function adopted by the group. For instance, in a dictatorial state the belief of the group corresponds to the belief held by a single individual (see List & Pettit 2011).
13 Take, for instance, a case where, due to their prejudice, none of the jurors can form the belief that the defendant is innocent. However, based on the evidence brought to light in the trial, they collectively judge that she is innocent.
14 Gilbert (1987).
15 Bird (2010).
16 A Ramsey sentence is a sentence that includes a collection of statements that quantify over a variable. In the case of group belief, the variable corresponds to the mental state of the group, and the collection of statements includes terms that refer to external stimuli, other mental states, behaviour, and causal relations among them.

Bibliography

Bergmann, M. (2009). Rational disagreement after full disclosure. *Episteme* 6: 336–53.

Bird, A. (2010). Social knowing: The social sense of 'scientific knowledge'. *Philosophical Perspectives* 24: 23–56.

Bird, A. (2019). Group Belief. In Fricker, Miranda, Peter J. Graham, David Henderson and Nikolaj J. L. L. Pedersen, "*The Routledge Handbook of Social Epistemology*" (Abingdon: Routledge, 07 Aug 2019)

Bogardus, T. (2009). A vindication of the equal-weight view. *Episteme* 6: 324–35.

Broncano-Berrocal, F., & Simion, M. (2020). Disagreement and epistemic improvement. Manuscript.

Chisholm, R. (1977). *Theory of knowledge*, 2nd edition. Englewood Cliffs: Prentice-Hall.

Christensen, D. (2007). Epistemology of disagreement: The good news. *Philosophical Review* 116: 187–217.

Christensen, D. (2009). Disagreement as evidence: The epistemology of controversy. *Philosophy Compass* 4: 756–67.

Conee, E. (2010). Rational disagreement defended. In R. Feldman & T. A. Warfield (eds.), *Disagreement*. Oxford University Press.

Elga, A. (2007). Reflection and disagreement. *Noûs* 4: 478–502.

Elga, A. (2010). How to disagree about how to disagree. In T. Warfield & R. Feldman (eds.), *Disagreement*. Oxford University Press, Oxford.

Feldman, R. (2005). Respecting the evidence. *Philosophical Perspectives* 19: 95–119.

Feldman, R. (2006). Epistemological Puzzles about Disagreement. In S. Hetherington (ed.), *Epistemic Futures*. New York: Oxford University Press, pp. 216–236.

Feldman, R. (2007). Reasonable religious disagreements. In L. Antony (ed.), *Philosophers without gods: Meditations on atheism and the secular*. Oxford University Press, Oxford: 194–214.

Feldman, R. (2009). Evidentialism, higher-order evidence, and disagreement. *Episteme* 6: 294–312.

Feldman, R. (2014). Evidence of evidence is evidence. In J. Matheson & R. Vitz (eds.), *The ethics of belief*. Oxford University Press, New York: 284–99.

Fricker, M. (2007). Epistemic injustice: Power and the ethics of knowing. Oxford University Press, Oxford and New York (Retrieved March 6, 2020).

Friedman, J. (2013). Suspended judgment. *Philosophical Studies* 162: 165–81.

Goldman, A. I., & Olsson, E. J. (2009). Reliabilism and the value of Knowledge. In A. Haddock, A. Millar, & D. Pritchard (eds.), *Epistemic value*. Oxford University Press, Oxford: 19–41.

Gilbert, M. (1987). Modelling collective belief. *Synthese* 73: 185–204.

Gilbert, M., & Pilchman, D. (2014). Belief, acceptance, and what happens in groups: Some methodological considerations. In J. Lackey (ed.), *Essays in collective epistemology*. Oxford University Press.

Hawthorne, J., & Srinivasan, A. (2013). Disagreement without transparency: Some bleak thoughts. In D. Christensen & J. Lackey (eds.), *The epistemology of disagreement: New essays*. Oxford University Press, Oxford.

Kappel, K. (2019). Bottom up justification, asymmetric epistemic push, and the fragility of higher order justification. Episteme. Cambridge University Press.

Kelly, T. (2005). The epistemic significance of disagreement. In T. Gendler & J. Hawthorne (eds.), *Oxford studies in epistemology, Vol. 1.* Oxford University Press, Oxford: 167–96.

Kelly, T. (2010). Peer disagreement and higher-order evidence. In R. Feldman & T. A. Warfield (eds.), *Disagreement.* Oxford University Press, Oxford: 111–74.

Kelly, T. (2013). How to be an epistemic permissivist. In M. Steup & J. Turri (eds.), *Contemporary debates in epistemology.* Blackwell, Oxford.

King, N. L. (2012). Disagreement: What's the problem? Or a good peer is hard to find. *Philosophy and Phenomenological Research* 85: 249–72.

Kornblith, H. (2010). Belief in the face of controversy. In R. Feldman & T. A. Warfield (eds.), *Disagreement.* Oxford University Press, Oxford.

Kornblith, H. (2013). Is philosophical knowledge possible? In D. E. Machuca (ed.), *Disagreement and skepticism.* Routledge.

Lackey, J. (2008). What should we do when we disagree? In T. S. Gendler & J. Hawthorne (eds.), *Oxford studies in epistemology.* Oxford University Press, Oxford: 274–93.

Lackey, J. (2010). A justificationist view of disagreement's epistemic significance. In A. Haddock, A. Millar, & D. Pritchard (eds.), *Social epistemology.* Oxford University Press, Oxford.

Lackey, J. (2014). Socially extended knowledge. *Philosophical Issues* 24(Extended Knowledge): 282–98. doi: 10.1111/phis.12034

Lackey, J. (2016). What is justified group belief? *Philosophical Review* 125(3): 341–96. doi: org/10.1215/00318108-3516946

Lasonen-Aarnio, M. (2013). Disagreement and evidential attenuation. *Noûs* 47: 767–94.

Levin, J. (2018). Functionalism. In E. N. Zalta (ed.), *The Stanford encyclopedia of philosophy* (Fall 2018 Edition). https://plato.stanford.edu/archives/fall2018/entries/functionalism/

List, C., & Pettit, P. (2016). *Group agency: The possibility, design, and status of corporate agents. Whose peace? Local ownership and United Nations peacekeeping.* Oxford University Press.

Matheson, J. (2015). *The epistemology of disagreement.* Palgrave, UK.

Miragoli, M. (2020). Group belief functionalism, Manuscript.

Quinton, A. (1975). Social-objects. *Proceedings of the Aristotelian Society* 75: 1–27.

Simion, M. (2019a). *Epistemic norms and epistemic functions.* Manuscript.

Simion, M. (2019b). *Knowledge-First Social Epistemology.* Manuscript.

Simpson, R. M. (2013). Epistemic peerhood and the epistemology of disagreement. *Philosophical Studies* 164: 561–77.

Steup, M., & Neta, R. (2020). Epistemology. In E. N. Zalta (ed.), *The Stanford encyclopedia of philosophy* (Summer 2020 Edition), forthcoming https://plato.stanford.edu/archives/sum2020/entries/epistemology/.

Strohmaier, D. (2019). Two theories of group agency. *Philosophical Studies.* doi: 10.1007/s11098-019-01290-4

Titelbaum, Michael G. 'Rationality's Fixed Point (or: In Defense of Right Reason).' Oxford Studies in Epistemology Volume 5, ed. Tamar Szabó Gendler, and John Hawthorne (Oxford, 2015; pubd online Apr. 2015). Oxford Scholarship Online, http://dx.doi.org/10.1093/acprof:oso/9780198722762.003.0009 accessed 09 Oct. 2020.

Tollefsen, D. (2015). *Groups as Agents*. Polity Press.

Tuomela, R. (2013): *Social Ontology: Collective Intentionality and Group Agents*. New York: Oxford University Press.

van Inwagen, P. (1996). It is wrong, everywhere, always, for anyone, to believe anything upon insufficient evidence. In J. Jordan & D. Howard-Snyder (eds.), *Faith, freedom and rationality*. Rowman and Littlefield: 137–54.

van Inwagen, P. (2010). We're right. They're wrong. In T. Warfield & R. Feldman (eds.), *Disagreement*. Oxford University Press, Oxford.

Weatherson, B. (2013). Disagreements, philosophical and otherwise. In D. Christensen & J. Lackey (eds.), *The epistemology of disagreement: New essays*. Oxford University Press, Oxford.

Weisberg, M. (2009). Three kinds of idealization. *Journal of Philosophy* 104: 639–59.

Williamson, T. (2000). *Knowledge and its limits*. Oxford University Press, Oxford.

8 Disagreement and Epistemic Injustice from a Communal Perspective

Mikkel Gerken

8.1 Introduction

In this paper, I will consider disagreement from a communal perspective. Thus, my focus will not primarily be on disagreement between different groups, although this case will figure as well. My main focus is on the epistemic pros and cons of disagreement for a community and on how the social structure of the community bears on these pros and cons. A central lesson will be that disagreement has more epistemic costs at the communal level than is often recognized and that these epistemic costs often yield epistemic injustice.

Much contemporary epistemology of disagreement is inspired by Mill's forceful defense of freedom of speech by appeal to the epistemic benefits of disagreement (Mill 1859/2002, Chap 2). In particular, the ensuing debate has inherited Mill's focus on the ways in which epistemic disagreement are epistemically *beneficial*. For example, Christensen has argued that peer disagreement "...should be welcomed as a valuable strategy for coping with our known infirmities" (Christensen 2007a: 216). The extent to which one should revise one's belief in the face of disagreement is debated. But the assumption that disagreement is often epistemically *good news* is widely agreed upon. Moreover, Mill's considerations centrally involve the social group that the disagreeing individual belongs to: The *community* that may benefit from disagreement in its marketplace of ideas.

In contrast, I will discuss how disagreement may defeat or diminish testimonial warrant.[1] This is not to oppose the view that there are epistemically positive aspects of disagreement. But I will argue that a balanced assessment of the epistemic significance of disagreement requires a better understanding of how and when varieties of it amount to epistemically *bad news*. Moreover, I will argue that these epistemic costs of disagreement may both be partly caused by the disagreeing parties' social community. Thus, the negative epistemic impact of contexts of disagreement requires more careful treatment than it has received. Furthermore, this treatment should not be individualistic in the sense that it only considers the epistemic effects on disagreeing individuals. Rather, it should consider the effects of disagreement within the wider social group.

The task of identifying and diagnosing the circumstances in which disagreement is epistemically problematic is especially important because the epistemically problematic aspects of disagreement are related to epistemic injustice (Fricker 2007). Indeed, I will argue that epistemically problematic disagreements may be both *generated by* and *resulting in* epistemic injustices. So, the overall effect may, in some circumstances, be a vicious circle. Consequently, an aim of applied epistemology should be that of articulating strategies for how to deal with the epistemically problematic aspects of disagreement. I will argue that lack of transparency about whether a disagreement is an epistemic peer disagreement may contribute to disagreement resulting in epistemically bad consequences and epistemic injustices. On the basis of this diagnosis, I conclude by briefly exploring strategies to address problematic consequences of disagreement. In line with the communal perspective, I will not focus on the strategies which individual agents may adopt but rather on the strategies that may be adopted on the communal level.

The paper is organized as follows: In **Section 8.2**, I characterize varieties of disagreement as well as the notion of epistemic peerhood. In **Section 8.3**, I consider a broad argument to the effect that disagreement may defeat or diminish epistemic warrant: *The Argument from Self-Doubt*. In **Section 8.4**, I argue that this negative impact of disagreement is more severe than is commonly recognized once we consider the effects of the disagreement at the level of the social group. In **Section 8.5**, I indicate how the noted epistemological problems with disagreement may breed epistemic injustice in the community. Finally, in **Section 8.6**, I briefly consider what measures a community may take in order to avoid the noted epistemological problems with disagreement.

8.2 Disagreement and Peerhood

Disagreement presents itself in many forms. In general, it may be characterized as the case in which two individuals or groups differ significantly in their doxastic attitude toward a proposition. For example, one person may believe that *p*, whereas another may believe that not *p*. However, two persons may also be said to disagree with regard to *p* if their attitudes toward *p* involve different degrees of credence. So, I will use the phrase 'disagreement' broadly to apply to any non-negligible difference in doxastic attitude toward a proposition.[2]

Much attention has been devoted to the possibility of *rational* disagreement among epistemic peers. As is customary, I use 'epistemic peers' (relativized to a proposition or a domain) to denote individuals who meet, at least in an approximate manner, the following three conditions:

i They share the same evidence
ii They are equally rational and competent (with respect to a proposition or a domain)
iii The have considered the proposition disagreed upon equally carefully

As indicated by the phrase 'at least in an approximate manner', a bit of slack must be given with regard to each condition in order to avoid making the subjects so similar that the occurrence of disagreement becomes a puzzle. Moreover, I am interested in an operational notion of epistemic peerhood that applies to a significant set of actual cases rather than only to heavily idealized cases. For the same reason, I assume that two people may be epistemic peers without having disclosed their evidence, reasoning, etc. That is, the present characterization does not include a 'disclosure' condition on epistemic peerhood itself.

Here is how the slack is given to each condition: As for (i), two individuals may be regarded as peers about *p* even if the evidence they share is not identical but merely relevantly similar (see also Hawthorne and Srinivasan 2013, fn. 15). As for (ii), it is hardly ever the case that two individuals are perfectly equi-competent with regard to a proposition or domain. Likewise, the final condition (iii) should allow for minor discrepancies. In particular, a *performance error* by one of the disagreeing parties may be responsible for a genuine peer disagreement.

Note that many of the cases in the literature, such as Christensen's Mental Math case, presuppose that the disagreement is explained by a performance error on the part of a peer (Christensen 2007a). So, I take this specification of peerhood to align with the notion that is operative in the literature (see also Kelly 2005; Gelfert 2011; Vorobej 2011).

It will be important for the following discussion to note that the above articulation of the notion of epistemic disagreement articulates *de facto*, rather than apparent, epistemic peer disagreement. So, whether two disagreeing people regard each other as epistemic peers does not determine whether they are epistemic peers (contrast Elga 2007). However, apparent peer disagreement may be articulated derivatively as follows: S is confronted with an apparent epistemic peer disagreement just in case it appears to S that (i)-(iii) hold (at least in an approximate manner) and there are no obvious indications that would make it irrational for S to regard the disagreement as a *de facto* epistemic peer disagreement.

The wide category of disagreement involves robust disagreement, which occurs in cases where the disagreeing parties recognize the disagreement and basic aspects of their opponents' epistemic reasons and reasoning. Moreover, robust disagreement is characterized by the fact that neither party revises her belief on the basis of a first round of critical reflection, and both parties lack disagreement-independent reasons to oppose the opponent's view or rationale (Christensen 2007a). So, whereas epistemic peer disagreement does not involve a disclosure condition, robust epistemic peer disagreement requires the main aspects of the disagreeing parties' evidence and reasoning to be disclosed. However, even robust peer disagreement may be apparent rather than *de facto* disagreement. For example, it may be the product of biased cognition, or it may be explained by seemingly minor but consequential discrepancies in the disagreeing parties' evidence or reasoning. Finally, robust disagreement may be distinguished from *deep* disagreement which is, roughly, disagreement that is not resolved, despite full disclosure of both evidence and the consciously available reasoning, from the evidence to the beliefs that yield the disagreement (Goldman 2009, 2010; Lynch 2010). Deep disagreement is often explained by epistemic diversity, which may, in turn, be characterized as variances of epistemically significant aspects of meaning or of variances in epistemic perspectives, worldviews, values or standards.[3] Apparent deep peer disagreements may also be merely apparent. For example, epistemically diverse people may not be epistemic peers since their cognitive values or worldviews may not be equally epistemically rational. However, this situation does not entail that the disagreement may be resolved (Goldman 2010).

While there is much more to be said about these different notions of disagreements, I hope to have said enough to consider some of their epistemically problematic ramifications.

8.3 The Argument from Self-Doubt

In this section, I will argue that a variety of epistemically negative effects may be grounded in forms of disagreement. I start out articulating an argument – *The Argument from Self-Doubt* – that concludes that disagreement can diminish and even defeat epistemic warrant.

8.3.1 Peer Disagreement and Conciliationism

Cogent arguments have been set forth in favor of conciliationism – the view that a subject who is confronted with robust peer disagreement should revise her belief to some extent (Christensen 2007a; Carter 2014; Matheson 2015a, 2015b).[4] However, a rational obligation to revise one's belief that *p* does not entail that the subject should *doubt* that *p* or suspend judgment about it. In many cases, one should simply lower one's degree of belief that *p* in the face of peer disagreement.

Since the 'should' in question is one of epistemic rationality, it is natural to discuss the issue in terms of degree of warrant for the belief in question. For example, Michael Thune argues that the verdict that S confronted with peer disagreement should (-of-epistemic-rationality) lower the degree of confidence in *p* (Thune 2010). This assumption may be motivated by the idea that peer disagreement is a higher-order defeater or diminisher of S's warrant for the belief that *p*. Indeed, the assumption that an epistemically rational decrease of degree of belief corresponds to a lower degree of warrant appears to follow by an appropriate specification of the slogan: *Proportion (the degree of) your belief to (the degree of) your warrant.* So, I shall simply speak of degree of warrant for a belief rather than speaking of epistemically rational degree of belief. This way of putting things has among its advantages the fact that we may consider doxastic (or *post ante*) warrant as well as propositional (or *ex ante*) warrant.

It is widely, although not universally, accepted that peer disagreement may defeat or diminish warrant (see Christensen 2009; Feldman and Warfield 2009). However, the circumstances in which peer disagreement defeats or diminishes warrant and the extent to which it does so are debated. Indeed, the underlying explanation as to *why* and *how* peer disagreement defeats or diminishes antecedent warrant is disagreed upon. For example, it is controversial whether the appearance of peer disagreement about *p* figures in the set of S's *total evidence* against the proposition *p* (Kelly 2005, 2010; Feldman 2009; Christensen 2009, 2010).

Here, I will consider an alternative argument to the conclusion that apparent peer disagreement defeats or diminishes the subject's antecedent warrant. Here is the gist of it. An agent, S, who is confronted with a robust disagreement with a rational peer should exhibit certain self-doubts.[5] For example, one might doubt whether one has made a performance error in the judgment that *p*, that one's evidence is flawed and so on. However, self-doubt in one's own judgment that *p* or its sources tends to defeat or diminish one's warrant for the belief that *p*. So, the appearance of a robust peer disagreement may defeat or diminish the antecedent warrant for the belief disagreed upon. The idea of self-doubt has been discussed in various contexts (Jones 2012; Medina 2013). But in order to consider it explicitly in relation to robust apparent peer disagreement, I will state the reasoning sketched above as an explicit deductive argument:

The Argument from Self-Doubt

D1: If S responds rationally to a robust apparent peer disagreement about *p*, S engages in self-doubt with respect to her judgment that *p*.
D2: If S engaged in rational self-doubt with respect to her judgment that *p*, it is frequently the case that S's warranted belief that *p* becomes unwarranted or that its warrant is diminished.
D3: If S responds rationally to a robust apparent peer disagreement about *p*, it is frequently the case that S's warranted belief that *p* becomes unwarranted or that its warrant is diminished.

Although my main interest is to shed light on the wider ramifications of the conclusion, D3, I will begin by briefly considering the argument for it. The argument is articulated in a manner that does not require that robust apparent disagreement amounts to evidence. However, it is compatible with such a view. D2 merely sets forth a doctrine that connects S's rational self-doubt about S's belief that *p* and S's warrant for that belief. Independently of what is taken to constitute warrant for a belief, it is plausible that self-doubt in cases of robust apparent peer disagreement will, at least frequently, defeat or diminish it.[6] This assumption is the core of D2.

In consequence, I will restrict my attention to the other premise, D1, and the conclusion, D3. Let me begin with the latter. D3 does not immediately have any negative epistemic consequences. After all, the engagement in self-doubt provides an occasion for checking one's reasoning, reconsidering one's evidence and so forth (Christensen 2007a). Such activities are often epistemically beneficial to the individual agent as well as to the wider community.

Yet the robust appearance of peer disagreement may have epistemically bad ramifications. Let me restate this with an important emphasis: The robust *appearance* of peer disagreement may have epistemically bad ramifications. The restatement emphasizes an under-discussed aspect of epistemic disagreement: It is frequently not transparent to a subject who is confronted with a robust apparent disagreement, whether it is a genuine peer disagreement that is explained by, for example, a performance error or not a peer disagreement at all. Often, this issue is sidestepped by focusing exclusively on known peer disagreement or idealized cases of peer disagreement with full disclosure of evidence and reasoning. But the issue, I shall argue, is too important to be sidestepped, and this is especially true once we consider the social community in which the disagreement is situated.

Turning to D1, facts about transparency are clearly significant. The notion of transparency deserves a more comprehensive treatment than I can provide here. Roughly, I will be concerned with the idea that the nature of a disagreement is transparent to S, to the extent that it is easy for S to form warranted beliefs about its nature. For example, it is highly transparent to S that the disagreement between her father and his doctor is not a peer disagreement because S can easily form a warranted belief that this is so by reflecting on the discrepancy in their medical training. In contrast, it may be highly non-transparent to S that he is not S*'s peer, if his reasoning leading to the disagreement with S* is under the influence of unconscious biases. Transparency is a matter of degree, but for the sake of simplicity, I will often use the categorical terms 'transparent' or 'non-transparent' when it is very easy or very difficult, respectively, for S to form a well-warranted belief about the aspects of the disagreement in question. I will be concerned with transparency concerning aspects of the nature or source of disagreements. Aspects of the nature of the disagreement concern whether it is a factual disagreement, a peer disagreement, a rational disagreement, etc. Aspects of the source of the disagreement concern whether it is produced by biased cognition, a performance error, a well-functioning cognitive process, etc. I will primarily be concerned with the transparency of aspects of the nature and source of disagreement as they pertain to epistemic peerhood, as characterized above. If such aspects of the nature or the source of a robust epistemic disagreement are not transparent to a disagreeing party, S, it is *ceteris paribus* rationally required of S to respond to a robust apparent peer disagreement by engaging in some degree of self-doubt. For example, one would not be responding rationally to an apparent robust peer disagreement by completely ignoring it or by only considering wherein the apparent peer might have erred. This assumption is not an epistemically internalist one. Epistemic externalists typically allow for both unrepresented defeaters, such as missed clues and higher-order defeaters (see, e.g., Bergmann 2006, Ch. 6; Gerken 2020a).

It appears, then, that there is a *prima facie* case for D1. It might be objected that the mere appearance of peer disagreement should not give occasion to self-doubt unless it is reasonable to suppose that the disagreement is a *de facto* peer disagreement (Lackey 2008a). There is something to this worry. However, I have sought to anticipate it by including a mild rationality constraint in the characterization of the term 'apparent' in D1: Recall that a disagreement is characterized as an apparent epistemic peer disagreement only if there are no obvious indications that would make it irrational for S to regard the disagreement as a *de facto* epistemic peer disagreement. So, both cases of *de facto* peer disagreement and non-transparent non-peer disagreement may qualify as apparent peer disagreement.[7] Furthermore, the argument is restricted to cases in which the appearance of a peer disagreement is robust. This entails, among other things, that neither peer has disagreement-independent reasons to dismiss the opponent. Given that 'robust apparent peer disagreement' is specified in the manner above, the premise D1 is *prima facie* plausible, and, given D2, so is D3.

Many of those who regard disagreement as good news accept D3. Consequently, my main ambition in this section is to indicate that D3 has some problematic consequences that both conciliationists and their opponents have underestimated. So, I will henceforth allow myself D3 as a sub-conclusion in order to consider its wider ramifications.

8.4 Transparency and Cornerstone Propositions

Robust apparent peer disagreements are frequently not *de facto* peer disagreements. Consider, for example, anonymous disagreement in an online discussion forum between laypersons. In such a case, the disagreement may amount to a robust apparent peer disagreement, although the disagreeing individual is not a peer but an overconfident ignoramus.

It appears, then, that the warrant for a subject's belief that *p* may be defeated or diminished, even if the disagreeing person is not a peer at all but merely an overconfident ignoramus. So, such an individual may defeat or diminish perfectly good warrant. This problem is particularly pertinent in societies with a lot of such individuals. However, whether there are many such individuals depends to a large extent on incentives and social norms. If individuals can benefit from posing as epistemic peers in cases where they are not, and social norms do not lead to sanctions of such behavior that match the benefits, it is only to be expected. This indicates the importance of considering the epistemic properties of disagreement from a communal perspective. According to a social externalist account, the social environment is a partial determiner of epistemic warrant (Graham 2010, 2016; Gerken 2013, 2020a). Cases of non-transparent and merely apparent peer disagreement make for another way in which the social environment bears on the warrant for disagreeing individuals as well as the more general epistemic position of the wider society. Consider, for example, a society in which it is non-transparent that a high ratio of apparent peer disagreements are not *de facto* peer disagreements. For example, it is not a far-fetched thought experiment to imagine a society in which various sorts of pundits weigh in on all sorts of issues with the authority of epistemic expertise that they, in fact, lack.[8] Thus, reasonably well-informed citizens may encounter apparent robust peer disagreements with such pundits who are, in fact, inferior to them. In accordance with *The Argument from Self-Doubt*, warranted individuals who encounter such disagreements may, in many cases, respond with self-doubt, which decreases their degree of warrant. Thus, diminished warrant through self-doubt in cases of disagreement may be partly but centrally explained by features of the general social environment. For example, pundits are incentivized to opine and provided with platforms in which they can do so. However, they may, in some contexts, do so in a manner that conveys epistemic expertise that they, in fact, lack. More generally, incentives to epistemic overconfidence and lack of social repercussions against it may lead to an overestimation of the cases of peer disagreement and, in the end, widespread self-doubt of the warrant-diminishing kind. Thus, features of the general epistemic community partly determine how prone disagreement is to diminishing warrant through self-doubt.

However, it is important to note that epistemic community's epistemic position may also be compromised by apparent peer disagreement in ways that do not centrally involve self-doubt. In consequence, I will invoke some perspectives beyond just those pertaining to self-doubt. One thing to note is that some disagreements may be about rather large domains of propositions. These may be direct, as when a coherent set of propositions is disagreed upon, but they may also be indirect when a proposition is foundational to a larger set of propositions. This idea is related to but subtly different from Wright's idea of a cornerstone proposition, according to which a proposition is a "*cornerstone* for a given region of thought just in case it would follow from a lack of warrant for it that one could not rationally claim warrant for *any* belief in the region" (Wright 2004: 167–168).[9]

Assume, for example, that disagreement about a proposition, *p*, is foundational to a domain, D. For example, *p* could concern the truth-conduciveness of a method used to generate beliefs about the propositions in D. Or *p*, such that its epistemic status is reasonably thought to be representative of the epistemic status of the majority of propositions in D. In such cases, it is plausible that the following principle governs the domain D: *If there is expert peer disagreement about a proposition that is foundational to D, it is likely that there is widespread expert peer disagreement about propositions that belong to D.*

Hence, a single but robust apparent expert peer disagreement may lead to a very general defeat of warrant in the community, and this may be an enormous epistemic cost. Indeed, the primary damage may not be the disagreeing individual's warrant but rather the general epistemic position of larger groups or even the general community. To illustrate this, consider the cornerstonish idea that scientific models are generally the most reliable source concerning a domain, D (this could be climate science Winsberg 2012, 2018). However, if there is pervasive, non-transparent apparent expert peer disagreement but not *de facto* expert peer disagreement about this proposition in the society, the result is a generally compromised epistemic environment. The point that apparent expert disagreement puts laypersons in a challenging epistemic position is familiar enough (Goldman 2001). However, it is not always appreciated that this epistemic cost of a prevalent type of disagreement should be taken into account when assessing the overall epistemic costs and benefits of disagreement for the wider community. In some cases, apparent expert peer disagreement may undermine testimonial warrant in the wider community because individuals may no longer be able to acquire warrant by testimony – even when the testifier is in fact a reliable expert.

A concrete case concerns the idea of *balanced reporting* – roughly, the idea that science reporters should, whenever feasible, report opposing hypotheses in a manner that does not favor any one of them. It has been argued that this principle of science reporting undermines warranted public belief by representing disagreement between superiors and inferiors as an expert peer disagreement (Boykoff and Boykoff 2004; Figdor 2018; Gerken 2020c). Interestingly, the rationale for a principle of *balanced reporting* is a broadly Millian epistemic one. However, if the critics (myself included) are correct that the epistemically misleading aspects of balanced reporting are more consequential than its purported epistemic benefits, this suggests a general lesson: One cannot assume, without empirical investigation and philosophical reflection, that furthering disagreement is epistemically beneficial to the general community. This lesson is important for an accurate assessment of the overall epistemic pros and cons of disagreement (Gerken Ms).

But the problems do not stop here. Testimonial warrant, or at least the externalist species of it – testimonial entitlement – is *particularly* endangered if it is often non-transparent whether robust apparent epistemic peer disagreement is *merely* apparent. For the present purpose,

I assume that a hearer, H, by accepting S's testimony, may acquire a kind of warrant that does not depend on H's reasons or cognitive access to the warranting force of S's testimony. That is, I suppose that H may acquire an *epistemically externalist* sort of testimonial warrant: Testimonial entitlement (Burge 1993; Graham 2010, 2016; Gerken 2013, 2020a).

Given the externalist nature of testimonial entitlement, it is vulnerable to disagreement. Since it does *not* involve any access to the testifiers' reliability and intentions, a completely unreasonable testimonial disagreement will defeat or strongly diminish the entitlement for testimonial belief. This may be problematic in social environments which contain a lot of "noise" that consists of unqualified opining.[10] Again, this indicates the importance of considering the social environment in which testimony – including expert testimony – takes place.

For example, if the experts in a community are not easily recognizable, laypersons may be more likely to voice their disagreement with the experts. Not only will this proliferate disagreements; it will increase the problematic cases in which disagreements between epistemic inferiors and superiors are *mis*taken for peer disagreements. Likewise, if the evidence for the disagreeing parties is not transparent, many disagreements that are in fact best explained by flawed or inferior evidence will have the effect of peer disagreement on an audience. If individuals who are engaged in disagreements and subjects who are confronted with opposing testimonies are deprived of (part of) their entitlement in such bad cases, non-transparent epistemic disagreement can be epistemically bad news for individuals as well as groups. As in the cases above, an important culprit in such cases is the non-transparency of the nature and source of disagreement. But the consequences for testimonial entitlement may be among the most troublesome epistemically negative consequences of apparent epistemic disagreement.

In this section, I have considered some ramifications of *The Argument from Self-Doubt* as well as a range of further perspectives on the putative epistemic costs of various forms of disagreement in society. I make no comparative claim to the effect that the overall epistemic consequences of disagreement are negative or positive. As the discussion indicates, this depends a great deal on the nature of the disagreement, the general features of the social environment and the more specific context. Moreover, I make no claim that, if the overall epistemic consequences of epistemic disagreement were negative, this would be a good reason to structure society less inclusively such that only epistemically privileged voices were heard. On the contrary, I believe that other reasons for inclusiveness would trump such an argument (see, e.g., Fricker 2007; Gerken 2019). On the other hand, I will argue that this issue is more complex than it might seem because certain types of epistemic injustice may be generated in contexts of disagreement.

However, even if the troublesome cases that I have called attention to are relatively rare, they should nevertheless figure in an overall assessment of the epistemic properties of disagreement. This should, in turn, figure in an overall assessment of disagreement from a communal perspective.

8.5 Disagreement, Social Cognition and Epistemic Injustice

So far, I have emphasized that there may be significant epistemic costs to both individuals and the wider community if it is not transparent whether a disagreement is a peer disagreement or merely an apparent one. In this section, I will continue to argue that these epistemic costs may yield further costs in terms of epistemic injustice. Fricker originally characterized epistemic injustice as "a wrong done to someone specifically in their capacity as a knower" (Fricker 2007: 1). One species of this – *distributive* epistemic injustice – is a consequence of "the unfair distribution of epistemic goods such as education or information" (Fricker 2013: 1318). However, my focus here will be *discriminatory* epistemic injustice ('DEI', for short) which tends to be explained by *identity prejudices* that pertain to gender, class, race or social power.

Fricker has come to substitute the knowledge-centric formulation for a broader one (Fricker 2013: 1320). This is reasonable since knowledge is not the only epistemic phenomenon that one may be wronged with regard to (see Gerken 2019 for explicit arguments). For example, discriminative epistemic injustice sometimes concerns the comparison between degrees of epistemic competence, trustworthiness and reliability, and it is implausible that all of these phenomena can be reductively analyzed in terms of knowledge (Gerken 2017b).[11] For example, someone who is better warranted than anyone else, although her degree of warrant is insufficient for knowledge, may unjustly be given a deflated level of credibility (see Gerken 2019 for a concrete case). Moreover, in the context of discovery, S's hypotheses may be taken less seriously than S*'s hypotheses for reasons pertaining to biases, stereotypes and prejudices.[12] Although hypotheses ventured in the context of the discovery are not typically known, these cases may exemplify epistemic injustice and, specifically, testimonial injustice. Hence, the characterization of epistemic injustice should be broadened from concerning knowers to concerning epistemic subjects. Hence, I will use the following generic characterization of discriminatory epistemic injustice (from Gerken 2019):

> *Generic DEI*
> S suffers a discriminatory epistemic injustice if (and only if) S is wronged specifically in her capacity as an epistemic subject.

The left-to-right direction of *Generic DEI* is left parenthetical because I want to leave open the possibility of counterexamples to it. However, these need not concern us here; at present, I will only consider the right-to-left direction – i.e., the sufficient condition.[13]

As noted, disagreement may undermine testimonial warrant in the wider community. Consequently, it is worth highlighting a sub-species of discriminatory epistemic injustice – namely, testimonial injustice which is, roughly, the sort of epistemic injustice that a testifier suffers. A central example of testimonial injustice occurs when a testifier is not believed due to a credibility deficit that is explained by the hearer's being prejudiced against her social group. Due to the fact that we are bounded agents, we rely heavily on social stereotypes in the cognitive heuristics that generate our day-to-day assessments of epistemic competence. Regrettably, such folk epistemological stereotypes are often inaccurate, and in consequence, our judgments about who are epistemic peers are biased (Gerken 2017a, forthcoming b; Spaulding 2016, 2018). There are multiple strands of evidence for these broad assumptions about social cognition. Given the overarching aim of considering disagreement from a communal perspective, it is worth considering some of them in a bit further detail.

Some of the most prominent strands of evidence for cognitive biases in assessment of epistemic competence are effects of gender and race in identical CVs (see, e.g., Steinpres et al. 1999; Moss-Racusin et al. 2012). The underlying explanation for such findings is that properties such as gender, race and age affect our social cognition to a considerable degree. We are extremely quick to categorize individuals according to such properties (Ito et al. 2004; Kubota and Ito 2007). However, evidence suggests that social categorization in terms of gender, race and age is interwoven with our ascription of personality traits, including cognitive ones such as competence and trustworthiness (Porter et al. 2008; Rule et al. 2013; Todorov et al. 2015).

Research on in-group/out-group dynamics in social cognition support this picture. For example, we are more inclined to trust and cooperate with in-group members than we are with out-group members (see Balliet et al. 2014 for a meta-analysis). Likewise, we tend to extrapolate our own perspective to members of in-groups, whereas we are more likely to rely on crude stereotypes in our assessment of out-group individuals (Robbins and Krueger 2005; Ames et al. 2012). Furthermore, some studies indicate that we tend to attribute achievements of out-group individuals to circumstantial and environmental facts, whereas we tend to attribute achievements of in-group members to personality traits (Brewer and Brown 1998; Brewer 2001). These tendencies reflect cognitive strategies that may be effective heuristics that allow us to make rapid social judgments and decisions. The cost is that they are biased in various ways. In particular, the in-group/out-group dynamics may lead to overestimation of members of one's in-group and underestimation of members of one's out-group (Brewer 2001; Spaulding 2018).

I have only noted a fraction of the empirical literature and methodological concerns about parts of social psychology that call for caution in drawing overly strong conclusions. Yet I take the empirical work on social cognition to motivate the following theses (see Gerken forthcoming c, Ms):

> ***Epistemic Overestimation***
> *Both accurate and inaccurate social stereotypes may lead evaluators to overestimate a subject's epistemic position.*

> ***Epistemic Underestimation***
> *Both accurate and inaccurate social stereotypes may lead evaluators to underestimate a subject's epistemic position.*

These theses reflect central aspects of our folk epistemology (Gerken 2017a). Unfortunately, both may lead to unjust patterns of credibility excesses and deficits, and thereby to direct and indirect epistemic injustice. Cases of direct epistemic injustice may occur when *Epistemic Underestimation* is in play. *Epistemic Overestimation*, in turn, may lead to indirect epistemic injustice insofar as the overestimated individuals may gain an unfair epistemic advantage – cases of white male privilege are examples.[14]

This upshot bears fairly directly on cases of apparent peer disagreement. If our assessment of whether disagreeing parties – whether they be individuals or groups – are biased in the ways described, it will yield cases of apparent peer disagreement that are not *de facto* peer disagreement. When *Epistemic Underestimation* is operative, the result may be that epistemic superiors are regarded as peers or even inferiors. Likewise, *Epistemic Overestimation* may result in epistemic inferiors or peers being regarded as superiors by other members of the group that they belong to. In each case, a disagreement that should be settled in the favor of one side will appear to be a peer disagreement. Specifically, the members of the same group as one of the disagreeing parties may epistemically overestimate her or underestimate her opponent. This is epistemically costly for the entire community. Moreover, it may yield epistemic injustice in the form of testimonial injustice to the epistemically underestimated groups. For example, the members of such groups may be wronged in their capacity as testifiers. But this type of discriminatory epistemic injustice may also interact with self-doubt in a manner that results in a vicious circle. To see this, let us return to the self-doubt that disagreement may cause.

Several philosophers have emphasized how credibility deficits generate epistemic self-doubt: "…if a history of such injustices gnaws away at a person's intellectual confidence, or never lets it develop in the first place, this damages his epistemic function quite generally" (Fricker 2007: 49;

Jones 2012; Medina 2013). Fricker is primarily concerned with how decreasing intellectual confidence can compromise general cognitive virtues such as intellectual confidence (see also Jones 2012). However, *The Argument from Self-Doubt* suggests that if social stereotypes compromise a person's confidence, this may have more specific bad epistemic consequences. After all, if one's self-confidence is undermined by social stereotypes, one is more likely to regard oneself as a peer, even though one is, in fact, a superior in a given disagreement. But, according to *The Argument from Self-Doubt*, the rational response is to engage in yet *further* self-doubt. Thus, the person's warrant for believing a specific proposition may be defeated or decreased as a result of the self-doubt generated by unjust assessments of her epistemic competence in conjunction with robust apparent peer disagreements. A further consequence may be that the person's warrant is rendered impotent in the communal belief revision. Both these outcomes are manifestations of a type of epistemic injustice for a group as well epistemic costs for the wider community. So, again, the communal perspective on disagreement indicates some bad news.

Fricker emphasizes how testimonial injustice may occur when speakers suffer credibility *deficits* that are due to our reliance on biased cognitive heuristics. However, unjust epistemic privilege in the form of credibility *excesses* may be equally harmful (Davis 2016). For a person who enjoys credibility excesses is more likely to be regarded as an epistemic peer, even if he is not, in fact, a peer. This is an epistemic injustice in its own right. Moreover, as *The Argument from Self-Doubt* indicates, it may also lead to increased self-doubt among those who do not enjoy credibility excesses. After all, systematic credibility excesses of certain people will situate others in more disagreements which misleadingly appear to be robust peer disagreements than they otherwise would experience. The consequence may be self-doubt that diminishes the individual's antecedent warrant. Furthermore, the systematic credibility excess of certain people may distort the process of rational communal belief revision in a manner that is not truth conducive. For example, disagreements between superiors and inferiors may be taken to be peer disagreements by observers who may, in consequence, be overly zealous in withholding judgment.[15] Thus, both epistemic privilege and epistemic marginalization may, in the context of disagreement, lead to epistemic injustice as well as to further bad epistemic consequences for the community as a whole.

Such epistemic injustices may reinforce the original epistemic injustices that cause them. For a person who acts deferentially is thereby conforming to the troublesome stereotypes. Hence, epistemic agents who endure unjust credibility deficits may easily be caught in a vicious self-reinforcing circle of increasing marginalization. Epistemic underestimation of the group may increase the cases of merely apparent peer disagreement, which, in turn, leads to self-doubt, which, in turn, leads to further epistemic underestimation. And so on. And so forth (see also, de Bruin forthcoming).

The vicious circle is not merely bad news in terms of epistemic justice for those individuals and the groups to which they belong; it is also epistemically bad news for the community as a whole. After all, the predicament skews the potentially beneficial process of rationally revising or calibrating our beliefs in the face of peer disagreement. The promise of peer disagreement as a means to rational communal belief revision requires us to be reasonably good at tracking epistemic peerhood. But the fact that we heavily rely on stereotype-driven cognitive heuristics in our epistemic assessments of others compromises our ability to meet this requirement (Spaulding 2018). Thus, disagreement may yield epistemic injustice, and this may have bad epistemic consequences that can reinforce and amplify such epistemic injustices. This too is a cost that should figure into the overall assessment of disagreements' epistemic properties.

8.6 Diagnosis and Steps toward a Cure

The arguments to the effect that epistemic disagreement can be epistemically problematic and epistemically unjust for certain groups do not provide a solid basis for *weighing* the potentially negative aspects of disagreement against their positive consequences. However, the same is true of many of the prominent arguments in *favor* of disagreement, in which its adverse effect rarely plays a role. Consequently, I have by no means sought to argue that the varieties of epistemic injustice associated with disagreement are worse than the injustices associated with suppressing disagreement.

Nevertheless, it may be worthwhile to briefly consider the putative negative consequences of epistemic disagreement considered so far. Likewise, it is worthwhile to briefly consider how the noted challenges due to disagreement may be countered.

8.6.1 Tentative Diagnosis

Before attempting to prescribe a cure, we should diagnose the problems. A diagnosis may begin by noting that the discussed cases of epistemic disagreement were problematic in part because of non-transparency. A rough and partial diagnosis of such cases, then, is that lack of transparency of whether the disagreement is a peer disagreement often contributes to their epistemically negative consequences. If this rough diagnosis is on the right track, some of the epistemically negative effects of disagreement may be partly countered if the nature of the disagreement is transparent to the disagreeing parties as well as to the broader community. Consider cases in which an expert disagrees with a layperson who she reasonably assumes to be another expert. Assume, for example, a meteorologist who, at a meteorology conference, encounters a layperson who is willing to bet that the next week will be exceptionally windy. Our expert carefully reviews the data and comes to disagree. However, given the reasonable presumption that the layperson is an epistemic peer, the meteorologist should be less confident in her belief that the next week will not be exceptionally windy. (Yet she might still do well in taking the bet). However, if it is made clear to her that the layperson is not a peer, she should discard the disagreement as an occasion for revising her belief. (Also, she should clearly take the bet).

Likewise, in many cases of expert disagreement, *sharing the evidential basis* for the verdict may well be central. In many such cases, the disagreeing experts are not really epistemic peers in virtue of violating (i). They do not, in fact, have relevantly similar evidence. Moreover, even genuine peer disagreement is often explained by a performance error by one of the sides. So, increasing the transparency of the evidence and reasoning underlying the verdict may contribute to resolving the disagreement in a rational manner. This is a central reason why scientists present not only their conclusions but also their evidence and methodology in order to subject it to the scrutiny of the scientific community (Longino 1990; Gerken 2015, Ms). In both scientific and everyday cases of apparent peer disagreement, increased transparency will help decrease the cases in which a disagreement is mistakenly taken to be a peer disagreement (Gerken 2020c). This too may, at least in some cases, help address epistemic injustices that arise from reliance on crude social stereotypes rather than a proper assessment of the agent's epistemic competences and resources.

A residual set of cases of rationally presupposed peer disagreement is likely to remain. But discerning at least some of the look-alike cases from the genuine cases of peer disagreement will be epistemically valuable insofar as it contributes to minimizing the noted negative impact of epistemic disagreement. I propose that transparency of the factors, (i)-(iii), that characterize peer disagreement is central to the process of weeding out cases of apparent peer disagreement and, more generally, over- and underestimation of epistemic competence.

Consider the empirical conjecture that a significant majority of cases of *apparent* peer disagreement are not *de facto* peer disagreement. If this conjecture is true, promoting transparency of (i)-(iii) may help counter the noted negative aspects of epistemic disagreement as well as some of the epistemic injustices that it gives rise to.

Of course, there are also considerations against this diagnosis. For example, I have only considered select cases of a couple of species of disagreement. So, the diagnosis may well lack generality. Moreover, I have not argued that the epistemically positive aspects associated with increasing transparency outweigh the putative negative aspects. For example, it might be that simply presupposing that apparent peer disagreement is genuine is a heuristic that is, in many cases, *boundedly rational*. After all, the suggested alternative may be too demanding, given our limited cognitive resources. However, this concern may be alleviated by considering the transparency-promoting measures that we might take as a community rather than as individuals.

8.6.2 Steps toward a Cure

What may be done in order to organize a community so as to minimize the problems discussed? As a manner of conclusion, I will pursue some tentative suggestions for amelioration. The ameliorative suggestions will be tentative, in part because I will rely on the diagnostic suggestion above that increasing the transparency of the nature of disagreement is epistemically beneficial.[16]

In any case, it is worth considering how a community may be structured, legally and otherwise, so as to further that disagreement is transparent wherever it may occur. One measure that can be taken, and which *is* taken in many societies, consists in a proper *labeling* of experts (Goldman 2001). However, despite some labeling of experts, one often finds cases in which disagreements are presented as peer disagreements, although they are not. As already noted, the free press in liberal democracies frequently invokes the journalistic norm of *balanced reporting* when reporting disagreement regarding some controversial topic – e.g., climate change – as a peer disagreement, although it is not (Boykoff and Boykoff 2004; Figdor 2018; Gerken 2020c). This practice of science communication is epistemically problematic, although it may be refined so as to minimize the misleading appearance of peer disagreements (Gerken 2020c, Ms). Furthermore, it is not clear that such refinements need decrease inclusiveness or that they otherwise generate epistemic injustices. Calling a layperson a layperson is compatible with giving him a hearing on a topic on which he disagrees with the experts.

Experts themselves also face a serious responsibility of clarifying when they are speaking qua experts and, in particular, when they are not. Very often an expert in some domain, D, will be treated as an expert in a different domain, D*. In such cases of what I call *expert trespassing testimony*, it is important for the expert to be explicit about the fact that she is not speaking qua expert (Gerken 2018; Ballantyne 2019).

A suggestion that is both more abstract and more controversial is to maintain a "culture of reason-giving" in cases of disagreement. If explicating the reasoning behind a disagreement is overall epistemically beneficial, it might be worth thinking about how to promote reason-giving in public debates as well as in science communication (Gerken forthcoming a, Ms). However, the suggestion is so abstract that it is not clear how to implement it. Moreover, it may be in tension with the epistemically beneficial properties of trust (see, e.g., Hieronymi 2008; Nickel 2009; Faulkner 2011; Hawley 2012, 2019). It may be that it is, in many contexts, important to trust someone rather than require reasons for believing them. If there is such a tension, the optimal trade-off between trust and transparency is an issue that requires considerable conceptual and empirical investigation (Gerken Ms).

Another set of issues concerns the degree of disagreement that should be promoted. These issues are extremely hard to resolve because they intersect with questions regarding liberal rights, such as freedom of speech. However, measures may be taken to minimize obvious noise without compromising liberal rights (Gerken 2018). For example, it is fairly uncontroversial that it is legitimate to maintain forums in which only scientific experts may voice opinions. Such forums are already upheld, and peer-reviewed journals and academic conferences are salient examples. These do not seem epistemically unjust in their own right, although they may manifest *distributive* epistemic injustice (Fricker 2007, 2013). As I have argued above, an excessive degree of disagreement may be epistemically problematic in various ways. Maintaining restricted forums of debate is a legitimate way of handling excessive disagreement without disallowing, or even hampering, it.

I reemphasize the tentativeness of these suggestions, which are conditional on the rough diagnosis above and involve some important empirical questions. However, I hope that the suggestions indicate why it is important to pursue a more precise empirical and philosophical diagnosis of the epistemic consequences of disagreement.

8.6.3 Concluding Remarks

Much contemporary epistemology has inherited the focus on the positive aspects of epistemic disagreement that Mill expressed so powerfully:

> [T]he peculiar evil of silencing the expression of an opinion is, that it is robbing the human race; posterity as well as the existing generation; those who dissent from the opinion, still more than those who hold it. If the opinion is right, they are deprived of the opportunity of exchanging error for truth; if wrong, they lose, what is almost as great a benefit, the clearer perception and livelier impression of truth, produced by its collision with error.
>
> (Mill 1859/2002, Chap 2)

Mill's picture is a compelling one because it goes hand in hand with the extra-epistemological case for freedom of speech. In contrast, the present consideration from a communal perspective suggests that the full *epistemological* picture is more complicated. However, I have not considered the arguments for the positive epistemic aspects of disagreement.

So, the discussion does not leave us in a position to adjudicate on the trade-off between disagreement's positive and its negative epistemic aspects. Thus, further philosophical and empirical work on epistemic disagreement is required. Likewise, the present discussion suggests that further research should pay attention to the issues regarding the transparency of disagreement.

While the present discussion is preliminary, it suggests that, though disagreement can be a good thing, there can be too much of a good thing in this case. This is especially so once we elevate the gaze from the disagreeing individuals to the groups and community that they are members of. So, I have sought to *counterbalance* the historical and contemporary emphasis on the epistemically positive features of disagreement. In particular, I have emphasized the idea that non-transparent disagreement may have epistemically bad consequences in a wider array of cases than has been appreciated. Since these consequences are non-negligible, they should figure in an overall account of the epistemic properties of disagreement.

Finally, I only briefly considered the relationships between the epistemic and the ethical sides of disagreement. But even the present preliminary discussion of epistemic injustice indicates that these relationships are extremely complex. It is safe to say, however, that the epistemological issues pertaining to disagreement have very significant ethical ramifications. So, if non-transparency is a major culprit, and it is possible to restructure aspects of society so as to diminish it, and do so without any bad consequences, we may be both epistemically wise and morally obliged to do so.[17]

Notes

1 Terminology: I use the term 'warrant' as a genus for a positive, but non-factive, epistemic property which harbors both epistemically internalist species – labeled 'justification' – and epistemically externalist ones – labeled 'entitlement' (Burge 2003). I assume that there are both testimonial justifications and testimonial entitlements (Gerken 2013, 2020a).

2 This is merely a terminological choice. Sometimes, 'disagreement' is characterized in a way that requires conflicting attitudes. I will leave it open what constitutes a non-negligible difference by focusing on clear cases of conflict.

3 While I will not thematize the nature of cognitive diversity here, I take it to differ from disagreement in that it may not be reflected in the attitudes of the diverse individuals or groups but rather reflected in norms, practices and values. In contrast, I take disagreement to be constituted by an attitudinal difference in doxastistic state or degree thereof (for further perspectives on diversity, see List 2006, Muldoon 2013).

4 The assumption is not uncontroversial (Kelly 2005, 2010, Lackey 2008a, 2008b). However, theorists who emphasize the epistemic benefits of peer disagreement typically uphold it.

5 For discussion of the relevant notion of doubt, see (Christensen 2007b, Jones 2012).

6 Of course, some theorists uphold a thesis that is stronger than D2 – viz. an *overtly* normative analog. For example, the argument appears to be compatible with Christsensen's central normative assumptions (Christensen 2007a).

7 The present-tense formulation is meant to indicate that the principle is synchronic. It concerns the appearance of a peer disagreement at the time of the disagreement (see Matheson 2015a for a discussion of synchronic vs diachronic principles).

8 This phenomenon is related to but subtly different from the problem of scientific expert trespassing testimony in which an expert in a domain, D, provides testimony in a domain, D*, in which she lacks epistemic expertise (Gerken 2018, forthcoming a, b, Ms; Ballantyne 2019).

9 One difference is that Wright's notion entails that if the warrant for the cornerstone is defeated, so is the warrant for all the propositions in the region of thought (Wright 2004). The present idea is compatible with the assumption that defeat of the proposition in question only *diminishes* warrant for many of the propositions in the region of thought. Moreover, the candidate cases of foundational propositions that I consider differ from the cases that Wright focuses on.

10 An epistemically externalist analysis would have to consider the circumstances in which apparent peer disagreement tends to occur. If disagreement tends to occur only when individual reliability is low, disagreement may be generally truth-conducive. If disagreement tends to occur despite high individual reliability, then disagreement may not be generally truth-conducive. It is an empirical question which antecedent holds.

11 While this assumption is controversial, I will here rely on previous arguments for it and against knowledge-first epistemology in general (cf. Gerken 2011, 2012, 2014, 2017a, 2017b).

12 Thanks to Miranda Fricker (in correspondence) for this type of case.

13 Note that Generic DEI is a genus that may harbor various species, such as testimonial and hermeneutical injustice (Fricker 2007). For example, testimonial injustice may be characterized by replacing 'epistemic subject' with 'testifier'.

14 Note that this account does not entail that the evaluators are culpable, although I think this is often the case – even when they are ignorant of their sub-conscious cognitive heuristics. Yet individuals and groups may suffer a systemic epistemic injustice, even if the relevant evaluator is not blameworthy for it.

15 Although the matter is complicated, it should also be noted that while credibility excess tends to come with practical advantages that accrue to being regarded as trustworthy and convincing, it may also come with epistemic costs. For example, if S is epistemically inferior to S* with regard to the domain, D, but it is regarded as an epistemic peer, S's ability to acquire warranted belief by deference may be compromised.

16 Here, it is worth noting a perspective on non-transparency due to Hawthorne and Srinivasan, who argue that prospects are bleak for articulating "perfectly operationalizable" norms that may guide an agent's responses to disagreement (Hawthorne and Srinivasan 2013). Their central reason is that the epistemic conditions figuring in the norms are not transparent to the disagreeing parties. Hawthorne and Srinivasan's proposed norm for disagreement, their notion of perfect operationalizability and their notion of transparency are articulated in terms of knowledge. I do not accept these "knowledge-centric" characterizations. But, as Hawthorne and Srinivasan note, much of their discussion applies more widely (Hawthorne and Srinivasan 2013: 13). In particular, their point, that non-transparency renders it

difficult to articulate norms that may guide agents situated *within the context* of epistemic disagreement, may be congenial to the present diagnosis. But this is compatible with considering how to minimize problematic cases of epistemic disagreement in the first place. This will be my approach.

17 This chapter is a descendent of a fraction of a paper first drafted around 2008 and presented at a conference at Vrije University, Amsterdam (2009); two workshops at the University of Copenhagen (2009, 2012); an epistemology workshop in McGill (2013); and Bled Epistemology Conference (2013). I am grateful to these audiences for feedback. Embarrassingly, my records of individuals who helped me are in shambles. I keep a file to keep track of interlocutors, but because the paper was broken up, restructured several times, I managed to mess it up in this case. I apologize to those who helped but who I failed to keep track of – my bad, not OK! However, I strongly suspect that Kristoffer Ahlström-Vij, Klemens Kappel and Nikolaj Jang Pedersen commented on an early draft, and I recall discussing/corresponding about material from the paper with David Christensen, Philip Ebert and Chris Kelp. Finally, Adam Carter and Fernando Broncano-Berrocal provided helpful substantive and editorial comments on a late draft.

Literature

Ames, D. R., Weber, E. U., & Zou, X. (2012). Mind-reading in strategic interaction: The impact of perceived similarity on projection and stereotyping. *Organizational Behavior and Human Decision Processes* 117 (1): 96–110.

Ballantyne, N. (2019). Epistemic trespassing. *Mind* 128 (510): 367–395.

Balliet, D., Wu, J., & De Dreu, C. K. (2014). Ingroup favoritism in cooperation: A meta-analysis. *Psychological Bulletin* 140 (6): 1556.

Bergmann, M. (2006). *Justification without awareness.* Oxford: Oxford University Press.

Boykoff, M. T., & Boykoff, J. M. (2004). Balance as bias: Global warming and the US prestige press. *Global Environmental Change* 14 (2): 125–136.

Brewer, M. B. (2001). Ingroup identification and intergroup conflict. *Social Identity, Intergroup Conflict, and Conflict Reduction* 3: 17–41.

Brewer, M. B., & Brown, R. J. (1998). *Intergroup relations.* McGraw-Hill.

Burge, T. (1993). Content preservation. *Philosophical Review* 102 (4): 457–488.

Burge, T. (2003). Perceptual entitlement. *Philosophy and Phenomenological Research* 67 (3): 503–548.

Carter, J. A. (2014). Disagreement, relativism and doxastic revision. *Erkenntnis* 79 (S1): 1–18.

Christensen, D. (2007a). Epistemology of disagreement: The good news. *Philosophical Review* 116 (2): 187–217.

Christensen, D. (2007b). Does Murphy's law apply in epistemology? Self-doubt and rational ideals. *Oxford Studies in Epistemology* 2: 3–31.

Christensen, D. (2009). Disagreement as evidence: The epistemology of controversy. *Philosophy Compass* 4 (5): 756–767.

Christensen, D. (2010). Higher-order evidence. *Philosophy and Phenomenological Research* 81 (1): 185–215.

Davis, E. (2016). Typecasts, tokens, and spokespersons: A case for credibility excess as testimonial injustice. *Hypatia* 31: 485–501.

de Bruin, B. (forthcoming). Epistemic injustice in finance. *Topoi*: 1–9.

Elga, A. (2007). Reflection and disagreement. *Noûs* 41 (3): 478–502.
Faulkner, P. (2011). *Knowledge on trust*. Oxford: Oxford University Press.
Feldman, R. (2009). Evidentialism, higher-order evidence, and disagreement. *Episteme* 6 (3): 294–312.
Feldman, R., & Warfield, T. (eds.) (2009). *Disagreement*. Oxford: Oxford University Press.
Figdor, C. (2018). Trust me: News, credibility deficits, and balance. In C. Fox & J. Saunders, *Media ethics, free speech, and the requirements of democracy*. Routledge: 69–86.
Fricker, M. (2007). *Epistemic injustice: Power and the ethics of knowing*. Oxford University Press.
Fricker, M. (2013). Epistemic justice as a condition of political freedom? *Synthese* 190 (7): 1317–1332.
Gelfert, A. (2011). Who is an epistemic peer? *Logos and Episteme* 2 (4): 507–514.
Gerken, M. (2011). Warrant and action. *Synthese* 178 (3): 529–547.
Gerken, M. (2012). Discursive justification and skepticism. *Synthese* 189 (2): 373–394.
Gerken, M. (2013). Internalism and externalism in the epistemology of testimony. *Philosophy and Phenomenological Research* 87 (3): 532–557.
Gerken, M. (2014). Same, same but different: The epistemic norms of assertion, action and practical reasoning. *Philosophical Studies* 168 (3): 745–767.
Gerken, M. (2015). The epistemic norms of intra-scientific testimony. *Philosophy of the Social Sciences* 45 (6): 568–595.
Gerken, M. (2017a). *On folk epistemology. How we think and talk about knowledge*. Oxford: Oxford University Press.
Gerken, M. (2017b). Against knowledge-first epistemology. In E. C. Gordon, B. Jarvis, & J. A. Carter (eds.), *Knowledge-first approaches in epistemology and mind*. Oxford: Oxford University Press: 46–71.
Gerken, M. (2018). Expert trespassing testimony and the ethics of science communication. *Journal for General Philosophy of Science* 49 (3): 299–318.
Gerken, M. (2019). Pragmatic encroachment and the challenge from epistemic injustice. *Philosophers' Imprint*.
Gerken, M. (2020a). Epistemic entitlement – Its scope and limits. In P. Graham & N. J. L. L. Pedersen (eds.), *Epistemic entitlement*Oxford: Oxford University Press: 150–178.
Gerken, M. (2020b). Public scientific testimony in the scientific image. *Studies in History and Philosophy of Science A*. 80: 90–101.
Gerken, M. (2020c). How to balance *balanced reporting* and *reliable reporting*. *Philosophical Studies*.
Gerken, M. (forthcoming b). Dilemmas in Science Communication. In N. Hughes (ed.), *Epistemic dilemmas*. Oxford University Press.
Gerken, M. (forthcoming c). Salient alternatives and epistemic injustice in folk epistemology. In S. Archer (ed.), *Salience: A philosophical inquiry*. Routledge.
Gerken, M. (Ms). *The Significance of Scientific Testimony*. Oxford: Oxford University Press (under contract).
Goldman, A. (2001). Experts: Which ones should you trust? *Philosophy and Phenomenological Research* 63 (1): 85–110.
Goldman, A. (2009). Epistemic relativism and reasonable disagreement. In R. Feldman & T. A. Warfield (eds.), *Disagreement*. Oxford: Oxford University Press, 187–215.

Goldman, A. (2010). Systems-oriented social epistemology. In T. Gendler & J. Hawthorne (eds.), *Oxford studies in epistemology*, Vol. 3, Oxford: Oxford University Press, 189–214.

Graham, P. (2010). Testimonial entitlement and the function of comprehension. In A. Haddock, A. Millar, & D. Pritchards (eds.), *Social epistemology*. Oxford: Oxford University Press, 148–174.

Graham, P. (2016). Testimonial knowledge: A unified account. *Philosophical Issues* 26 (1): 172–186.

Hawley, K. (2012). *Trust – A very short introduction*. Oxford: Oxford University Press.

Hawley, K. (2019). *How to be trustworthy*. Oxford: Oxford University Press.

Hawthorne, J., & Srinivasan, A. (2013). *Disagreement without transparency: Some bleak thoughts, the epistemology of disagreement: New essays*, D. Christensen & J. Lackey (eds.). Oxford: Oxford University Press: 9–30.

Hieronymi, P. (2008). The reasons of trust. *Australasian Journal of Philosophy* 86 (2): 213–236.

Ito, T. A., Thompson, E., & Cacioppo, J. T. (2004). Tracking the timecourse of social perception: The effects of racial cues on event-related brain potentials. *Personality and Social Psychology Bulletin* 30 (10): 1267–1280.

Jones, K. (2012). The politics of intellectual self-trust. *Social Epistemology* 26 (2): 237–251.

Kelly, T. (2005). The epistemic significance of disagreement. In J. Hawthorne & T. Gendler (eds.), *Oxford studies in epistemology, Volume 1*. Oxford: Oxford University Press, 167–196.

Kelly, T. (2010). Peer disagreement and higher order evidence. In A. I. Goldman & D. Whitcomb (eds.), *Social epistemology: Essential readings*. Oxford: Oxford University Press, 183–220.

Kubota, J. T., & Ito, T. A. (2007). Multiple cues in social perception: The time course of processing race and facial expression. *Journal of Experimental Social Psychology* 43 (5): 738–752.

Lackey, J. (2008a). What should we do when we disagree? In T. S. Gendler & J. Hawthorne (eds.), *Oxford studies in epistemology*, Vol. 3, Oxford: Oxford University Press, 274–293.

Lackey, J. (2008b). A justificationist view of disagreement's epistemic significance. In A. M. A. Haddock & D. Pritchard (eds.), *Social epistemology*. Oxford: Oxford University Press, 298–325.

List, C. (2006). Episteme. *Special Issue on Epistemic Diversity* 3 (3).

Longino, H. (1990). *Science as social knowledge*. Princeton, NJ: Princeton University Press.

Lynch, M. P. (2010). Epistemic circularity and epistemic disagreement. In A. Haddock, A. Millar & D. Pritchard (eds.), *Social Epistemology*. Oxford: Oxford University Press, 262–277.

Matheson, J. (2015a). *The epistemic significance of disagreement*. Palgrave Macmillan.

Matheson, J. (2015b). Disagreement and the ethics of belief. In J. Collier (ed.), *The future of social epistemology: A collective vision*. Lanham, MD: Rowman and Littlefield: 139–148.

Medina, J. (2013). *The epistemology of resistance: Gender and racial oppression, epistemic injustice, and resistant imaginations*. Oxford: Oxford University Press.

Mill, J. S. (1859/2002). *On liberty*. Dover Publications.

Moss-Racusin, C. A., Dovidio, J. F., Brescoll, V. L., Graham, M. J., & Handelsman, J. (2012). Science faculty's subtle gender biases favour male students. *Proceedings of the National Academy of Sciences* 109 (41): 16474–16479.
Muldoon, R. (2013). Diversity and the division of cognitive labor. *Philosophy Compass* 8 (2): 117–125.
Nickel, P. (2009). Trust, staking, and expectations. *Journal of the Theory of Social Behaviour* 39 (3): 345–362.
Porter, S., England, L., Juodis, M., ten Brinke, L., & Wilson, K. (2008). Is the face a window to the soul? Investigation of the accuracy of intuitive judgments of the trustworthiness of human faces. *Canadian Journal of Behavioral Science* 40: 171–177.
Robbins, J. M., & Krueger, J. I. (2005). Social projection to ingroups and outgroups: A review and meta-analysis. *Personality and Social Psychology Review* 9 (3): 2–47.
Rule, N. O., Krendl, A. C., Ivcevic, Z., & Ambady, N. (2013). Accuracy and consensus in judgments of trustworthiness from faces: Behavioral and neural correlates. *Journal of Personality and Social Psychology* 104: 409–426.
Spaulding, S. (2016). Mind misreading. *Philosophical Issues* 26 (1): 422–440.
Spaulding, S. (2018). *How we understand others: Philosophy and social cognition*. Routledge.
Thune, M. (2010). 'Partial defeaters' and the epistemology of disagreement. *Philosophical Quarterly* 60 (239): 355–372.
Todorov, A., Olivola, C. Y., Dotsch, R., & Mende-Siedlecki, P. (2015). Social attributions from faces: Determinants, consequences, accuracy, and functional significance. *Annual Review of Psychology* 66: 519–545.
Vorobej, M. (2011). Distant peers. *Metaphilosophy* 42 (5): 708–722.
Winsberg, E. (2012). Values and uncertainties in the predictions of global climate models. *Kennedy Institute of Ethics Journal* 22 (2): 111–137.
Winsberg, E. (2018). Communicating uncertainty to policymakers: The ineliminable role of values. In E. A. Lloyd, & E. Winsberg, (eds.), *Climate Modelling: Philosophical and Conceptual Issues*. Springer., 381–412.
Wright, C. (2004). Warrant for nothing (and foundations for free)? *Aristotelian Society Supplementary* 78 (1): 167–212.

9 Group Disagreement in Science

Kristina Rolin

9.1 Introduction

The epistemology of disagreement has mainly focused on disagreement between individuals who are epistemic peers. Given the fact that numerous philosophers have examined group beliefs and group justification (e.g., Gilbert 2000; List 2005; Rolin 2010; Schmitt 1994), the investigation of group disagreement is timely. In addition to analyzing what it takes to revise a group's belief, such investigation gives rise to the question of whether a group should revise some of their beliefs, or their degree of confidence in these beliefs, when it is faced with peer disagreement over the beliefs (Carter 2016; Skipper and Steglich-Petersen 2019).

In this chapter, I direct attention to a slightly different set of questions. I aim to understand what kind of action would be epistemically responsible when a group is faced with peer disagreement over some of their beliefs and what it takes for a group, not just for individuals, to be epistemically responsible. These questions are of interest not only to epistemologists but also to philosophers of science worried about the epistemic and political effects of scientific dissent, such as skepticism over climate change or the safety of vaccines (Biddle and Leuschner 2015; Kitcher 2011; Leuschner 2018; de Melo-Martín and Intemann 2013, 2014, 2018; Nash 2018; Rolin 2017b). Granting that scientific dissent is sometimes epistemically and politically harmful (Michaels 2008; Oreskes and Conway 2010), philosophers of science have raised such questions as: Do scientific communities always have an obligation to respond to dissenters? Are there situations in which scientists can legitimately ignore scientific dissent? Is it permissible for scientists to discredit dissenters by questioning their expertise or motivations, for instance, by revealing their financial or political ties to think tanks or private industry?

A widespread view in philosophy of science is that scientific communities have an obligation to engage scientific dissent only when it is normatively appropriate from an epistemic point of view; otherwise, scientific communities have no such obligation (see also Intemann and de Melo-Martín 2014). Engaging scientific dissent involves evaluating arguments with the aim of judging the extent to which they are correct or not and responding to dissenters accordingly. Given this view, one challenge is to understand how scientists can distinguish normatively appropriate from inappropriate dissent. In this chapter, I discuss one way of tackling this question.

Many of the cases which philosophers of science and science studies scholars have identified as problematic dissent (e.g., exaggerating uncertainty over well-established scientific knowledge of tobacco smoking, DDT, and climate change) seem to have one thing in common. They are created in bad faith. In some cases, there is evidence suggesting that dissenters "manufacture" doubt over widely held scientific views in order to promote political ideologies or the economic interests of their paymasters (Michaels 2008; Oreskes and Conway 2010). Yet dissenters' motivations can hardly be used as the main criterion to tell normatively inappropriate dissent apart from more appropriate versions. This is partly because purely epistemic motivations are not necessary for creating good scientific research (Kitcher 1993). Scientists often have mixed motivations, including both epistemic and non-epistemic interests, such as the advancement of their own careers or the promotion of human well-being (Rolin 2017b, 212; see also de Melo-Martín and Intemann 2018). While non-epistemic interests may sometimes lead scientists to violate epistemic standards or principles of research ethics, this kind of thing is not inevitable. Epistemic and non-epistemic interests can coexist peacefully in scientific practices.

Acknowledging that the bad-faith criterion is insufficient to identify normatively inappropriate dissent, philosophers of science have proposed other criteria. One proposal is that scientific dissent is normatively inappropriate when dissenters violate at least one norm that is part of the social organization of epistemically well-designed scientific communities. According to an influential account, epistemically well-designed scientific communities are governed by four norms: Those of "venues," "uptake," "public standards," and "tempered equality of intellectual authority" (Longino 2002, 129–131). According to Helen Longino, the norm of venues requires criticism to be presented publicly in recognized scientific conferences, journals, or other publications (2002, 129). The norm of uptake demands that each party to a controversy engage criticism and change their beliefs accordingly, instead of merely "tolerating dissent" (2002, 129–130). The norm of public standards states that criticism must appeal to some standards of evidence and argumentation accepted by the scientific community (2002, 130–131). Finally, the norm of tempered equality of intellectual authority requires each community member to be recognized as someone with cognitive and intellectual skills which enable them to make cogent comments about the subject matter of inquiry (2002, 133, note 19). Such equality is tempered only insofar as scientists differ in their domain-specific knowledge.

When dissenters conform to these four norms (to be explained further in Section 9.2), scientific dissent is normatively appropriate, and the scientific community as a whole has an obligation to respond to it in some way. A community that ignores normatively appropriate dissent can be blamed for violating the norm of uptake. However, when dissenters fail to play by the rules of epistemically well-designed communities, dissent is normatively inappropriate from an epistemic point of view, and it does not deserve to be taken seriously by other community members.

Like some other philosophers of science (de Melo-Martín and Intemann 2018), I argue that there are limits to the applicability of the four norms. While Longino's account rules out *deep* disagreement, that is, disagreement about the four norms, dissenters and the advocates of a consensus view can still disagree about the *interpretation* of those norms. When the two parties to a controversy interpret a norm in different ways, there is no guarantee that they will reach a shared understanding of whether someone has actually followed the norm. Disagreements about the interpretation of norms make it difficult to settle disagreements about whether scientific claims are well-established or not. Thus, a scientific controversy may reach an impasse due to ambiguity in the norms of epistemically well-designed scientific communities.

In this chapter, I propose a way out of that impasse by elaborating on Longino's account of epistemically well-designed scientific communities. I argue that the supporters of a consensus view, as well as the dissenters, have a moral reason to be epistemically responsible for their knowledge claims, including claims to the effect that the other party should suspend judgment due to insufficient evidence. Even when there is disagreement over the interpretation of the norms of uptake, public standards, and tempered equality, the norm of epistemic responsibility provides scientists with a moral reason to be epistemically responsible toward the other party. A moral reason for this is the belief that their actions contribute to the well-being of other human beings by showing them respect. The norm of epistemic responsibility does not require scientists to revise their views (or the degree of confidence they have in their views), whenever they are faced with disagreement. However, in case scientists do not revise their views, the norm of epistemic responsibility requires them to communicate these views and their reasons for holding them in a more accessible and explicit way than what they have done so far or to provide further explanations for their views.

This chapter is organized as follows. In Section 9.2, I explain how Longino's account of epistemically well-designed communities can be used to distinguish between normatively appropriate and inappropriate dissent. In Section 9.3, I turn to a criticism of Longino's account. In their book *The Fight against Doubt* (2018), Inmaculada de Melo-Martín and Kristen Intemann argue that Longino's account fails to pinpoint normatively inappropriate dissent in a reliable way. In response to this concern,

I introduce the norm of epistemic responsibility in Section 9.4. In Section 9.5, I argue that the norm of epistemic responsibility gives scientists a moral reason to respond to the other party, even when there is disagreement over the interpretation of the norms of uptake, public standards, and tempered equality.

Before discussing normatively appropriate dissent, a clarification of the terms "scientific dissent" and "consensus view" is in order. "Scientific dissent" refers to views that run contrary to widely held scientific theories, methods, or assumptions (de Melo-Martín and Intemann 2018, 6). It is not enough to have a disagreement; to have scientific dissent, the disagreement must challenge a consensus view. A "consensus view" refers to a view that has been accepted by a scientific community, either in a summative or a non-summative way. According to a summative understanding of a consensus view, to claim that a scientific community has accepted that p is merely to a shorthand statement of the claim that all or most community members have accepted that p. According to a non-summative understanding of a consensus view, the claim that a scientific community has accepted that p is *not* equivalent to the claim that all or most community members have accepted that p. As Margaret Gilbert explains, a non-summative account of a consensus view means that scientific communities have "scientific beliefs of their own" (2000, 38). While some philosophers believe that scientific communities are capable of having collective knowledge in a non-summative sense (e.g., Bird 2010; Gilbert 2000; Miller 2015; Rolin 2008), others hold that only research teams are capable of having such knowledge (e.g., de Ridder 2014; Wray 2007).

It is important to notice that the existence of a consensus view does not exclude the possibility of dissent in scientific communities. On a summative account of a consensus view, some community members can disagree with the majority of the community. On a non-summative account, some community members can harbor personal doubts over the community's collective view and eventually challenge it by voicing their dissent in public (Gilbert 2000, 44–45). Even when there is a consensus over a scientific view, it is possible that the scientific view is not true (Miller 2019).

9.2 Normatively Appropriate Dissent

A prominent approach to normatively appropriate dissent suggests that dissent is normatively appropriate from an epistemic point of view when dissenters conform to norms and standards that govern epistemically well-designed scientific communities. Given this approach, one task is to understand what such norms and standards are. In this section, I explain how I understand the notion of scientific community and, especially, the notion of an epistemically well-designed scientific community.

After these preliminary clarifications, I turn to Longino's account of the norms and standards that scientific communities should implement in their activities.[1]

The concept of scientific community can be applied to various social groups in science, including the community of all scientists, disciplinary communities, and specialty communities within and between disciplinary communities. I use the term "scientific community" in the sense of a specialty community. In philosophy of science, such communities are believed to be "the producers and validators of scientific knowledge" (Kuhn 1996, 178). As Thomas Kuhn explains, in specialty communities, scientists share concepts, beliefs, and standards because they have received similar educations, and they are familiar with the basic literature on the subject matter of inquiry (1996, 177). That community members can take for granted many assumptions about the world and the method of studying it partly explains why specialty communities are efficient units for conducting scientific research (Wray 2011, 174).

While community members share some concepts, beliefs, and standards, they can also endorse slightly different constellations of these elements, with the consequence that there may not be any unambiguous way to define the boundaries of communities or distinguish members from non-members. Specialty communities may overlap, and individual scientists may belong to several communities either simultaneously or in succession (Kuhn 1996, 178). Most importantly, specialty communities are arenas for scientific disagreement and dissent. I maintain that conflicting views are not recognized as *scientific* disagreement or dissent unless they are made public in the arenas of specialty communities. It is not uncommon for there to be disagreement over some scientific views due to ignorance among laypeople. Such disagreement rarely has any bearing on scientific debates. Things are different for disagreement or dissent that has crossed the threshold of a recognized scientific venue. Such disagreement or dissent can make an impact on a scientific debate. Scientific disagreement and dissent may concern not only hypotheses, theories, and methods but also background assumptions and standards shared by many community members. For example, a standard can be criticized and transformed in reference to other standards, goals, and values which had temporarily held constant (Longino 2002, 131).

By epistemically well-designed communities, I mean scientific communities that are organized so that, by operating according to their norms and standards, scientists are likely to be successful in achieving their epistemic goals (Kitcher 1993, 303). Such communities may be engaged with basic or applied research. While applied research typically pursues solutions to practical problems, it has epistemic goals in addition to practical ones (Niiniluoto 1993, 12). Applied research can achieve a practical goal by producing recommendations of the form "If you want A, and you believe that you are in a situation B, then it is instrumentally rational for you to do X." The recommendation depends on scientific knowledge to the effect that doing X is likely to bring about A under the circumstances. In order to be able to deliver such recommendations, applied research needs to pursue an epistemic goal, the goal of establishing a connection between X and A. For the purpose of this chapter, I assume that the epistemic goals of scientific communities, both in basic and in applied research, include significant truth (Kitcher 1993) and empirical success (Solomon 2001).

Given this understanding of epistemic goals, the norms and standards of epistemically well-designed communities are such that they promote significant truth or empirical success. Norms and standards can promote epistemic goals directly, by leading us toward them, or indirectly, by being connected to some other factor that leads us toward them. By norms in general, I mean behavioral rules that people are accountable for conforming to in suitable conditions. Holding someone to account typically involves imposing a sanction on them (Kauppinen 2018, 3). For example, the rule of assertion is a norm stating that "One must: assert that p only if C(p)," where C(p) specifies the condition that p fulfills (Williamson 1996, 492). When a person violates the norm by asserting that p when not C(p), such a violation is likely to elicit a sanction. The hearer may believe that the speaker has cheated, and then they respond accordingly. By standards, I mean standards that make it possible to assess evidence, inferences, hypotheses, models, and theories from an epistemic point of view. An example of a standard would be a rule dictating that, in statistical hypothesis testing, the significance level should be 5%. While I focus on norms and standards, I do not thereby suggest that having the right norms and standards is all that it takes to make scientific communities epistemically successful. Epistemically well-designed communities can have other features that are responsible for their epistemically successful performance.

The very idea of an epistemically well-designed community presupposes an instrumentalist account of epistemic rationality (Kitcher 1993, 179). According to an instrumentalist account, norms and standards are epistemically rational insofar as they are means to achieve desired epistemic goals. As Ronald Giere explains, "To be instrumentally rational is simply to employ means believed to be conducive to achieving desired goals" (1989, 380). An instrumentalist account of epistemic rationality appeals to an objective rather than a subjective sense of instrumental rationality. An objective instrumental rationality consists in "employing means that are not only believed to be, but are in fact conducive to achieving desired goals" (1989, 380). Thus, instrumental epistemic rationality amounts to objective instrumental rationality in the service of desired epistemic ends. Instrumental epistemic rationality is conditional since it involves the view that epistemic norms and standards exert their normative force on a person only insofar as she is pursuing epistemic goals.[2]

So far, I have suggested that an epistemically well-designed community is such that, when its norms and standards are followed, they promote significant truth or empirical success. With a working definition of an epistemically well-designed community on hand, we can assess one proposal for the norms of such a community. Longino argues that the norms of venues, uptake, public standards, and tempered equality promote epistemic goals indirectly by ensuring that criticism can transform scientists' beliefs or the confidence they have in their beliefs (2002, 129–131). When criticism is effective in changing scientists' beliefs, it is conducive to achieving epistemic goals because it is likely correct false beliefs and biased research: For example, research in which the selection or interpretation of evidence is skewed such that other bodies of relevant evidence or interpretations of evidence are overlooked. Even when criticism does not give scientists a reason to change their beliefs, it can promote epistemic goals in other ways. It can force scientists to provide better arguments for their views or to communicate their views in a more accessible and explicit way than what they have done so far. Criticism can help scientists avoid dogmatic beliefs.

According to Longino, the norm of "venues" facilitates transformative criticism by requiring that criticism be made public in scientific venues and the norm of "uptake" by demanding that each party to a controversy evaluate criticism and respond to the other party accordingly (2002, 129–130). The norm of "public standards" makes transformative criticism possible by requiring that criticism appeal to some standards of evidence and argumentation accepted by the scientific community (2002, 130–131). While Longino acknowledges that different specialty communities may subscribe to slightly different sets of epistemic standards, she emphasizes that the set must include the standard of empirical adequacy (1990, 77). Finally, the norm of "tempered equality" serves transformative criticism by disqualifying those communities in which certain views dominate because of the political or economic power of their adherents (1990, 78). The norm of "tempered equality" also makes room for a diversity of perspectives, which is likely to generate epistemically fruitful criticism (2002, 131). While Longino proposes that scientific communities "take active steps to ensure that alternative points of view are developed enough to be a source of criticism and new perspectives" (2002, 132), she recognizes that it is not just any diversity that is welcomed in scientific communities. The scope of diversity is constrained by the norm of "public standards."

By arguing that the four norms promote epistemic goals, Longino also provides an explanation of why dissenters ought to comply with the rules of epistemically well-designed communities. When dissenters play by the rules, scientific dissent has the potential to be epistemically beneficial for the community as a whole. Like some other philosophers of science (Solomon 2001), Longino believes that the epistemic advantages of dissent are potentially so significant that scientific communities should actively seek and cultivate dissent (2002, 132).

By focusing on the norms guiding scientists' behavior, Longino's account addresses common concerns about the behavior of dissenters. For example, Justin Biddle and Anna Leuschner argue that scientific research is in danger of stagnation if scientists are forced to spend a significant amount of their time and energy on repeating their responses to dissenters (2015, 262; see also Kitcher 2011, 221). The norm of uptake is relevant to this concern as it requires dissenters, like other scientists, to respond to criticism. When dissenters are not capable of responding to criticism of their views, they should stop repeating their objections (Longino 2002, 133). While the norm of uptake can bring many controversies to an end, there is also the possibility that the two parties do not agree about when the obligation to respond to criticism ends. I will return to this problem in the next section.

Another worry raised by Biddle and Leuschner is that aggressive dissenters will succeed in "winning" a scientific debate by creating an atmosphere in which other scientists are afraid to express their views openly (Biddle and Leuschner 2015, 269). The norm of tempered equality is relevant to this concern because it forbids attempts to intimidate or threaten scientists. Insofar as criticism leads to a transformation in scientific views, the transformation should be an outcome of a debate in which participants enjoy equal intellectual authority as well as sufficient resources. The latter condition is needed to ensure that scientists are actually capable of performing their duties (Rolin 2017b). If scientific communities lacked adequate resources, dissenters could easily wear them down by demanding responses to numerous objections.

Another concern is that dissent leads to scientific polarization, that is, a situation in which two groups hold increasingly opposing views (Leuschner 2018, 1262). Insofar as scientific polarization is an outcome of a social process by which scientists give more weight to evidence from like-minded colleagues than they give to evidence from disagreeing colleagues (O'Connor and Weatherall 2018), the norm of tempered equality can mitigate it. The practice of giving more weight to evidence from like-minded colleagues than is given to evidence from disagreeing colleagues is a violation of this norm. By requiring the advocates of a consensus view and dissenters to treat each other as equals (provided that they abide by the norm of public standards), the norm of tempered equality can block a social process that produces scientific polarization.

It is important to notice that the obligation to engage scientific dissent belongs to the community as a whole (Longino 2002, 129). Yet, the norm of uptake should not be taken to mean that each individual community member has an obligation to analyze arguments and respond to dissenters. If this were the case, scientists with political and economic agendas could use dissent as a tool to exhaust the resources of scientific communities. Rather, the norm of uptake suggests that a community can discharge its obligations by distributing them so that only some community members evaluate arguments and respond to dissenters (Rolin 2017b, 216). Other community members let these individuals do the work of engaging dissent on behalf of the whole community. Such a division of epistemic labor does not need to be an outcome of a collective decision-making process. It can take place informally, with some community members voluntarily responding to criticism and others supporting and endorsing their work.

In sum, I have explained how Longino's account of epistemically well-designed communities would draw the line between normatively appropriate and inappropriate dissent. Whereas the norm of tempered equality of intellectual authority makes room for scientific dissent by requiring scientific communities to pay attention to criticism from a variety of sources, the three other norms set constraints on dissenters. Dissenters need to express their objections in recognized scientific venues, be responsive to criticism of their views, and follow at least some of the standards of evidence and argumentation accepted by the scientific community. In the next section, I discuss concerns that other philosophers of science have about Longino's account.

9.3 Uptake, Public Standards, and Tempered Equality

de Melo-Martín and Intemann (2018) argue that Longino's account of epistemically well-designed scientific communities fails to distinguish between normatively appropriate and inappropriate dissent in a reliable way. The reason for this is that, in some cases, the norms of uptake, public standards, and tempered equality are ambiguous. As these norms are implicit in scientific practices, they can be interpreted in many ways. Consequently, it is possible that dissenters and scientists upholding a consensus view might disagree over whether someone has actually conformed to them. Each party can blame the other one for a failure to meet the three norms. Before proposing my own solution to disagreements over their interpretation, I explain why de Melo-Martín and Intemann are not satisfied with these norms.

Let me begin with the norm of uptake. The norm states that when dissenters have expressed their objection in a recognized scientific venue, the community as whole has an obligation to engage dissent instead of ignoring it (Longino 2002, 129). According to de Melo-Martín and Intemann, it is not an easy task to determine what "engaging" dissent actually amounts to. They argue that engaging dissent should not be taken to mean that scientists capitulate to any criticism "as this would demand that all participants simply agree with each other whenever objections are proposed, which is not warranted in many cases" (2018, 46). Also, they argue that "it cannot be that uptake involves merely the acknowledgment of a challenge, as this would also fail to contribute to scientific progress" (2018, 46). In their view, engaging dissent amounts to evaluating evidence and arguments with the aim of judging the extent to which evidence is relevant and arguments are correct, and responding to dissenters accordingly. While this suggestion is reasonable, it gives rise to further questions. If dissenters and advocates of a consensus view are to address each other, and not talk past each other, it is necessary that they share some standards of evaluation. The crucial question is whether the two parties have reached an overlapping consensus on the norm of public standards. How many standards and which standards should they both accept? As de Melo-Martín and Intemann explain, it is difficult to apply the norm of uptake without first specifying what the norm of public standards means (2018, 48).

They argue also that, even when dissenters and the advocates of a consensus view reach an overlapping consensus on the norm of public standards, they may still disagree over whether someone has "engaged" dissent successfully. Insofar as engaging dissent involves evaluating evidence and arguments, and responding to dissenters accordingly, the process can end in many ways. One possible scenario involves mainstream scientists revising their views in response to criticism and openly expressing this change. Another scenario involves them suspending their judgment and acknowledging that more evidence is necessary to settle the disagreement. Yet another scenario involves them explaining to dissenters why their criticism is irrelevant or mistaken in some other way. This response may elicit yet another round of objections from dissenters demanding uptake and so on. As there are many ways to end the process of "engaging" dissent, dissenters and the advocates of a consensus view can disagree over whether the process has been brought to an end in a satisfying way (2018, 46–47). Similarly, there is no straightforward method to determine when someone has "ignored" criticism or a response to criticism. Does silence in the face of dissent mean that scientists have ignored it? Does it mean that scientists have conceded privately that there is something right in the criticism? Does it mean that scientists have decided to postpone judgment and wait for more evidence to arrive?

Like the norm of uptake, the norm of public standards is open to many interpretations. It requires that both dissenters and the advocates of a consensus view be committed to the standard of empirical adequacy (Longino 1990, 77). Yet, as de Melo-Martín and Intemann argue, empirical adequacy is an ambiguous concept (2018, 49). The supporters of a consensus view and dissenters may diverge on the question of *what kind of evidence* is relevant for the controversy. Some scientists may emphasize the *depth* of empirical adequacy by demanding that scientific theories account accurately for a particular body of evidence (2018, 50). Others may stress the *breadth* of empirical adequacy by requiring that scientific theories apply to a range of domains (2018, 50). Moreover, the supporters of a consensus view and its dissenters may diverge on the question of *how much evidence* is required for accepting a hypothesis. This is because they may have different views of the risks involved in accepting a false hypothesis or rejecting a true one. For example, if dissenters believe that the consequences of accepting a false hypothesis are severe, they are likely to demand a higher degree of evidential warrant than others. If the advocates of a consensus view believe that the consequences of rejecting a true hypothesis are damaging, they are likely to set the bar for acceptance lower than others.

According to de Melo-Martín and Intemann (2018), the norm of tempered equality of intellectual authority is no less ambiguous than the norm of uptake and public standards. The norm demands that mainstream scientists take criticism seriously independently of the social position of the scientist who presents the criticism (Longino 2002, 131). Yet the term "tempered" is meant to suggest that dissenters ought to have a reasonable degree of expertise in a relevant domain in order to be able to participate in scientific controversies in a meaningful way (de Melo-Martín and Intemann 2018, 53). According to a widespread view, a reasonable degree of expertise requires that a person have a PhD in a relevant scientific discipline and publications in peer-reviewed scientific journals (Anderson 2011). While this seems plausible, dissenters and the supporters of a consensus view can disagree over the *degree* of expertise that is required to participate in a scientific controversy. Moreover, they can disagree over the *domain* of expertise that is relevant for the controversy. de Melo-Martín and Intemann warn against constructing expertise too narrowly in terms of disciplinary accomplishments (2018, 54). In their view, a narrow understanding of expertise runs the risk of excluding potentially valuable criticism from the category of normatively appropriate dissent (2018, 55). Since certain scientific areas, such as climate science, require scientists to collaborate across disciplines and specialties, potentially relevant domains of expertise can be found in many disciplines and specialties.

There is yet another ambiguity in the norm of tempered equality. The "equality" aspect of the norm encourages scientists to keep the assessment of evidence and arguments separate from the assessment of the person who presents them. Ideally, scientists focus on the former and refrain from the latter. The "tempered" aspect of the norm recognizes that in some cases, the assessment of evidence and arguments cannot be fully separate from the assessment of the expertise of the person who has put them forward. Given that equality of intellectual authority is tempered, one might ask how much weight is appropriate to give to the assessment of expertise when evaluating evidence and arguments. This question can divide dissenters and supporters of a consensus view.

Erin Nash (2018) argues that the assessment of evidence and arguments should *not* be kept apart from the assessment of the person who has put them forward. This is because our knowledge of the person's expertise, its degree, and its domain functions as higher-order evidence that has some bearing on our assessment of first-order evidence. Higher-order evidence is likely to play a role, especially in a situation of expert disagreement (2018, 334). In such a situation, higher-order evidence concerning a person's expertise is likely to have an impact on whether they are capable of functioning as a credible testifier (2018, 335–336). Nash argues that since higher-order evidence concerning a person's expertise is relevant for assessing her evidence and arguments, it is permissible for scientific communities to draw attention to dissenters' expertise – or lack thereof. Revealing information about dissenters' academic backgrounds is not an illegitimate attack on their person. Instead, such information is valuable higher-order evidence (2018, 340).

In sum, I have reviewed arguments suggesting that the norm of uptake, public standards, and tempered equality can be interpreted in many ways. Insofar as these norms are ambiguous, there is no guarantee that dissenters will agree with the supporters of a consensus view when it comes to deciding whether someone has fulfilled her obligations. de Melo-Martín and Intemann take this to mean that Longino's account of epistemically well-designed community is not a practically useful way in which to distinguish normatively appropriate from inappropriate dissent (2018, 58).

While I believe that Longino's four norms are often capable of drawing the line between appropriate and inappropriate dissent, I grant that, in some cases, there is a need for more guidance. In the next section, I introduce the norm of epistemic responsibility and explain how it enables dissenters and the advocates of a consensus view to avoid a stalemate. The norm of epistemic responsibility is meant to supplement Longino's four norms, not replace them. Even when there is a disagreement over the interpretation of the norms of uptake, public standards, and tempered equality, the norm of epistemic responsibility provides scientists with a moral reason to respond to the other party.

9.4 What is Epistemic Responsibility?

While some philosophers understand epistemic responsibility as a virtue that a person can have (Code 1984), I understand it as a property that the act of making a knowledge claim can have. I introduce the norm of epistemic responsibility: When a person makes a knowledge claim, she ought to do so in an epistemically responsible way. A person violates the norm of epistemic responsibility when she makes a knowledge claim in an epistemically irresponsible way. In this section, I explain the norm of epistemic responsibility and its epistemic justification. This differs from the rule of assertion (introduced in Section 9.2) in an important way. While the latter is meant to be a *constitutive* rule of assertion, that is, a rule that *necessarily* governs every act of assertion (Williamson 1996, 489–490), the former is *not* meant to be such a rule. The norm of epistemic responsibility guides acts *contingently*, when inquires pursue epistemic goals, and the norm promotes the achievement of those goals.

As I understand it, epistemic responsibility is a *relational* property holding between the act of making a knowledge claim and an audience. A person is not just responsible for her knowledge claim but responsible to someone. According to one account of epistemic responsibility, a person makes a knowledge claim that p in an epistemically responsible way when she provides (or takes steps toward providing) evidence in support of p or commits herself to defending p (Williams 2001, 23–24). What counts as an appropriate kind and amount of evidence depends on what the audience accepts without further inquiries or challenges, at least for the moment. To be epistemically responsible, the person does not need to cite evidence in support of all her claims. She can put forward a knowledge claim with a commitment to defend it. Such a commitment means that she accepts an obligation to defend the claim whenever it is challenged with counter-evidence or some other kind of argument. Suspending or withdrawing a knowledge claim is an epistemically responsible thing to do when the person does not have sufficient evidence for the claim and is not capable or willing to defend it by other means.

Given this account of epistemically responsible knowledge claims, epistemic responsibility is not merely a relational but, more significantly, a *contextual* property of the act of making a knowledge claim. A contextual account of epistemic responsibility aims to do justice to the contextual nature of evidence as it is understood, especially in philosophy of science. Evidence is contextual in two ways. First, in the sense that it depends on a context of background beliefs or assumptions. A series of observations or data are rarely evidence in their own right. They become evidence for a scientific knowledge claim when they are made public and placed in a context of background beliefs or assumptions that explain how the observations or the data are connected to the phenomenon that is the object of inquiry (Longino 1990, 44). Background beliefs or assumptions are necessary to establish that the phenomenon under study is among the causal processes by which the observations or the data are generated in the particular research setting (Boyd 2018, 407). Sometimes, background beliefs or assumptions are needed to decide which alternative hypotheses – hypotheses that could also account for the observations or the data – are to be considered and how they are to be eliminated in order to have indirect support for the hypothesis (Reiss 2015, 357–358).

Beyond depending on a context of background beliefs or assumptions, evidence is contextual in the sense that it depends on the context of a scientific community. This is because the context of background beliefs or assumptions that is necessary to establish the idea that observations or data are relevant to a hypothesis – and, hence, can function as evidence in favor of or against it – may vary from one scientific community to another. For example, some scientific communities subscribe to what Julian Reiss (2015) calls the "experimental" paradigm of evidence, whereas some others subscribe to the "pragmatist" paradigm. The experimental paradigm holds that a well-designed and well-executed randomized controlled trial is the "gold standard" of evidence, and all other methods are assessed in terms of how closely they resemble that "gold standard" (Reiss 2015, 341). Yet many scientific communities, especially in the social sciences and humanities, settle for the pragmatist paradigm which accommodates diverse types of evidence, such as ethnographic observations, interview transcriptions, pictures, published texts, and artifacts. In accordance with the pragmatist paradigm, evidence may include evidence in favor or against the hypothesis as well as evidence in favor or against relevant alternative hypotheses (Reiss 2015, 360). In both cases, evidence is contextual in the sense that it depends on "background knowledge about how the world works" (Reiss 2015, 360).

The norm of epistemic responsibility aims to do justice to the contextual nature of evidence by requiring epistemically responsible knowledge claims to satisfy the standards of evidence and argumentation recognized by the scientific community that is the main audience. For example, the authors of a scientific paper have followed the norm when they have met the standards of evidence and argumentation endorsed by the editors and the reviewers of a scientific journal. They have also acted in accordance with the norm when they have defended their arguments successfully in the scientific debates following the publication of their paper.

The contextual nature of evidence helps explain why knowledge, as it is often understood in epistemology, is too strong a requirement for epistemic responsibility. If epistemic responsibility required knowledge (and knowing that p entails that p is true), then a speaker could claim that p in an epistemically responsible way only when p is true. However, the requirement that p is true is too strong for an account of epistemic responsibility that is meant to accommodate a fallibilistic understanding of scientific knowledge. By fallibilism, I mean the view that scientific knowledge claims are rarely justified in a conclusive way, and hence, it is possible to doubt their truth. In accordance with fallibilism, to make a knowledge claim is to put forward a hypothesis rather than to make an assertion. To make room for fallibilism, I maintain that it is not necessary for the speaker to know that p in order to claim that p in an epistemically responsible way.

That epistemic responsibility does not require knowledge, as it is often understood in epistemology, is also easier to understand if one keeps in mind the social function that the norm of epistemic responsibility is meant to serve. While the knowledge rule of assertion (one must assert that p only if one knows that p) is designed for the purpose of transmitting knowledge from the speaker to the listener (Williamson 1996, 520), the norm of epistemic responsibility has a different social function: To ensure that both the speaker and the listener have mutual epistemic obligations when they are participating in a joint knowledge-seeking practice (Rolin 2017a).

The epistemic justification for the norm of epistemic responsibility is of the instrumentalist type. Like Longino's four norms, the norm of epistemic responsibility serves epistemic goals by facilitating transformative criticism, which helps scientists eliminate false and avoid dogmatic beliefs. The norm of epistemic responsibility promotes the achievement of epistemic goals in tandem with Longino's four norms. Yet it goes beyond these other norms in that it is also a moral norm (as I will argue in Section 9.5). The moral dimension of the norm of epistemic responsibility is key to understanding how it can help scientists solve disagreements over the interpretation of the other epistemic norms.

Let me explain how the norm of epistemic responsibility works in tandem with Longino's four norms. Two of the four (uptake and tempered equality) follow from the norm of epistemic responsibility, while the two other (venues and public standards) are necessary to make the norm of epistemic responsibility feasible for individual scientists. The norm of uptake follows from the norm of epistemic responsibility because this demands that a challenge that is appropriate by the standards of the scientific community receives a response. The norm of tempered equality also follows from the norm of epistemic responsibility because it demands that an appropriate challenge be taken seriously, independently of the social position of the person who presents it. Things are different for the norm of venues and public standards. For individual scientists to be able to fulfill the norm of epistemic responsibility, it is necessary that scientific communities provide venues for scientific debates. Similarly, to be able to fulfill the norm of epistemic responsibility, both parties to a controversy must have access to the standards of evidence and argumentation which constrain what can count as an epistemically responsible knowledge claim and a challenge to the claim. By implementing the norm of venues and public standards, scientific communities ensure that the norm of epistemic responsibility is feasible for individual community members.

An instrumentalist epistemic justification for the norm of epistemic responsibility can acknowledge that the norm may not promote epistemic goals when it is applied outside of the context of epistemically well-designed scientific communities. For example, when a speaker addresses a listener who subscribes to standards that are not truth-conducive, it is unlikely that the norm of epistemic responsibility will lead the speaker or the listener toward true claims. Insofar as the norm of epistemic responsibility leads scientists toward true claims and helps them avoid false ones, this is because the norm is applied in the context of epistemically well-designed scientific communities. In such a context, all community members have an obligation to be epistemically responsible vis-à-vis other community members, and they share standards of evidence and argumentation which have been tested in the actual practice of science. The epistemic success of science is not due to the norm of epistemic responsibility alone; it is also partly due to the social organization of scientific communities, which determines to whom scientists have an obligation to be epistemically responsible and to which standards.

In order to understand what it takes for a scientific community, and not just for individuals, to be epistemically responsible, it is necessary to introduce the idea of the distribution of epistemic obligations. For a scientific community to hold a view in an epistemically responsible way, it is necessary that at least one recognized member of the community provides (or takes steps toward providing) evidence in support of the view (or commits herself to defending the view). It is not necessary that each community member provides (or takes steps toward providing) evidence in support of the view (or commits herself to defending p). A scientific community can discharge its epistemic obligations by distributing them so that some community members perform the obligations on the behalf of the community.

How does the norm of epistemic responsibility help dissenters and the advocates of a consensus view avoid a stalemate due to their disagreement over the interpretation of the other epistemic norms (e.g., the norm of uptake, public standards, and tempered equality)? The norm of epistemic responsibility requires dissenters to tailor their arguments to meet at least some of the epistemic standards tested and accepted by the scientific community. The norm also requires at least some of the supporters of a consensus view to reply to dissenters by tailoring their counter-arguments so that they communicate with dissenters. Tailoring may involve explaining and defending a background assumption or an epistemic value that is widely accepted in the community. It may also involve explaining why a body of evidence is relevant to the consensus view or why there is enough evidence to support this view. The norm of epistemic responsibility advises each party to extend their arguments so that they come closer to meeting the other party's standards of evidence, be they experimental or pragmatist. However, the norm of epistemic responsibility cannot guarantee that scientific controversies are never blocked by insurmountable obstacles. For example, deep disagreement over any of the norms of uptake, public standards, and tempered equality may lead to a deadlock.

In this section, I have introduced the norm of epistemic responsibility to supplement Longino's account of an epistemically well-designed scientific community. An instrumentalist epistemic justification of the norm of epistemic responsibility is not undermined by the objection that conforming to the norm of epistemic responsibility doesn't always help a person achieve true beliefs and avoid false ones. For an instrumentalist, what matters is not as much the epistemic success of individuals as the epistemic success of communities. The epistemic justification for the norm of epistemic responsibility lies in the claim that when scientists systematically act in epistemically responsible ways toward the other members of their scientific communities, they promote the epistemic goals of the communities, even if not directly, by facilitating transformative criticism (Rolin 2017a).

9.5 The Norm of Epistemic Responsibility as an Epistemic and a Moral Norm

Thus far, I have argued that Longino's four norms help scientists identify normatively appropriate dissent. However, it is possible that dissenters and the advocates of a consensus disagree over the interpretation of the four norms. In this section, I argue that, despite such disagreement, dissenters and the advocates of a consensus should comply with the norm of epistemic responsibility (provided that their disagreement is not deep, that is, a disagreement over the four norms themselves, not just their interpretation). This is because the norm of epistemic responsibility is a *moral* norm, not merely an epistemic one. When scientists understand the norm of epistemic responsibility as a moral norm, they conform to it because they believe that they thereby contribute to the well-being of other human beings.

In order to see why the norm of epistemic responsibility is both a moral and an epistemic norm, we need to consider two questions: One, what is a *justification* for the norm, and two, what is an appropriate *sanction* for violating the norm? It is important to notice that the term "epistemic" in the norm of epistemic responsibility refers to the *content* of the norm. The content of the norm is epistemic because the norm tells us how we should act when we *make a knowledge claim*. That the content of the norm is epistemic does not yet make the norm itself exclusively epistemic (Simion 2018). Nor does it exclude the possibility that the norm is moral.

In Section 9.4, I have argued that there is an instrumentalist epistemic justification for the norm of epistemic responsibility. While this may not yet be a sufficient reason to believe that the norm of epistemic responsibility is an epistemic norm, there is a further reason to believe that it is epistemic. As Antti Kauppinen (2018) argues, a norm is epistemic when a violation of it calls for an *epistemic* sanction. I argue that the norm of epistemic responsibility is epistemic because it is likely to elicit an epistemic sanction. For example, when a person violates a norm by making a knowledge claim in an epistemically irresponsible way, the audience may deny her credibility. They may also advise others not to rely on her, especially in the domain in which she has acted in an epistemically irresponsible way (see also Anderson 2011, 146).

Similarly, I argue that the norm of epistemic responsibility is a *moral* norm not only because it has a moral justification but also because it calls for a moral sanction. When acting in an epistemically responsible way, a person contributes to the well-being of other human beings by showing respect for them, especially in their capacity as knowers. This provides moral justification for the norm of epistemic responsibility. By "respect," I mean the kind of respect that all human beings are owed morally merely because they are human beings, regardless of their social position or individual achievement. As Miranda Fricker argues, our capacity to give reasons, to understand reasons, and to respond to reasons is essential to human value (2007, 44). Thus, if not all human beings, at least all well-functioning adult human beings are entitled qua human beings to be taken seriously as an epistemic audience (Rolin 2017a).

Moreover, the norm of epistemic responsibility is a moral norm because it is appropriate to respond to a violation of the norm with a moral sanction. A moral sanction is typically moral blame, which the audience can express in the form of disapproval or resentment (Kauppinen 2018, 5). For example, when a person advances a knowledge claim in an epistemically irresponsible way, she may be perceived as someone whose intention is to deceive or mislead her audience. While lying is objectionable from an epistemic point of view, it is also morally wrong. Hence, it is appropriate to respond to such an action with moral condemnation. Similarly, when a person who has made a knowledge claim refuses to engage appropriate criticism, she may be perceived as behaving in an arrogant and disrespectful way toward the critique. While such behavior is regrettable from an epistemic point of view, it is also morally blameworthy.

The upshot is that, when there is disagreement over the interpretation of the norms of uptake, public standards, and tempered equality, dissenters as well as the advocates of a consensus view have a moral reason to be epistemically responsible toward the other party. What is at stake in cases of scientific dissent is not merely the well-being of the two parties of the scientific controversy but also the well-being of the third parties: People who do not participate in the controversy but have an interest in its outcome. The third parties include members of the public and policymakers who rely on scientific knowledge for their policy decisions. By being epistemically responsible vis-à-vis other scientists, scientists also fulfil their moral obligation to meet the informational needs of the third parties.

9.6 Conclusion

According to a widespread view, scientific communities have an obligation to engage scientific dissent only when it is normatively appropriate from an epistemic point of view. Recently, this view was challenged by de Melo-Martín and Intemann (2018), who argue that the norms of epistemically well-designed scientific communities are ambiguous. While such norms rule out deep disagreement – disagreement about the norms themselves – they are vulnerable to disagreement about the interpretation of norms. In response to this concern, I have argued that scientific communities have a moral reason to be epistemically responsible toward dissenters, even when there is disagreement over the interpretation of the norms of uptake, public standards, and tempered equality. When the norm of epistemic responsibility functions as a moral norm, it goes beyond the norms of uptake, public standards, and tempered equality by providing scientific communities with a moral reason to respond to dissenters. The norm of epistemic responsibility is a moral norm, not merely an epistemic one, because a violation of the norm calls for a moral sanction (moral blame) in addition to an epistemic one (reduced credibility). The norm of epistemic responsibility can also be given a moral justification. Its moral justification lies in the view that human value in itself requires us to take others seriously as an epistemic audience (Rolin 2017a, 479).

Notes

1 Longino's account of an epistemically well-designed community involves norms that scientists can follow, not norms for an idealized epistemic community. In this respect, it differs from Philip Kitcher's (2011) "well-ordered science," which is meant to be an ideal that cannot be implemented in scientific communities. Kitcher believes that scientists can aim to move toward the ideal of "well-ordered science," even though the ideal cannot be fully realized (2011, 125).

2 I do not claim that epistemic rationality is nothing but a species of instrumental rationality. I maintain, rather, that instrumental epistemic rationality supplements non-instrumental accounts of epistemic rationality. According to a *non-instrumental* account, a person can have epistemic reasons for believing something such that the normative force of her epistemic reasons is categorical and not dependent on her having epistemic goals (Kelly 2003, 621).

References

Anderson, E. (2011), "Democracy, Public Policy, and Lay Assessment of Scientific Testimony," *Episteme* 8 (2): 144–164.

Biddle, J. and A. Leuschner. (2015), "Climate Skepticism and the Manufacture of Doubt: Can Dissent in Science Be Epistemically Detrimental?" *European Journal for Philosophy of Science* 5 (3): 261–278.

Bird, A. (2010), "Social Knowing: The Social Sense of 'Scientific Knowledge'," *Philosophical Perspectives* 24 (1): 23–56.

Boyd, N. M. (2018), "Evidence Enriched," *Philosophy of Science* 85: 403–421.

Carter, J. A. (2016), "Group Peer Disagreement," *Ratio* 29 (1): 11–28.

Code, L. (1984), "Toward a 'Responsibilist' Epistemology," *Philosophy and Phenomenological Research* 45 (1): 29–50.

Fricker, M. (2007), *Epistemic Injustice: Power & the Ethics of Knowing*, Oxford and New York: Oxford University Press.

Giere, R. (1989), "Scientific Rationality as Instrumental Rationality," *Studies in History and Philosophy of Science* 20 (3): 377–384.

Gilbert, M. (2000), *Sociality and Responsibility: New Essays on Plural Subject Theory*, Lanham MD: Rowman & Littlefield Publishers.

Intemann, K. and I. de Melo-Martín. (2014), "Are There Limits to Scientists' Obligations to Seek and Engage Dissenters?" *Synthese* 191: 2751–2765.

Kauppinen, A. (2018), "Epistemic Norms and Epistemic Accountability," *Philosophers' Imprint* 18 (8): 1–16.

Kelly, T. (2003), "Epistemic Rationality as Instrumental Rationality: A Critique," *Philosophy and Phenomenological Research* 66 (3): 612–640.

Kitcher, P. (1993), *The Advancement of Science: Science without Legend, Objectivity without Illusions*, New York and Oxford: Oxford University Press.

Kitcher, P. (2011), *Science in a Democratic Society*, Amherst, NY: Prometheus Books.

Kuhn, T. (1996), *The Structure of Scientific Revolutions*, 3rd ed., Chicago, IL: The University of Chicago Press.

Leuschner, A. (2018), "Is It Appropriate to "Target" Inappropriate Dissent? On the Normative Consequences of Climate Skepticism," *Synthese* 195: 1255–1271.

List, C. (2005), "Group Knowledge and Group Rationality: A Judgment Aggregation Perspective," *Episteme* 2 (1): 25–38.

Longino, H. (1990), *Science as Social Knowledge*, Princeton, NJ: Princeton University Press.

Longino, H. (2002), *The Fate of Knowledge*, Princeton, NJ: Princeton University Press.

de Melo-Martín, I. and K. Intemann. (2013), "Scientific Dissent and Public Policy: Is Targeting Dissent a Reasonable Way to Protect Sound Policy Decisions," *EMBO Reports* 14 (3): 231–235.

de Melo-Martín, I. and K. Intemann. (2014), "Who's Afraid of Dissent?: Addressing Concerns about Undermining Scientific Consensus in Public Policy Developments," *Perspectives on Science* 22 (4): 593–615.

de Melo-Martín, I. and K. Intemann. (2018), *The Fight against Doubt: How to Bridge the Gap Between Scientists and the Public*, New York: Oxford University Press.

Michaels, D. (2008), *Doubt Is Their Product: How Industry's Assault on Science Threatens Your Health*, Oxford and New York: Oxford University Press.

Miller, B. (2015), "Why (Some) Knowledge Is the Property of a Community and Possibly None of Its Members," *The Philosophical Quarterly* 65 (260): 417–441.

Miller, B. (2019), "The Social Epistemology of Consensus and Dissent," in *The Routledge Handbook of Social Epistemology*, edited by M. Fricker, P. J. Graham, D. Henderson, and N. J. L. L. Pedersen, New York and London: Routledge, 230–239.

Nash, E. (2018), "In Defense of 'Targeting' Some Dissent about Science," *Perspectives on Science* 26 (3): 325–359.

Niiniluoto, I. (1993), "The Aim and Structure of Applied Research," *Erkenntnis* 38: 1–21.
O'Connor, C. and J. O. Weatherall. (2018), "Scientific Polarization," *European Journal for Philosophy of Science* 8 (3): 855–875.
Oreskes, N. and E. Conway. (2010), *Merchants of Doubt*, New York: Bloomsbury Press.
Reiss, J. (2015), "A Pragmatist Theory of Evidence," *Philosophy of Science* 82 (3): 341–362.
de Ridder, J. (2014), "Epistemic Dependence and Collective Scientific Knowledge," *Synthese* 191 (1): 37–53.
Rolin, K. (2008), "Science as Collective Knowledge," *Cognitive Systems Research* 9 (1–2): 115–124.
Rolin, K. (2010), "Group Justification in Science," *Episteme* 7 (3): 215–231.
Rolin, K. (2017a), "Scientific Community: A Moral Dimension," *Social Epistemology* 31 (5): 468–483.
Rolin, K. (2017b), "Scientific Dissent and a Fair Distribution of Epistemic Responsibility," *Public Affairs Quarterly* 31 (3): 209–230.
Schmitt, F. F. (1994), "The Justification of Group Beliefs," in *Socializing Epistemology: The Social Dimensions of Knowledge*, edited by F. F. Schmitt, Lanham MD: Rowman & Littlefield Publishers, 257–287.
Simion, M. (2018), "No Epistemic Norm for Action," *American Philosophical Quarterly* 55 (3): 231–238.
Skipper, M. and A. Steglich-Petersen. (2019), "Group Disagreement: A Belief Aggregation Perspective," *Synthese* 196: 4033–4058.
Solomon, M. (2001), *Social Empiricism*, Cambridge, MA: MIT Press.
Williams, M. (2001), *Problems of Knowledge: A Critical Introduction to Epistemology*, Oxford and New York: Oxford University Press.
Williamson, T. (1996), "Knowing and Asserting," *The Philosophical Review* 105 (4): 489–523.
Wray, K. B. (2007), "Who Has Scientific Knowledge?" *Social Epistemology* 21 (3): 335–345.
Wray, K. B. (2011), *Kuhn's Evolutionary Social Epistemology*, Cambridge: Cambridge University Press.

10 Disagreement in a Group

Aggregation, Respect for Evidence, and Synergy

Anna-Maria Asunta Eder

10.1 Introduction

We often have to decide what to do. We do so based on our credences or beliefs. Decisions are often hard to make when we act as individual agents; however, they can be even harder when we are supposed to act as members of a group, even if we agree on the values attached to the possible outcomes. Consider, for instance, decisions of members of a scientific advisory board or research group, or of friends who are deciding which hiking path to take. Decisions in groups are often harder to make because members of a group doxastically disagree with each other: they have different doxastic attitudes, for instance, different credences or beliefs. And when they disagree, they are supposed to find an epistemic compromise.

In this paper, I focus on disagreement among members of a group who have different rational credences, where such credences are represented probabilistically and the rationality involved is epistemic rationality.[1] My main aim is to answer the following question:

> ***Main Question*** How do members of a group reach a rational epistemic compromise on a proposition when they have different (rational) credences in the proposition?

A standard method of finding such an epistemic compromise is based on *Standard Bayesianism*. According to the method, the only factors among the agents' epistemic states that matter for finding the compromise are the group members' credences. What I refer to as the "*Standard Method of Aggregation*", *or* "*Weighted Straight Averaging*", proposes to settle on the weighted average of the group members' credences as the epistemic compromise.[2] The respective weights represent "the level of relative competence" of group members within the group, where the level is relative to the competence of the other members (Brössel and Eder 2014:2362). The *Standard Method of Aggregation* faces several challenges, of which I focus on two. They are both due to the fact that the method takes only the (rational) credences of the members of a group into account and neglects other factors pertaining to agents' (rational) epistemic states.

I take the *Standard Method of Aggregation* as a starting point, criticize it, and propose to replace it by what I refer to as the "*Fine-Grained Method of Aggregation*", which is introduced in Brössel and Eder (2014) and further developed here.[3] According to this method, the members' (rational) credences are not the only factors concerning the group agents' rational epistemic states that matter for finding an epistemic compromise. The method is based on a non-standard framework of representing rational epistemic states that is more fine-grained than *Standard Bayesianism*. I refer to this framework as "Dyadic Bayesianism".[4] It distinguishes between an agent's rational reasoning commitments and the agent's total evidence. Rational reasoning commitments reflect how the agent rationally judges the evidential support provided by some evidence and how the agent rationally reasons on the basis of the evidence. Furthermore, like Levi's (1974/2016, 1980, and 2010) confirmational commitments, they are like rules from the evidence to the doxastic state. The total evidence of the agent and the agent's rational reasoning commitments then determine the agent's rational credences. On the basis of this framework, the method of aggregation that I defend, the *Fine-Grained Method of Aggregation*, suggests that disagreeing members of a group aggregate their total evidence and their reasoning commitments, instead of their credences alone.[5]

In Section 10.2, I introduce some assumptions that clarify the focus of the paper: I present different kinds of doxastic disagreements and specify on which kind of disagreement I concentrate. In Section 10.3, I make some idealizing assumptions and introduce the *Standard Method of Aggregation*, which builds on *Standard Bayesianism*. I end the section by presenting two challenges to the *Standard Method of Aggregation*: one concerning the fact that the method does not respect the evidential states of agents, and the other that the method cannot account for synergetic effects. In Section 10.4, I propose *Dyadic Bayesianism* as an alternative to *Standard Bayesianism*. I compare it with Levi's (1974/2016, 1980, and 2010) framework for representing epistemic states, to which it can be traced, yet from which it slightly differs. The comparison will help provide a better understanding of *Dyadic Bayesianism*. Building on *Dyadic Bayesianism*, I propose the *Fine-Grained Method of Aggregation* as a means of providing an answer to the *Main Question*, and I discuss the challenges to the *Standard Method of Aggregation* in relation to the *Fine-Grained Method of Aggregation*. Finally, I summarize my results in Section 10.5.

10.2 Kinds of Doxastic Disagreement and Social Settings

In the following section, I present different kinds of doxastic disagreement and their social settings, albeit without aspiring to present a complete list of either. The kinds of disagreement and the settings that I introduce will suffice to clarify the focus of the present paper.

10.2.1 Shared vs. Different Total Evidence

Agents might disagree when they do not share the same total evidence but also when they do. The following example by Feldman describes a case in which agents don't share the same total evidence:

> ***Criminal Case Example*** "Consider [...] the example involving the two suspects in a criminal case, Lefty and Righty. Suppose now that there are two detectives investigating the case, one who has the evidence about Lefty and one who has the evidence incriminating Righty. They each justifiably believe in their man's guilt. And then each finds out that the other detective has evidence incriminating the other suspect".
>
> (Feldman 2007:208)

Elga presents an example that shows a case in which the agents share the same total evidence:

> ***Death-Penalty Example*** "Suppose that you and your friend independently evaluate the same factual claim—for example, the claim that the death penalty significantly deterred crime in Texas in the 1980s. Each of you has access to the same crime statistics, sociological reports, and so on, and has no other relevant evidence. Furthermore, you count your friend as an **epistemic peer**—as being as good as you at evaluating such claims.
>
> You perform your evaluation, and come to a conclusion about the claim. But then you find out that your friend has come to the opposite conclusion".
>
> (Elga 2007:484)

Recent literature on disagreement has focused on cases where disagreeing agents share the same total evidence (before facing disagreement).[6,7] However, in social epistemology, we also need answers to the questions of whether and how to revise credences or how to find an epistemic compromise for both kinds of cases: when agents who face disagreement share the same total evidence (before they face disagreement), and when agents who face disagreement do not share the same total evidence (before they face disagreement). In this paper, I propose a method that is apt for finding an epistemic compromise when disagreeing agents share the same total evidence. In addition, given certain circumstances, the method is also apt when disagreeing agents do not share the total evidence.

10.2.2 Coarse-Grained vs. Fine-Grained Disagreements

Agents doxastically disagree with each other with respect to a proposition just in case they have different doxastic attitudes toward the proposition. It is straightforward to distinguish between coarse-grained and fine-grained disagreement.[8] Imagine, for example, the above *Criminal Case* to be such that one detective believes that Lefty is guilty, while the other disbelieves this or suspends judgment on it. I refer to such cases of disagreement as "cases of coarse-grained disagreement" because they concern coarse-grained doxastic attitudes such as belief, disbelief, and suspension of judgment. Now imagine the *Criminal Case* to be such that one of the agents has a specific credence in the proposition that Lefty is guilty and the other agent has a higher or lower credence in it. I refer to such cases of disagreement as "cases of fine-grained disagreement". They concern credences which are fine-grained doxastic attitudes. Note that there are cases where there is no coarse-grained disagreement, but there is fine-grained disagreement: for instance, cases where both agents believe a proposition but to different degrees. In this paper, I focus exclusively on *fine-grained* disagreement, and will understand or represent credences in probabilistic terms.

10.2.3 Revealed vs. Unrevealed Disagreement

Many agents disagree with each other without being aware of it. And when they are aware of it, they might still be unaware whether they share the same total evidence. Or they might be aware that they disagree with each other and that they share the same total evidence. More complicated are cases in which the agents are aware that they disagree and that they do not share the same total evidence. In some of these cases, they know what different pieces of evidence they have; in many cases, however, they do not know the extent to which their evidence differs. And even when they are aware of the difference in their total evidence, they might not be aware of how the evidence is judged. And sometimes they are aware of all those factors and are still in disagreement. I refer to the latter kind of disagreement as "revealed disagreement". In this paper, I focus exclusively on such disagreement.

10.2.4 Social Settings

In the literature, one can find different social settings in which agents face disagreement, and these might call for different methods for dealing with the disagreement. Following Wagner (2010:336–337) and Brössel and Eder (2014:2361–2362), I distinguish three kinds of social settings.[9] The first two concern agents as individuals, and the third concerns agents as members of a group.

First, agents as individuals might disagree with other agents.[10] In such a setting, the individual agents are all involved in the disagreement: think, for example, of a dispute which you might have with a friend. Second, agents as individuals might come into contact with disagreement among other agents. In this kind of setting, an agent who is not involved in the disagreement experiences other agents who disagree with each other: think of a case where you have to consult experts who disagree, and who might or might not be aware of each other. In both kinds of settings, we usually focus on the doxastic attitude that is rational for an individual agent to hold after becoming aware of the disagreement. Now consider the third kind of setting: agents as members of a group might face disagreement and seek to find an epistemic compromise. This compromise is not to be mistaken for the doxastic states of the members of the group. The crucial difference between this and the first two kinds of setting is that it does not concern how agents as individuals revise their doxastic state in the face of disagreement. In the latter, third, kind of social setting, the members of the group might stick to their individual credences but, for example, decide to act on the basis of the epistemic compromise as long as they are in that social setting. (I am neutral on whether one has to stick to the compromise when one is no longer a member of the group.) The epistemic compromise is also not to be equated with the group credence. I am neutral on whether there is such a thing as group credences. Even if there is such a thing, the method for finding an epistemic compromise might be different from the method for finding the group credences.[11] The *Criminal Case Example*, as well as the *Death-Penalty Example*, can be extended to provide examples of the mentioned social settings (I leave it to the reader to make the required adjustments to these examples). In this paper, I focus on epistemic compromises.[12]

In Brössel and Eder (2014), we assumed that disagreements in all three social settings should be resolved in the same way. I'm now more cautious, however, and won't take a stance here on whether one should treat all of them in the same way. In this paper, I focus on disagreement among agents as members of a group who are required to find a (rational) epistemic compromise.

To sum up, in this paper, I focus on cases where agents as members of a group are in revealed, fine-grained (doxastic) disagreement with respect to a proposition, and they are required to find an epistemic compromise on that proposition. In some such cases, they share the same total evidence, and in others, they do not.

10.3 The *Standard Method of Aggregation*

Before I proceed with a first candidate answer to the *Main Question*, I introduce idealizing assumptions, most of which are common in probabilistic debates on disagreement. The idea is to take as starting points precise accounts of representations of epistemic states and accounts of aggregation and to investigate what follows under the given idealizing assumptions. The plan is that, based on the results, later investigations will, step-by-step, eliminate some of the idealizing assumptions.

10.3.1 Idealizing Assumptions

10.3.1.1 Stable Truth-Value

Here, I ignore the possibility that an agent has credences in propositions that change their truth-values over time: for example, propositions that change their truth-value as soon as the agent holds a doxastic attitude toward the propositions. To be on the safe side, I also ignore the possibility that an agent has credences in propositions that lose or gain evidential support as a consequence of the agent adopting a doxastic attitude toward the propositions. Including propositions that change their truth value over time, or that lose or gain such evidential support, would require us to deal with problems that are not specific to the problem of finding an epistemic compromise.

10.3.1.2 True Evidence

I assume that the evidence available to agents is true. This allows us to ignore questions concerning whether one can rely on the evidence available to other agents or to oneself. For simplicity, perception and testimony—the primary sources of information about the world—are taken to be perfectly reliable (see, similarly, Eder and Brössel 2019).

10.3.1.3 Ideally Rational Doxastic States

I focus on ideally rational doxastic states. Since I focus on fine-grained disagreement, I focus on credences as doxastic states. In particular, I assume that the group members who are required to form an epistemic compromise are agents whose credences are (ideally) rational in the sense that they do not violate the probability calculus (they are understood as probabilities) and are updated by a conditionalization rule. Furthermore, by saying that a credence is (ideally) rational, I do not want to indicate that one is obliged to adopt it; rather, the credence is merely evaluated as ideal, where the notion of ideal rationality that I have in mind is evaluative.[13]

In probabilistic frameworks, it is common to equate rational epistemic states with rational credences in the following way:[14]

> ***Standard Bayesianism*** "First, a (rational) agent's epistemic state is best represented by her (rational) credences alone. Second,

> (rational) credences obey the probability calculus and they are updated by strict conditionalization".
>
> (Brössel and Eder 2014:2360)[15]

If the members of a group disagree with each other, this is due to them having different rational credences, or credence functions. The task of finding a (rational) epistemic compromise amounts to finding another probability function that all members of the group can accept as an epistemic compromise, even if they do not accept it as their new credence.

Note that I am happy to accept further principles that restrict the scope of when a credence or credence function is rational. For instance, I am willing to adopt principles such as Lewis's (1980) *Principal Principle* and van Fraassen's (1984) *Reflection Principle*, or variants thereof. While such principles restrict the set of permissible or rational credence functions, which are then updated by strict conditionalization when new evidence is acquired, they do not necessarily single out a unique rational credence function. That is, I do not assume an inter-personal uniqueness principle, according to which two agents ought to agree on a credence in response to shared evidence.[16]

10.3.2 Weighted Straight Averaging

Now that I have specified the setting, let us return to the *Main Question*: How do members of a group reach a rational epistemic compromise on a proposition when they have different (rational) credences in the proposition? To answer this question, I first look at approaches in the literature on how to rationally deal with disagreement. In particular, I focus on accounts of whether, and if so how, it is rational for individual agents to revise their credences in the light of disagreement.

According to some approaches in the literature, after becoming aware of the disagreement, it is rational for individual agents not to revise their credences at all (see Frances and Matheson (2019) for an overview of such approaches). Whatever the merits of such approaches for disagreeing agents as individuals, it is certainly not an option to adopt the credence as an epistemic compromise among members of a group.

Other approaches suggest it is not (necessarily) rational for agents to retain their doxastic states, but rather to revise them. There are two prominent approaches of this kind that fit our probabilistic setting here. According to the first, it is rational for the agent to revise her credence as she always does: by conditionalizing on the evidence—in this particular case, by conditionalizing her old credences on the new evidence about the disagreement with other agents.[17] This kind of approach also seems to be wrong-headed for finding an epistemic compromise. If the group members start with different credence functions, then they presumably will also have different credence functions after conditionalizing on the evidence concerning their disagreements. Their *a priori* credence functions would have to satisfy various as-yet-unspecified principles to ensure that the group members agree on some rational epistemic compromise after learning about their disagreement. It is far from clear how members of a group might end up having an epistemic compromise when they use a conditionalization rule. I agree with Easwaran et al. (2016), who acknowledge that the approaches in terms of a conditionalization rule are overly demanding.[18] One could only apply such a rule if it were clear how to react to disagreement before one is aware of the disagreement. So this approach, even if successful, would presuppose that we have found an answer to our *Main Question*.

According to the second kind of approach that fits our probabilistic setting here, the agents' credences are aggregated via rules that combine the individual credence functions of the disagreeing agents to obtain a single probability function. According to the standard interpretation of these rules in the context of disagreement, the latter function should be adopted as the new credence function of the disagreeing agents. The most prominent and most often used aggregation rule will take center stage in the following: the *Standard Method of Aggregation*, or *Weighted Straight Averaging*.[19] According to it, the result of the aggregation should be the weighted average of the initial individual credences.[20] The respective weights of the agents reflect their level of relative (epistemic) competence. It is assumed that agents have a level of absolute competence which is independent of the level of competence of other agents. The level of relative competence puts the level of absolute competence of agents in relation to each other. It does so in such a way that the sum of the levels of relative competence is one. (I will say more about the weights after presenting the aggregation rule.)

In detail, *Weighted Straight Averaging* says the following:

> ***Weighted Straight Averaging*** Consider agents $s_1, \ldots, s_n$, with credence functions $\mathrm{Pr}_{Cr_{s_1}}, \ldots, \mathrm{Pr}_{Cr_{s_n}}$: the epistemic compromise $EC_{SA}\left[\mathrm{Pr}_{Cr_{s_1}}, \ldots, \mathrm{Pr}_{Cr_{s_n}}\right]$ is determined as follows:
> for all propositions p
>
> $$EC_{SA}\left[\underset{Cr_{s_1}}{\mathrm{Pr}}, \ldots, \underset{Cr_{s_n}}{\mathrm{Pr}}\right](p) = \sum_{i=1}^{n}\left[w_i \times \underset{Cr_{s_i}}{\mathrm{Pr}}(p)\right]$$
>
> where each agent's epistemic weight is $w_i \in \mathbb{R}^+$, and for the sum of their weights, it holds that $\sum_{i=1}^{n} w_i = 1$ (see, very similarly, Brössel and Eder 2014:2367).[21]

Instead of interpreting the result of the aggregation as the new credence of the agents, I propose to understand it as providing the rational epistemic compromise of the group. According to the *Standard Method of Aggregation,* or *Weighted Straight Averaging*, finding the epistemic compromise amounts to more than just averaging the group members' credences: it also takes the weights of the individual agents into account. As mentioned before, these weights are typically taken to reflect the level of relative competence of the agents in comparison to the other group members' competence (see Brössel and Eder 2014). It is common in social epistemology to focus on peer disagreement, where the agents involved in the disagreement all have the same competence and thus the same weight. *Death-Penalty Example* is a case in point. According to this example by Elga, you disagree with a peer, who is a peer in virtue of "being as good as you at evaluating" the relevant claims.[22] It is common to assume that we can distinguish agents' competence in a fine-grained way. I assume that one can assign to each member $s_1, \ldots, s_n$ of a group a precise weight w_i within this group.[23] As mentioned before, this weight reflects the level of *relative* competence of an agent within this group.[24] However, the weight w_i of a group member can be assumed to depend on her level of (unrelativized) competence. Suppose that for each member s_i of a group, one quantifies her level of absolute competence with some number $c_{s_i} \in \mathbb{R}^+$. The weights are then calculated as follows:

$$w_i = \frac{c_{s_i}}{\sum_{i=1}^{n} c_{s_i}}.$$

This would ensure that the weights of all members of the group sum to one (i.e., $\sum_{i=1}^{n} w_i = 1$) and that equally competent group members receive the same weight within the group. Note, furthermore, that our assumption that $\sum_{i=1}^{n} w_i = 1$ excludes cases where for all agents s_i: $c(s_i) = 0$ (see also Brössel and Eder 2014:2375). That said, I won't present a general account of competence that tells us how to measure the unrelativized notion of competence for any situation but I simply assume its existence.

Before I turn to objections to the *Standard Method of Aggregation*, I highlight two important, well-known properties of the method.[25] I will return to them when I discuss the challenges to the *Standard Method of Aggregation* in the subsequent sections.

The first property is characterized by the following:

> ***Irrelevance of Alternatives*** Consider agents $s_1, \ldots, s_n$ with credence functions $\Pr_{Cr_{s_1}}, \ldots, \Pr_{Cr_{s_n}}$. Their epistemic compromise on a proposition p depends only on their individual credences in the proposition p, that is, $EC_{SA}\left[\Pr_{Cr_{s_1}}, \ldots, \Pr_{Cr_{s_n}}\right](p)$ is a function of $\Pr_{Cr_{s_1}}(p), \ldots, \Pr_{Cr_{s_n}}(p)$.[26]

Irrelevance of Alternatives seems attractive because it says that, in finding an epistemic compromise, we do not need to discuss and compromise on any other proposition than the one at hand.

The second well-known property of the *Standard Method of Aggregation* is that the method preserves existing agreement. In particular, if the group members all assign the same credence to a proposition, then the epistemic compromise will settle on the same credence. This is expressed by the following:

> ***Unanimity*** If all agents $s_1, \ldots, s_n$ with credence functions $\mathrm{Pr}_{Crs_1}, \ldots, \mathrm{Pr}_{Crs_n}$ assign the credence r to the proposition p, then their epistemic compromise on p equals r too, that is, $EC_{SA}\left[\mathrm{Pr}_{Crs_1}, \ldots, \mathrm{Pr}_{Crs_n}\right](p) = r$, if $\mathrm{Pr}_{Crs_i}(p) = r$, for all $s_1, \ldots, s_n$.[27]

This feature is initially appealing because it is in line with the purpose of finding an epistemic compromise: if the agents already agree on a proposition, applying the *Standard Method of Aggregation* does not change anything.

10.3.3 First Challenge: No Respect for Evidence

In the following, I present a challenge that can be raised against the *Standard Method of Aggregation*. The challenge is to present an account of aggregation that respects the evidence. The *Standard Method of Aggregation* is based on *Standard Bayesianism*, which only takes the doxastic state, the credences, of an agent into account. Since *Standard Bayesianism* ignores the agent's evidential state, it ignores important factors of the epistemic state of the agent.[28] As a first consequence of this, it is not able to accommodate the relevant difference in competence in acquiring and processing evidence. As a second consequence, it is not able to accommodate disagreements involving different total evidence.

Let me start by discussing the first consequence. Consider the following example, which hints at the challenge:

> ***Disagreeing-Physicists Example*** "[S]uppose, first, theoretical physicist s_1 considers experimental physicist s_2 an expert with respect to gathering evidence, but a fool with respect to the confirmational import of the respective evidence. Accordingly, s_1 would like to assume s_2's evidence, but to ignore s_2's judgement of the confirmational import of the evidence. Or suppose, second, experimental physicist s_3 considers theoretical physicist s_4 a fool with respect to gathering evidence, but an expert with respect to the confirmational import of the given evidence. Accordingly, s_3 would like to ignore what agent s_4 accepts as evidence, but to assume s_4's judgement of the confirmational import of s_3's evidence".
>
> (Brössel and Eder 2014:2372; notation adapted)

This example makes clear that one better not ignore the evidential states of the agents—as *Standard Bayesianism* does. We therefore do not focus on the credences of an agent alone.

As Weatherson emphasizes: "There are two things we assess when evaluating someone's beliefs [...] we evaluate both their collection and processing of evidence" (Weatherson 2008:565). If we dropped our idealizing assumption that the evidence is always true, we would have to admit that some agents are better at acquiring evidence, and others are better at processing it. This should also be mirrored in their weights. Accordingly, an agent can receive different weights, one concerning the agent's evidence and another concerning the agent's processing of the evidence. Discussing group disagreement and epistemic compromise in the light of evidence that may not be true goes beyond the scope of this paper. Here, I neglect the weights with respect to the evidential states since I assume that the agents' evidence is true and that the agents are perfectly reliable in acquiring it (see Sect. 10.3.1.). However, it is a defect of *Standard Bayesianism* that it can't even allow for the difference between the mentioned kinds of weights.[29]

Let's consider the second consequence of ignoring the agent's evidential state. Members of a group might disagree for different reasons. They might disagree because they judge their evidence differently or because they do not share the same total evidence. An agent who is better informed and has acquired more evidence might have a different credence in a proposition than an agent who is less informed and has less evidence. If the members of a group aggregate their credences, the different total evidence should be considered. Even if the members of the group are equally competent and receive the same weights, the difference in their evidence should be taken into consideration. The *Standard Aggregation Method* does not account for the difference in evidence, or, to be more precise, it is not adequate when disagreeing members of a group don't share the same total evidence. According to this method, only the agents' credences in a proposition are aggregated. Recall, the *Standard Method of Aggregation* satisfies *Irrelevance of Alternatives*. According to it, only the credences are aggregated. Due to this, the *Standard Method of Aggregation* and *Irrelevance of Alternatives* are not as attractive as they might initially seem.

10.3.4 Second Challenge: No Synergy

The following challenge is one that has been presented in the context of peer disagreement where agents disagree as individuals; however, it is straightforward to apply it analogously to the *Standard Method of Aggregation* as a method of finding an epistemic compromise. Examples of the following kind motivate the challenge:

> ***Birthday Party Example I*** Suppose two peers, Anma and Alma, remember that Peter promised them a year ago that he would

> come to their birthday party on the weekend. Both know that Peter never breaks a promise, but they do not consider their memory to be infallible. Anma ends up with a credence of .7 that Peter will come to the party. Alma is slightly more confident and assigns credence .9 to the same proposition.[30]

According to epistemologists such as Christensen (2009), Easwaran et al. (2016), and Grundmann (2019), it can sometimes be rational for the disagreeing agents to raise their credence in a proposition even above each of the agents' initial credences;[31] the above example is provided here as a case in support of this position. Roughly put, even though the agents disagree on the exact credence, the fact that they both assign a high credence to the proposition in question makes it rational in the particular situations for them to increase their probability above both their initial credences. This has been considered a synergetic effect. Let me be clear: I do not think that the credences alone determine whether there is a synergetic effect—the circumstances matter. In the example above, there is no doubt about whether Peter breaks promises—both know that he does not. The little doubt that Anma and Alma have concerns the reliability of their memory. However, the evidence that the other peer also assigns a high probability to Peter coming to the party provides further evidence that their memory is not failing, which makes it rational for them to increase a credence even above .9. I think this would also hold if both had a credence of .9 that Peter will come to the party. A synergetic effect can seem rational even when the agents share the same credence in a proposition. Thus, a part of the second challenge is that cases like the one above speak against the *Standard Method of Aggregation* and against methods that satisfy *Unanimity*. In particular, contra *Unanimity*, examples such as *Birthday Party Example I* suggest that even in the light of an agreement between two agents, the agents should sometimes increase their probability in a proposition. Applied to epistemic compromises, this has as a consequence that even if the group members already agree, the epistemic compromise might differ from their initial credences.

Another part of the challenge is that there are also cases in which a synergetic effect seems counter-intuitive. I take the following example to be a case in point:

> ***Birthday Party Example II*** Suppose a few seconds ago, the peers, Anma and Alma, heard Peter promise that he would come to their birthday party at the weekend. Both share the same evidence. They both know that Peter sometimes cannot fulfill his promises and might miss their party. Based on the shared evidence, Anma ends up with a credence of .7 that Peter will come to the party. Alma is slightly more confident and assigns credence .9 to the same proposition.

This example supports that it is not always rational to increase one's probability above both the initial credences even when they are high. Both agents are aware that circumstances might be such that they prevent Peter from attending the party. This time, the doubt does not concern the reliability of Anma's and Alma's memories, for they know for certain that Peter just made the promise and that the other person heard it too. That they both agree that such circumstances are unlikely is, in that case, not a reason to increase the probabilities for them even further. If this is correct, it also means that it cannot be a function of the agents' credences whether or not a synergetic effect is rational. In *Birthday Party Example I* and *Birthday Party Example II*, both agents have high credences in the proposition in question, and in only one example does it seem plausible that both agents should increase their probability above both their initial credences. The challenge is to answer the question of how agents can rationally increase their probability above their initial credences in the face of disagreement, and the answer should not exclusively depend on the agents' credences. In both examples, the distribution of credences is the same, but the examples call for different verdicts. The *Standard Method of Aggregation* exclusively considers the credences of the disagreeing agents, thus *Irrelevance of Alternatives* holds for it. However, in light of both examples, this does not seem appropriate.

10.4 An Alternative Method of Aggregation

The discussion of both challenges indicates that we are in need of an alternative method of aggregation that considers factors additional to the agents' credences. The *Standard Method* cannot meet the challenges. From the discussion of the challenges, it is apparent that we need a more fine-grained representation of epistemic states, which does not exclusively consider the credences of agents. I follow Brössel and Eder (2014), and Eder and Brössel (2019), in suggesting such a representation of epistemic states: *Dyadic Bayesianism*. Since the framework is non-standard in epistemology in general, and in social epistemology in particular, I will spend some time introducing it, and comparing it with Levi's (1974/2016, 1980, and 2010) similar representation of epistemic states to which it traces back. Subsequently, I propose what I refer to as the "*Fine-Grained Method of Aggregation*".

10.4.1 Dyadic Bayesianism

Dyadic Bayesianism represents different factors of agents' epistemic states that are relevant for finding a well-informed epistemic compromise. Let's start with the following example by Elga, which displays such factors:

Weather Forecaster Example "When it comes to the weather, I completely defer to the opinions of my local weather forecaster. [...] In treating my forecaster this way, I defer to her in two respects. First, I defer to her *information*: 'As far as the weather goes,' I think to myself, 'she's got all the information that I have—and more.' Second, I defer to her *judgment*: I defer to the manner in which she forms opinions on the basis of her information".

(Elga 2007:479)

The example shows that the following factors concerning an agent's epistemic state are relevant: the agent's evidence and how the agent reasons on the basis of the evidence. The following framework takes these factors into account:

Dyadic Bayesianism "An agent s's (rational) epistemic state is

1 a dyad/ordered-pair $ESs = \langle Pr_{R_s}, tev_s \rangle$ consisting of (i) *s*'s [rational] reasoning commitments, Pr_{R_s}, and (ii) *s*'s total evidence, tev_s, such that
2 *s*'s [rational] credences are as follows: $Pr_{Cr_s}(p) = Pr_{R_s}(p/tev_s)$, and
3 both Pr_{Cr_s} and Pr_{R_s} obey the probability calculus"

(Brössel and Eder 2019:69)

An agent's (rational) epistemic state is represented by, first, the agent's rational *reasoning commitments* and, second, the agent's *total evidence*. Rational credences are then equated with reasoning commitments conditional on the total evidence. This framework is inspired by, and in many respects similar to, Levi's framework for representing epistemic states: he distinguishes between total evidence and confirmational commitments (see, e.g., Levi 1974/2016, 1980, 2010). Discussing crucial similarities and differences between these accounts will clarify *Dyadic Bayesianism* and what it owes to Levi's account.[32]

10.4.1.1 Reasoning Commitments and Levi's Confirmational Commitments

An agent's (rational) reasoning commitments, as I understand them, are captured by a probability function that reflects the agent's (rational) commitments concerning which (rational) credences to adopt on the basis of bodies of total evidence.[33] That is, they reflect how to reason from the evidence. In some sense, my reasoning commitments can be understood as bearing a close similarity to Williamson's (2000) objective evidential probabilities and Carnap's (1950) logical probabilities. However, reasoning commitments are understood in a more subjective fashion. According to Williamson, objective evidential probabilities measure "something like the intrinsic plausibility of hypotheses prior to investigation" (2000:211). The objective evidential probability of a proposition, or hypothesis, on some evidence, reflects the plausibility of the proposition given the evidence, before the evidence is acquired. For Carnap, logical probabilities represent the logical plausibility of a proposition given the evidence in question. The logical probability of the proposition given the evidence reflects a logical or *a priori* relation between the evidence and the proposition.[34] One can understand the reasoning commitments in a similar way, except that they are subjective evidential probabilities that measure the "intrinsic plausibility of hypotheses prior to investigation" as subjectively judged by the agent. Note that, as with credences or credence functions, I do not assume that there is a unique rational reasoning commitment function. Reasoning commitments also reflect how agents are committed to processing their evidence, that is, what credences to adopt on various evidential bases. In particular, the reasoning commitment concerning a proposition conditional on some total evidence reflects the agent's subjective judgment of the evidential support provided by the evidence for the proposition. The reasoning commitment concerning a proposition conditional on some total evidence is tightly linked to the plausibility of the proposition given the evidence prior to any investigation and prior to acquiring any evidence. (Connoisseurs of Carnap and Levi might notice that my account is in this respect more in line with Carnap than with Levi (cf. Levi 2010:Sect.7). Note that for Levi, judgments of evidential support make sense only when they concern an expansion of the agent's total evidence, that is, the agent's full belief. However, we are not concerned with full belief here.

Reasoning commitments reflect "the judgements of the confirmational import of the evidence, which capture how agents justify their credences" (Brössel and Eder 2014:2373). Reasoning commitments play an important role for agents in justifying their credences. For justifying one's credence in a proposition, one states one's evidence and the reasoning commitments that lead to the credence. And when we criticize someone's credences as unjustified, we can trace them back to either their evidence or their reasoning commitments (or both). Similarly, Carnap (1950) envisioned that we would use logical probabilities to justify credences. Accordingly, one's credence would be justified by stating one's evidence and by referring to the logical probability of the proposition conditional on the available evidence.

Levi characterizes confirmational commitments as rules that do not need to be understood or represented as probabilities:

> "X's state of full belief **K** cannot, in general, determine X's state **B** of credal probability judgements by itself. It needs to be supplemented by what I call a 'confirmational commitment' (Levi 1974, 1979,

> 1980, Chap. 4) which is a rule specifying for each potential state of full belief relevantly accessible to X what X's credal state should be, when X is in that set of full belief".
>
> (Levi 2010:99)

Analogous to my position concerning reasoning commitments, Levi assumes that confirmational commitments determine an agent's credal state. In particular, an agent's credal state is determined by the agent's full beliefs and her confirmational commitments.

It is noteworthy that reasoning commitments, as well as confirmational commitments, can change over time. Sometimes such changes are adequate when agents face disagreement with other agents, and the evidence about the disagreement indicates that one had better change one's reasoning commitments. (See Levi 2010 for changes in confirmation commitments upon facing disagreement, and Brössel and Eder 2014 for such changes in reasoning commitments upon facing disagreement.)

A main difference between reasoning commitments and Levi's confirmational commitments is that confirmational commitments are rules that assign a set of probability functions to each logically closed set of full beliefs. I assume reasoning commitments are a single probability function, a position that Levi rejects (Levi 2010:102).

10.4.1.2 Credences and Levi's Credal States

As mentioned several times, according to *Dyadic Bayesianism*, agents' credences are determined by the agents' reasoning commitments and their total evidence. Similarly, for Levi, agents' credal states are determined by the agents' confirmational commitments and their total evidence. However, for Levi (2010), an agent's credal state is *a set* of conditional probability functions defined for all pairs of propositions $\langle p,q \rangle$ such that p is a proposition and q is a proposition compatible with the agent's total evidence. For me, an agent's credal state is (represented by) a single probability function.

10.4.1.3 A Merit of Dyadic Bayesianism

Following many epistemologists engaged in this debate, I have focused on doxastic disagreement. In Section 10.2.2, I characterized it as a mismatch between the doxastic states of agents toward a proposition. Unfortunately, the literature tends to neglect other kinds of relevant mismatches. Doxastic disagreement is not the only form of mismatch relevant for finding an epistemic compromise. A merit of the current approach, and of *Dyadic Bayesianism* in particular, is that it allows us to distinguish different kinds of mismatches. In addition to doxastic disagreement, agents might have different reasoning commitments;

I refer to such mismatches as "reasoning mismatches". (Recall *Birthday Party Example II*. This example reveals a reasoning mismatch between Anma and Alma. They have the same total evidence, but they process it differently—which is reflected in different reasoning commitments—and, thus, end up having different credences.) Agents might also have different evidence. I refer to such mismatches as "evidential mismatches" (see similarly Brössel and Eder 2014:2373, where we use the term "disagreement" instead of "mismatch"). These two additional notions of mismatch allow us to more thoroughly analyze the potential reasons for doxastic disagreement. Agents are in doxastic disagreement because they are in evidential mismatch or because they are in reasoning mismatch. Note, however, that agents might be in doxastic *agreement* and still be in evidential or reasoning *mismatch*. Consider, for example, cases where we doxastically agree with a colleague with respect to a proposition but have different reasoning commitments that lead to the doxastic agreement.[35] It is not possible to do justice to such a case within *Standard Bayesianism*, and it is a merit of *Dyadic Bayesianism* that it makes it possible to model the mentioned sources of doxastic disagreement as well as the various mismatches that might underlie doxastic agreement.

10.4.2 The Fine-Grained Method of Aggregation

In *Dyadic Bayesianism*, the framework advocated here, an agent's (rational) evidential state and (rational) reasoning commitments together determine the agent's (rational) credences. Thus, as mentioned before, when the members of a group doxastically disagree with each other, this is so because they are either in evidential mismatch or in reasoning mismatch. These mismatches are then the source of the doxastic disagreement. Instead of merely aggregating the credences of the agents in order to find an epistemic compromise, what need to be aggregated are their evidential states and their reasoning commitments. The epistemic compromise concerning a proposition is then the result of both aggregations.

10.4.2.1 Aggregating Evidential States

As a first step to finding an epistemic compromise, group members need to come to a compromise concerning their evidential states. Given the strong idealizing assumption that we introduced in the previous subsection, coming to such an epistemic compromise is straightforward. I assumed that the group members are fully reliable in collecting evidence. Recall that I assume that they only receive true propositions as evidence (see Sect. 10.3.1). As a consequence, the evidential states of all agents are true, and they are logically compatible with each other. Given this assumption, it is rational for the group members to accept each others' pieces of evidence (cf. *Disagreeing-Physicists Example* and *Weather Forecaster Example)*. The aggregated evidential state is the conjunction of the members' evidential states.[36] As a consequence, if the members share the same total evidence, then the aggregated evidential state is just this shared evidence. The members' total evidence is not double-counted since the conjunction of the members' total evidence is logically equivalent to each member's total evidence. A further consequence is that if a group member receives a piece of evidence, then the whole group would accept this piece of evidence.

Method for Aggregating Evidential States Consider agents $s_1, \ldots, s_n$, with epistemic states $ES_1, \ldots, ES_n$ and corresponding evidential states $tev_{s_1}, \ldots, tev_{s_n}$. Then the compromise for the evidential states of the group $EC_{ES}\left[tev_{s_1}, \ldots, tev_{s_n}\right]$ is determined as follows:

$$EC_{ES}\left[tev_{s_1}, \ldots, tev_{s_n}\right] = tev_{s_1} \wedge \ldots \wedge tev_{s_n}$$

The idealizing assumptions that lead to this method for aggregating evidential states are strong. They need to be relaxed, and this would lead us to use a more nuanced method for aggregating evidential states. Konieczny and Pino Pérez (2011) introduce and discuss various merging operators that deal with conflicting bodies of evidence. To my knowledge, probability-based methods for aggregating evidential states have not been discussed in the literature on disagreement.[37] To discuss them, however, is a task for another time.

10.4.2.2 Aggregating Reasoning Commitments

In addition to a method for aggregating evidential states, we need a method for aggregating reasoning commitments. Following Brössel and Eder (2014: 2375), I propose to aggregate reasoning commitments as follows:

Method of Aggregating Reasoning Commitments Consider agents $s_1, \ldots, s_n$, with epistemic states $ES_1, \ldots, ES_n$ and corresponding reasoning commitments $Pr_{R_{s_1}}, \ldots, Pr_{R_{s_n}}$: the epistemic compromise concerning the reasoning commitments $EC_R\left[Pr_{R_{s_1}}, \ldots, Pr_{R_{s_n}}\right]$ for all propositions p is determined as follows

$$EC_R\left[\Pr_{R_{s_1}}, \ldots, \Pr_{R_{s_n}}\right](p) = \sum_{i=1}^{n} w_i \times \Pr_{R_{s_i}}(p)$$

where $w_i \in \mathbb{R}^+$ and $\sum_{i=1}^{n} w_i = 1$.

The weights w_i in this method are best understood as reflecting the level of relative competence of an agent concerning how the agent reasons on the basis of various possible evidential states. As an example of someone who is highly competent in this regard, consider our (theoretical) physicist who can judge the evidential import of various pieces of evidence better than her colleagues. Such a physicist might be assigned a high weight, regardless of whether she collects evidence herself.

According to the method, the reasoning commitments of the group members are aggregated into a single probability function. The result is considered to be the epistemic compromise concerning how to reason on the basis of various potential evidential states.[38]

10.4.2.3 Epistemic Compromise

The two aggregation methods together provide us with an epistemic compromise concerning the epistemic states of the group members. It is determined as follows:

> ***Fine-Grained Method of Aggregation*** Consider agents $s_1, \ldots, s_n$, with epistemic states $\mathrm{ES}_{s_1}, \ldots, \mathrm{ES}_{s_n}$: the epistemic compromise $\mathrm{EC}\left[\mathrm{ES}_{s_1}, \ldots, \mathrm{ES}_{s_n}\right]$ is determined as follows:

$$\mathrm{EC}\left[\mathrm{ES}_{s_1}, \ldots, \mathrm{ES}_{s_n}\right] = \left\langle \mathrm{EC}_{\mathrm{R}}\left[\underset{R_{s_1}}{\mathrm{Pr}}, \ldots, \underset{R_{s_n}}{\mathrm{Pr}}\right], \mathrm{EC}_{\mathrm{ES}}\left[tev_{s_1}, \ldots, tev_{s_n}\right]\right\rangle$$

In what follows, I discuss how the new method for finding an epistemic compromise deals with the mentioned objections.

10.4.3 Respect for Evidence

A challenge that the *Standard Method of Aggregation* does not adequately meet is to respect the evidence of the disagreeing members of a group. It cannot respect it because it focuses only on the (rational) credences of the agents. This is so because it is based on *Standard Bayesianism*, which does not differentiate between evidence, (rational) reasoning commitments, and (rational) credences.

The *Fine-Grained Method of Aggregation* is based on a framework for representing epistemic states that is fine-grained in the sense that it differentiates between evidence, reasoning commitments, and credences; that is, *Dyadic Bayesianism*. Consequently, the method allows us to take the difference between evidence, reasoning commitments, and credences into account. One can aggregate the evidence of the agents who are required to find an epistemic compromise while considering their competence in acquiring evidence. At the same time, one can separately aggregate the reasoning commitments of the agents, taking into account their competence in responding to the evidence. Once one has the evidence and the reasoning commitments aggregated, one also has the epistemic compromise as a result.

As a further consequence, the *Fine-Grained Method of Aggregation* can be employed to find an epistemic compromise even when the disagreeing members of a group do not share the same total evidence. If, as we assumed, the group members' evidence only includes true propositions, they can accumulate their evidence to obtain a larger body of evidence. This method respects the evidence of each group member.

10.4.4 No Synergy

The second challenge is to answer the question of how agents can rationally increase their probability above their initial credences in the face of disagreement, and the answer should not exclusively depend on the agents' credences. The *Standard Method of Aggregation* cannot meet the challenge, because it is built on a framework for representing epistemic states that focuses solely on credences. According to it, the new probability (i.e., the epistemic compromise) is between the initial credences. Contra the *Standard Method of Aggregation*, the answer to the challenge should not depend exclusively on the agent's credences. In Section 10.3.4, I presented two examples of disagreement that involve the same credence distributions: *Birthday Party Example I* and *Birthday Party Example II*. Only in one of them did increasing the probability above the initial credences seem rational for the agents.

Based on the *Fine-Grained Method of Aggregation*, I propose the following to meet the challenge: the differentiating feature between the examples is the evidence. In some situations, if a member of a group learns that the other members have additional pieces of evidence in support of a proposition that the member does not have, the member acquires extra evidence in support of the proposition: evidence of evidence. According to Feldman's slogan, evidence of evidence is evidence. Although the slogan is not always correct,[39] in those cases in which evidence of evidence *is* evidence (for some proposition), it can provide a reason to agree to an epistemic compromise above the initial credences of the group members. This evidence of evidence would provide extra evidence for the proposition in question. The resulting evidential states are aggregated and allow for a synergetic effect.

In contrast, imagine members of a group who disagree concerning a proposition and share the same total evidence. Imagine furthermore that by revealing the doxastic disagreement, the members do not receive any evidence of evidence in support of the proposition. Since the members share the same total evidence and have different credences in the proposition in question, they just learn that the reasoning commitments are different. However, that the members judge the evidential support provided to the proposition in question differently provides no reason for adopting more extreme reasoning commitments that assign an even higher credence to the proposition. There is no reason to change the evidential states. The result of the aggregation of the evidential states is the same as the members' initial total evidence. And according to our *Method for Aggregating*

Reasoning Commitments, the result of the aggregation of the different initial reasoning commitments is between them. Consequently, the epistemic compromise is also between the group members' initial credences.[40] I cannot think of a reason that allows for a synergetic effect in such a case.

In the following, I illustrate the answer to the second challenge by applying it to our two examples: *Birthday Party Example I* and *Birthday Party Example II*.

First, consider *Birthday Party Example I*. For both agents, Anma and Alma, it is each one's memory that is the relevant evidence that supports high credence in the proposition that Peter will attend their joint birthday party at the weekend. In disclosing the disagreement, the agents receive evidence that the other agent also remembers Peter making the promise: this is the relevant evidence of evidence. The fact that they both remember him making the promise is what provides extra evidence for assuming that Peter indeed promised he would come to the party. And since they know that Peter keeps his promises, it is rational to increase the probability of Peter's attendance above both initial credences. Learning that different pieces of evidence, that is, different memories, support the same proposition is why it is rational for both agents to increase the probability above their initial credences. Imagine there were more group members who remembered Peter making the promise: this would provide more evidence for the group in support of Peter's attendance. Since he always keeps his promises, the group would be rational in assigning a very high probability, a probability higher than the group member's initial credences, in the proposition that Peter will attend Anma and Alma's joint birthday party.

Now consider *Birthday Party Example II*. Here, both agents have the same total evidence—a few seconds ago, Peter promised he would come to Anma and Alma's joint birthday party. Anma and Alma do not fully rely on Peter's promise. They know that circumstances might prevent him from attending the party. Their predictions differ only slightly. In disclosing the disagreement, the agents do not receive relevant evidence of evidence in support of the proposition in question. There is no reason to add something to their evidential states that supports the proposition. The aggregation of the shared evidential states results in the same evidential state. That Anma has reasoning commitments that assign a credence of .7 to the proposition that Peter will attend Anma and Alma's joint birthday party at the weekend, and Alma assigns a credence of .9 is not a reason for them to assume reasoning commitments that commit them to an even higher probability. And even if more and more agents had similar reasoning commitments, this would not be a reason to adopt reasoning commitments that make it certain that Peter will come—after all, everyone agrees that Peter does not always keep his promises. The result of the aggregation of the reasoning commitment is between the initial reasoning commitments, and the same holds for the credences (recall there is no change in evidential states). No synergetic effect arises.

10.5 Conclusion

In this paper, I have focused on revealed, fine-grained disagreement among members of a group who are required to find a rational epistemic compromise. A promising way of finding such a compromise is by aggregating the members' epistemic states. *Standard Bayesianism* focuses on the agents' credences and represents the credences as probabilities; and the *Standard Method of Aggregation* aggregates the credences, or probabilities. I discussed challenges to that method: first, it does not respect the evidential state of agents, which, however, is crucial for finding an epistemic compromise. Second, it is not able to account for cases with synergetic effects, where the epistemic compromise is not to be found between the agents' credences. The method that I propose, the *Fine-Grained Method of Aggregation*, is able to meet the challenges adequately.

Acknowledgments

I am grateful to Fernando Broncano-Berrocal, Peter Brössel, Adam Carter, and Thomas Grundmann for extensive and insightful commentaries on previous versions of this paper.

Notes

1 In this paper, I assume that rational credences obey the probability calculus and are updated in response to the evidence by some conditionalization rule. I say more on rational credences in Sect. 10.3.1. Admittedly, many interesting cases of disagreement arise because it is not clear whether the credences involved are rational. However, I have my hands full with cases that involve rational credences and postpone the discussion of cases where it is not clear whether the credences that are involved are rational.

2 For accounts that are in the spirit of *Weighted Straight Averaging*, see, e.g., Christensen (2007), Elga (2007), and Jehle and Fitelson (2009). And for literature that discusses it in the context of finding an epistemic compromise, see Brössel and Eder (2014), Frances and Matheson (2019), and Moss (2011).

3 I must leave it to another occasion to defend aggregation methods *per se* and also to discuss alternative ways of finding compromises.

4 In Brössel and Eder (2014), we use the term "Pluralistic Bayesianism" in contrast to what Schurz (2012) and Unterhuber and Schurz (2013) call "Monistic Bayesianism"; the latter corresponds to what we call "*Standard Bayesianism*".

5 In Brössel and Eder (2014), we focus on the formal properties of the *Fine-Grained Method of Aggregation*. Here, my focus is more on the philosophical motivation of the account. Furthermore, in Brössel and Eder (2014), only reasoning commitments are aggregated. Here, evidential states are also aggregated, and I make room for synergetic effects, which are rejected in Brössel and Eder (2014). I discuss this in more detail in Sect. 10.4.4.

6 Exceptions are, for example, Feldman (2007) and Grundmann (2013).

7 I am concerned with revealed disagreement (Sect. 10.2.3), where agents who share the same total evidence continue to share their total evidence after the disagreement is revealed.

8 See also Frances and Matheson (2019) and MacFarlane (2009). This distinction is similar to the distinction between weak and strong disagreement (for this latter distinction, see, e.g., Grundmann 2019).

9 See also Easwaran et al. (2016) for different social settings in the context of disagreement.

10 See Christensen (2009), Frances and Matheson (2019), Goldman and O'Connor (2019), Lackey (2010) for a discussion of prominent views on what to do when one faces such a situation.

11 For an appealing account of group credence that is analogous to the *Standard Method of Aggregation*, see Pettigrew (2019). While our *Standard Method of Aggregation* refers to epistemic compromises, Pettigrew's method concerns group credences. Similarly, Easwaran et al. (2016:Sect. 2) address aggregation rules as rules that represent the opinion of a group. However, the opinion may have the same function as the epistemic compromise: to assist the group in finding decisions.

12 Discussions of judgment aggregation are related to the discussions in this paper. However, judgment aggregation concerns the aggregation of categorical doxastic attitudes or of judgments of acceptance and rejection—as opposed to aggregation of credences (see List 2012, Sect. 6.3 for a comparison, and List and Pettit 2002, 2004 for judgment aggregations and their problems).

13 For an evaluative understanding of (ideal) rationality, see, for example, Christensen (2004), Easwaran and Fitelson (2015), Eder (2019), and Titelbaum (2015).

14 Following Schurz (2012) and Unterhuber and Schurz (2013), Brössel and Eder (2014) refer to this position as "*Monistic Bayesianism*".

15 For an account in these terms that concerns disagreement, see, e.g., Jehle and Fitelson (2009).

16 For literature on uniqueness principles, see Feldman (2007), Kelly (2014), Kopec and Titelbaum (2016), Rosa (2018), and White (2005, 2014).

17 I take Kelly's (2010) *Total Evidence View* to be along these lines. Grundmann describes Kelly's view as an account of aggregation of evidence (Grundmann 2019:130–131).

18 Nevertheless, Easwaran et al. (2016) provide an account that mimics conditionalization given certain assumptions.

19 There is no room here to discuss all such aggregation rules in detail. In particular, I will ignore the *Geometric Mean Rule*. For an extensive discussion of variants of this rule, see Brössel and Eder (2014), Easwaran et al. (2016), and Genest and Zideck (1986).

20 Since it is a method that results in a single credence (function), Frances and Matheson (2019:Sect. 5.1) refer to it (or a special case of it) as "a kind of doxastic compromise".

21 This rule or variants thereof are often referred to as the "Linear Opinion Pooling Rule".

22 Alternative accounts of peerhood not only assume that peers are equally competent but also that they share the same total evidence (for such an account, see Grundmann 2019). In this paper, I do not assume that the agents are epistemic peers and that peerhood requires that the agents share the same total evidence.

23 It is common to use such weights in a formal setting (see, among others, Brössel and Eder (2014), Easwaran et al. (2016), Genest and Zidek (1986), Moss (2011), and Pettigrew (2019)).

24 In the context of peer disagreement between agents as individuals, there are approaches according to which it is rational for an agent to move her credence in a proposition toward the credence in the proposition of a peer with whom she disagrees but put more weight on her own credences. This way she ends up with a credence closer to her initial credence than to the other peer's initial credence. Within the present formal setting, she can do justice to this by assigning more weight to her own credence even though all agents involved are equally competent. (See Elga (2007) and Feldman (2007) for a discussion of what Elga refers to as the *Extra Weight View*, which is in this spirit. But Elga and Feldman do not endorse the view. Enoch (2010) argues for the related *Common Sense View*.) In such a case, the weights do not reflect the level of relative competence alone. Although such an approach might be adequate in the context of disagreement between agents as individuals, it is certainly not adequate in the context of disagreement between agents as members of a group that are supposed to find an epistemic compromise. I cannot think of any reason that would justify putting more weight on the credences of a member of the group in finding a rational epistemic compromise where all members are equally competent. And in our setting, there is no reason to take into account non-epistemic factors that determine the weight of an agent within the group. Here, I assume that the group members' weights represent their relative competence.

25 For a more detailed discussion of these and further properties, see Brössel and Eder (2014) and, especially, Genest and Zideck (1986), and Jehle and Fitelson (2009).

26 This label of the property is common in the literature (see, for example, Jehle and Fitelson 2009). Sometimes it is also referred to as the "Strong Setwise Function Property".

27 "Unanimity" is also the label Jehle and Fitelson (2009) use.

28 My criticism is related to Kelly's (2010) criticism of the *Equal Weight View* but different from it. There is no room here to compare them.

29 Note that I am not claiming that this difference is ignored in social epistemology in general. It might be standard to make the difference in non-formal epistemology, which does not focus on formally precise accounts.

30 See Christensen (2009), Easwaran et al. (2016), and Grundmann (2019) for similar examples. Along these lines, Easwaran et al. (2016) argue for a variant of the *Geometric Mean Rule* that does justice to such intuitions. Brössel and Eder (2014) discuss a slightly different variant of the *Geometric Mean Rule* that is, in its essence, the same as that of Easwaran et al. But we reject it based on the rule's synergetic effect.

31 See Easwaran et al. (2016:Sect. 6) for further references to the literature in favor of such synergetic effects.

32 For related frameworks and discussions, see Brössel (2012), Hawthorne (2005), Lange (1999), Schurz (2012), and Unterhuber and Schurz (2013). Unfortunately, there is no room here to deal with those frameworks and discussions.

33 Here Levi and I agree, see the next paragraph.

34 For literature on Carnap's logical probabilities, see Hájek (2019), Leitgeb and Carus (2020), Levi (2010), and Maher (2006).

35 This difference in reasoning commitments may also yield doxastic disagreement about higher-order propositions, e.g., propositions about which reasoning commitments or ways of processing evidence are more adequate. However, this disagreement about higher-order propositions would be different to a disagreement with respect to the original proposition in question or to the reasoning mismatch.

36 Things are more complicated when we do not assume that the evidence is true. Unfortunately, there is no room here to develop a formally precise account of aggregation of evidential states that works without this assumption.
37 Such methods should be able to deal with uncertain evidence, that is, evidence we are not certain of. The latter kind of evidential input is the input required for Jeffrey conditionalization.
38 Lasonen-Aarnio (2013) briefly considers views such as the one presented here and in Brössel and Eder (2014), and a similar view by Rosenkranz and Schulz (2015); however, she ultimately rejects them, among other reasons because she believes "the resulting views raise a plethora of technical worries. For instance the kinds of updates may not leave [the agents] with a probabilistically coherent function" (Lasonen-Aarnio 2013:782). At least some of the technical worries can be overcome by the view presented here and in Brössel and Eder (2014). I leave a discussion of her arguments against positions such as ours for another occasion, and here concentrate on demonstrating the merits of our view.
39 See Eder and Brössel (2019).
40 See Brössel and Eder (2014:2380).

References

Brössel, P. 2012. *Rethinking Bayesian confirmation theory.* PhD thesis, Konstanz: University of Konstanz.

Brössel, P. and Eder, A.M.A. 2014. How to resolve doxastic disagreement. *Synthese* 191:2359–2381.

Carnap, R. 1950. *Logical foundations of probability.* Chicago: University of Chicago Press.

Christensen, D. 2004. *Putting logic in its place.* Oxford: Oxford University Press.

Christensen, D. 2007. Epistemology of disagreement: The good news. *Philosophical Review* 116:187–217.

Christensen, D. 2009. Disagreement as evidence: The epistemology of controversy. *Philosophy Compass* 4:756–767.

Easwaran, K. et al. 2016. Updating on the credences of others: Disagreement, agreement and synergy. *Philosophers' Imprint* 16:1–39.

Easwaran, K. and Fitelson, B. 2015. Accuracy, coherence, and evidence. *Oxford Studies in Epistemology* 5:61–96.

Eder, A.M.A. 2019. Evidential probabilities and credences. *The British Journal for the Philosophy of Science.* https://doi.org/10.1093/bjps/axz043.

Eder, A.M.A. and Brössel, P. 2019. Evidence of evidence as higher order evidence. In: M. Skipper and A. Steglich-Petersen (eds.), *Higher-order evidence: New essays.* Oxford: Oxford University Press:62–83.

Elga, A. 2007. Reflection and disagreement. *Nou^s* 41:478–502.

Enoch, D. 2010. Not just a truthometer: Taking oneself seriously (but not too seriously) in cases of peer disagreement. *Mind* 119:953–997.

Feldman, R. 2007. Reasonable religious disagreements. In: L. Antony (ed.), *Philosophers without God: Meditations on atheism and the secular life.* New York: Oxford University Press:194–214.

Frances, B. and Matheson, J. 2019. Disagreement. In: E.N. Zalta (ed.), *The Stanford encyclopedia of philosophy* (Winter 2019 Edition), https://plato.stanford.edu/archives/win2019/entries/disagreement/.

Genest, C. and Zidek, J. 1986. Combining probability distributions: A critique and annotated bibliography. *Statistical Science* 1:114–135.

Goldman, A. and O'Connor, C. 2019. Social epistemology. In: E.N. Zalta (ed.), *The Stanford encyclopedia of philosophy* (Fall 2019 Edition), https://plato.stanford.edu/archives/fall2019/entries/epistemology-social/.

Grundmann, T. 2013. Doubts about philosophy? The alleged challenge from disagreement. In: T. Henning and D. Schweikard (eds.), *Knowledge, virtue, and action: Putting epistemic virtues to work*. Routledge:72–98.

Grundmann, T. 2019. How to respond rationally to peer disagreement: The preemption view. *Philosophical Issues* 29:129–142.

Hájek, A. 2019. Interpretations of probability. In: E.N. Zalta (ed.) *The Stanford encyclopedia of philosophy* (Fall 2019 Edition), https://plato.stanford.edu/archives/fall2019/entries/probability-interpret/.

Hawthorne, J. 2005. Degree-of-belief and degree-of-support: why Bayesians need both notions. *Mind* 114:277–320.

Jehle, D. and Fitelson, B. 2009. What is the "equal weight view"? *Episteme* 6:280–293.

Kelly, T. 2010. Peer disagreement and higher order evidence. In: R. Feldman and T. Warfield (eds.), *Disagreement*. New York: Oxford University Press:111–174.

Kelly, T. 2014. Evidence can be permissive. In: M. Steup et al. (eds.), *Contemporary debates in epistemology*. Malden, MA: Wiley-Blackwell:298–312.

Konieczny, S. and Pino Perez, R. 2011. Logic based merging. *Journal of Philosophical Logic* 40:239–270.

Kopec, M. and Titelbaum, M. 2016. The uniqueness thesis. *Philosophy Compass* 11:189–200.

Lackey, J. 2010. What should we do when we disagree? In: T. Szab´o Gendler and J. Hawthorne (eds.), *Oxford studies in epistemology*, Vol. 3. Oxford: Oxford University Press:274–293.

Lange, M. 1999. Calibration and the epistemological role of Bayesian conditionalization. *The Journal of Philosophy* 96:294–324.

Lasonen-Aarnio, M. 2013. Disagreement and evidential attenuation. *Nou^s* 47:767–794.

Leitgeb, H. and Carus, A. 2020. Rudolf Carnap. In: E.N. Zalta (ed.), *The Stanford encyclopedia of philosophy* (Spring 2020 Edition), https://plato.stanford.edu/archives/spr2020/entries/carnap/.

Levi, I. 1974/2016. On indeterminate probabilities. In: H. Arl-Costa, V.F. Hendricks, and J. Van Benthem (eds.), *Readings in formal epistemology*. Dordrecht: Springer:107–129.

Levi, I. 1979. *Serious possibility. Essays in Honour of Jaakko Hintikka*. Dordrecht: Reidel.

Levi, I. 1980. *The enterprise of knowledge: An essay on knowledge, credal probability, and chance*. Cambridge, MA and London: MIT Press.

Levi, I. 2010. Probability logic, logical probability, and inductive support. *Synthese* 172:97–118.

Lewis, D. 1980. A subjectivist's guide to objective chance. In: R.C. Jeffrey (ed.), *Studies in inductive logic and probability*, Vol. 2. Berkeley: University of California Press:263–293.

List, C. 2012. The theory of judgment aggregation: An introductory review. *Synthese* 187:179–207.

List, C. and Pettit, P. 2002. Aggregating sets of judgments: An impossibility result. *Economics and Philosophy* 18:89–110.

List, C. and Pettit, P. 2004. Aggregating sets of judgments: Two impossibility results compared. *Synthese* 140:207–235.

MacFarlane, J. 2009. Varieties of disagreement. http://johnmacfarlane.net/varieties.pdf (Accessed March 20, 2020).

Maher, P. 2006. The concept of inductive probability. *Erkenntis* 65:185–206.

Moss, S. 2011. Scoring rules and epistemic compromise. *Mind* 120:1053–1069.

Pettigrew, R. 2019. On the accuracy of group credences. In: T. Szab´o Gendler and J. Hawthorne (eds.), *Oxford Studies in Epistemology*, Vol. 6. Oxford: Oxford University Press:137–160.

Rosa, L. 2018. Uniqueness and permissiveness in epistemology. *Oxford Bibliographies.*

Rosenkranz, S. and Schulz, M. 2015. Peer disagreement: A call for the revision of prior probabilities. *Dialectica* 69:551–586.

Schurz, G. 2012. Tweety, or why probabilism and even Bayesianism need objective and evidential probabilities. In: D. Dieks et al. (eds.), *Probabilities, laws, and structures. The philosophy of science in a European perspective*, Vol. 3. New York: Springer.

Titelbaum, M. 2015. Rationality's fixed point (or: In defense of right reason). In: T. Szab´o Gendler and J. Hawthorne (eds.), *Oxford Studies in Epistemology*, Vol. 5. Oxford: Oxford University Press:253–294.

Unterhuber, M. and Schurz, G. 2013. The new Tweety puzzle: Arguments against Monistic Bayesian approaches in epistemology and cognitive science. *Synthese* 190:1407–1435.

Van Fraassen, B. 1984. Belief and the will. *The Journal of Philosophy* 81:235–256.

Wagner, C. 2010. Jeffrey conditioning and external Bayesianity. *Logic Journal of the IGPL* 18:336–345.

Weatherson, B. 2008. Deontology and Descartes's demon. *The Journal of Philosophy* 105:540–569.

White, R. 2005. Epistemic permissiveness. *Philosophical Perspective* 19:445–459.

White, R. 2014. Evidence cannot be permissive. In: M. Steup et al. (eds.), *Contemporarydebatesinepistemology.* Malden,MA:Wiley-Blackwell:312–323.

Williamson, T. 2000. *Knowledge and its limits*. Oxford: Oxford University Press.

11 Why Bayesian Agents Polarize

Erik J. Olsson

11.1 Introduction

Many societal debates are polarized in the sense that a substantial proportion of the population holds one view, while the remaining part is of the diametrically opposite opinion. Abortion, climate change, immigration and the merits of Donald Trump's presidency come to mind as issues upon which, at the time of writing, opinions are seriously divided in many Western societies. A somewhat comforting thought is that this only means that one party must be not only wrong but wrong because they are irrational. If people end up on the wrong side in a dispute because they are irrational, that would suggest that we could avoid or even eradicate polarization by educating people in the normatively correct way of reasoning and weighing evidence.[1]

But what if polarization is not irrational, but even rational? More carefully put: what if even people who carefully consider their evidence in conformity with impeccable principles of rationality may still end up divided on the issues at hand, and what if this happens, not only once in a while, but frequently?

In fact, a number of studies have concluded that polarization may result from rational processes (Cook and Lewandowsky, 2016, Easwaran, Fenton-Glynn, Hitchcock, and Velasco, 2016, Jern, Chang, and Kemp, 2014, Kelly, 2008). One such body of work stems from the Bayesian community and, in particular, from research exploring the Laputa simulation model for social network communication developed by Staffan Angere and Erik J. Olsson (see Olsson, 2011, for an introduction and overview). To convey the main ideas, in Laputa, two or more inquirers are concerned with the same question whether a factual proposition p ("Climate change is man-made", "Trump will be re-elected" ...) is true or false. Their inquiry is an on-going process that takes place over time in a network of connected inquirers. Each inquirer can, at any time, consult her own outside source as to whether p is true. The inquirers can, at any time, ask other inquirers in the social network to which they are connected whether p. The outside sources are somewhat but (typically) not fully reliable. The inquirers (typically) do not fully trust their outside sources, nor do they fully trust each other; rather, they update trust dynamically as they receive information from their outside source and/or their network peers. The situation allows for different social practices to be implemented (e.g. much, little or no communication), and the question arises which practice is most beneficial in the interest of inquirers' arriving at the true answer to the underlying question.

Olsson (2013) showed by computer simulation how communication in Laputa among ideally rational agents leads to polarization under various plausible conditions. He concluded (p. 130):

> [t]o the extent that Bayesian reasoning is normatively correct, the perhaps most surprising, and disturbing, results of this study are that polarization and divergence are not necessarily the result of mere irrational 'group thinking' but that even ideally rational inquirers will predictably polarize or diverge under realistic conditions.

How robust is polarization in Laputa? This question is thoroughly investigated in an extensive (55 page) study by Pallavicini, Hallsson and Kappel (2018). The authors also consider and eventually rule out a number of intriguing hypotheses about what causes polarization in Laputa networks. Vindicating Olsson's study, the authors find that "groups of Bayesian agents show group polarization behavior under a broad range of circumstances" (p. 1).[2] However, rather than concluding that polarization may be rational, they argue that the results are, in the end, explained by an alleged failure of Laputa to capture rationality in its full sense. In particular, they notice that agents in Laputa lack the ability to respond to "higher-order evidence". This lack is what, according to the authors, ultimately explains the fact that agents polarize. As a remedy, they sketch a revised updating mechanism that they think does justice to higher-order evidence. Pallavicini *et al.* do not provide a detailed rule, nor do they demonstrate analytically or by computer simulation that their proposal would prevent groups from polarizing.

In this paper, I show that incorporating higher-order evidence in the way Pallavicini and her colleagues suggest fails to block polarization in Laputa. Thus, failure to comply with the revised updating rule cannot be the root cause of polarization. Rather, what drives polarization, on closer scrutiny, is expectation-based updating in combination with a modeling of trust that recognizes the possibility that the source is biased, that is, gives systematically false information. Finally, I demonstrate that polarization is rational in a further sense: epistemic practices that lead to polarization can be, and often are, associated with increased epistemic value at the group level. I conclude that the case for the rationality of polarization has been significantly strengthened rather than weakened.

In Section 11.2, having given a brief snapshot of relevant parts of the Laputa model, I summarize the findings in Pallavicini *et al.*'s (2018) concerning the ubiquity of polarization in the model. In Section 11.3, I consider the authors' argument for a revised rule intended to take higher-order evidence into account in order to block polarization among deliberating agents. Section 11.4 is devoted to an investigation into polarization and epistemic value. In the final section, I summarize the results and draw some additional conclusions.

11.2 Background on Laputa and Polarization

The Laputa framework for studying epistemological aspects of deliberation in social networks is in many ways a Bayesian model. For instance, an agent's belief state is represented by a probability distribution corresponding to the agent's degree of belief in the proposition in question. Moreover, updating of degrees of belief (credence) takes place through conditionalization on the evidence. The evidence here means evidence coming either from inquiry (a personal outside source not part of the network) or from a source in the network. While the model is generally complex, the messages that can be sent and received by agents are only of two kinds: p or not-p, for a proposition p. Thus, Laputa models network activity in response to a binary issue: guilty or not guilty, climate change is man-made or not and so on. At any step in a deliberation, agents can communicate with other agents to whom they are connected, or they can conduct inquiry in the sense of receiving information from their outside source. The distributions that determine the chance of communication, of conducting inquiry and so on at a given point in the deliberation are parameters in the model. The information obtained leads to a new credence through conditionalization on the evidence. An important point here is that the evidence will be of the kind "Source S reported that p", rather than p itself. This opens up for the possibility of not taking what a source says at face value.

A novel feature is that the Laputa framework incorporates a Bayesian mechanism for representing the degree to which an agent trusts her own inquiry (outside source) as well as her network peers. Trust here means perceived reliability and is represented as a "trust function" over all possible reliability profiles – from being systematically biased/anti-reliable to being systematically truth-telling – representing how likely those profiles are taken to be at a given stage in the deliberation. It turns out that, for some purposes, trust can be represented by a single number: the expected value of the trust function. An inquirer's new trust function after having received information is obtained via conditionalization on the evidence.[3] In the simple case in which the inquirer has a normally distributed trust function with expected value 0.5 and assigns p a degree of belief exceeding 0.5, the inquirer will, upon receiving repeated confirming messages from one source, update her trust function so that it approaches a function having expected value 1, representing full trust in the source. Interestingly, representing trust by a function rather than a single number allows for complex interactions between different parameters. Two agents who assign the same degree of belief to p have trust function with the same expected value and receive exactly the same information (say, from inquiry) may nevertheless, depending on their initial trust functions, end up with very different degrees of belief and new trust functions.

Updating in Laputa is quite complex, especially the updating of trust. Fortunately, there exists a computer implementation that does the computations automatically which, as we will see, greatly facilitates investigation into the model and its consequences (see Olsson, 2011, for an overview). For the purposes of this paper, there is very little the reader needs to know about Laputa in addition to what has already been explained. An exception is the "Laputa table" (Table 11.1) containing the derived updating rules for belief (credence) and expected trust (see Olsson, 2013, for derivations).

Table 11.1 is a condensed representation of how updating in Laputa works. Consider, for example, the upper left-most cell in the table. This is the case in which an agent receives an expected message from a trusted source. That the message, let us say p, is expected means that the receiving agent assigns p a credence higher than 0.5. That the source is trusted means that the receiving agent assigns a trust function to the source such that the expected value of that function is higher than 0.5. What should happen in this case? The plus sign here means that the receiving agent will strengthen her current belief. In our example, it means that she will believe even more strongly that p is the case. The up-arrow means that the receiving agent will trust the source even more. Similarly, the minus sign in Table 11.1 means that the receiving agent weakens her current belief, and the down-arrow means that she trusts the source less than she did before. It is important to understand that the rules described in Table 11.1 are derived rules in the sense that they follow from the underlying Bayesian machinery.[4,5]

In the following, I will use the terminology put forth in Pallavicini *et al.* (2018) regarding polarization and related concepts. Thus, "polarization", as the term is often used in social epistemology to denote the tendency of deliberation to strengthen the pre-existing attitudes in a

Table 11.1 Derived updating rules for belief (credence) and trust

	Message expected	*Neither nor*	*Message unexpected*
Source trusted	+(↑)	↑()	−(↓)
Neither nor	0(↑)	0()	0(↓)
Source distrusted	−(↑)	↓()	+(↓)

group of like-minded people, will instead be called "escalation". Escalation will not play any major role in this paper. The term "group polarization", or simply "polarization", will be reserved for the phenomenon of a group being seriously divided on an issue. In the extreme case, half the group believes p, and the other half believes not-p.

The degree of polarization for a given network of agents can be computed as the average (root mean square of the) deviation of individual credence from the mean. Thus, a network in which every agent has the same credence in p has polarization 0 (minimum). A network in which half the inquirers are certain that p, and half are certain that not-p has polarization 0.5 (maximum). We are often interested in the extent to which polarization has increased or decreased following deliberation. We can find this out by simply computing the final (post-deliberation) degree of polarization minus the initial (pre-deliberation) degree of polarization. A positive value means that agents in the network have become more polarized as the result of deliberation. A negative value means that they have become less so.

Olsson (2013), in Section 11.5, studied polarization by means of computer simulation for what he called a "closed room" debate without anyone in the network undertaking inquiry (inquiry chance set to 0). Rather, all the activity consisted in communication between mutually trusting agents in the network, where the initial trust values were drawn from a (truncated) normal distribution with a mean value of 0.75. The initial degree of belief (credence) in p was assumed to be normally distributed with a mean value just above 0.5. Laputa was instructed to generate 1,000 networks satisfying these and some other reasonable constraints, allowing each network to evolve ten time steps ("rounds"). The simulation was run in "batch mode", with Laputa collecting average results over all the network runs. The result was belief escalation toward degree of belief 1 in p. In fact, after ten rounds, virtually all agents believed fully that p, with very few exceptions.

Olsson (2013) also studied some conditions under which agents in Laputa polarize. The three remaining cases were considered: people trust but are biased to give false reports, people distrust but tell the truth and people distrust and are biased to give false reports. Olsson concluded that the first two cases, characterized by a lack of social calibration in the sense that there is a mismatch between trust and actual reliability, give rise to polarization (p. 128). Additionally, Olsson walked through a simplified case involving just two communicating agents under similar circumstances to see how polarization arises, step-by-step.

Pallavicini *et al.*'s study (2018) contains a much more detailed analysis of the conditions under which agents in Laputa polarize and, in particular, how the agents' initial beliefs in p affect subsequent polarization. Trust is also varied, but in a different way than in Olsson's study, making the two studies non-trivial to compare. Pallavicini *et al.* look at five different cases concerning initial beliefs (Figure 11.1). In the first case, initial credence is drawn from a normal distribution, with mean 0.5 (undecided group). They also consider two cases in which agents are already polarized, in one case more so than in the other. Finally, in two of the examples, the distributions of initial belief are tilted toward believing p, thus corresponding to the setting in Olsson (2013), in one case more so than in the other (called the "suspecting groups").

The other parameters studied by Pallavicini and her colleagues involve inquiry trust and communication trust, that is, peer trust. It should be noted that both communication chance and inquiry chance are set to be governed by a uniform distribution over [0, 1] in the study (see their Appendix B.2). Thus, there will usually be both communication and inquiry going on in a particular network generated by Laputa in batch mode. The cases considered regarding trust are the following (p. 16): agents generally trust themselves (inquiry) as much as they trust others (i.e. the inquiry trust distribution is the same as for the communication trust distribution), agents generally trust themselves (inquiry) more than they trust others (i.e. the inquiry trust distribution has a higher mean than the communication trust distribution) and agents generally trust others more than they trust themselves (inquiry) (i.e. the communication trust distribution has a higher mean than the inquiry trust distribution). Combined with the five belief distributions, this leaves the authors with 15 (5*3) possibilities to consider.

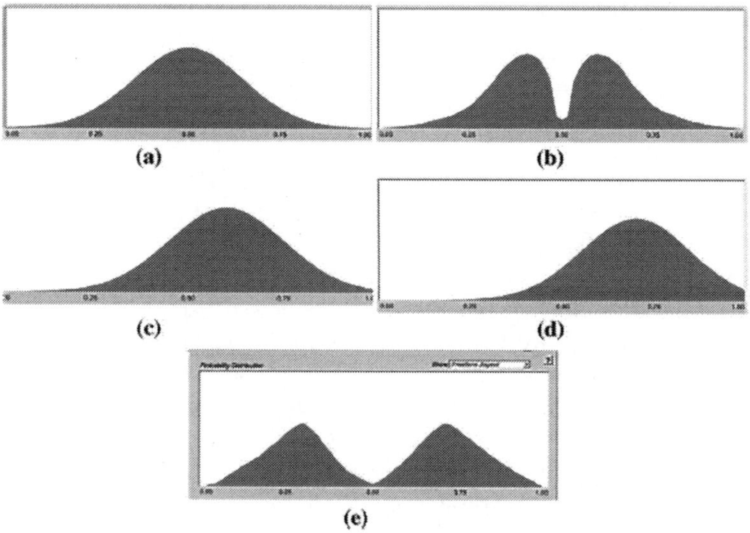

Figure 11.1 Initial distributions of degrees of belief for the five different groups: the undecided group (a), the polarized group (b), the suspecting group (c), the very suspecting group and (d) the very polarized groups (e). Adapted from Pallavicini *et al.* (2018), p. 15.

The striking result is that groups polarize under all conditions. In the undecided and polarized cases, agents end up divided into two equally large camps: one camp assigning credence 1 to p and the other assigning credence 1 to not-p (credence 0 to p). The suspecting cases (in which inquirers are initially statistically inclined to believe p) lead to polarization as well, although here, the camp assigning credence 1 to p is bigger than the camp assigning credence 1 to not-p. The different trust conditions studied basically do not affect these results. Pallavicini and her colleagues also perform a very extensive robustness study by varying trust in more fine-grained ways, which effectively means that they simulate 285 different groups. Their conclusions are noteworthy (p. 22): "The very surprising result of this simulation is all of the groups polarized to some degree. In fact, most groups polarized to the maximum level. There were no conditions under which depolarization occurred". Thus, "the observed polarization behavior is a very stable phenomenon for these Bayesian agents" (p. 20).

At this point, it would seem that Pallavicini *et al.* have achieved a striking vindication of the "disturbing" conclusion of Olsson's 2013 study to the effect that even ideally rational Bayesian agents polarize under a broad range of conditions. Surprisingly, however, this is not the moral Pallavicini and her colleagues draw from their investigation.

11.3 Pallavicini, Hallsson and Kappel on the Cause of Polarization

Pallavicini and her co-authors devote several sections of their paper to inquiring into the root causes of group polarization in Laputa. For instance, one might think that it is the way trust is updated in Laputa that ultimately causes polarization. However, the authors show that polarization occurs even if trust updating is turned off in the Laputa simulation program, finding that "deactivating trust-updating does not stop the polarization behavior" (p. 26); rather "the trust-updating speeds up an already existing process" (p. 27).

Another possible explanation of polarization considered by Pallavicini *et al.* is the fact that once Bayesian agents research a credence of 1 in a proposition, they cannot – for familiar reasons – change their mind. However, this, too, does not explain polarization (p. 32): "The aspect of Bayesian agents that they cannot change their minds after reaching an extreme credence is not the cause either, it just means that the results will be stable after a certain point". They also look into the possibility that "double-counting the evidence" might be causing polarization. In Laputa, an agent A updates belief and trust every time a network peer B sends a message to A, regardless of whether B has already asserted the same message before without performing any inquiry in-between. Pallavicini *et al.* test the hypothesis that double counting causes polarization by turning on a feature of Laputa which prevents agents from sending messages without having received an intermediate message from inquiry, observing that "[i]n all cases the groups reached maximal polarization within the 30 time steps of the original simulation" (p. 31). Hence, double-counting is not the root cause of polarization either. Finally, they manage to exclude the possibility that polarization results from networks having a certain density, that is, a high proportion of communication connections between agents.

So what, then, is responsible for the ubiquitous polarization we see in social networks in Laputa? Researchers working in the Bayesian tradition have shown how their models are compatible with polarization among agents. Pallavicini *et al.* consider two such accounts at some length, one due to Jern *et al.* (2014) and the other due to Kelly (2008). Both studies conclude that Bayesian updating is compatible with polarization in cases in which agents have different background beliefs. Jern *et al.* make this point as follows (p. 209):

> [S]uppose that a high cholesterol test result is most probable when a patient has Disease 1 and low blood sugar, or when a patient has Disease 2 and high blood sugar. Then two doctors with different prior beliefs about the patient's blood sugar level may draw opposite conclusions about the most probable disease upon seeing the same cholesterol test result D.

This explanation seems to transfer directly to Laputa. In Laputa, agents may have different background beliefs, not only regarding the proposition p but also regarding the trustworthiness of a source. Suppose, to consider a case similar to that investigated by Jern *et al.* (2014), that A has a high credence in p and trusts the source, and B has a low credence in p (high credence in not-p) and distrusts the same source, that is, considers it to be potentially biased (reporting false propositions). Now the source says that p. For A, this is an expected message coming from a trusted source. By the Laputa updating table (upper left-most cell in Table 11.1), A will believe p even more strongly than before. For B, it is an unexpected message coming from a distrusted source. By the Laputa table (lower right-most cell in Table 11.1), B will believe not-p even more strongly than before. Thus, agents polarize, and what is responsible for this are differences in background beliefs and the effects those differences have, given the underlying Bayesian machinery. Those effects essentially mean, in the case of credence updating, that evidence coming from sources believed to be trustworthy is taken at face value, whereas evidence coming from sources believed to be biased is taken as "evidence to the contrary".

Yet Pallavicini *et al.* disagree with this explanation, writing (p. 35): "The group polarization we see in our simulations does not depend on any particular prior assumptions made by subjects in the group, as our polarization results are robust for more than 200 different groups".

Their conclusion is that "we can not amend the explanation from Jern *et al.* to argue that our polarization results are rational" (ibid.). One could object that it is not necessary for Laputa agents to polarize in the way just demonstrated that "particular prior assumptions" are made by subjects in the group, whatever this might mean more precisely, so long as agents have qualitatively different beliefs concerning p and the trustworthiness of the source.

Pallavicini *et al.* (p. 36) consider a similar explanation due to Kelly (2008):

> [I]t may be possible to give an interpretation of what goes on in the simulations which is compatible with Kelly's account. The information in the Bayesian network consists of agents communicating with each other and the agents doing inquiries on their own. The received messages and results of inquiry are what would be the narrow evidence on Kelly's view. All of the agents in the simulation update their beliefs in the same way, based on a formula that incorporates the agent's prior belief, all of the information that an agent receives at a given time (the narrow evidence) and how much the agent trusts the sources that are giving the information ... This updating based on the collection of the prior belief, the narrow evidence and the trust in the sources could be understood as the broader evidence.

Furthermore (p. 36):

> Since in none of our simulations the agents have the same narrow evidence and since the agents do not share their broad evidence when communicating ..., it makes sense on Kelly's view that the agents update their degrees of beliefs in different directions.

Yet, once more, Pallavicini *et al.* find this sort of explanation problematic (p. 36):

> However, this interpretation seems insufficient to explain why agents polarize in our simulation. The interpretation assumes a very detailed process for how the agents treat and generate evidence, which is not captured by the mechanics of the model. In the model the agents just receive some information and update their degrees of belief and degrees of trust accordingly. This setup means that the model is compatible with various different interpretations for how to understand this behavior.

However, as demonstrated above in connection with the discussion of Jern *et al.*, it follows directly from the Laputa updating table that agents will polarize if they have qualitatively different prior beliefs concerning p and qualitatively different trust assignments. Following Jern *et al.* (2014) and Kelly (2008), these differences in background beliefs, together with the underlying Bayesian machinery, fully explain how polarization can arise in models like Laputa.

Note that the only thing that is needed to explain how polarization can occur in Laputa in the above "Jern-style" example are the rules for updating credences in the Laputa table; the rules for updating trust play no role in the explanation. This is, of course, completely in accord with the previously mentioned finding by Pallavicini *et al.* that polarization takes place in simulations even when trust-updating is turned off.

Having, clearly incorrectly, rejected this kind of explanation of polarization in Laputa, what do Pallavicini *et al.* propose in its stead? Their own analysis is that Laputa lacks a certain feature that they think is required of a full model of epistemic rationality: namely, a mechanism that takes "higher-order evidence" into account. In their view, this is what explains polarization in Laputa. The idea is that two agents who see each other as epistemic equals, in terms of diligence, carefulness and the like, but disagree regarding a proposition p following communication should not only update by adjusting their credence in p and adjusting their trust in the source, as is the case in the Laputa model as it stands, but should also downgrade their trust in their own abilities to inquire properly. In Laputa, this would mean that disagreement should lead not only to lower trust in one's peer but also to lower trust in one's own inquiry. Pallavicini *et al.* are silent on how, exactly, to implement this proposal for a revised updating rule in Laputa.

Pallavicini *et al.* think that taking this proposal seriously would have beneficial effects in simulations (p. 37):

> Now consider the implications of this for the simulation. Can the Bayesian agents in our simulations represent and process higher-order evidence in the way suggested by the above cases? The answer is 'yes' when it comes to information from inquiry, but 'no' when it comes to information from communication. Since the vast majority of information in the simulation comes from communication, this partial Bayesian agent blindness towards higher-order evidence might be quite significant for explaining why they polarize to the surprising extent that they do, and why this polarization is much stronger than what we would expect to see among ordinary epistemically well-functioning human beings.

We note that the ambition has been lowered from explaining polarization *per se* to explaining the surprising extent of polarization. At any rate, Pallavicini *et al.* clarify their view as follows (p. 39):

> Here we have a hypothesis about why ideally rational Bayesian agents in the simulation behave so surprisingly. Agents are responsive to first-order evidence in communication for or against p, but

> the fail to treat the fact of disagreement as higher-order evidence and fail to adjust their first-order beliefs in their own abilities [i.e. their inquiry trust] accordingly. If they did, we might speculate, they would tend not to be as confident in their ever more extreme views as they are. Moreover, if we assume that fully rational epistemic agents should be responsive to higher-order evidence, then these Bayesian agents are not fully rational. It is not that they are irrational, rather a Bayesian agent only constitutes a partial model of full rationality.

My first point is that the cause of polarization in Laputa, or its extent, is not that the model lacks a mechanism for handling "higher-order evidence" along the lines suggested by Pallavicini *et al.* One way to see this is to observe that polarization, as we noted in connection with Olsson's 2013 study, occurs even if we turn off inquiry altogether. We recall that Olsson's examples concerned a "closed-room debate" in which inquiry chance was set to 0, and yet, as he observed, polarization occurred, indeed to a very considerable extent. Why is this a relevant observation here? The reason is that an updating rule of the kind proposed by Pallavicini *et al.*, according to which communication in the network should affect not only credences in p and social trust among agents but also the receiving agent's inquiry trust, can obviously have any effect only if agents actually engage in inquiry. If they don't, inquiry trust may be updated as much as you like during communication; it won't have any effect on what transpires in the network. In particular, it won't have any effect on whether or not, or the extent to which, agents update their credence in p and, as an effect thereof, polarize.

It is still possible that a revised rule like the one suggested by Pallavicini *et al.* could affect polarization if inquiry is turned on (that is, if inquiry chance is set to a non-zero value). Even so, because, as Pallavinici *et al.* note, "the vast majority of information in the simulation comes from communication" (p. 37), it is unlikely that a rule that differs from the current updating rule for communication only in the effect it has on inquiry should have a major effect on simulation results. In the absence of a formally precise specification of the rule, we cannot know for sure, however.

To clarify, even though I think the study by Pallavicini and her co-authors fails to identify the root cause of polarization in Laputa, their investigations into the impact of various factors on the extent of polarization, and many other insightful observations, add greatly to our understanding of the model.

11.4 Polarization and Epistemic Value

The net effect of the simulations carried out by Pallavicini *et al.* is, in fact, a stronger argument for the rationality of polarization. Not only is polarization compatible with Bayesian updating; polarization is, as their study amply demonstrates, omnipresent in social networks governed by such updating. Now, besides Bayesian updating, there is a further standard of epistemic rationality that is relevant in connection with polarization, namely, whether or not deliberation can increase epistemic value. More precisely, can deliberation that leads to higher epistemic value for the group leave that group seriously divided on the issue at hand, and, if so, under what conditions does this transpire? This issue is not studied in the article by Pallavicini and her co-workers. Of course, "epistemic value" may mean different things. I will explain the account I favor in a moment.

In shedding light on this matter, let us return to the simple case of two agents, let us call them John and Mary, with opposing prior beliefs, who both strengthen their beliefs after receiving the same information from the same source (Figure 11.2). Let us assume that the source says that p is true. Both John and Mary receive this message and no other information. Mary is initially inclined to believe that p is true, whereas John is initially inclined to believe that not-p is true. Both John and Mary are unsure about the reliability of the source: it is probably no better than tossing a coin, but it may also be somewhat reliable or somewhat biased.

Formally:

- The source's degree of belief in p = 1, its certainty threshold is below that value (0.72), and communication chance is set to 1
- Mary's degree of belief in p = 0.75
- John's degree of belief in p = 0.25
- Inquiry chance = 0 for both John and Mary
- Both John and Mary have a trust function corresponding to a normal distribution with mean (expected trust) 0.5 and standard deviation 0.1

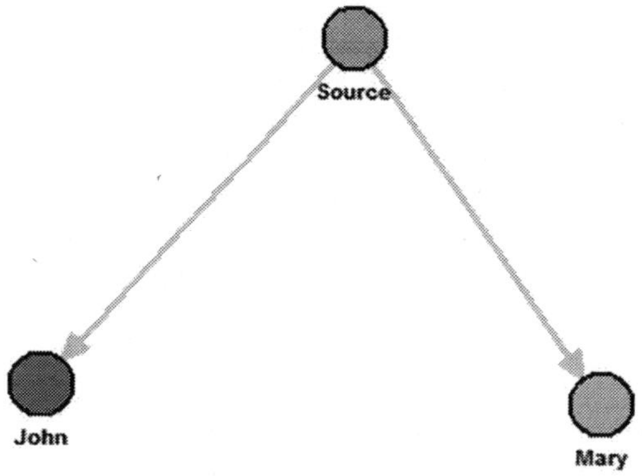

Figure 11.2 Network of John and Mary listening to the same source.

First, a few observations about polarization. If we run this network in Laputa single network mode, nothing happens at time 0. Polarization kicks in only at time 2, after the source has repeated that p. If, as in this case, both agents have an expected trust of 0.5 in the source, believing it to be no better than chance, two rounds are required to obtain belief polarization.

Let us now adjust the situation so that John is initially inclined to think that the source is probably biased, and Mary has an inclination in the opposite direction. Specifically, John and Mary both have a trust function corresponding to a normal distribution with standard deviation 0.1, but John's trust function has the mean 0.46 and Mary's trust function has the mean 0.54. Then we obtain belief polarization after just one round. This confirms what we already knew: where agents have qualitatively different views about the trustworthiness of a source, the same evidence can prompt them to update their degrees of belief in opposite directions, and this happens even when no inquiry is taking place.[6]

To return to the present issue, it remains to be investigated whether polarization is rational in the further sense of being the outcome of a practice that has positive epistemic value. We will assume that one proposition, p, is true and, following the authoritative account in Goldman (1999), focus on epistemic value, or E-value for short, in the sense of "veritistic value". The main intuition is that the closer an inquirer's degree of belief in a true proposition p is to 1, the better it is. Thus, having a credence of 0.9 in p is better than having a credence of 0.8 in p, for a true proposition p. The veritistic value of an inquirer's degree of belief in the true proposition p can be identified with that degree of belief. For example, if an inquirer assigns credence 0.6 to the true proposition p, then the veritistic value of that assignment is simply 0.6.

The E-value of a network state can be defined as the average degree of belief in the true proposition p among the agents in the network. Thus, a network in which every agent has degree of belief 1 in the truth has E-value 1 (maximum), and a network in which every agent has degree of belief 0 in the truth has E-value 0 (minimum). We are, above all, interested in whether a given epistemic practice of deliberation, as defined by the initial constraints on the network parameters, raises or lowers epistemic value. For this purpose, we define E-value ∇ to be the final E-value (after the simulation) minus the initial E-value (before the simulation) of the network. Thus, a positive E-value ∇ means that agents in the network, on average, have come closer to (full belief in) the truth as the effect of engaging in inquiry or communication. A negative E-value ∇ means that agents, on average, have moved farther away from (full belief in) the truth.

Let us consider John and Mary again. We will study three cases, differing in how, exactly, John and Mary assign initial credences to p.

<u>Case 1:</u> John and Mary are equally far from 0.5 in their belief. To be specific, we assume that John assigns credence 0.25 to p and Mary

assigns credence 0.75 to p. Simulation reveals that, in this case, John and Mary will polarize (Figure 11.3). After 20 time steps, John almost fully believes not-p, whereas Mary almost fully believes p. Meanwhile, E-value does not change at all. In particular, there is no increase in E-value resulting from John and Mary engaging with the source. It is easy to see why: since John and Mary are initially equally far from 0.5 in their initial credences, and John distrusts the source as much as Mary trusts it, their credences will move apart symmetrically from 0.5, meaning that the E-value (average credence in p, the true proposition) will remain 0.5.

Case 2: Mary is farther away from 0.5 than John is. To be specific, we assume that John, as before, assigns credence 0.25 to p, but Mary now assigns credence 0.90 to p. This assignment leads to polarization as well (Figure 11.4), but this time there is a change in E-value, but the change is negative (–0.05, to be precise). This means that John and Mary, as a collective, have moved farther away from (full belief in) the truth. Again, the explanation is straightforward. Given the circumstances, the average credence in p is initially 0.575. After 20 simulation rounds, however, since John and Mary have reached opposite poles, the average credence in p is 0.5. So there has been a decrease in E-value.

Case 3: Finally, we consider a case in which John is farther way from 0.5 than Mary is. As in the first case, Mary assigns credence 0.75 to p, but now, John assigns a mere 0.1 credence to p. In this case, we do not only get polarization, but also – lo and behold – a positive E-value (Figure 11.5)! The reason why this is so should be clear by now: the average credence in p was initially slightly below 0.5, or 0.425 to be precise.

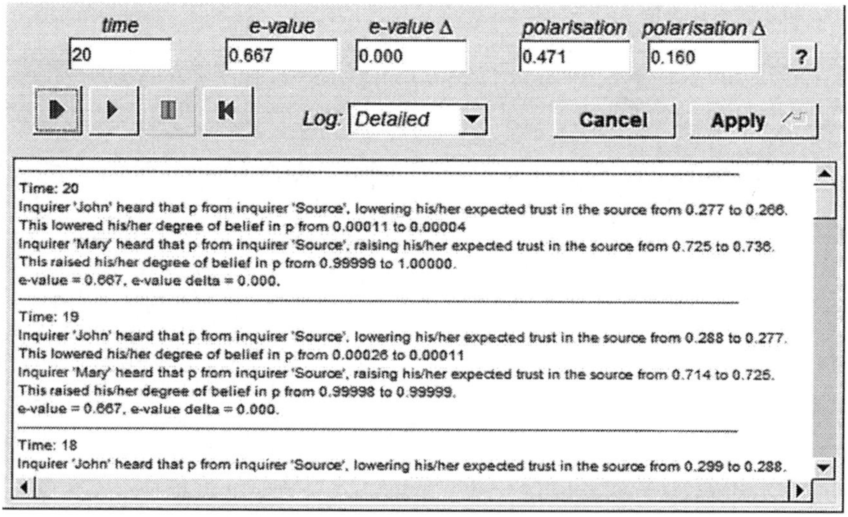

Figure 11.3 Output of Laputa in Case 1.

After 20 rounds of activity, John and Mary have reached opposite poles, and so the average credence is 0.5, that is, slightly higher than it was initially.

What I have done so far is giving an "existence proof": there exist scenarios in Laputa in which agents that collectively benefit from increased veritistic value polarize. This shows that collective rationality in the sense of increased average veritistic value in the group is compatible

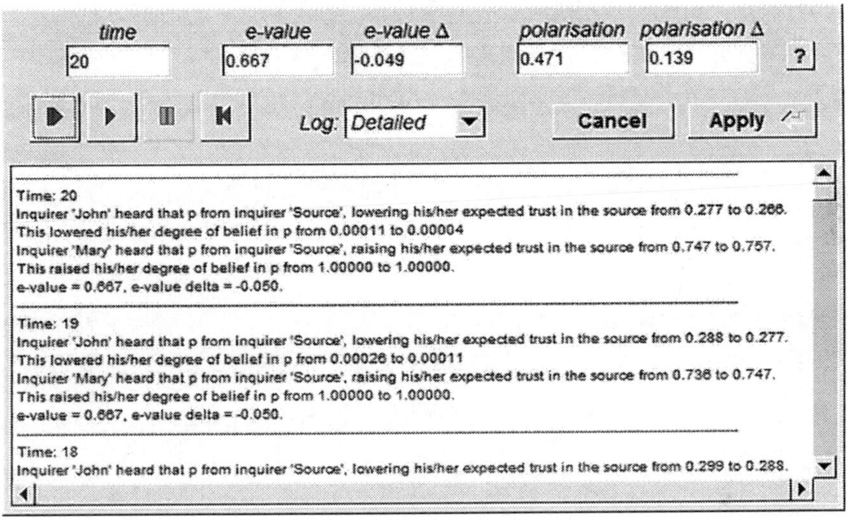

Figure 11.4 Output of Laputa in Case 2.

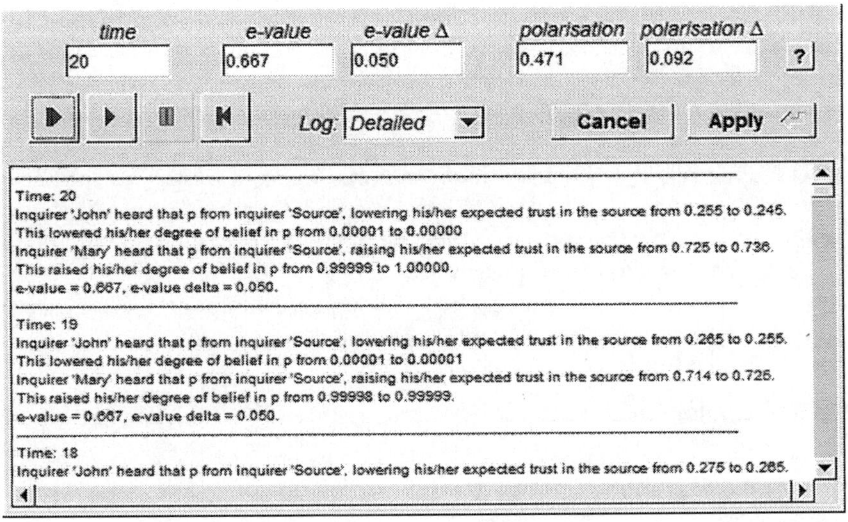

Figure 11.5 Output of Laputa in Case 3.

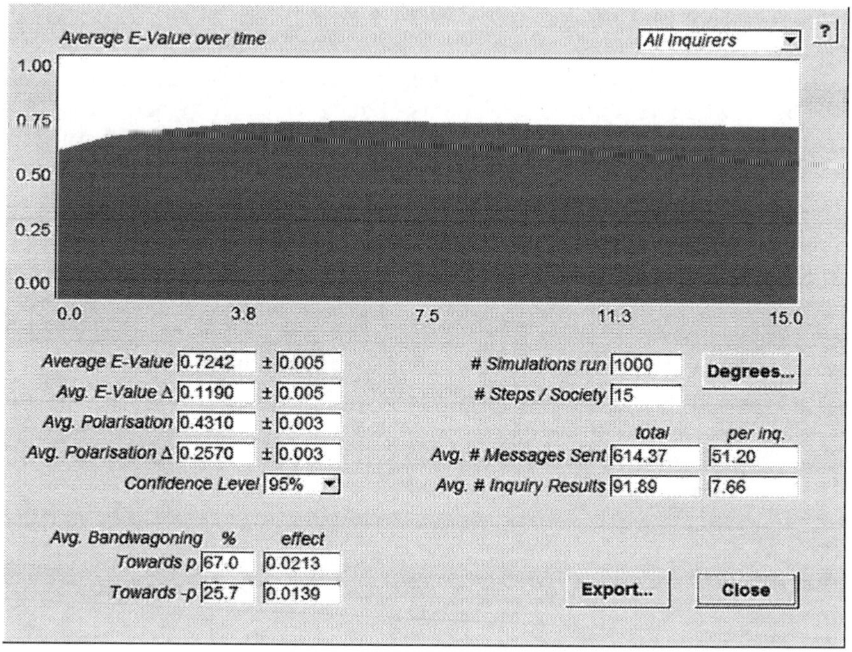

Figure 11.6 Typical result of simulation in batch mode with increase in epistemic value as well as polarization. E-value has increased by 0.1190 and polarization has increased by 0.2570.

with polarization. A stronger claim would be that polarization is rational in the sense that it arises from a practice of social inquiry that increases average veritistic value in the long run. In fact, it is quite common in Laputa that agents that benefit, collectively, from increased veritistic value also become increasingly polarized. A typical case is depicted in Figure 11.6.

The upshot is that polarization is rational not only in the sense that it emerges from Bayesian updating in the cases under consideration but also in the sense that a situation in which agents polarize can be one in which the collective benefits from positive epistemic value, a situation that commonly occurs in Laputa simulations, although assessing the precise extent to which this happens would require a more detailed study.

11.5 Conclusion

Pallavicini *et al.* (2018) is an important study into the robustness of polarization in the Bayesian Laputa model. The authors extend the results reported in Olsson (2013) quite considerably, showing that groups of Bayesian agents polarize under a surprisingly broad range of circumstances. However, rather than concluding that polarization may be rational, they argue that the results are, in the end, explained by an alleged failure of Laputa to capture rationality in its full sense. What, in their view, is not accounted for in Laputa is the role of higher-order evidence in cases in which network peers disagree. They think this lack is what ultimately explains the fact that agents polarize. As a remedy, they propose a revised updating mechanisms, though without providing a detailed rule, let alone demonstrating analytically or by computer simulation that their proposal would prevent groups from polarizing.

I showed that incorporating higher-order evidence in the manner proposed by Pallavicini *et al.* in fact fails to block polarization in Laputa. Instead, a closer examination revealed that what drives polarization is simply Laputa rules for updating credences on the basis of the expectedness of a message in conjunction with a recognition that the source might be biased, that is, systematically giving false information. A criticism of the rationality of polarization in Laputa style frameworks would need to address the rationality of expectation-based updating or the rationality of countenancing the possibility that a source might be biased – or, possibly, both.[7] Finally, I demonstrated, by means of simulations, that polarization is rational in a further sense: epistemic practices that lead to increases in epistemic value at the group level can be, and in practice often are, associated with increased polarization, if epistemic value is construed, following Alvin Goldman (1999), as (average) veritistic value. Pace Pallavicini *et al.*, the upshot of all this is a strengthened case for the rationality of polarization.

Notes

1 Acknowledgment: I would like to thank Fernando Broncano-Berrocal and Adam Carter for their valuable comments on an earlier version of this article.
2 All references to page numbers in Pallavicini *et al.* (2018) are to the online version; no printed version had appeared at the time of writing.
3 Derivations of the credence and trust updating functions can be found in Angere and Olsson (2017). Pallavicini *et al.* (2018) is also rich in background information on Laputa.
4 Since the Laputa model was first described (Olsson, 2011), it has been applied to a number of issues in epistemology, such as norms of assertion (Angere and Olsson, 2017, Olsson and Vallinder, 2013), the argument from disagreement (Vallinder and Olsson, 2013a), the epistemic value of overconfidence (Vallinder and Olsson, 2013b), the problem of jury size in law (Angere, Olsson, and Genot, 2015), peer disagreement (Olsson, 2018) and the epistemic effect of network structure (Angere and Olsson, 2017, Hahn, Hansson, and Olsson, 2018).
5 Collins, Hahn, von Gerber, and Olsson (2018) examined, theoretically and empirically, the implications of using message content as a cue to source reliability in the spirit of Laputa. They presented a set of experiments examining the relationship between source information and message content in people's responses to simple communications. The results showed that

people spontaneously revise their beliefs in the reliability of the source on the basis of the expectedness of a source's claim and, conversely, adjust message impact by perceived reliability, much like how updating works in Laputa. Specifically, people were happy downgrading the reliability of a source when presented with an unexpected message from that source.

6 It might be argued that, since the agents assign different trust values to the same source, one of them must be wrong. Being wrong about the trustworthiness of a source is, one might think, a sign of irrationality. For instance, if John assigns a lot of trust to the reports of a creationist, he is irrational. If so, the above simulation does not establish that *rational* agents can update their beliefs in opposite direction. Against this, one could object that rationality is a matter of internal coherence as opposed to one's connection to the world. On this picture, even an ideally rational agent may be utterly mistaken in his beliefs. Similarly, according to classic Bayesianism, rationality does not dictate what initial beliefs an agent should have (including beliefs about the reliability of sources) so long as they are coherent in the sense of satisfying the Kolmogorov axioms. The present work is situated in this influential tradition.

7 See Hahn, Merdes and von Sydow (2018) for an extensive and insightful discussion of expectation-based credence updating and its role in reasoning.

References

Angere, S., and Olsson, E. J. (2017). Publish late, publish rarely! Network density and group performance in scientific communication. In T. Boyer, C. Mayo-Wilson, and M. Weisberg (Eds.), *Scientific collaboration and collective knowledge*, New York: Oxford University Press: 34–62.

Angere, S., Olsson, E. J., and Genot, E. (2015). Inquiry and deliberation in judicial systems: The problem of jury size. In C. Baskent (Ed.), *Perspectives on interrogative models of inquiry: Developments in inquiry and questions*, Dordrecht: Springer: 35–56.

Collins, P. J., Hahn, U., von Gerber, Y., and Olsson, E. J. (2018). The bi-directional relationship between source characteristics and message content, *Frontiers in Psychology*, 9. https://doi.org/10.3389/fpsyg.2018.00018

Cook, J., and Lewandowsky, S. (2016). Rational irrationality: Modeling climate change belief polarization using Bayesian networks, *Topics in Cognitive Science*, 8(1): 160–179.

Easwaran, K., Fenton-glynn, L., Hitchcock, C., and Velasco, J. D. (2016). Updating on the credences of others: Disagreement, agreement and synergy, *Philosophers' Imprint*, 16: 1–39.

Goldman, A. I. (1999). *Knowledge in a social world*, New York: Oxford University Press.

Hahn, U., Hansen, J. U., and Olsson, E. J. (2018). Truth tracking performance of social networks: How connectivity and clustering can make groups less competent, *Synthese*: 1–31. https://link.springer.com/article/10.1007/s11229-018-01936-6

Hahn, U., Merdes, C., and von Sydow, M. (2018). How good is your evidence and how would you know? *Topics in Cognitive Science*, 10: 660–678.

Jern, A., Chang, K.-M. K., and Kemp, C. (2014). Belief polarization is not always irrational, *Psychological Review*, 121(2): 206–224.

Kelly, T. (2008). Disagreement, dogmatism, and belief polarization, *Journal of Philosophy*, 105(10): 611–633.

Olsson, E. J. (2011). A simulation approach to veritistic social epistemology, *Episteme*, 8(2): 127–143.

Olsson, E. J. (2013). A Bayesian simulation model of group deliberation and polarization. In Zenker, F. (Ed.), *Bayesian argumentation: The practical side of probability*, Synthese Library, New York: Springer: 113–134.

Olsson, E. J. (2018). A diachronic perspective on peer disagreement in veritistic social epistemology. *Synthese*: 1–19. https://link.springer.com/article/10.1007%2Fs11229-018-01935-7

Olsson, E. J., and Vallinder, A. (2013). Norms of assertion and communication in social networks, *Synthese*, 190: 1437–1454.

Pallavicini, J. Hallsson, B., and Kappel, K. (2018). Polarization in groups of Bayesian agents, *Synthese*: 1–55. https://link.springer.com/article/10.1007/s11229-018-01978-w

Vallinder, A., and Olsson, E. J. (2013a). Do computer simulations support the argument from disagreement? *Synthese*, 190(8): 1437–1454.

Vallinder, A., and Olsson, E. J. (2013b). Trust and the value of overconfidence: A Bayesian perspective on social network communication, *Synthese*, 191(9): 1991–2007.

12 The Mirage of Individual Disagreement

Groups Are All that Stand between Humanity and Epistemic Excellence

Maura Priest

12.1 Introduction

Many of us (i.e. academics, especially philosophers, alongside other educated and not so educated civilians) believe that the world would be better if the population improved epistemically. Such improvement is often understood as avoiding false unjustified beliefs and acquiring beliefs which are true and justified. Sometimes, also, the *type* of belief is thought to matter, with some beliefs considered more valuable than others. However, there is disagreement over just which beliefs are valuable.[1] For this paper's purpose, however, we can push these specifics aside, and focus on what is less controversial: *beliefs which are true, justified, or both (ceteris paribus) are epistemically good (let us call these good beliefs), and beliefs that are false, unjustified, or both (ceteris paribus) are epistemically bad (i.e., bad beliefs).* We can, of course, note that we mean this only with a *ceteris paribus* clause. Still, to maintain our focus, we will assume that the cases are basic and that all other things are indeed equal. Hence, one significant form of epistemic improvement amounts improving one's ratio of true and justified beliefs (good beliefs) to false and unjustified beliefs (bad beliefs). Anything that improves the former while keeping the latter the same, or, even better, while diminishing the latter, amounts to epistemic improvement. Likewise, the following is also an epistemic improvement: anything that lowers the total number of an agent's bad beliefs while maintaining the same number of good beliefs, or, even better, while raising the number of good beliefs.

Of course, truth and justification can come apart. An agent might have a belief that is true but not justified or a belief that is justified but false. In these cases, whether such beliefs are viewed as good or bad, that is, whether they are viewed as improving or diminishing one's standing as an epistemic agent, will depend on which theoretical stance an epistemologist takes on contentious issues. Epistemologists known as "internalists" are more likely to view a justified and false belief as "good," that is, improving one's status as an epistemic agent, than epistemologists known as "externalists." Externalists are more likely to see a true, reliably formed, belief as improving one's status as an epistemic agent, regardless of whether the agent has consciously accessible justification. That said, for this paper's purposes, it will suffice to discuss those issues that most epistemologists do agree on. Internalist and externalist camps come together where true beliefs and (internally) justified beliefs come together, and where false and unjustified beliefs come together. I am not claiming that what I call good and bad beliefs are exhaustive of all beliefs. Rather, I am narrowing the class of all possible beliefs down to a subset: in particular, a subset of beliefs where the epistemic values of diverse camps come together, that is, internalists, externalists, and those who have never studied epistemology at all.

We can look at epistemic improvement in terms of individual epistemic agents *or* in terms of society at large. All things being equal, an epistemic agent improves *qua epistemic agent* if she acquires good beliefs; likewise, her status as an epistemic agent diminishes if, all things being equal, she acquires bad beliefs. The same thing could be said of society, or really any group at all. All things being equal, groups improve epistemically if they acquire good beliefs, and, all things being equal, groups are made epistemically worse by bad beliefs.

For those who wish for grand-scale epistemic improvement, a hopeful outlook might include the society-wide (or world-wide) adaption of epistemic strategies that markedly increase the acquisition and preservation of good beliefs, while simultaneously decreasing the acquisition and preservation of bad ones. If this is your hope, this paper might crush your epistemic spirits.

This paper aims to convince the reader that a large number of important and long-standing disagreements, typically understood as between individuals, are actually disagreements between collectives. (So far, so good, but the bad news will come.) More pointedly, in many long-standing disagreements where one disagreeing party claims p, and the other party claims not-p, *the parties are collectives*. This might be confusing, because it is individuals who assert these beliefs, but collectives who actually hold them. Hence, I must make clear that S asserting the belief that-p does not imply that it is S who believes p. Rather, that assertion might imply that some group of which S is a member believes p (but not S herself). One last time for clarity: often, the bearers of beliefs p and not-p (the bearers of disagreeing beliefs) are not individuals, *nor an aggregate of individuals;* instead, the bearers of the beliefs are collectives. Of course, it may or may not hold that the group members, in addition to the group, also believe p. This includes the group member who asserts p. Agents might assert p in a group setting even if they do not personally believe p. Another way to think of it is that, often, individual assertions that p are meant to express a group belief in particular, regardless of whether the individual also believes p.[2]

Many of the argumentative claims in this paper follow from this first claim that many disagreements, while they appear to be between individuals, are actually between collectives. Understanding certain disagreements as collective illuminates *why* these disagreements are long-standing. This takes us to the paper's second claim, which is that collectives are often epistemically obligated (i.e. they would make an epistemic mistake if they refrained) to reconsider their belief in light of a disagreement. Despite this, *few such disagreements will result in reconsideration.* This is claim number three. The dismal epistemic conclusion is claim four, which follows from 1-3:

> Dismal Epistemic Conclusion (DEC): *Many long-standing disagreements will remain unresolved because the relevant parties are not properly motivated by epistemic ends.*

The lack of proper motivation will come to be as follows: the motivational forces at play in many long-standing disagreements are overwhelmed by the motivating force to remain loyal to a group. The motivation stemming from loyalty is not, by logical necessity, in conflict with epistemic motivation. However, in practice, conflicts are frequent, and the two typically come together by accident rather than design. After all, epistemic motivation is one phenomemon, and the motivation to display loyalty to a group another. The epistemic end is truth, justified belief, knowledge, or all of them. But the end of group loyalty is to avoid betrayal. Whenever evidence against a group belief arises, that is, when evidence suggests a group holds a false belief, group members, if they are to act with *epistemic integrity*, must point out the group's past epistemic mistakes. However, pointing out such mistakes often means abandoning certain commitments to the group: for example, the commitment to go along with a group agreement, such as an agreement to act as though a certain proposition is true. Here, we have epistemic motivation pitted against motivation grounded in group loyalty. The strength of the latter, I contend, often overwhelms the former. When it does, this is because group members are more motivated by group loyalty than the epistemic good and hence are not properly epistemically motivated.

The paper finishes by switching perspectives from the collective to the individual, and, sadly, the resolute is again dismal—this time in the form of a dilemma. Given the epistemically unfortunate circumstances in respect to groups, what ought *independent epistemic agents* to do? The independent epistemic agent is faced with a dilemma. There are two clean paths that an individual might take after recognizing the epistemic shortcomings of collective entities. Each path brings with it one epistemic good at the cost of losing another:

> Dismal Individual Epistemic Dilemma (DIED): *The choice between avoiding bad beliefs and gaining good ones.*

To summarize, this paper makes four claims, which lead to a fifth claim, that is, the DEC that follows from the first four claims. This conclusion, in turn, introduces a bonus part of the paper—the introduction of an epistemic dilemma that follows from the DEC. The four claims are:

1 Many disagreements that appear to be between individuals are actually between collectives.
2 Collectives are often epistemically obligated to reconsider p in light of disagreement.
3 Members of the collective, however, are obligated to uphold group agreements, including the agreement to act as though p is true.
4 Because of (3), despite being obligated to do so, collectives will rarely reconsider their beliefs in light of disagreement.

   Therefore,

5 DEC = Many long-standing disagreements will remain unresolved because the relevant parties are typically not properly motivated by epistemic ends but instead are more strongly motivated by group loyalty.

   From 1-4, I will argue that what follows is a dismal individual epistemic dilemma (DIED):

   DIED = Agents are forced to choose between acquiring good beliefs or avoiding bad beliefs, and they cannot choose both.

In what I have shown, it is not yet clear how DIED follows from 1-4. This will be explained in what is to come. For now, I will just note that members of collectives sometimes face situations where they must choose between group loyalty and epistemic loyalty. I argue that group members often show more loyalty to the group than they do to epistemology. However, let us imagine some especially independent thinking group members. These agents have an easier time going against the grain than most, and hence, they are actually more motivated by epistemic ends than group loyalty. This is the situation in which DIED arises. The brief story (to be detailed later) is that when agents choose to "betray" their group for the sake of epistemology, both good and bad epistemic results can follow. The good that can follow is that both their group and the independent agents themselves avoid false belief. However, this comes at a cost. The independent thinking agents, by demonstrating disloyalty and hence distancing themselves from the group, will have a harder time acquiring true beliefs in the future. Or so, I will argue.

12.2 Literature Overview: The Epistemology of Disagreement

The epistemology of disagreement literature, insofar as it is a systematic study of the epistemic importance of disagreement, does not begin until the 21st century.[3] During its short tenure, philosophers studying the epistemology of disagreement have huddled around a cluster of issues that seem to derive from the following questions: If a competent and informed epistemic agent, let us call him "Aristotle," believes p, and Aristotle runs into someone he regards to be another informed and competent epistemic agent who believes not-p (let us call him Bentham), what ought Aristotle to do? Moreover, what ought Bentham to do?

There are a number of background assumptions that the literature typically assumes, stipulates, or takes for granted. The first is that questions of disagreement are most interesting, difficult, and/or relevant when they are between *epistemic peers*. For example, in the words of Frances and Matheson (2019), "The literature on peer disagreement has instead focused on disagreement between competent epistemic peers, where competent peers with respect to P are in a good epistemic position with respect to P—they are likely to be correct about P" (Section 12.4, final paragraph).This is why I described both Aristotle and Bentham as "informed and competent." Later sections in this paper will delve more into the details of peerhood. For now, just note that peer disagreement is between agents who possess the same (or about the same) epistemic competence with regard to whether p. It is only when we meet disagreeing parties who are similarly competent (or perhaps of greater competence) that we have grounds to take their word seriously. Once this happens, the circumstance begs the following question, "Who should we trust about p's truth? Should we trust ourselves, or the (equally competent) disagreeing party?"

Interestingly, the disagreement the literature has been largely silent on is how we *actually* handle disagreements.[4] Disagreement discussions largely attempt to justify an epistemically normative position about what *we ought to do*, without considering first what we *actually* do. It seems plausible, however, that normative recommendations regarding how we ought to handle disagreements are, at least partly, dependent upon how we actually handle them. They would seem relevant if we cared about making recommendations in our actual world instead of, or in addition to, in an ideal world. At the least, *any* normative recommendations that aim at even some level of applicability (i.e. working in the real world) should consider the plausibility of the recommendations, that is, given how human beings actually behave, what are the odds that such recommendations are ever implemented? The plausibility of humans adhering to recommendations is dependent upon certain epistemic limitations. Hence, in knowing how we actually behave, we can consider what is the easiest and the most efficient way to adjust this behavior to achieve the best results, given human imperfections (*not* the best results, given *ideal epistemic agents*.)

If this paper is right, and it is indeed true that many disagreements are best understood as between collectives rather than between individuals, then normative recommendations about disagreement (or at least some of them) should be geared toward collectives rather than individuals. Because collectives do not always behave like individuals, we might expect that the normative landscape will change. So even if a reader rejects most of my claims, the paper does something worthwhile if it does nothing but make a plausible argument for the following: many disagreements that we *prima facie* assume are between individuals are actually between collectives.

12.3 What Is Collective Disagreement

There is a common tendency, both in and outside of philosophy, to see all beliefs as arising from individuals. On the one hand, the epistemology of disagreement literature has long recognized that disagreements often arise between *aggregates of individuals*.[5] If C, a theist, disagrees with D an atheist, about God's existence, C is probably aware that D is far from the only atheist. We can assume C knows that thousands of epistemically competent persons are atheists. Likewise, D probably knows the converse. D knows that there are probably thousands of epistemically competent persons who are theists. The disagreement, then, extends far beyond just C and D, even if each of them finds themselves in a "real-time," here and now disagreement with the other.

The situation I describe above—disagreements between aggregates of individuals—might be what some intuitively label a "collective disagreement." After all, the disagreement is between many individuals, and some understand a "collective" to be nothing more than multitudes of individuals. If this is indeed the best way to understand collectives, then collective disagreement will be of little importance. Imagine an individual who disagrees with a "collective," where this collective is understood as nothing more than the individual members. In this case, we should assume that the greater the number of individuals that constitute this "collective," the more the reason the lone disagreeing individual has for questioning their belief. After all, if *prima facie*, many persons disagreeing holds more force than just one person.[6] There is no need to focus on a *collective agent* and, hence, no need to focus on how beliefs of collective agents might differ from beliefs of "many individuals." Collective *just are* multitudes of individuals.

I argue for key conceptual differences between some collections of individuals and other kinds. More specifically, sometimes collections of individuals consist of *collective agents*, and other times they do not. Tracy Issacs (2011), for instance, has described a conceptual account of collective agents that epistemically and metaphysically distinguishes *collections*—individuals sharing a property—from *collective agents*—individuals joined together in such a way that the group itself is *its own agent* (one separate from the constituting group members). If there are such collective agents with beliefs distinct from the individual group members, then, contra Lackey, the *number* of individuals constituting a collective is epistemically irrelevant (for the purposes of understanding collective disagreement.)[7]

This paper contends that collective disagreements are between two disagreeing *collective agents*. Taking an approach similar to Isaacs' (2011), I contend that collective disagreement is simply a *disagreement between collectives* (typically two collectives, but sometimes more). Likewise, a disagreement between two or more individuals is something we can call an *individual disagreement*. Disagreements between one individual and one collective might also arise; this needs some other name: we might call these *mixed disagreements*. The remainder of this paper focuses on disagreements where at least one of the disagreeing agents is a collective agent. This focus can be distinguished from focusing on one-to-one disagreement or one-to-many (i.e. multiple individuals who do not constitute a collective agent). Disagreements of the latter two simply face distinct philosophical complications.

Here is one example of a collective disagreement. Imagine an adult softball team and a homeowner's association. Suppose these collectives disagree about whether or not stadium lights should be used after 8 pm. The two disagreeing agents are (1) the softball team and (2) the homeowner's association. Note that, regardless of the total number of players or the total number of team members, the disagreement is between two and only two agents. These two agents both, of course, are collective agents. Hence, the disagreement is a collective disagreement. So we see that collective disagreement, contra some previous literature, is not just about the number of disagreeing agents. The softball team and the homeowner's association are just two agents. Two is also the number of disagreeing parties in most paradigmatic cases of individual disagreement. What makes the disagreement a collective one is not the number of agents but *the type* of agents, that is, the agents themselves are collective agents.

I appeal to Margaret Gilbert's account of collective belief to illuminate this phenomenon.[8] Gilbert's account focuses on an agreement-like process that she calls *joint commitment*. While joint commitments are sometimes formed amongst persons who already share group membership, in other instances, joint commitments are made between two or more *individuals*, and in so doing, these two individuals *will become a collective agent*[9] (but this paper will focus on cases involving existing groups).

The process of joint commitment resulting in collective belief formation is described via the steps below. The list is my own interpretation of Gilbert's joint commitment process gathered from a wide variety of her publications, all of which discuss joint commitment and many of which specifically discuss collective belief.[10] The steps are meant to describe a paradigm instance of collective belief formation. This is not a list of necessary steps, it is only a list of sufficient ones.

1 A proposition (or set of propositions) is suggested to the group (the whole group or just part of it) via an assertion or a question. For example, a group member might make the following proposal: "Plato was the best philosopher to ever live, wasn't he?"
2 Often (but not always) a discussion ensues, and reasons in favor and against the proposal are considered. (Sometimes a discussion of the relevant sort has *already* taken place, or perhaps it is common knowledge that members have already looked into the matter themselves.)
3 The group and/or the group members (or potential group or group members) reflect on the proposition. (This step is optional but common.)
4 A person with the required authority expresses a (tentative) group belief, often leaving room for others to object. For example, "Okay, so we are all on the same page about Plato being the greatest philosopher of all time?"
5 Group members, future group members, or some relevant contingent thereof express agreement that the proposed proposition is true. This expression results in the collective belief (if the group does not express confirmation, the potential group belief dissipates).
6 Members of the collective are now obligated (via the collective belief) to "act as a body" in respect to the truth of the collective belief (i.e. members will make clear, in the relevant circumstances, that the collective indeed holds the relevant belief).

This is an outline only. There are many caveats and clarifications to draw, depending on circumstance.

Groups vary tremendously in size, purpose, and belief forming procedures. The collective might have a policy, for instance, that allows elected members to speak on behalf of other members or there might be committees delegated to express group beliefs on select issues. Here is the heart of Gilbertian collective belief formation: *a proposal is made; the necessary agents express a willingness to jointly commit to that belief and in so expressing solidify the collective belief. This belief does not necessarily bear any relation to the personal beliefs of group members.*

12.4 Responding to Gilbert's Critics

This section answers two common criticisms of Gilbert's account: (1) collective belief is nothing over and above the beliefs of the members of the collective, and (2) this account does not describe collective belief but rather something like collective acceptance. I deem this section necessary for the rest of the paper is grounded in Gilbert-style collective beliefs. Hence, clarifying the following matters, (1) these beliefs are a frequent phenomenon, and (2) collective "beliefs" are rightly called beliefs as opposed to some other term.

Imagine that Harvard releases a statement denying prejudice in its admission process. A reasonable interpretation of these events, likely to be described by the press and the public, is that *Harvard believes it has a fair admissions process*. Note that it seems irrelevant whether the majority of Harvard associates actually suspect the opposite, that is, that Harvard's admission process is, in fact, prejudiced. While reading *Inside Higher Education* and sipping morning coffee, we can still aptly say, "Harvard believes it has fair admission procedures." Because Harvard has institutional practices for arriving at a collective assertion, there is no need for majority agreement. In sum, there is an important sense of collective belief, a sense we often use in everyday discourse, that bears no relationship to the personal beliefs of group members.

Some critics contend that Gilbert's account, and/or any potential account of group belief, does not and cannot explain something best called collective "belief." Because groups are different from individuals in important ways, this line of thinking assumes that it makes little sense to attribute "beliefs" to groups. After all, if the term "belief" implies anything like a human mind, then group belief doesn't even seem possible.[11] Hence, some assume that collective or group 'beliefs' must be closer to the something often called 'acceptance.' Gilbert-style collective beliefs, critics contend, are voluntary and/or not responsive to evidence. Hence, they cannot be real beliefs. This criticism rests on mistaken assumptions about (1) what phenomenon Gilbert is attempting to describe, and (2) the way in which the selected phenomenon actually arises in most "real world" cases.

Suppose a committee at Harvard is discussing accusations of prejudice. The following conversation ensues:

Committee Member 1: If we are so prejudiced, why do we have the highest non-white enrollment of all the ivies?

Committee Member 2: Good point, and why are we one of only two east coast schools with a triple-blind application review process?

Committee Member 3: This whole prejudiced idea is just based in a fantasy. After all, we just committed five million dollars into research projects on anti-discriminatory hiring practices.

Committee Member 1: (after a discussion of this kind has gone on for several more minutes) So I think we all agree that Harvard denies any accusation of prejudice?

Notice that the above conversation involves sharing evidence with respect to the proposed belief. There is not merely a belief proposal and then agreement or denial with no discussion of epistemic support. The point is not that the above discussion is the only way in which collective beliefs might be formed. Rather, the point is that the above conversation is both plausible (similar conversations often take place, and often result in something like a collective belief) and typical (these conversations do occur, and their occurrence is not unusual.)

In contrast to the conversation above, consider another possible conversation, assuming the same background circumstances:

Committee Member 1: Well, we were accused of being prejudiced. Which, we are, of course.

Committee Member 2: Yes. We are prejudiced. But why don't we just believe that we are not. After all, believing that we are not prejudiced is more useful.

Committee Member 1: Good idea. So, who wants to believe we are not prejudiced?

It seems quite unlikely that the above conversation would unfold in the fashion displayed. There is infelicity in saying, "We are prejudiced. But why don't we believe that we are not." If anything of this deceptive nature were to occur, it seems likely that the suggestion would have a different tone, such as "We are prejudiced, sure. But why don't we just *deny it anyway*?" Notice that the phrase "deny it anyway" does not involve any type of belief proposal. Nor would the phrase "Why don't we just *say we believe* we are fair?" The proposal to "deny" or to "say" argues in favor of *making a specific assertion*—not in favor of holding a specific belief. If E plans to "say she knows nothing about discrimination," few of us would interpret this as plans to hold a certain belief. The obvious interpretation, rather, is that it is simply plans to *assert a certain belief*. The same should apply to collectives, that is, plans to assert a belief do not result in what can properly be called a collective belief.[12]

12.5 Identifying Collective Disagreements

Hence far, we have discussed the epistemology of disagreement literature, the criteria for a collective disagreement (i.e. a disagreement between at least two subjects that are about collectives), and what qualifies a belief as a collective one (i.e. the belief came about via a joint-commitment). It follows that a collective disagreement is between two entities, both of which hold collective beliefs.

This section will address the following: How can we even know a disagreement is a collective disagreement? After all, I have claimed that collective disagreements are often present when it is an individual who asserts a proposition. Although an individual might be speaking on behalf of a collective, the individual asserting the belief might not always clarify that they are speaking on the collective's behalf.[13] Instead, they are simply following through with their end of the bargain as a member of a group that jointly committed to a collective belief, that is, they are acting as though the beliefs true.[14]

The list below is a non-exhaustive list of "signals of collective disagreement." The combined signals are neither necessary nor sufficient for a collective disagreement; these factors are merely evidence markers in favor of collective disagreement without guaranteeing it. Moreover, I am leaving out the most obvious cases, that is, those in which an agent says something like "I am not speaking on my own behalf, but rather, on behalf of the SPCA." Similarly, "We, the American Philosophical Association, make the following statement of support…." While these are phrases that *can* make group disagreement obvious, I am focusing on group disagreement that has often been mistaken as individual disagreement. In other words, I am focusing on the non-obvious cases of group disagreement.

SIGNALS OF COLLECTIVE DISAGREEMENT

1 *Collective Correspondence*: Agents asserting the disputed belief are also members of collectives known to hold the same belief.
2 *Dependent Revision*: Revision of the disputed belief is closely linked (perhaps even dependent upon) to group revision.
3 *Group Projection*: Individuals expressing the disputed belief project a sense of speaking on behalf of a larger collective.
4 *Collective Evidence*: Agents expressing the disputed belief appeal to evidential merits tied to a group.
5 *Collective Rebuke*: If the agent(s) asserting the disputed belief were to reverse paths and acquiesce to a disagreeing party, the agent(s) would face rebuke from a group member.

I will say a bit more about each of these signals: (1) In *Collective Correspondence*, if an agent S asserts p, and p is also a belief that is (a) held by a collective, and (b) S is member of that collective, then what follows is (c) that the assertion might be a means of fulfilling a joint commitment to uphold belief in p. Suppose that S asserts that same-sex marriage ought to be prohibited. If S is also a member of the Baptist Church, and we know that the Baptist Church also believes that same-sex marriage should be prohibited, then we have at least one signal that S's assertion is a means of fulfilling his end of a joint commitment to uphold the belief of the Baptist Church.

Collective Correspondence is certainly not enough to *know* that a disagreement is collective. It is merely a signal that it *might be*. Yet it is an important signal because the conditions that fulfill it make collective disagreement possible. After all, if S asserts p, and S is *not* a member of a collective (or they are a member but not of a collective that believes p), then S is not asserting p on the collective's behalf. Collective disagreement requires collective belief. Suppose, for instance, that Sam is *not* a member of the American Philosophical Association. Notwithstanding, Sam asserts, "On behalf of the American Philosophical Association, I confirm that David Hume is unquestionably the best philosopher of the last 5 centuries." Sam is "seeming" to speak on behalf of a group. Seeming to speak on their behalf but not actually doing so because Sam not only lacks the authority to speak on the group's behalf, but also "speaking on behalf" must *accurately reflect a group belief.* Speaking on behalf is not simply expressing the speaker's own opinion or the speaker's opinion about the group's belief. It must be expressing the actual group belief.

The second signal, *dependent revision*, concerns the conditions that greatly increase the odds that an agent alters her expressed belief. Imagine a committed Catholic who is unlikely to alter her expressed stance on birth control unless the church alters theirs. This signals that the just mentioned assertions are a means of fulfilling a joint commitment owed to the Catholic Church. It is unlikely a matter of coincidence when an belief expressed by an agent alters in accordance with group belief.

Speaking on behalf of a collective (i.e. fulfilling a joint commitment to uphold a collective belief) might have a different "feel" than stating a personal opinion. Coincidentally, I myself recently experienced this type of "collective feeling." I was defending virtue ethicists against accusations of egoism. The experience in offering this defense was notably different from a seemingly similar experience I had the day before, when I defended my own paper against various critiques. When defending virtue ethics, I felt as though I was speaking on behalf of *all* virtue ethicists, or even anyone who might find virtue ethics compelling.

The "on behalf of" feeling is a vague concept. Perhaps this is the least helpful signal on the list. Notwithstanding, many long-standing disagreements involve parties who see themselves as defending a perspective that stretches far beyond themselves (political theories, religious theories, moral commitments, etc.). This might exacerbate the difficulty of arriving at a resolution.

Signal 4 (Collective Evidence) references the phenomenon of individual group members depending on (or appealing to, making use of, etc.) evidence that belongs to the collective itself, but not to the individual. By "belongs to," I am referencing the ability to gain full access and understanding to a piece of evidence.

In small collectives, it might be difficult to distinguish between the collective's evidence and member evidence. Imagine that S is a member of the American Council for Mental Health. While the ACMH is world-wide, there are local chapters, and S attends monthly meetings where she learns about developments in mental health research. Several months earlier, a survey was distributed that asked ACMH members with relevant experience to convey their thoughts about a new depression treatment, "XX." S lacks experience with XX, so she refrained from completing the survey. At the next meeting, S learns that the ACMH concluded that they cannot recommend XX. ACMH not only commits to this collective belief privately; they also make a public statement condemning XX as ineffective and dangerous.

Imagine that S finds herself in an argument with a pharmaceutical lobbyist who speaks on behalf of XX's manufacturer. As the argument intensifies, a small crowd coalesces. In her attempt to win the argument, S asserts that the treatment is ineffective and dangerous, appealing to the survey of the ACMH. She mentions that two patients lost their life using the drug, and that the drug's manufacturer already has multiple complaints filed against it through various consumer protection agencies.

S is epistemically and morally justified in doing all of the above. Group members appealing to "collective evidence" (supporting information that is only accessible via or in virtue of her group membership) would not normally raise epistemic eyebrows. Insofar as S acts on behalf of the group, the relevant body of evidence includes the email surveys, member testimony, feedback from local chapters, and more. This is evidence that the collective itself possesses, as a unified subject. (Collective Evidence is different from the aggregate of member evidence, because members might keep some evidence to themselves.)

While S can appeal to Collective Evidence when she speaks as a group member, arguably she *cannot* do the same if she is speaking on behalf of herself. After all, she has no idea what any of the members wrote in the survey. Moreover, because this area is not within her realm of expertise, she is unsuited to assess whether the group decision sounds plausible. For all these reasons, S using Collective Evidence as personal evidence is suspect. There seems a difference between citing evidence when group members speak on a group's behalf, and when group members speak as mere individuals. Someone might argue that trust in the group ought to justify using the group's evidence. But using testimony as evidence is different than using the group evidence itself. Speaking only for herself, S might say that she is skeptical of XX's efficacy because she trusts the testimony of the ACMH. This is different than appealing to specific surveys that were sponsored by the ACMH. Trusting a what a friend tells you is different than trusting your friend's evidence.

The last signal of collective disagreement concerns Gilbert's concept of rebuke. *Collective rebuke* is a potential consequence violating joint commitments. And it is only through joint commitment that agents might acquire what Gilbert calls the "standing" to issue this rebuke.[15]

One sign that a disagreement is collective occurs when (1) an agent, let us call her S, is engaged in a disagreement over p: (2) suppose S has been asserting p for some time, and (3) S suddenly has a reverse course and asserts *not-p*, now expressing agreement with whom she previously disagreed, then (4) a collective of which S is a member issues a rebuke against S for this change. For instance, imagine S is a well-known vegan, public intellectual, and PETA member. S has long asserted that animal "kill" shelters are immoral. However, imagine S surprisingly writes an editorial defending kill shelters as sad but necessary. We can easily imagine the following:

1. S gets angry phone calls from PETA governing associates, who ask her questions like, "What were you thinking?" and "Do you realize how much damage you have done?"
2. PETA writes an editorial condemning S and her newly expressed stance on kill shelters. The article includes phrases like, "S does not speak for us," and "PETA is united in our continued condemnation of kill shelters."
3. There are many angry emails in S's inbox from low-rank, dues-paying, PETA members that include criticisms along the lines of "How could you have said that?" or "You know that there are hundreds of alternatives to heartless execution, don't you?"

Regardless of what anyone thinks of PETA, these reactions are understandable. An explanation is that S, in previously condemning kill shelters, was expressing the collective belief of PETA, not her personal views. While group members can and often do speak against a group belief, other members thereby possess "the standing" (i.e., it makes sense for them to do so, the rational consequences of the situation support them doing so, etc.). *Hence, when an agent faces rebuke for switching sides, this is a sign that they have been speaking on behalf of a collective.*

12.6 Lasting and Passionate Disagreements are Frequently Collective Disagreements

This section contends that many disagreements that we assume to be between individuals are actually between collectives. This is owing to the social nature of the way we form beliefs, especially beliefs about values or beliefs that otherwise have what you might call a "normative tinge."

Imagine a University of Rochester student sitting in his adviser's office. The adviser says to the student, "And see, doesn't that seem plausible grounds to think agents must have access to some type of epistemic justification?" This is a collective belief proposal, that is, a Gilbertian extension to join a collective belief. Will the student accept this invitation? Acceptance, of course, is not necessary. But there is undoubtedly social pressure arising from the desire to please a supervisor. There might also be (plausible) epistemic grounds to do so. After all, an expert has just offered a reasoned defense of internalism. If the student expresses acceptance, he becomes a member of a collective, that is, the collective consisting of the student and the supervisor. As part of this collective, the student becomes obligated, via joint commitment, to uphold the relevant collective belief (i.e. the belief in epistemic justification).

Because humans are social creatures, we tend to discuss all sorts of theoretical and/or normative issues, even if the discussion never rises to expert philosophical theory. Even gossip at the lunch table can touch on theory (Why would the boss make Julia work Saturday?), the normative (It is foolish to make Julia work Saturday.), and the ethical. (It is wrong to make Julia work Saturday.) Because these issues are frequently discussed together (collectively), there is a high chance that corresponding collective beliefs arise.

There is no sense in making statistical claims about the percentage of normative beliefs that are collective beliefs, nor regarding what percentage of disagreements are collective disagreements. But it is reasonable to believe that *many* normative beliefs are collective ones, and that many disagreements, especially normative disagreements, are between collectives rather than individuals.

I will now argue that *if* I am correct that many normative disagreements are between collectives, this changes the philosophical landscape (in respect to peer disagreement) in noteworthy ways. Let's remember that the disagreement literature has long focused on individual belief and individual disagreement.[16] However, if (1) many beliefs and many disagreements are actually between collectives, and (2) many disagreements often considered most "important" (i.e., those about values) are in fact collective disagreements, then two results follow. First, the literature has ignored, overlooked, or undertheorized a meaningful class of disagreements. And second, normative recommendations regarding disagreements might be misleading or incomplete. At the very least, it makes sense to reexamine these recommendations in light of the realization that many disagreements are collective disagreements. After all, why would we assume that the best epistemic response for *individual* disagreement is also the best for *collective* disagreement? Advice for individuals, in many areas of life, proves inapt or irrelevant for collectives. This shouldn't be surprising as the mechanism of action in individuals is often different from the mechanism of action in collectives. At the least, philosophers should *consider* whether individual and collective disagreements require distinct normative recommendations.

12.7 Problems with Peerhood

In this section I will make an argument for why, epistemically speaking, groups often are *epistemically* obligated to reevaluate their beliefs in response to disagreement. The gist of my argument is that, given the nature of group belief (on the Gilbert model I described), there is a high propensity for error. Because of this, the epistemic obligation to reconsider arises frequently. Notwithstanding, you can disagree with this entire section, and the main thesis of the paper will still have significant philosophical import. All that is necessary to take on board is the following non-controversial claim: groups *sometimes* have good reason to reevaluate their beliefs in response to disagreement.

The epistemology of disagreement literature typically focuses on disagreement between peers. I want to quickly explain why peerhood is a difficult, and less relevant, concept for groups.

In the (mostly individual) disagreement literature, there is much disagreement about peerhood. What most *agree* to is that peers are some type of intellectual equal and that this equality status supports taking the opinion of peers seriously. Many think peerhood requires some vague type of equality of evidence and vague equality of cognitive ability. There is much variance between scholars regarding who should count as a peer and when.[17]

The problems about peerhood are worse with groups. And things get exponentially worse as groups get larger. Consider disagreements between the Republican Party and the Democratic Party. If a small Democrat Committee in New Orleans has information about the local election, this is plausibly group evidence. Notwithstanding, it is unlikely most democrats are aware of this evidence, much less the republicans. The upshot is this: because group evidence is terribly hard to assess, and because evidence is almost always relevant to peerhood, evaluating group evidence is immensely difficult. While there might be circumstances in which such an evaluation is possible, this seems the exception, not the rule. So, if "group peers" exist, groups will nonetheless, in typical circumstances, lack justified reasons for thinking this peerhood exists. Even in the best cases, such peer assessment would be little more than a guess.

Some might argue that peerhood can be evaluated via *track record*. But one problem is that peerhood is tied to a particular question or at least a particular topic/area of study. How to define the scope of the subject to assess track record will be disputed. And because groups are often ideological, there ought to be real concerns that track record defining would be biased.[18] Disagreeing groups are unlikely to be the best ones to judge the historical epistemic success of the disagreeing party. However, since there is rarely a central agency evaluating track records of expressed group opinion, there is not an easy alternative. So groups should be hesitant to discount other opinions unless they have *especially strong* evidence regarding abysmal track records.

If collectives are often in the dark about peerhood, are there epistemic grounds for reevaluating belief in response to disagreement? There's reason to think, "yes." We can use the same justification that was used to doubt the efficacy of track record assessment: because groups are prone to ideological biases, epistemic honesty requires a healthy skepticism toward their own positions. The more reason to believe an agent is prone to error, the more seriously this agent should take countervailing evidence. After all, this needs little argument: if S's odds of epistemic error are 80%, then S has more reason to take disagreement seriously than if S's error odds are 5%. Of course, it will matter where that disagreement is coming from, at least to some degree. But the point about bias is often, especially with "big issue" disagreements, groups are ill-equipped to evaluate where that disagreement is coming from.

Given well-documented tendencies of group behavior, there is strong reason to err on the side of reevaluation, that is, to think that the world would be better off epistemically if groups spent a lot more time reevaluating their beliefs.[19] This does not require them to change beliefs; it only asks them to assess their beliefs in light of new evidence, that is, the evidence of the disagreement itself, and perhaps any argument/evidence presented by the disagreeing agent. Moreover, epistemic reconsideration is not that risky. It is not the demand that the group *change* belief or enter a state of doubt. Reconsideration *might* result in a state of doubt, or a change of belief, but it often it will not. "Often" because, as will be argued below, structural features of group belief impose pragmatic difficulties regarding revision. If changing group belief is indeed difficult, then the risk/reward calculation speaks much in favor of reevaluation: there is a non-trivial chance that a group belief is wrong, or at least not fully right (due to ideological/in-group bias). Reconsideration might get closer to the truth. The odds that the group has the correct belief but upon reconsideration will have an incorrect belief are low. First, because changing beliefs are difficult; second, because groups will be inclined to support their own position. If already inclined to "over-support" their own view, change will require demonstrable evidence pointing toward the falsity of the group's belief before. There is little risk, then, of going from a true belief to a false one.

Besides empirical reasons, there are conceptual reasons to worry about ideological stubbornness, that is, the very thing that defines a group is often, and maybe always, ideological. By "ideological" I mean committed to a specific idea, belief, value, and so on. The commitment (the loyalty) to this value can hinder epistemic honesty. Groups might judge the ideological value of greater importance than epistemic value. For instance, the Catholic Church is committed to values that uphold the "sanctity" of human life. Suppose there is a collective gathering of Catholics, and evidence is presented that suggests young fetuses lack many life-like features that older fetuses possess. If the church were to form the belief that "young fetuses lack important life-like features," this threatens the church's values. Or at the least, the belief could be *interpreted* as threatening the church's values. Hence, the group might refuse to hold this belief, despite the epistemic evidence. Catholic values can help explain why epistemology loses this particular battle.

Groups are often formed via shared values or common causes: for example, those who work together want good pay, benefits, a stress-free work environment, and many other goods along these lines. Likewise, religious organizations have a shared set of values and often a shared commitment to a particular way of life. The campus atheists club, also, can have similarly shared values and commitments. One commitment might be overturning the hold of theism on contemporary society, while the campus Christian club might have the opposite commitment.

Often the purpose of a group, that is, the justification for its existence, is advocacy. An LGBT advocacy group fights for the rights and needs of the LGBT community, a teacher's union for the rights and needs of the teachers, and a victims' advocacy group for the special interests of victims. Even if we look at small groups formed *merely on the basis of a collective belief*, this group still shares a common commitment, that is, the commitment to their shared belief. Suppose S1 meets S2 at a bus stop. S1 laments to S2, "I can't stand the new buss advertisement, it's an eyesore." S1's statement is a Gilbertian collective belief proposal. Suppose S2 responds as follows: "You are absolutely right. It is such a shame the public will have such an ugly advertisement roaming through their streets." S2's statement finalizes the joint commitment, so S1 and S2 hold a collective belief along the lines of, "The new advertisement is an eyesore." They are together committed to uphold the truth of this statement. This, itself, is a form of ideological commitment. Suppose a third person came along and said, "You know, I love the new bus advertisement because the artist using amazing color matching." S1 and S2 are under pressure to reject this statement, pressure they would not have been under without the presence of the relevant collective belief. Even if S2 finds this new claim compelling, they might not express as much, for the fear of getting rebuked from S1. If situations like this create ideological pressure, then nearly any collective belief can do so.

I will end by stressing what was mentioned at the start of this section: even if you reject the dismal assessment of group epistemic reliability, that is, the problems with group bias, you can still agree that, *at least sometimes*, groups ought to reconsider their opinion in response to disagreement. If so, what follows will still be important. I argue that the structural features of groups make it very unlikely that groups will reevaluate belief in response to disagreement, (including when they epistemically ought to.)

12.8 Why Group Belief Is Stagnant

This section (Section 12.8) explains why groups are unlikely to reevaluate belief. Some will think this is obvious, from what has already been said about group bias, that is, groups are unlikely to reevaluate belief because they are unlikely to think that they need to do so, because they are biased about the truth of their belief, and true beliefs need no revision. This is all compelling. But let us suppose that the disagreeing group has a compelling case, strong enough to overcome this bias. There are still problems.

12.8.1 Problems Getting Started

Groups are hesitant to change belief, insofar as members will be hesitant to make a suggestion contrary to the group belief (for the members will fear rebuke).[20] But it is only by making a suggestion to change a group belief that the group can change it.

12.8.2 Changing Belief Hurts Credibility

Changing a group belief might work against the purpose of the group itself. Suppose a worker's union disagrees with the city council about safe working conditions. Imagine that the best epistemic response for the worker's union is to reconsider their relevant claims in light of the city council's disagreement, and also disagreement from others. But reconsidering can do nothing to help the cause. If working conditions are actually safe, the union loses public respect.

12.8.3 The False Belief is Beneficial

Not only will group members avoid starting the reevaluation process (for doing so risks rebuke), but, even more, group goals are often in direct conflict with epistemic goals. If a group holds a belief that furthers their group's values, ideals, and pragmatic ends, then little good can come from reevaluating that belief. At the least, reevaluating can seem like an unforced error that fails to serve not only the purposes to which the group is committed but often the purposes that justify the very existence of the group in the first place. Of course, individuals may sometimes refuse to reconsider beliefs for similar reasons. Notwithstanding, the problem is particularly pronounced in groups. Groups are prone to what has been called "pluralistic ignorance." This occurs when individual group members all believe p, yet individual group members also believe that *the other* group members believe *not-p*. For instance, a group member might think it is best for the group to change believes, but this group member also believes that he is the *only member who thinks this way.* Hence, he assumes he will be rebuked, mocked, criticized, and so on for proposing a change. Individuals, on the other hand, don't fear their own rebuke in the same way group members fear group rebuke. Moreover, it is typically easier for an individual to change their mind about values than for a group to do so. Group values are often grounded in tradition, and the very purpose of the group might be to uphold these values. So if the group were to discard these values, they might threaten their existence. Individuals, however, change values frequently, and changing values does not threaten individual existence.

12.8.4 Pragmatic Difficulties

Let us contrast change/reconsideration of group belief with the same regarding individuals. Suppose S1 finds out that he disagrees with S2; S1 can almost immediately start reconsidering. Perhaps he cannot immediately alter belief, but he can at least pause and reflect on whether the reasons he has for believing are good ones. But with groups, not only changing or revising but also just reconsidering might demand that a certain segment of the group, or the whole group, find the time to get together. In a group, especially a large one, the exchange of information and the offering of reasons are far more practically demanding than with an individual. Even more so is the discussion and the negotiation. Sometimes, individual belief revision requires deep, systematic thought and evidence gathering. But often, just hearing a different opinion is enough. Not so with groups. Often, groups have a hard time getting members to do all kinds of pragmatic tasks: for example, the Catholic Church has a hard time getting its members to go to mass, and the Philosophy Undergraduate Club has a difficult time getting enough to show at weekly meetings. Groups might find it unfeasible to garner the necessary contingent to make reconsideration possible. Even if groups find this feasible, they might not wish to spend their resources on this end; resources could be spent on other ends that more directly serve the group's purpose. Individual belief reconsideration usually requires much less resources. Individuals do not need to find a common time to meet on Skype, nor must individuals pay to fly themselves all the way from both Florida and Wisconsin.

12.9 The Individual Epistemic Dilemma

Suppose an agent, let us call her the *Independent Epistemologist*, knows that humans are prone to join collectives and that collectives often engage in epistemically suspect belief forming and maintaining practices, or otherwise fall short of epistemic ideals. Supposing that our Independent Epistemologist cares about forming true and/or justified beliefs and avoiding false and/or unjustified ones. More generally, she cares about epistemic excellence. How ought she to approach this reality?

Perhaps the Independent Epistemologist should keep collective and personal beliefs in specially marked and distinct cognitive components. Gilbert's theory makes clear that collective beliefs need not concur with member beliefs; there is no contradiction in belonging to a group that thinks P and personally believing not-P.[21] Likewise, our Independent

Epistemologist can aim to acquire epistemic habits apart from the habits of her group. For instance, even though her group might approach belief revision with a closed mind, she might have an open mind. However, spending time in groups who assert a class of p-like beliefs, while holding no sympathies to p-like beliefs oneself, is difficult. Groups committed to p-like beliefs will not spend much time discussing evidence contra to p. More probably, they will spend time collecting evidence that *supports p*. Hence, group membership, other things being equal, results in one's being exposed to evidence supporting group belief and lack of access to contrary evidence.

To balance out evidential bias, group members must collect evidence on their own terms. Not only are most persons busy, but members of groups committed to p have all sorts of social pressures to refrain from this practice. A member of a Christian church, for instance, seems unlikely to search for evidence against God's existence or against the divinity of Jesus. A vegan club member is unlikely to search for evidence supporting the health benefits of meat-eating or to spend hours reading testimonies from "ethical meat-eaters." Even if members of these groups desired to do so for genuine epistemic reasons, they would need to balance this desire against the possibility of social sanction. Hence, compartmentalization is pragmatically difficult, for both emotional and social reasons (i.e. it "feels" wrong for members of group G to research evidence in conflict with G's principles; moreover, even without internal guilt, groups might fear external sanctions. Moreover, spending time in a group results in exposure to selective evidence. And one's evidence, however, gathered, will influence belief).[22]

While advocacy groups, on average, might leave little room for belief divergence, other groups might fall in between demanding belief confirmation and accepting belief divergence. But the more a member diverges, the less accepting most groups will be. Hence, even though members can hold contrary beliefs to the group, especially with Gilbert's personal disclaimer (i.e. "I personally believe" or, popular today, "This opinion is mine alone), divergence, especially repeated divergence, still comes with the risk of group rebuke. Rebuke, moreover, is a signal of alienation. Those who frequently express "group-conflicting beliefs" might face problems with close intellectual relationships or moving up the inner-group hierarchy, even if they are not removed from the group entirely. This, the inability to form close in-group bounds and move up in social status, is *intellectually* costly in addition to being personally costly. We learn much from others, often more than we would learn by ourselves.[23]

Group membership can be epistemically valuable for many other reasons. There is the simple division of labor. We lack time to read and research everything of interest. Trusting members to do some of the reading and research helps us acquire information, perhaps even knowledge.

Likewise, the collective in its entirety shares a collective body of evidence which is often superior to the evidence of one individual. Simply hearing group testimony, belief aside, can provides an epistemic edge. For example, if Dr. Smith listens to Dr. Johnson regarding an exciting new cancer treatment, Smith might be tipped off to a new area of research that wouldn't have otherwise crossed his path.

While *epistemic independence* is epistemically valuable, that is, persons who think for themselves will be less likely to fall prone to epistemically troublesome group-think, this is compatible with *epistemic isolation* being detrimental. *Often an agent has to choose between an action which shows independent thought and an action which will curry favor with his group.*

Thus, the Dismal Individual Epistemic Dilemma

> *DIED:* avoiding bad beliefs is in conflict with acquiring true beliefs.

So, again, what should the Independent Epistemologist do? What is the best way to respond to the dilemma? First, the best epistemic agents are careful in which groups they join. While all collective beliefs create partisan pressure, groups can be more or less problematic. Groups of scholars are probably less problematic than groups of ideologically motivated political parties or religious sects.[24] Moreover, the best epistemic agents will be skilled in distinguishing between different groups within the same class. For instance, a scholar might notice the opportunity to join several different research groups. The best epistemic agent will take care to consider which group has the most, and which group the least, problematic collective belief forming processes.

Choosing one's group wisely is important, but there is more to the story. The best epistemic agent must develop a more general all-purpose skill, something similar to what Aristotle called practical wisdom.[25] *This wisdom will involve balancing independent thought with collective intellectual engagement.* It involves knowing when it makes sense to voice opinion that diverges from group opinion, and when this divergence is not worth the intellectual cost. This wisdom involves thinking about whether embarking on a conversation is wise, given that it will result in a collective belief (or the awkward refusal to accept a collective belief proposal). There are many others, as that is the nature of this type of wisdom. The situations that must be epistemically evaluated stretch wide.

12.10 Conclusion

This paper argued for a number of related points that suggest that the epistemology of disagreement literature has overlooked important aspects of the phenomenon. One central point is that many disagreements assumed to be between individuals are better understood as disagreements between collectives. Other points follow. Collective belief reconsideration, in response to collective disagreement, is often merited. Yet it is rarely acted upon. This epistemic failure is best explained via collectives prioritizing non-epistemic ends. These groups might be capable of understanding that belief revision is justified, but they make no attempt to revise belief because doing so would undermine prioritized, non-epistemic ends.

Since group members are not themselves the group, it need not follow that epistemic failures of the former will fall upon the latter. Members can aim for independence, and to avoid holding the same unjustified beliefs as their group. But this independent epistemic agent faces a dilemma; she often must choose between avoiding false beliefs and acquiring true ones (because the group helps her acquire the latter, and doing the former alienates her from her group). The best epistemic agents have the wisdom to balance between these epistemic ends.

Notes

1 Discussions on just which beliefs are valuable, or whether all of them are valuable, and to what degree, include: Baehr, 2011; Marian, 2001; Carter & Pritchard, 2015; Haddock et al., 2009; Hu, 2017, and Kvanvig, 2005.

2 How I describe this situation bears some similarities to what Jennifer Lackey, 2015, has described as a group speaking through a "spokesperson." But there are also important distinctions. Lackey argues that if a spokesperson speaks on behalf of the group, the group's testimony is identical to the speaker's testimony. In some sense I agree. I think a spokesperson of the group claiming p often amounts to nothing more than the group claiming p. However, I understand *the group as primary* in the following way: often it is not that the spokesperson asserts p on their own belief, and therefore p automatically becomes the group belief. Rather, the spokesperson says "that p," regardless of whether the spokesperson personally believes p. The spokesperson says p because this is what the group believes. I am not denying that sometimes a spokesperson can do as Lacky describes. But that situation is not the focus of this paper, and there are other situations in which the spokesperson belief comes after the group's belief.

3 "While the discussion of disagreement isn't altogether absent from the history of philosophy, philosophers didn't start, as a group, thinking about the topic in a rigorous and detailed way until the 21st century" (Frances & Matheson, 2019).

4 Frances & Matheson, 2019, offer a comprehensive summary of the literature, and as their article and reference lists show, very little space in the literature is devoted to discussions of actual disagreement, to the distinction between theoretical and actual disagreement or to the plausibility of the normative recommendations in the disagreement literature.

5 See Boyce & Hazlett, 2016, and Frances & Matheson, 2019, Section 6.

6 In Lackey's 2015 piece, she suggests something similar, i.e., she argues that group testimony should be "...subsumed in my Statement View of (Individual) Testimony." (89.) In her 2018 publication, Lackey puts a different spin on things and argues that a "spokeperson" can speak on behalf of a group, regardless of what individual group members actually believe.

7 Tracy Isaacs has distinguished "collections" from "collective agents." Collections are simply aggregates of individuals that share a property(s).
8 The basic phenomenon of collective belief is described in the following (non-exhaustive list of) publications by Gilbert: 1987, 1989, 1990, 1993, 1999, 2001, 2006, 2008. See also these co-authored works: Gilbert & Priest, 2016, 2019, forthcoming; Gilbert & Pilchman, 2014.
9 This is explained clearly in Gilbert, 1987, and Gilbert & Priest, 2014.
10 See footnote 5 for the list of articles that helped me develop the description of collective belief.
11 This critical line of thought is sometimes called "rejectionism." Discussions that express such skepticism toward the very idea of "literal" collective belief include: Cohen, 1989, 1995; Pascal, 2000; Hakli, 2006; Mathiesen, 2006;Meijers,1999; Pettit, 2010; Schmitt, 1994; Tuomela, 1992, and Wray, 2001, 2003.
12 In Section 12.4, I aimed to show that (1) contra critics, many cases of group belief arising from joint commitment do, in fact, involve an exchange of evidence and appear to be based on epistemically justifying reasons, and (2), in at least typical cases, groups simply "choosing" to hold a belief despite of, and in contradiction to, the evidence, is not intuitively a case of group belief at all. Instead, what we have is a case of *apparent group belief*, or said differently, a group lie, i.e., a group claiming to believe p, even though they do not. I have not ruled out special cases in which Gilbert's critics are correct, and in which joint commitment results in a belief that is either voluntary and/or unreceptive to evidence. I will take no stance on whether this is possible. What I will say is that Gilbert's account describes many common instances of epistemically responsible group belief. Even if her account is not airtight (I take no stance on whether it is airtight), it still captures an important epistemic phenomenon. Maybe her account is best modified to fend off criticisms that arise in extreme cases, but many valuable epistemic theories have the same type of shortcoming, and still offer value because most cases are not extreme.
13 "Speaking on behalf of" is similar to Lackey's, 2015, "spokesperson" noted earlier.
14 Evidence in social psychology supports the thesis that group members can speak on behalf of a group even though the assertions are made from the first-person perspective. For example, Turner, 2000, argues that becoming a member of a group can have the effect of minimizing the individual's personal concept of the self and instead see their own personal concept as part of the group. Because individuals see themselves as part of a group, they can make assertions in the first person while really thinking of group opinion.
15 See Gilbert, 1987, 1989, 1990, 1993, 1999, and Priest & Gilbert, 2016.
16 For an exception, see Carter, 2016. Carter focuses on problems with groups being obligated to revise opinion in response to disagreement. One problem he suggests is that if a group is obligated to revise belief, then it is unclear how or who within the group might be obligated to take action in order for this revision to take place. I agree that in order for a group to revise belief, an individual member of the group will have to act in a certain way. And indeed, I show there are difficulties with persons actually acting this way. But I disagree with Carter that the problem is one about who within the group is obligated to do what. Groups, as I see them, are singular, collective agents. And groups can be obligated to A even if no individual within the group is obligated to take steps toward Aing. And even if members were obligated to take action that is the impetus for the group's Aing, those obligations would be distinct from the group's obligation for Aing. Imagine, for instance, a community group that has a book lovers club. The club promotes

the enjoyment of reading via various interactions with the community. Now imagine the club plans a book fare, and sells tickets to the community in an effort to raise money toward the remodel of the local library. However, on the day of the book fair, an emergency arises and the fair is canceled last minute. It makes sense to say that the book lovers club is obligated to do something to compensate those who purchased tickets. Maybe they can redo the event, or refund the money, or put on a different event, etc. But something must be done. It is easy to see why this is an obligation that falls on the book club. However, it is not obvious that any individual within the club would be obligated to take any act toward this end. Assuming the volunteer structure is non-hierarchical, there might not be one "obvious" step, nor any specific individual who must start the process. It still makes sense to say the book lovers club is obligated in the relevant way. If the book club does nothing, then the book club violated its obligation, regardless of whether any member of the group violated its obligation. The foundation of non-summative Gilbert-style collective theory is that groups, their actions, their obligations, and their other characteristics are divorced from the corresponding states in the group members. Carter's next worry is about a conflict between obligations—the conflict from the group's obligation to change belief and the member's obligation to act as though the belief is true. I discuss this later in the paper, and I have at least a connected worry. However, not the same conceptual worry Carter seems to have. There is no contradiction in obligations that can't be explained by different obligation types. A member's obligation to act as though p is true is a *non-epistemic* obligation, and the to act to revise the belief (in so far as it falls on the individual at all, it might, it might not) is an *epistemic obligation*. We are all familiar with conflicts between distinct obligation types.

17 Some articles discussing epistemic peers include Benjamin, 2015; Conee, 2009; King, 2011 & 2013; Licon, 2013; Schafer, 2015; Simpson, 2013.

18 Chambers et al., 2013 found that liberals and conservatives would evaluate groups better if the group aligned with their values, and worse if the group did not align with their values. The study, of course, attempted to control so that the groups, if evaluated objectively, would have received similar ratings. Interestingly, liberals and conservatives showed roughly equal bias in this respect. Of course, this study was of individuals evaluating groups, not groups evaluating groups. But if I am correct that individual belief is often a stand-in for group belief, the participants might have actually been evaluating the group as a member of their own group. I would argue this is what explains the bias. Other studies that show similar problems with group bias include: Tetlock, 2000; Chatman & Von Hippel, 2001; Wann & Grieve, 2005; Reingewertz & Lutmar, 2018, and Lyengar & Westwood, 2015. All of the just cited is more specific evidence of a very well documented phenomenon of in-group bias. By virtue of being a group, or in virtue of being a member of a group, agents are skewed toward assuming the truth of (1) statements that arise from members of their group, (2) statements that support the values that the group supports, (3) statements that confirm propositions that the group has already affirmed, especially publicly affirmed, and (4) statements from agents known to have values, beliefs, and commitments that oppose the group's values beliefs and commitments. All of this causes clear trouble for one group's ability to accurately assess the track record of another group, especially another group that has an active disagreement with the first group.

19 Relevant research on group behavior includes Mendleberg, 2002; Thau et al., 2015; Smelser, 2015; Chen & Li, 2009; Coie et al., 1990; Mintz,

1951; Barsade, 2002; Howard & Rothbart, 1980; Hogg, 2001; Swann et al., 2009; Slater et al., 2000 and Branscombe et al., 2010.

20 As mentioned, earlier in note 11, Carter, 2016 discusses something similar.

21 See Gilbert, 1987, 1989, and Gilbert & Priest, 2016.

22 Confirmation bias, a well-known phenomenon in individual psychology, has also been shown to be a problem in groups, i.e., groups also exhibit confirmation bias. See Schulz-Hardt et al., 2000

23 Johnson & Johnson, 2009, summarize the literature in interdependence theory and social learning and argue that, overall, the literature shows that persons learn better via activities that involve social interaction rather than on their own. See also Rusbult & Arriaga, 1997; Yamarik, 2007; Bowen, 2000; Maldonado et al., 2005, and Glynn et al., 2006.

24 (Perhaps epistemic excellence is in conflict with other sorts of excellence, like excellent public service or spiritual excellence.)

25 For more on Aristotle's practical wisdom, see Aristotle & Reeve, 2013.

References

Aristotle, & Reeve, C. D. (2013). *Aristotle on practical wisdom: Nicomachean ethics VI*. Cambridge, MA: Harvard University Press.

Baehr, J. (2011). Credit theories and the value of knowledge. *The Philosophical Quarterly*, 62(246), 1–22.

Barsade, S. G. (2002). The ripple effect: Emotional contagion and its influence on group behavior. *Administrative Science Quarterly*, 47(4), 644–675.

Benjamin, S. (2015). Questionable peers and spinelessness. *Canadian Journal of Philosophy*, 45(4), 425–444.

Bowen, C. W. (2000). A quantitative literature review of cooperative learning effects on high school and college chemistry achievement. *Journal of Chemical Education*, 77(1), 116.

Boyce, K., & Hazlett, A. (2016). Multi-peer disagreement and the preface paradox. *Ratio*, 29(1), 29–41.

Branscombe, N. R., Spears, R., Ellemers, N., & Doosje, B. (2002). Intragroup and intergroup evaluation effects on group behavior. *Personality and Social Psychology Bulletin*, 28(6), 744–753.

Carter, J. A. (2016). Group peer disagreement. *Ratio*, 29(1), 11–28.

Carter, J. A., & Pritchard, D. (2015). Knowledge-how and epistemic value. *Australasian Journal of Philosophy*, 93(4), 799–816.

Chambers, J. R., Schlenker, B. R., & Collisson, B. (2013). Ideology and prejudice: The role of value conflicts. *Psychological Science*, 24(2), 140–149.

Chatman, C. M., & Von Hippel, W. (2001). Attributional mediation of in-group bias. *Journal of Experimental Social Psychology*, 37(3), 267–272.

Chen, Y., & Li, S. X. (2009). Group identity and social preferences. *American Economic Review*, 99(1), 431–457.

Cohen, G. L. (2003). Party over policy: The dominating impact of group influence on political beliefs. *Journal of Personality and Social Psychology*, 85(5), 808.

Cohen, J. (1989). Belief and acceptance. *Mind*, 98 (391), 367–389.

Cohen, J. (1995). *An essay on belief and acceptance*. Oxford, UK: Clarendon Press.

Coie, J. D., Dodge, K. A., & Kupersmidt, J. B. (1990). Peer group behavior and social status. In S. R. Asher & J. D. Coie (Eds.), *Cambridge studies in social and emotional development. Peer rejection in childhood* (pp. 17–59). Cambridge, UK: Cambridge University Press.

Conee, E. (2009). Peerage. *Episteme*, 6(3), 313–323.

Frances, B., & Matheson, J. (2019). Disagreement. In E. N. Zalta (Ed.), *The Stanford encyclopedia of philosophy* (Winter 2019 Edition), forthcoming, https://plato.stanford.edu/archives/win2019/entries/disagreement/.

Gilbert, M. (1987). Modelling collective belief. *Synthese*, 73(1), 185–204.

Gilbert, M. (1989). *On social facts*. London, UK: Routledge.

Gilbert, M. (1990). Walking together: A paradigmatic social phenomenon. *MidWest Studies in Philosophy*, 15(1), 1–14.

Gilbert, M. (1993). Group membership and political obligation. *The Monist*, 76(1), 119–131.

Gilbert, M. (1999). Obligation and joint commitment. *Utilitas*, 11(2), 143–163.

Gilbert, M. (2001). Collective preferences, obligations, and rational choice. *Economics & Philosophy*, 17(1), 109–119.

Gilbert, M. (2006). Rationality in collective action. *Philosophy of the Social Sciences*, 36(1), 3–17.

Gilbert, M., & Pilchman, D. (2014). Belief, acceptance, and what happens in groups. In J. Lackey (Ed.), *Essays in collective epistemology* (pp. 189–212). Oxford, UK: Oxford University Press.

Gilbert, M. & Priest, M. (2014). Social rules. In B. Kaldis (Ed.), *Encyclopedia of philosophy and the social sciences*. Thousand Oaks, CA: Sage Publications.

Gilbert, M., & Priest, M. (2016). Conversations and collective belief. In A. Capone (Ed.), *Perspectives on pragmatics and philosophy* (pp. 1–33). New York, NY: Springer.

Gilbert, M., & Priest, M. (forthcoming). Collective responsibility and its relationship to member responsibility. In D. Tollefsen, & S. Bazargan-Forward (Ed.), *Routledge handbook of collective responsibility*. Oxford, UK: Routledge.

Gilbert, M., & Priest, M. (2013). Conversation and Collective Belief In A. Capone, F. LoPiparo, & M. Carapezza (Eds.), *Perspectives on Pragmatics and Philosophy*. New York NY: Springer.

Glynn, L. G., MacFarlane, A., Kelly, M., Cantillon, P., & Murphy, A. W. (2006). Helping each other to learn–A process evaluation of peer assisted learning. *BMC Medical Education*, 6(1), 18.

Haddock, A., Miller, A., & Pritchard, D. (2009). *Epistemic value*. Oxford, UK: Oxford University Press.

Hakli, R. (2006). Group beliefs and the distinction between belief and acceptance. *Cognitive Systems Research*, 7(2–3), 286–297.

Hogg, M. A. (2001). Social categorization, depersonalization, and group behavior. In Hogg, M.A. & S. Tindale (Eds.), *Blackwell handbook of social psychology: Group processes* (Vol. 4) (pp. 56–85). Hoboken, NJ: Wiley-Blackwell.

Howard, J. W., & Rothbart, M. (1980). Social categorization and memory for in-group and out-group behavior. *Journal of Personality and Social Psychology*, 38(2), 301.

Hu, X. (2017). Why do true beliefs differ in epistemic value? *Ratio*, 30(3), 255–269.

Isaacs, T. L. (2011). *Moral responsibility in collective contexts*. Oxford, UK: Oxford University Press.

Johnson, D. W., & Johnson, R. T. (2009). An educational psychology success story: Social interdependence theory and cooperative learning. *Educational researcher*, 38(5), 365–379.

Iyengar, S., & Westwood, S. J. (2015). Fear and loathing across party lines: New evidence on group polarization. *American Journal of Political Science*, 59(3), 690–707.

King, N. L. (2011). Disagreement: What's the problem? Or a good peer is hard to find. *Philosophy and Phenomenological Research*, 85(2), 249–272. doi:10.1111/j.1933-1592.2010.00441.x

King, N. L. (2013). Disagreement: The skeptical arguments from peerhood and symmetry. In D. Machuca (Ed.), *Disagreement and skepticism* (pp. 193–217). New York, NY: Routledge.

Kvanvig, J. (2005). Truth is not the primary epistemic goal. In Steup, M., & Sosa E. (Eds.), *Contemporary debates in epistemology* (pp. 285–296). Oxford, UK: Blackwell.

Lackey, J. (2015). A deflationary account of group testimony. In J. Lackey (Ed.), *Essays in collective epistemology* (pp. 64–94). Oxford, UK: Oxford University Press.

Lackey, J. (2018a). Group assertion. *Erkenntnis*, 83(1), 21–42.

Lackey, J. (2018b). Group lies. In E. Michaelson & A. Stokke (Eds.), *Lying: Language, knowledge, ethics, and politics* (pp. 262–284). Oxford, UK: Oxford University Press.

Licon, J. A. (2013). On merely modal epistemic peers: Challenging the equal-weight view. *Philosophia*, 41(3), 809–823.

Maldonado, H., Lee, J. E. R., Brave, S., Nass, C., Nakajima, H., Yamada, R., & Morishima, Y. (2005, May). We learn better together: Enhancing e-learning with emotional characters. In C. Chinn, G. Erkens, & S. Puntambkar (Eds.), Taipei, Tawain: *Proceedings of 2005 conference on computer support for collaborative learning: learning 2005: The next 10 years!* (pp. 408–417). International Society of the Learning Sciences.

Marian, D. (2001). Truth as the epistemic goal. In M. Steup (Ed.), *Knowledge, truth, and duty: Essays on epistemic justification, responsibility, and virtue* (pp. 151–169). New York, NY: Oxford University Press.

Mathiesen, K. (2006). The epistemic features of group belief. *Episteme*, 2(03), 161–175.

McMahon, C. (2002). Two modes of collective belief. *Protosociology*, 18(19), 347–362.

Meijers, A. W. M. (1999). Believing and accepting as a group. In *Belief, cognition and the will* (pp. 59–73). Tilburg, Netherlands: Tilburg University Press.

Mendleberg, T. (2002). The deliberative citizen: Theory and evidence. In M. Delli Carpini, L. Huddy, & R. Shapiro (Eds.), *Political decision making, deliberation and participation* (Vol. 6) (pp. 151–193). Cambridge, MA: Elsevier.

Mintz, A. (1951). Non-adaptive group behavior. *The Journal of Abnormal and Social Psychology*, 46(2), 150.

Pettit, P. (2010). Groups with minds of their own. In A. Goldman, & D. Whitcomb (Eds.), *Social epistemology: Essential readings*. New York, NY: Oxford University Press.

Reingewertz, Y., & Lutmar, C. (2018). Academic in-group bias: An empirical examination of the link between author and journal affiliation. *Journal of Informetrics*, 12(1), 74–86.

Rusbult, C. E., & Arriaga, X. B. (1997). *Interdependence theory*. In H. T. Reis, & S. Sprecher (Ed.), *Encyclopedia of human relationships*. Thousand Oaks, CA: Sage Publications.

Schafer, K. (2015). How common is peer disagreement? On self-trust and rational symmetry. *Philosophy and Phenomenological Research*, 91(1), 25–46.

Schmitt, F. (1994). The justification of group beliefs. In F. Schmitt (Ed.), *Socializing epistemology*. Lanham, MD: Rowman & Littlefield.

Schulz-Hardt, S., Frey, D., Lüthgens, C., & Moscovici, S. (2000). Biased information search in group decision making. *Journal of Personality and Social Psychology*, 78(4), 655.

Simpson, R. M. (2013). Epistemic peerhood and the epistemology of disagreement. *Philosophical Studies*, 164(2), 561–577.

Slater, M., Sadagic, A., Usoh, M., & Schroeder, R. (2000). Small-group behavior in a virtual and real environment: A comparative study. *Presence: Teleoperators & Virtual Environments*, 9(1), 37–51.

Smelser, J. (2013). *Theory of collective behavior*. New York, NY: Free Press/ Old South Books.

Souva, M. (2004). Institutional similarity and interstate conflict. *International Interactions*, 30(3), 263–280.

Swann, Jr., W. B., Gómez, A., Seyle, D. C., Morales, J., & Huici, C. (2009). Identity fusion: The interplay of personal and social identities in extreme group behavior. *Journal of Personality and Social Psychology*, 96(5), 995.

Tetlock, P. E. (2000). Cognitive biases and organizational correctives: Do both disease and cure depend on the politics of the beholder? *Administrative Science Quarterly*, 45(2), 293–326.

Thau, S., Derfler-Rozin, R., Pitesa, M., Mitchell, M. S., & Pillutla, M. M. (2015). Unethical for the sake of the group: Risk of social exclusion and pro-group unethical behavior. *Journal of Applied Psychology*, 100(1), 98.

Tuomela, R. (1992). Group beliefs. *Synthese*, 91(3), 285–318.

Turner, J. C. (2010). Social categorization and the self-concept: A social cognitive theory of group behavior. In T. Postmes & N. R. Branscombe (Eds.), *Key readings in social psychology. Rediscovering social identity* (p. 243–272). Psychology Press.

Wann, D. L., & Grieve, F. G. (2005). Biased evaluations of in-group and out-group spectator behavior at sporting events: The importance of team identification and threats to social identity. *The Journal of Social Psychology*, 145(5), 531–546.

Wray, B. (2001). Collective belief and acceptance. *Synthese*, 129 (3), 319–333.

Wray, B. (2003). What really divides gilbert and the rejectionists. *Protosociology*, 18(19), 363–376.

Yamarik, S. (2007). Does cooperative learning improve student learning outcomes? *The Journal of Economic Education*, 38(3), 259–277.

13 A Plea for Complexity

The Normative Assessment of Groups' Responses to Testimony

Nikolaj Nottelmann

13.1 Introduction

It is far from uncommon to judge that some group has responded inappropriately to testimony. The long-standing historic disagreement between the official position of "Big Tobacco"[1] and credible scientific testimony on cancerogenesis has aroused strong public sentiments (Brandt 2012). The Trump administration's disputes with the scientific community over anthropogenic climate change has led prominent commentators to hold it in contempt (see, e.g., Mecklin 2019). And the opinion is often heard that the Roman Catholic Church should have responded much earlier and more decisively to allegations of widespread child abuse among parts of its clergy (Rojas 2019 is representative of many voices in this debate).

In each such case, we must take seriously the claim that a group's response to testimony and disagreement has fallen short of important normative standards. Also, in each case, the relevant criticism befalls the group as a group, rather than just its individual members. Surely, for example, in the cases of Big Tobacco and the Catholic Church, some may single out specific members of those organizations for special criticism, such as the pope or the CEO of Philip Morris International Inc. Yet the matter is hardly settled by a change of personnel or the shaming of individuals. Rather, the common attitude is that said *organizations* ought to apologize and compensate their victims, no matter which specific individuals fill up their ranks.

However, spelling out exactly which norms have been violated in such cases is no easy feat. As we shall see shortly, nor is explaining exactly why a group could legitimately be held blameworthy for its failure to meet the relevant standards.[2] This presents an important theoretical challenge.

This chapter is organized as follows. In Section 13.2, I discuss the basic problems endemic to the normative assessment of an individual's responses to testimony. Section 13.3 presents the Transfer Problem of re-employing lessons from the individual level to the collective level. Section 13.4 then examines how extant accounts of group-level epistemic justification and its relationship to ethical concerns have arguably proceeded from highly questionable methodological assumptions. Not least, typically, theorists have presumed that basic criteria for groupness and group belief must be settled by appeal to some generic theory before contextualized epistemological and ethical evaluation even begins. Section 13.5 presents reasons to attack the Transfer Problem differently. A sequence of contexts is presented, each requiring the epistemological and/or ethical evaluation of a group agent. It emerges that plausibly adequate criteria of *groupness*, *group membership*, *group attitudes*, and *group belief justification* could radically shift between such contexts. Not least, it is crucially important whether we are interested in evaluating a group as a collective moral agent or merely as a collective epistemic performer. I sketch a model of a "group mind" adequate for the former purpose. Section 13.6 concludes.

13.2 The Normative Assessment of Individual Responses to Testimony

Consider a possible community, much smaller than ours, where the role of Big Tobacco is performed by an individual person named Big Toby. Even though originally, Toby's community agreed that a moderate consumption of his tobacco products is relatively harmless, over time, more and more of its respected scientists began to present strong written and verbal evidence to the effect that those products present a serious health hazard. Toby clearly assesses and understands at least central parts of this scientific testimony. Yet he continues his arduous efforts to recruit new customers. In his public statements, he clearly aims to manifest his disagreement with the scientific reports concerning their evidential strength. Overall, he publicly presents himself as a respectable marketeer, providing a product at a reasonable price, which helps customers enjoy themselves and express their personalities. Moreover, he invests significant parts of his profits in funding research aiming to undercut the alleged evidence of the concerned scientists. He also aims at influencing lawmakers not to disallow or hinder his traditional methods of manufacture, marketing, and sale.

How are we to judge Big Toby based on this story? Obviously, much hinges on how we assess his sincerity. He clearly communicates that his products are perfectly safe and that the conclusions of differing scientists are ill-grounded, but does he also *believe* this, despite knowing of the scientists' contrary statements? Suppose he does. In that case, his failure is primarily epistemic. He has failed appropriately to upgrade his beliefs based on his evidence. His current evidence indicates that the scientists' conclusions are most likely true. His conservative beliefs do not reflect that epistemic situation. However, given Toby's beliefs, his speech-acts and general behavior do not, by themselves, reflect badly on him. He could be guided entirely by intentions either morally neutral or praiseworthy, such as the intention to earn a decent profit by marketing a beneficial and much-demanded product. Still, his epistemic failure may indicate a deeper moral failure. Even if it would seem highly contentious to argue that epistemic unjustifiedness is morally bad *per se* (see Haack 1997), perhaps Toby's particular epistemic failure is down to him, morally speaking. Not least, his epistemic failure perhaps reflects a deeper moral failure, such as the failure to devote enough energy to evaluating his evidence, given the moral stakes of getting such important matters right. On the other hand, it might also be that Toby is morally excused, even if we judge his belief evidentially unjustified. For instance, for whatever reason, due to no fault of his, he may simply be psychologically unable to adapt to his new evidential situation (BonJour 2002, p. 236).

Suppose now that Toby's assertions are *insincere*: really, he is deeply affected by the evidence against tobacco safety and no longer believes that his products are safe. Rather, when performing his role as a tobacco marketeer, he merely chooses to *pretend* that his products are safe for purposes of marketing and public communication; that is to say, for those purposes, he adopts a policy of deeming that proposition true, of using it as a premise in his practical reasoning (i.e., his pretense is an *acceptance* in the technical sense of Cohen 1989, p. 368). This policy reflects a reprehensible configuration of conative states, not least the intention to put his preference for easy profit above anything else. Here, Toby's failure is clearly and primarily moral. His epistemic failure is merely apparent due to his policy of performing insincere assertive speech-acts (at least if we do not consider his false assertions epistemic failures *per se*).

To sum up, when an individual agent A accepts that p for the purposes of performing some social role and her testimonial evidence does not warrant her believing p, this is consistent with at least three ways she could be at fault:

1 A believes p, and this belief falls short of epistemic standards. We have nothing else to criticize.
2 A believes p, and this belief falls short of epistemic standards, but additionally, A is morally at fault for this epistemic shortcoming.
3 A does not believe p. Her acceptance of p for the purposes of performing her social role is insincere and opportunistic. It reflects a morally blameworthy disregard for the goal of accepting the true answer to the question whether p for the purposes of performing her relevant social role.

13.3 The General Transfer Problem

How many of the considerations from Section 13.2 translate to the case of an actual group agent like Big Tobacco, composed out of five international tobacco companies, interacting in a host of ways and each constituted by thousands of individuals organized in a highly complex hierarchy? Any hope of an easy solution to this *Transfer Problem* seems frustrated by a set of problems comprising at least the following elements:

3.1 When and how does a piece of testimony enter a group's evidence pool? While we have a reasonably clear idea of what it means for a piece of testimony to count as an individual's evidence, the issue is far murkier at the collective level. A group does not literally have collective eyes and ears with which to pick up testimony, nor a group cognitive system with which to process and understand it. And even if all individual members of a group have heard and understood a piece of testimony, it seems controversial to count it among the *group*'s evidence, if this testimonial evidence cannot penetrate the processes, by which the group settles upon its actions or collective attitudes.[3]

3.2 What does it mean for a group to be sincere in its assertions and other communications? The naïve answer: it means that the group only communicates what it actually believes! Yet, in general, the distinction is blurry between what a group actually believes and what it merely pretends or accepts for its purposes of communication. Even when a group has an individual spokesperson, some of whose communications commit the entire group (e.g., a pope speaking *ex cathedra* for the Catholic Church), this spokesperson's private beliefs are not for that reason obviously the group's beliefs. Seemingly then, we have no obvious way to tell whether we should criticize a group for believing against its evidence or whether we should criticize it for opportunistic insincerity in its communicative behavior. And we can hardly criticize a group for not revising its beliefs in the face of contrary evidence, if we cannot specify what it believes to begin with.

3.3 When a group is *chartered*, how does its charter affect which types of criticism it merits? In Frederick Schmitt's terms, "a chartered group is one founded to perform a particular action or actions of a certain kind" (1994, p. 272). "A chartered group has no life apart from its office, as a specialist individual has a life apart from his or her occupation" (ibid.). A paradigm case of a chartered group is a jury at a criminal trial. This case also demonstrates how a group's charter may be of great epistemological relevance (ibid., p. 274): a jury's charter involves not paying any attention to hearsay evidence in its deliberation about the defendant's guilt, even when doing so would result in a more reliable verdict. A jury verdict based on hearsay might be epistemically superior, yet it would be legally – and perhaps also morally – unjustified (see also Lackey 2016, p. 355). The case of a jury is normatively simple, though, since its charter is rigidly defined, and, normally, we have no reason to criticize a jury for abiding by its charter. But what are we to make of groups whose charters are less clearly defined, or epistemically and morally pernicious? In such cases, when a group ignores evidence in a way dictated by its charter, how shall we untangle the epistemic and moral threads[4]?

3.4 How does motivation work in the case of group agents? In the case of individual agents, our folk psychological and moral theories provide us with some understanding of whether an agent's fault is doxastic or merely conative. Even if there is considerable disagreement concerning the circumstances under which an agent is blameworthy for her failure to be aware of the morally bad-making features of her actions, it is generally agreed that an agent is excused for perpetrating morally significant harm, if she acted "in good faith," that is, in blameless unawareness of the risk of perpetrating such harm (see e.g. Smith 2017). And arguably, such unawareness could be blameless, even if strictly speaking, the beliefs shaping the agent's actions are epistemically unjustified (see here Nottelmann 2013a, Booth 2014). On the other hand, we have cases where an agent's beliefs are epistemically flawless, yet her actions are blameworthy due to their being motivated by a reprehensible configuration of desires (Smith 2017, p. 98). Such distinctions, however, depend on applying a belief-desire theory of action motivation. It is highly unclear how generally to do this for group agents. Again, this makes it difficult to transfer mundane normative assessments from the individual level to the group level. Which makes it hard to assess whether a group merits epistemic criticism, when, as often is the case, we can only access its public communications.

In conclusion to this section, the combination of the problems highlighted in Sections 13.3.1–13.3.4 clearly complicates the normative assessment of group responses to testimony well beyond the intricacies found at the individual level. In order to make any progress, we must carefully consider our methodological approach.

13.4 Some Methodological Flaws in the Literature

The extant literature on the epistemic evaluation of group belief has shown considerable sophistication in treating chartered groups of various kinds as well as groups with exotic and problematic pools of evidence. Except from Carter (2015, 2016) and Skipper & Steglich-Petersen (2019), no one has focused exclusively on group responses to testimony. Skipper & Steglich-Petersen do not focus on epistemic justification, whereas Carter does not offer any positive theory of group epistemic evaluation but treats various problems that might hinder any such account from getting off the ground. In contrast, Schmitt (1994), Goldman (2014), Lackey (2016), Silva (2018), and Dunn (2019) each offer positive accounts of epistemic justification for group belief, at least tentatively.[5] In the following, I shall aim to target their shared methodological assumptions.

Schmitt's pioneering article begins by endorsing a version of Margaret Gilbert's joint commitment account of group beliefs. Roughly, a group belief p equals the members' joint acceptance of p for the purposes of future joint cognition and action. To join this hegemony, a group member must express to her fellow members her willingness to endorse p as the group's joint acceptance, at least in so far as p is justified (or "warranted") by the group's joint reasons (1994, p. 262, following Gilbert 1989).

On this basis, Schmitt argues that a group's epistemic charter must govern its epistemic evaluation, for "as far as the use of beliefs in group action, goes, there is no point in permitting beliefs that fall short of special standards" (p. 273). Schmitt's guiding idea seems to be that any attitude not satisfying the group's epistemic charter would not even be a full-blown group belief; hence, *a fortiori*, it could not be a justified group belief. Yet, ultimately, Schmitt contends that no internalist theory of epistemic justification is plausible for group beliefs, since higher-order group attitudes are too scarce and exotic to matter for the more mundane phenomenon of first-order group justification (pp. 276–282). In contrast, an externalist process-reliabilist theory remains "a live option" (p. 283).[6]

Goldman (2014) has as his main objective canvassing how a process-reliabilist theory of group belief justification could be fruitful (p. 19). Unlike Schmitt, he assumes Christian List and Philip Pettit's Belief Aggregation Function (BAF) conception of group belief, where a group belief must be the output of some relevant aggregation function. According to Goldman, this conception forces two central constraints on group process reliabilism. The larger the portion of aggregated individual beliefs are individually justified on independent bases, the more justified the group belief engendered by a BAF becomes (p. 28). And, conditional on the justifiedness of its inputs, the process by which the BAF operates must be highly reliable (p. 29). In contrast, Dunn's "Simple Group Reliabilism" maintains that process-reliabilist conditions for group belief justification are both necessary *and* sufficient.[7] Also, he rejects Goldman's idea that aggregation functions must literally be BAFs; group members need not *believe* their inputs to the function. To yield a genuine group belief that p, it is enough that the function operates in the context of the group's "taking up the question whether p" as a group (2018, p. 3).

Lackey endorses the gist of Goldman's proposal that justification at the group level emanates from the epistemic justification of member beliefs through a process of aggregation (p. 381), even if she does not commit to Goldman's process reliabilism. To square this idea with her intuitions across a range of cases, Lackey constrains Goldman's conception of "vertical dependence" with a number of complex provisos. First, she takes to heart the general formal result that no BAF short of unanimity will invariantly output a consistent set of group beliefs (2016, fn25, following List & Pettit 2002). Since she finds it intuitively unacceptable that a group could ever have justification for each element of an inconsistent set of beliefs, she introduces the proviso that the sum of the individual bases of the group members partaking in the BAF must cohere and must still be able to support the target proposition after full disclosure and collective deliberation among relevant members (p. 381). Second, she adopts the idea from Schmitt that group justification depends in part on the group's charter or the moral demands on the group. Especially if a group membership incurs obligations of evidence gathering, Lackey thinks that this sometimes induces "normative defeaters" for individualized epistemic justification. As she puts it, if by virtue of her group membership a member "ought to have been aware of [contrary?] evidence [relevant to the target belief], this is enough for preventing epistemic justification" (p. 373). So, individual justification in abstraction from group membership does not simply flow upward to the group level. Rather, it only counts toward group justification, provided the relevant member has met her evidence-related duties qua member of the group.

Silva (2018) essentially accepts the BAF framework from Goldman and Lackey. However, he proposes slightly different provisos to Goldman's vertical dependence account. According to his "Evidentialist Responsibilism for Groups," there must not be defeaters for the group's collective evidence base among the individual evidence bases possessed by the members partaking in the BAF. And, overall, the group must be "epistemically responsible" in holding its belief on the relevant basis (p. 2).

Each author thus proceeds on the assumption that matters of group belief metaphysics must be roughly settled, before we enter the domain of group belief epistemology proper. And each seems happy with putting a specific generic theory of group attitude psychology in the epistemological driving seat: Schmitt employs Gilbert's joint-acceptance account, whereas the other authors work within the framework of List and Pettit's BAF conception. Whereas Schmitt is very explicit that justified group beliefs must be capable of acting as bases for group action (1994, p. 262), this idea is less prominent in the other treatments. Still, it often seems implicit, such as in Lackey's many examples from the practical and moral realm. Firmly rooted within their respective group psychological frameworks, each author then proceeds to work out a theory of group belief justification based on their intuitions across a range of problematic cases. In doing so, their respective accounts of group belief play a very significant role as a guide to positive theses regarding the nature of group belief justification.

Here is the main problem with this methodology:

> Not least since Edmond Gettier's seminal 1963 article, it has been standard fare in the epistemology of individual beliefs to mold one's theories of knowledge and justification over a range of thought experiments. This, since arguably any adequate epistemological

> theory must be consistent with widely shared intuitive verdicts on such cases. Still, it has not been general practice to constrain one's epistemological theory by specific metaphysical assumptions regarding the nature of belief. Arguably, there are two main reasons for this. First, the metaphysical nature and status of individual beliefs is such a hotly disputed and difficult topic that any epistemological account wedded to a specific account within this domain would immediately come under the threat of parochialism (Nottelmann 2013b). Secondly, it seems hard to make sense of relevant epistemological intuitions hedged by metaphysical frameworks. When considering a scenario such as an envatted brain fed deceptive stimuli, epistemologists may e.g. appeal to intuitions that the brain justifiedly believes it has a body. The basic verdict in this and many similar cases is whether justified belief or unjustified belief occurs. In contrast, it seems hard even to make sense of the question whether we intuit that the envatted brain justifiedly believes that it has a normal body, *provided* we make a number of metaphysical assumptions about its beliefs. Nor has answers to such questions played much of a role in the mainstream epistemology of individual belief.[8]

But perhaps the likes of Schmitt, Goldman, and Lackey rather suggest that we consult our "straight" intuitions whether a group justifiedly believes this or that under a set of specified circumstances. Only then do we consult our metaphysical theory of group belief, such as to construct a theory of *group belief justification* consistent with those intuitions. On a first blush, this seems far less problematic. However, let us suppose that we attempt to proceed along similar lines within individual level epistemology. Suppose that we begin our construction of a theory of epistemically justified individual belief by committing to the metaphysical idea that individual beliefs are simply acceptances or pretenses of some special kind. We next harness our intuitions that a belief's degree of justifiedness is an involuntary matter and that justified beliefs must be properly based on the believer's epistemic reasons. This clearly presents a problem within the conception of belief just adopted: beliefs can be epistemic reasons for other beliefs, and acceptances are, at least sometimes, voluntary occurrences based on practical rather than purely epistemic reasons. So, we try to fix those issues, for example, by appealing to the idea that the relevant acceptances must be "responsible" in a certain special sense or that the practical reasons underlying them must concern special epistemic goals. However, we now seem to run a high risk of running afoul of the concept of epistemic justification altogether since those new notions were introduced merely to make an inherently practical notion of belief more epistemologically respectable, which was not adopted out of epistemological concerns to begin with.

Another pressing issue is what the relevant intuitions at the group level are really about. Suppose, to take one of Lackey's primary cases, that we consider a group of museum janitors, composed of five subgroups of equal size. Each subgroup has decisive evidence that *someone* is planning to steal a painting at their museum. Unfortunately, however, each of the subgroups bases this common conclusion on an argument, whose premises are inconsistent with the corresponding premises of any other subgroup. For instance, one subgroup's evidence suggests that only Albert plans the heist, another subgroup's evidence suggests that only Bernard plans the heist, and so on (2016, p. 359. See also Goldman 2014, p. 16). It would strongly seem that if all the janitors were to deliberate about the issue without sharing their evidence across subgroups, they would come collectively to believe that a museum heist is underway. But would that group belief be epistemically justified? Based on her intuitions, Lackey proceeds to construct a complex theory of group justification consistent with a negative answer. But how, given the basic problem of keeping apart group belief and group acceptance, can Lackey be sure that she is not rather answering in the negative a question about the total janitor group's *moral* status, were its subgroups to reach the relevant collective conclusion without sharing their evidence?

To sum up my methodological worries thus far, by relying on a preconception of the nature of group belief, while trying to harness epistemological intuitions within that conception, theorists run a great risk of providing an account of group epistemically justified belief that is either parochial, based on intuitions of an obscure nature, or really an attempt to turn an inherently practical phenomenon into a fundamental object of epistemic evaluation while losing track of our basic epistemological concepts.

Here's another problem. To argue that propositional attitudes like beliefs are natural kinds, is at least a highly contentious issue in the case of individual psychology (Nottelmann 2013b). It seems futile to argue that the beliefs and desires of a tobacco company are natural kinds. When we ascribe such attitudes, we are hardly merely describing naturally occurring psychological phenomena. Rather, we express our interests in certain modes of prediction, explanation, and evaluation. Plausibly, the same concern also often arises for the delimitation of the groups to which we ascribe such attitudes. The focus in the extant group epistemological literature on clearly circumscribed groups like a trial jury or the janitors of British Museum is deceptive. For typical groups, like ethnic groups or even business companies, no clear and objective standards for group membership seem forthcoming. Suppose a company has laid off an employee and sent her home, while still paying her salary for a while. Is she still part of the company? For some legal purposes she might be. For most epistemological purposes, she is clearly not.

The above concerns make salient the possibility that our conceptions of a group and its beliefs need not be invariant across evaluative interests and purposes. More specifically, at least we should not simply assume the invariance of relevant criteria for *groupness*, *group membership*, and *group belief* across all modes of evaluation.[9] By tacitly assuming such invariance, the extant literature may well have failed to provide a maximally useful and well-motivated conception of group epistemic justification. This is far from saying that we should simply discard the conclusions and considerations offered by that literature. But, as I hope to demonstrate below, its insights come into a clearer light, once we consider our framing interests as evaluators.

13.5 A New Beginning

13.5.1 Interest in a Group as a Reliable Indicator

Below, I consider the epistemological evaluation of a group's responses to testimonial evidence as framed by various evaluative interests. I hope to make plausible the idea that our relevant criteria for *groupness*, *group membership*, *group belief*, and possibly even *group justification* should vary across those frameworks.

In the first and simplest case, our interest in a group is purely epistemic in the following sense: we regard the group simply as a mechanism by which some truths are hopefully revealed to us. This is often the primary way an esoteric diagnostic team is of interest to other subjects. We know there is a malfunction in our complex computer network. A team of putative computer experts is hired to diagnose the malfunction. Of course, we want their diagnosis to be a correct one. Under the scope of this interest, criteria for *groupness* can be held minimal: The relevant group must have some "mouthpiece" making its relevant verdicts known to us. But in theory, this "mouthpiece" need not even be one or more persons producing speech acts; it could simply be the publicized output of an algorithm into which group members plot their individual observations. Criteria for *group membership* and *group belief* can be held minimal too. In short, we could consider anything a group belief, which has assertive form, expresses a proposition, and is an output of the group's mouthpiece.

In such minimalist cases, the epistemic good of interest is reliable indication. We want the verdict concerning p related by the group's mouthpiece reliably to indicate whether p is the case. When the *mouthpiece* is sufficiently reliable, in a loose sense, we may perhaps talk of the group's verdicts as "justified," employing the notion of justification as a mere indicator concept for truth (cf. Chase 2004). But arguably, such a use of the term "justification" is not indicative of its general meaning within epistemological contexts.

13.5.2 Interest in a Group as Sustaining a Reliable Process

We now move to a slightly different case. Here, our interest in not merely in group outputs but also in the group itself. In this second type of case, for some reason or other, we are also interested in how the same group would perform under a range of circumstances, some perhaps counter-factual. For example, a diagnostic team of putative computer experts has just presented us with a solution to our department's computer problems, and we consider whether we should call on the very same group in future cases of electronic emergency. Hence, we want to gauge whether the group is recommendable for similar diagnostic jobs over a range of possible future circumstances. As before, we can safely hold minimal our criteria for *groupness*, *group membership*, and *group belief*. But unlike before, we have a clear interest in the group's characteristic internal processes. It matters to us, whether the group's processes for creating its verdicts are reliable within its topical domain across the circumstances in which the group could be called upon to function. Here, *process reliability* enters the picture. Again, at least loosely, we might naturally say things like: "I am impressed. Whatever that team comes up with is always justified. They are so reliable in detecting errors in our software systems, even under pressure." This might suggest a process-reliabilist theory of epistemic justification for group beliefs, as has been endorsed by Schmitt, Goldman, and Dunn. But arguably, we should be wary of concluding from the naturalness of epistemic justification ascriptions under the perspective of one particular evaluative interest that such ascriptions track the justification concept employed in more mundane epistemic evaluations at the collective level.

13.5.3 *Interest in a Group as a Reliable Indicator while Abiding by its Charter*

We now turn to chartered groups. As we saw above, some group charters include aspects of clear epistemological relevance, such as local standards for admitting and assessing evidence. We may, of course, have an interest in the epistemic performance of such groups, which is entirely indifferent to the group's charter, or whether the group continues to abide by it. But the evaluative perspective paradigmatically exemplified by typical assessments of trial jury performances is a different beast altogether. A jury's primary function is to deliver a legally legitimate verdict. Failure to comply here screens off the epistemic quality of its verdict since, in that case, the trial will not have been successfully concluded. Still, in so far as the jury's verdict is legally legitimate, we have a strong interest in a minimal risk of a conviction, if the defendant is in fact innocent. And arguably, this risk must be minimized, even at the expense of enlarging the risk of the jury acquitting a guilty defendant.[10] The jury's epistemic charter reflects such concerns of legal normativity. Therefore, a jury must ignore some evidence that could otherwise have helped secure a more reliable indication of the defendant's guilt: for example, hearsay from highly reliable sources. How should this evaluative perspective affect relevant criteria of *groupness*, *group membership*, and *group belief*?

The introduction of charters makes a crucial difference relative to the perspectives considered in Sections 13.3.1–13.3.2. As for *groupness*, there must now be a set of people normatively bound by a common purpose constitutive of the group (Schmitt 1994, p. 273). This is false of many *bona fide* groups like a bunch of old friends willingly hanging out together (ibid., p. 272). As for *group membership*, only people bound by the charter can be considered members. Still, we can remain very liberal concerning *group beliefs*. As before, we only need a mouthpiece to assertively express some proposition, though this must now happen in a way not conflicting with the relevant charter.

Now, let us suppose that a jury's verdicts are considered quite reliable for this type of chartered group. What should we say about the jury's epistemic status? This is not so clear. Schmitt's guiding idea is that its exclusion of epistemic reasons not allowed by its charter should not count negatively toward the chartered group's epistemic assessment, since "chartered groups must rely in their activities only on beliefs that meet their special standards" (p. 273). But even if a typical jury's charter is epistemically and morally benign, we can easily imagine groups with epistemically pernicious charters, e.g., a religious cult, whose charter forbids its members from bringing into the group's deliberations any evidence undercutting its absurd central dogma. It would seem wrong to declare a collective verdict of such a group justified, when it crucially rests on such chartered neglect of evidence. Rather than integrating group charters into our conception of group epistemic status, then, it seems more natural to conceive of epistemic evaluations hedged by charters as cases, where our interest in seeing epistemic standards met take second seat to non-epistemic goals. When ignoring epistemically valuable and undefeated evidence out of its charter, a jury is not naturally considered equally *epistemically* justified in its verdicts. At best, it performs as reliably and conscientiously as we could ask for within its chartered epistemic limitations.

13.5.4 Interest in a Group as Sustaining a Reliable Process while Abiding by Its Charter

This perspective we can treat briefly. We adopt it, for example, when we are interested in using a specific jury for a series of tasks, e.g., if we want the jury to judge admission exams at a music conservatory. Here, as with a trial jury, the charter will typically involve serious epistemic restrictions. For example, jury members must judge the actual musical performances of applicants on the admission exams while not bringing into the group's deliberations any previous experiences with the applicants as students or performers. Within such restrictions, however, we want the jury's verdict-forming process to be reliable. We especially want to minimize the risk that the jury decrees an applicant sufficiently skilled, when, in fact, she is not. This introduces no need for new criteria of *groupness, group membership,* or *group belief* compared to Section 13.3.3. But, as noted there, unlike under the perspective considered in Section 13.3.2, it no longer seems natural to say that our normative assessments track epistemic justification.

13.5.5 Interest in a Group as a Morally Responsible Believer – A Model Perspective

Quite often, when we evaluate some group's response to evidence from testimony or other sources, our primary interest is in a *moral* evaluation of the group. Above, we noted prominent cases like Big Tobacco's responses to scientific testimony or the Catholic Church's responses to the testimonies of sexual abuse victims. Many have felt that those responses reflect significant moral shortcomings, and that therefore those groups are seriously blameworthy. On a theoretical level, as we saw in Section 13.2, matters get complicated: for an ethics of belief to get a grip, there must be a well-defined distinction between the group's blameworthily believing the relevant propositions and its merely accepting them (in the sense of Cohen 1989) against its better doxastic judgment. Else, we have no way to tell whether the group's primary failure is doxastic or merely agential. At least three considerations complicate this matter beyond the parallel controversies at the level of individual agents, which are as follows.

First, often it is easy enough to specify what a group officially accepts by analyzing the official assertions of its spokespersons or the actions of its key members when acting in their office as group leaders. Clearly, for many years, the communications of Big Tobacco denied the scientific validity of the key findings of oncologists relating tobacco to lung cancer. And equally clearly, for many years, the Catholic Church denied what emerged as the true scale and systematicity of the child abuse perpetrated by parts of its clergy. It is far more difficult to say what a group *believes* in a more substantial sense and what evidence undergirds such *group beliefs*.

Second, if a group has mechanisms preventing members' evidence and propositional attitudes from penetrating its collective processes of deliberation, a question arises whether the group is *blameworthy* for this cognitive encapsulation. This opens an important flank in the ethics of group belief, which has no equally important parallel at the individual level. Of course, there are cases in which an individual manages to ignore parts of her evidence or side-rail important beliefs of hers, such as not to influence her actions.[11] But on the individual level, such cases seem an exotic phenomenon. On the group level, however, such phenomena are common-place and very often central to moral evaluation. For instance, one well-studied phenomenon is the way in which certain companies have viciously aimed to deter employees from making executives aware of the need for financially unpleasant company action, known as "gagging" (see e.g. Henik 2008).

Third, to a significant extent, a group's doxastic life is shaped by actions, be those the actions of the group or its members. For a group to undergo doxastic changes, someone must act. In contrast, at least some of an individual agent's beliefs are formed, abandoned, and revised automatically, not least her perceptual beliefs. Group belief revision can require a complex and lengthy pattern of action involving changes in how the group and its members conceive of – and understand – certain matters, even changes in group membership. Glen Pettigrove offers the illuminating example of the Presbyterian Church, whose revisions of its original Biblical literalist and infallibilist dogma took part by way of a historical process involving radical re-conceptualizations of theological research and divine guidance perpetrated in various social contexts within the church's life (2016, p. 127). Now, when we judge a group's belief as blameworthy, at least sometimes, this must be because we judge that the group or its members have not acted sufficiently to ensure that the group believes the truth on the relevant matter. Above, we saw that such failures might consist in the group's construction – or tolerance – of internal mechanisms excluding relevant evidence from collective deliberation. But other blameworthy failures could include insufficient gathering of evidence or willfully skewed evaluation thereof.

Since we are now considering a group as a morally responsible agent capable of acting on its beliefs, obviously our criteria of *groupness*, *group membership*, and *group belief* must be far more substantial relative to those considered earlier above, where a group was merely considered as a possibly chartered collective producer of an epistemically evaluable output. But faced with the massive complexities just considered, arguably the most fruitful way forward is to construct an idealized generic model of group mind for the relevant evaluative purpose. We may then hope that the basic lessons learned from this model will fruitfully apply to more realistic cases marred with the complexities of actual group life.

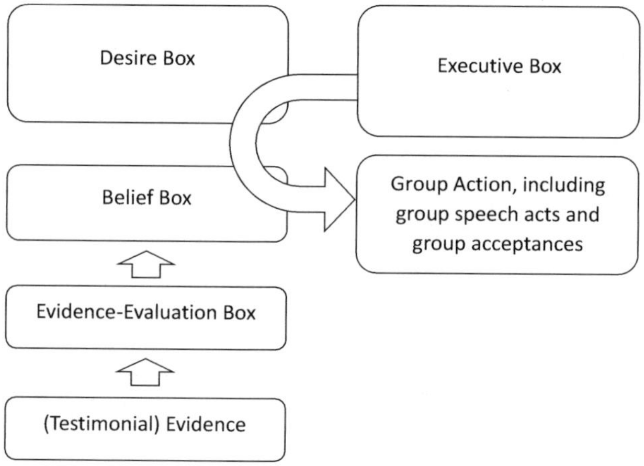

I propose a functional model of a "group mind" mimicking the basic functional assumptions of a folk psychology for individual agents as employed in typical moral evaluations. In that case, as we saw above, the difference between belief and acceptance was of crucial moral relevance. Also, a key difference between belief and acceptance was a functional one. While beliefs can be part of the motivational basis of acceptances, the opposite is psychologically impossible as the notions were defined. My proposed model group mind has five functional modules or "boxes," reflecting five basic ways in which the life of a collective agent could be morally problematic in its relations to (testimonial) evidence: *The Evidence Gathering Box*, *The Evidence Evaluation Box*, *The Belief Box*, *The Desire Box*, and, finally, *The Executive Box*. Each Box is constituted by a subset of group member activities. In principle, each member or subgroup of the group can partake in activities co-constituting any box, synchronically or diachronically. In highly idealized fashion, let us suppose that any individual or joint member activity co-constituting a box is informationally shielded from any activity co-constituting any other box, except through the informational channels created by the following functional architecture:

> *The Evidence Gathering Box* has as its defining function the collection of the group's evidence. In figurative terms it is the group's open eyes and ears vis-à-vis testimony, but also its means of locating its eyes and ears. Thus, the box takes as its input evidence from the world outside of the group's inner life, but nothing prevents it from also processing inputs concerning the group itself and its operations and structure.

The evidence gathered by *The Evidence Gathering Box* feeds into *The Evidence Evaluation Box*. This Box has as its function the epistemic evaluation of the evidence gathered by *The Evidence Gathering Box*. In carrying out this evaluation, the contents of *The Belief Box* are consulted.

Propositions judged sufficiently supported by the group's total evidence are then output into *The Belief Box* for fixation. If any older token representations in *The Belief Box* are inconsistent with new token representations fed into it, the older tokens must be destroyed. In figurative terms, then, *The Belief Box* is the group's active and consistent memory, the doxastic basis of the group's agency. It is consulted whenever *The Executive Box* must shape the group's actions, including speech-acts and acceptances, such as to aim at the satisfaction of one or more preferences picked from the group's *Desire Box* – for a business company, for example, the preference for profit, solvency, and growing stock value; for a Church, the expansions of lay membership and political goodwill. No subset of the group's preferences need necessarily be jointly satisfiable by the group's actions.

Finally, the defining function of *The Executive Box* is to pick out one or more preferences from *The Desire Box* for the group to aim at satisfying at some relevant time. For matters of ease, let us assume that our model group is a *Communitas Economica* (i.e. a collective *Homo Economicus*). Thus, its actions are shaped such as to maximize satisfaction of its executive preferences according to the assumptions presently contained in its *Belief Box*.

Surely, such a model is highly idealized and realistically would never be perfectly instantiated by any actual group under moral evaluation. Also, I am in no position to argue that no other group mind model is superior to the one suggested here. Thus, I shall simply focus on the theoretical benefits of the present model. First, the model allows us to make more precise and fruitful Tuomela's (2013) and Lackey's (2016s) talk of a group's "operative members"; "those who have the relevant decision-making authority" (2016, p. 350). Tuomela and Lackey both consider this member-subset of special epistemological and moral significance. But rather than attributing special significance to any special *member* subset, my model highlights that perhaps it is special subsets of member *activities* that ought primarily interest epistemic and moral evaluators. Also, the precise direction of this focus must vary with our evaluative purposes: if we are merely out to evaluate the group's epistemic performance vis-à-vis its actions and take a somewhat internalistic perspective, it is the relation between the input to the group's *Evidence Evaluation Box* as compared with *The Belief Box's* input to *The Executive Box* that should interest us. If we are interested in a moral evaluation of the group's doxastic life, we should focus on the relation between the activities constituting *The Evidence-Gathering Box* as compared with the updating of *The Belief Box* as mediated by *The Evidence-Evaluation Box*. If, finally, we are interested in morally evaluating the group as based on the moral quality of its intentions, we should focus on its *Executive Box* and interpret its preferred actions in the light of the contents of its *Belief Box*. In theory, however, the very same group members could be involved in the relevant activities in each case. Tuomela and Lackey's focus on a subset of "operative group members" thus serves to gloss over the intricate details involved in maintaining a relevant focus, when adopting various evaluative perspectives on a group agent.

Second, for a group conforming to the functional architecture of my model, the distinction between group acceptance and group belief makes clear sense. We may define a group's beliefs as the contents of its *Belief Box*. In contrast, a group's acceptances are the factual premises its *Executive Box* chooses to employ for its "official" justification of the group's public actions, including its direct and indirect communicative acts. Thus, even if a group's acceptances may perfectly coincide with the contents of its *Belief Box*, there is a crucial functional difference to consider: group acceptances are constituted by patterns of group actions shaped by the group's *Belief Box*, whereas group beliefs are simply *Belief Box* contents. When, as is often the case, a group's acceptances are not backed by corresponding beliefs, we may aptly call its deviant acceptances the group's *policy of pretense*. To exemplify, for a long time, Big Tobacco adopted a policy of pretending that its products were safe. This claim was part of its official justification for its marketing and sales strategies. But, arguably, this policy of pretense was based on its beliefs that its products constituted a serious health hazard and that it was in its best commercial interest that public knowledge of this fact be suppressed.

Employing my model, ethically to judge a group's conduct, we need evidence concerning the contents of its *Belief Box*. Since contents of *The Belief Box* are functionally defined, we must look for contents playing the proper role in the group's life. For a commercial company, perhaps we will be able to find at least some of the factual assumptions *actually* (rather than merely apparently) underlying its executive decisions in transcripts of board meetings or in the memories of former executives easing their conscience in interviews, memoirs, or legal testimony. In some cases, an organization might even have relevant clandestine handbooks and manuals playing the functional role of *Belief Box* contents. In the case of Big Tobacco, critics could ideally hope for a smoking (sic!) gun in the form of clandestine internal notes, stating that all employees must publicly denounce the cancerogenic effects of tobacco smoking, since those effects are obviously a real threat to the company. Given we can only access a group's public communications, however, we can hardly say whether we should blame it for its doxastic life or the weighing of its preferences. Of course, we may sometimes be in a position to judge that very likely a group is *at least* blameworthy in one of those ways. It does not seem unreasonable to feel this way about organizations like Big Tobacco or the Catholic Church. But without a suitable functional model, arguably even such disjunctive condemnations are jeopardized. If we cannot explain what it would mean for Big Tobacco to believe blameworthily as opposed to its accepting blameworthily based on its beliefs, it seems hard to make sense of the verdict that most likely Big Tobacco is blameworthy in at least one of those ways.

Let us return now to the ethics of group belief. Within my model, this topic is now clearly defined, at least if we adopt a simplified general tracing account of blameworthiness for doxastic states (see e.g. Levy 2005, Nottelmann 2007): Overall, we must investigate whether the group has done enough to secure that its *Belief Box* contains truths, and only truths, on the relevant topic. If in fact this box contains topical falsehoods, we must see if this is due to suboptimal performance of the group's *Evidence Gathering*, *Evidence Evaluation*, and *Belief Boxes*, that is, does *The Belief Box* not contain relevant truths because, morally speaking, the group has not done enough to secure evidence on the relevant topic and evaluate it according to legitimate epistemic standards? Has the group been too sloppy in keeping the contents of its *Belief Box* consistent? Or has the group perhaps deliberately tampered with its relevant functional modules, such as strategically to hamper their epistemic performance? If we can answer any such question in the positive, we have at least the outlines of a moral case against the group firmly based in the ethics of (group) belief.

Finally, we can approach an answer to the question of relevant criteria for *groupness*, *group membership,* and *group belief* in the maximally committing case of regarding a group as a morally responsible agent. In as far as the group conforms to the model architecture, criteria for *group belief* were already given above. As for *groupness*, it seems hard to provide a final list of necessary criteria. However, arguably a *sufficient* criterion is instantiating a functional architecture as devised by my model. And for any practical purpose, plausibly, we can also regard a reasonably close approximation of this architecture as sufficient for *groupness*. As for *group membership*, anyone partaking in actions co-constituting any of the group's five boxes could be considered a group member, even if we might want to apply a special label such as "core member" or "executive member" to members partaking in actions co-constituting the group's *Executive Box*. If we are out also to evaluate the moral complicity of individual group member in the group's wrongdoings, matters of relevant group membership might get far more complicated, but luckily this has not been my errand here (See e.g. Kutz 2000, Isaacs 2011).

How closely do actual groups under moral scrutiny conform to my model functional architecture? A substantial answer to this question lies outside the scope of the present paper. However, I do not find it far-fetched to claim that, for many evaluative purposes, the model fits well enough in the case of big hierarchical organizations like Big Tobacco or the Catholic Church. Indeed, supposedly the Catholic Church has fairly well-established protocols for questioning alleged victims of abuse, for deciding what to do with the reports of such questionings, and for deciding when and whether to take such reports into account when it aims to maximize its preferences for political power, widespread membership, and pristine public reputation. It does not seem far-fetched that a solid and substantial case could be built, rooted in my functional model, for blaming The Catholic Church on account of its doxastic life as well as its practical conduct. Yet obviously, building such a case in detail is an empirical matter far outside the scope of the present chapter.

13.6 Conclusions

The main message of this chapter has been a plea for complexity. The epistemic evaluation of group performance in the face of testimony and disagreement is a highly complex matter. Not least since it is often far from clear whether our evaluation of a group's responses to testimony is primarily epistemic or moral, and, in the latter case, how epistemic standards play into our moral assessment. The matter is further complicated by the difficulty of keeping apart a group's beliefs from its mere acceptances or pretenses for its purposes of communication. Also, arguably, most groups under such evaluation are not natural kinds. Neither are their propositional attitudes. Thus, we must take seriously the idea that relevant appropriate criteria of *groupness*, *group membership*, and *group belief* vary according to our evaluative perspectives. By ignoring or bracketing too many such complications, arguably the extant group epistemological literature has prematurely jumped to conclusions concerning the general nature of *group belief justification*.

Above, I have argued that matters are in fact so complicated that our best hopes of clarity and understanding rest on devising a relatively simple model for the mind of a group agent, for which the main evaluative problems are at least tractable. I have proposed one such model and demonstrated how epistemological and moral issues relating to a group's responses to testimony may be disentangled for a group agent conforming to it.

Hopefully, the work undertaken here has helped put at least parts of the difficult fields of group epistemology and the ethics of group belief on a surer methodological footing. Space has not permitted me to explore how closely actual problematic group agents like tobacco companies or powerful churches conform to the suggested model, or how normatively significant the actual discrepancies are. Much work remains for future research.

Notes

1 "Big Tobacco" is a colloquial collective term for five companies: Philip Morris International, British American Tobacco, Imperial Brands, Japan Tobacco International, and China Tobacco.

2 See Isaacs (2011, Chap. 2) for a forceful general argument that collective responsibility is a real phenomenon.

3 Thus, Lackey seems too quick when she claims that if all executive members of Philip Morris Inc. individually believe that the company's customers should be warned, then *the company* is blameworthy for not warning them (2016, p. 351). But, of course, given plausible background assumptions, each executive is individually blameworthy for not voicing his or her concerns to fellow board members. For illustration, consider a theist Church, whose reasons for endorsing theism are very clearly stated in its catechism. Still, each of its priests may be an atheist for perfectly fine personal reasons, even if she is forced to keep this a secret. But those secret individual reasons are hardly the Church's reasons or even reasons which the Church is at fault for not taking into account.

4 E.g. suppose that a small group of American jurists become marooned on a tiny island and decide formally to set up a miniature court system for settling their disputes. Now, their public prosecutor decides to let an

irate fellow undergo a trial by jury related to the disappearance of another community member. Since the community lives very closely together and everyone regularly share their evidence on matters of common interest, all testimonial evidence relevant to the case is already known to the jurors as "hearsay," which is now inadmissible in court. This is highly epistemically pernicious. However, morally speaking, the jurists ought to have realized that such problems would result from the inadmissibility rule and would lead to the harms resulting from the acquittal of dangerous criminals among them.

5 I have left Hakli (2011) out of consideration here. Despite its title, this article explicitly focuses on group acceptances only.

6 Lackey (2016, p. 346) takes Schmitt's relativistic account of what constitutes a group's reasons to also constitute his positive account of group epistemic justification. This, however, is a misreading of a passage in Schmitt (1994, p. 266), where Schmitt merely states that a group's having such reasons in favor of p is *necessary* for its justified belief p.

7 Dunn (2019, p. 5) takes Goldman as also offering sufficient conditions for group justification, but this is clearly at odds with Goldman's careful reservations.

8 This is not to claim that belief metaphysics should not play a much larger role in mainstream epistemology than is currently the case. See Gerken (2018).

9 See also the suggestion of Klausen (2015, p. 823) that the delimitation of groups for ascriptions of group knowledge must consider the "epistemic tasks" relevant to the ascriber.

10 This is the legal principle commonly known as Blackstone's Ratio, so often maligned by authoritarian governments. See e.g. Bown (2019).

11 This is the theme of W.K. Clifford's classic Ship-Owner Example (1999, p. 70).

Bibliography

BonJour, Laurence. 2002. "Internalism and Externalism." In *The Oxford Handbook of Epistemology*, edited by Paul K. Moser. Oxford: Oxford University Press: 234–263.

Booth, Anthony. 2014. "Epistemic Ought Is a Commensurable Ought." *European Journal of Philosophy* 22(4): 529–539.

Bown, William Cullerne. 2019. "Killing Kaplanianism: Flawed Methodologies, The Standard of Proof, and Modernity." *International Journal of Evidence & Proof* 23(3): 229–254.

Brandt, Allan M. 2012. "Inventing Conflicts of Interest. A History of Tobacco Industry Tactics." *American Journal of Public Health* 102(1): 63–71.

Carter, J. Adam. 2015. "Group Knowledge and Epistemic Defeat." *Ergo* 2(28): 711–735.

Carter, J. Adam. 2016. "Group Peer Disagreement." *Ratio* 29(1): 11–28.

Chase, James. 2004. "Indicator Reliabilism." *Philosophy and Phenomenological Research* 69(1): 115–137.

Clifford, William Kingdon. 1999. "The Ethics of Belief." In *The Ethics of Belief and Other Essays*, edited by Timothy J. Madigan. New York: Prometheus Books: 70–96.

Cohen, L. Jonathan. 1989. "Belief and Acceptance." *Mind* 98: 367–389.

Dunn, Jeffrey. 2019. "Reliable Group Belief." *Synthese*. https://doi.org/10.1007/s11229-018-02075-8

Gerken, Mikkel. 2018. "The New Evil Demon and the Devil in the Details." In *The Factive Turn in Epistemology*, edited by Veli Mitova. Cambridge: Cambridge University Press: 102–122.

Gettier, Edmond. 1963. "Is Justified True Belief Knowledge?" *Analysis* 23: 121–123.

Gilbert, Margaret. 1989. *On Social Facts*. London: Routledge.

Goldman, Alvin I. 2014. "Social Process Reliabilism: Solving Justification Problems in Collective Epistemology." In *Essays in Collective Epistemology*, edited by Jennifer Lackey. Oxford: Oxford University Press: 11–41.

Haack, Susan. 1997. "The Ethics of Belief' Reconsidered." In *The Philosophy of Roderick M. Chisholm*, edited by Lewish Hahn. Lasalle, IL: Open Court: 129–144.

Hakli, Raul. 2011. "On Dialectical Justification of Group Beliefs." In *Collective Epistemology*, edited by Hans Bernhard Schmid, Daniel Sirtes and Marcel Weber. Heusenstamm: Ontos: 119–153.

Henik, Erika. 2008. "Mad as Hell or Scared Stiff? The Effects of Value Conflicts and Emotions on Potential Whistle-Blowers." *Journal of Business Ethics* 80(1): 111–119.

Isaacs, Tracy. 2011. *Moral Responsibility in Collective Contexts*. Oxford: Oxford University Press.

Klausen, Søren Harnow. 2015. "Group Knowledge: A Real-World Approach." *Synthese* 192(3): 813–839.

Kutz, Christopher. 2000. *Complicity. Ethics and Law for a Collective Age*. Cambridge: Cambridge University Press.

Lackey, Jennifer. 2016. "What is Justified Group Belief?" *The Philosophical Review* 125(3): 341–396.

Levy, Neil. 2005. "The Good, The Bad, and The Blameworthy." *Journal of Ethics and Social Philosophy* 1(2): 1–16.

List, Christian and Philip Pettit. 2002. "Aggregating Sets of Judgement: An Impossibility Result." *Economics and Philosophy* 18: 89–110.

Mecklin, John. 2019. "Trump Administration's Attack on Climate Science Goes Full-Orwell." *Bulletin of the Atomic Scientists*, May 28. https://thebulletin.org/2019/05/trump-administrations-attack-on-climate-science-goes-full-orwell/

Nottelmann, Nikolaj. 2007. *Blameworthy Belief. A Study in Epistemic Deontologism*. Dordrecht: Springer.

———. 2013a. "The Deontological Conception of Epistemic Justification: A Re-Assessment." *Synthese* 190(12): 2219–2241.

———. 2013b. "Belief Metaphysics. The Basic Questions." In *New Essays on Belief. Constitution Content, and Structure*, edited by Nikolaj Nottelmann. Houndsmills: Palgrave-Macmillan: 9–29.

Pettigrove, Glen. 2016. "Changing Our Mind." In *The Epistemic Life of Groups: Essays in the Epistemology of Collectives*, edited by Michael S. Brady and Miranda Fricker. Oxford: Oxford University Press: 111–131.

Rojas, Rick. 2019. "They Hoped the Catholic Church Would Reveal Their Abusers. They Are Still Waiting." *New York Times*, May 21. https://www.nytimes.com/2019/05/21/nyregion/catholic-church-sexual-abuse.html

Silva, Jr., Paul. 2018. "Justified Group Belief is Evidentially Responsible Group Belief." *Episteme*. https://doi.org/10.1017/epi.2018.5

Skipper, Mattias and Asbjørn Steglich-Petersen. 2019. "Group Disagreement: A Belief Aggregation Perspective." *Synthese* 196(10): 4033–4058
Smith, Holly M. 2017. "Tracing Cases of Culpable Ignorance." In *Perspectives in Ignorance from Moral and Social* Philosophy, edited by Rik Peels. London: Routledge: 95–119.
Tuomela, Raimo. 2013. "An Account of Group Knowledge." In *Collective Epistemology*, edited by Hans Bernhard Schmid, Daniel Sirtes and Marcel Weber. Heusenstamm: Ontos: 75–118.

Notes on Contributors

Fernando Broncano-Berrocal is a Talent Attraction Fellow in Philosophy at the Autonomous University of Madrid. ORCID ID: 0000-0001-6472-2684

J. Adam Carter is a Reader in Epistemology at the University of Glasgow and Deputy Director of COGITO Epistemology Research Centre. ORCID ID: 0000-0002-1222-8331

Javier González de Prado Salas is an Assistant Professor of Philosophy at UNED (Spain). ORCID ID: 0000-0003-2020-058X

Xavier de Donato-Rodríguez is a researcher at the Faculty of Philosophy at the University of Santiago de Compostela (Spain). ORCID ID: 0000-0002-8464-9960

Mattias Skipper is a PhD student in the philosophy department at Aarhus University, Denmark. ORCID ID: 0000-0003-3383-2762

Asbjørn Steglich-Petersen is a Professor at Aarhus University, Department of Philosophy and the History of Ideas. ORCID ID: 0000-0002-5023-3449

Nathan Sheff is an adjunct faculty member in Philosophy at the University of Connecticut. ORCID ID: 0000-0002-6783-5980

Simon Barker has recently received his PhD in Philosophy at the University of Sheffield and is now a lecturer at The University of Tartu, Estonia. ORCID ID: 0000-0002-2133-980X

Mona Simion is Lecturer in Philosophy at the University of Glasgow and Deputy Director of the COGITO Epistemology Research Centre. ORCID ID: 0000-0001-7289-0872

Martin Miragoli is a PhD student in Philosophy at the University of Glasgow. ORCID ID: 0000-0002-8255-8985

Mikkel Gerken is Professor of Philosophy at the University of Southern Denmark. ORCID ID: 0000-0002-0266-9838

Kristina Rolin is Lecturer in Research Ethics at Tampere University. ORCID ID: 0000-0003-3893-7184

Anna-Maria Asunta Eder is a *Wissenschaftliche Mitarbeiterin* at the Department of Philosophy of the University of Cologne. ORCID ID: 0000-0002-4803-9786

Erik J. Olsson is a Professor in Theoretical Philosophy at Lund University. ORCID ID: 0000-0002-4207-3721

Maura Priest is an Assistant Professor and bioethicist in the Department of Philosophy in the School of Historical, Philosophical, and Religious Studies at Arizona State University. ORCID ID: 0000-0001-6962-993X

Nikolaj Nottelmann is Associate Professor of Philosophy at the University of Southern Denmark. ORCID ID: 0000-0002-8621-6640

Index

Made in the USA
Las Vegas, NV
31 October 2024

29f5d888-ab3a-4661-a77a-25f054eecc1eR01